...IEU TERRITORY

OCCUPIED TERRITORY

POLICING BLACK CHICAGO FROM RED SUMMER TO BLACK POWER

SIMON BALTO

The University of North Carolina Press | Chapel Hill

This book was published with the assistance of the
Authors Fund of the University of North Carolina Press.

Designed by April Leidig

Set in Arnhem by Copperline Book Services

The University of North Carolina Press has been a
member of the Green Press Initiative since 2003.

Cover photograph courtesy of the Chicago History Museum

Library of Congress Cataloging-in-Publication Data
Names: Balto, Simon, author.
Title: Occupied territory : policing black Chicago from Red Summer
    to black power / by Simon Balto.
Other titles: Justice, power, and politics.
Description: Chapel Hill : University of North Carolina Press, [2019] |
    Series: Justice, power, and politics | Includes bibliographical references
    and index.
Identifiers: LCCN 2018049256| ISBN 9781469649597 (cloth : alk. paper) |
    ISBN 9781469659176 (pbk. : alk. paper) | ISBN 9781469649603 (ebook)
Subjects: LCSH: Chicago (Ill.) Police Department—History—20th century. |
    Discrimination in law enforcement—Illinois—Chicago—History—20th
    century. | African Americans—Civil rights—Illinois—Chicago—History—
    20th century. | Chicago (Ill.)—Race relations—History—20th century.
Classification: LCC HV8148.C4 B35 2019 | DDC 363.2/308900977311—dc23
    LC record available at https://lccn.loc.gov/2018049256

*For those who dream and work
to bring about a better world,
and in memory of my mother,
who spent her life doing both
of those things*

CONTENTS

ILLUSTRATIONS

ABBREVIATIONS

AAPL	Afro-American Patrolmen's League
ACLU	American Civil Liberties Union
BCC	Black Crime Commission
BPP	Black Panther Party
CCC	Chicago Crime Commission
CCCCP	Chicago Campaign for Community Control of Police
CCHR	Chicago Commission on Human Relations
CCRR	Chicago Commission on Race Relations
CCWWC	Coalition of Concerned Women in the War on Crime
CFM	Chicago Freedom Movement
CHA	Chicago Housing Authority
CIO	Congress of Industrial Organizations
COP	Chicago Confederation of Police
CORE	Congress of Racial Equality
CP	Communist Party
CPA	Chicago Patrolmen's Association
CPD	Chicago Police Department
CRC	Civil Rights Congress
CUCA	Coalition for United Community Action
CUL	Chicago Urban League
DNC	Democratic National Convention
FBI	Federal Bureau of Investigation

FBN	Federal Bureau of Narcotics
FHA	Federal Housing Administration
FOP	Fraternal Order of Police
GIU	Gang Intelligence Unit
GLCC	Greater Lawndale Conservation Commission
HOLC	Home Owners' Loan Corporation
IAD	Internal Affairs Division
IID	Internal Investigations Division
LEAA	Law Enforcement Assistance Administration
MCHR	Mayor's Commission on Human Relations
NAACP	National Association for the Advancement of Colored People
NLRL	Negro Labor Relations League
NNC	National Negro Congress
OKPA	Oakland-Kenwood Property Association
PWOC	Packinghouse Workers Organizing Committee
SCLC	Southern Christian Leadership Conference
SNCC	Student Non-Violent Coordinating Committee
SWOC	Steel Workers Organizing Committee
UC	Unemployed Council
YSA	Young Socialist Alliance

OCCUPIED TERRITORY

MAP 1. Chicago community areas, indicating areas of major black residency, 1920.
Map based on original map by the Chicago Area Geographic Information Study at
the University of Illinois at Chicago.

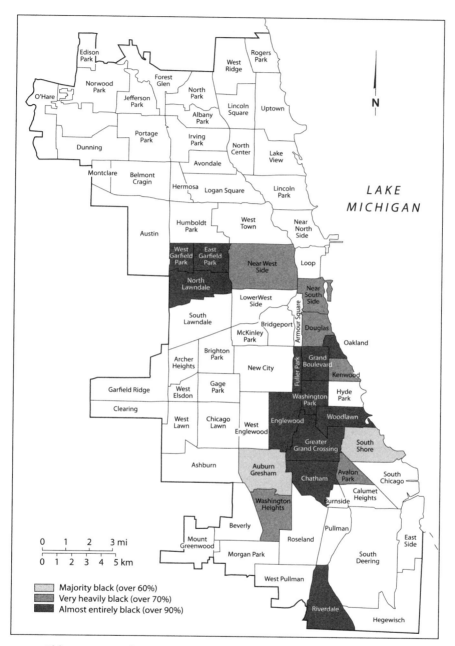

MAP 2. Chicago community areas, indicating areas of major black residency, 1970. Map based on original map by the Chicago Area Geographic Information Study at the University of Illinois at Chicago.

Introduction

OVERPOLICED AND UNDERPROTECTED IN AMERICA

"Chicago's black neighborhoods are the most overpatrolled and under-protected in the city," testified Howard Saffold, a black police officer with the Chicago Police Department (CPD). An assemblage of community members, experts, and activists looked on from their seats inside the Everett Dirksen Federal Building in downtown Chicago.[1] It was the summer of 1972, and this was the third in a series of four days of testimony called by black congressman Ralph Metcalfe on "the misuse of police authority" in Chicago. The first two had been devoted to community members' stories—those who had been beaten and harassed, whose family members had been killed, who had been called "black mother fuckers," "wetbacks," and "niggers."[2] The hearing's third day was turned over to comment from experts on the police department like Howard Saffold. A black man, concerned citizen, and CPD patrolman, Saffold was also president of the Afro-American Patrolmen's League (AAPL)—an organization of black CPD officers who, seeing the department as "a white racist institution," hoped to bend it toward some measure of functionality for black citizens.[3] To them, the department's primary failings were twofold: first, black people were constantly subjected to abuse, harassment, and hypersurveillance (overpatrolled). Second, they were continuously at risk within their neighborhoods anyway (underprotected).

The black neighborhoods that Saffold talked about were suffering badly from neglect and violence. As the by-product of numerous socioeconomic and political processes, and as the more intentional result of others, Chicago was roughly as segregated a place as one might find in America. The Dirksen Building where Saffold testified sat only five miles north of the heart of the black South Side, and even closer to the largest concentration of black communities on the West Side. From the chain-link-enclosed balconies of the Robert Taylor Homes and the Cabrini Green projects, people could see the towering majesty of the downtown Loop's skyscrapers—material prosperity, embodied in steel, glass, and concrete. But the Loop's residents rarely looked back in a meaningful way. If they had, they would have seen their fellow citizens living in terror. The blood of more than seven hundred murder victims soaked the city's streets that year—the vast majority on the West and South Sides. Before the decade closed, more than eight thousand Chicagoans, most of them black, would be registered on police homicide ledgers.[4]

At the same time, black citizens also lived in constant fear of police harassment, infringement on their civil liberties and bodily security, and, ultimately, violence. The specter of police violence was so great that, as the black construction contractor and community leader Lester Jackson told the Metcalfe panel, "When I leave my home in the morning, I don't know if I'll ever see it again."[5] Officer-involved shootings of black men and women had been escalating for years.[6] Much of black Chicago acknowledged a particular strand of antiblack racism that seemed endemic to the police department—a suspicion that was borne out in numerous studies and interviews and that received the strongest possible stamp around Christmastime of 1967, when a Ku Klux Klan cell that included the Illinois Klan's grand dragon was discovered to be operating and recruiting within the CPD.[7]

This book is an exploration of how Chicago and cities like it arrived at such a point. Between the late 1910s and the early 1970s, Chicago built an intricate, powerful carceral machinery whose most constitutive feature was an extreme racial selectivity. Within the cogs and wheels of that machinery, black communities increasingly became both overpatrolled and underprotected, and faced harassment, violence, and neglect from the police department that their taxes helped fund. The city's power structure consistently ignored, sidestepped, or crushed black critiques of these realities. The rest of the city generally looked on without offering much comment. In tracing the construction of that machinery and its reverberations across Chicago's social fabric, this book exposes a series of complex and troubling histories of African America, urbanism, American politics, and criminal justice. As it does, it raises challenging questions about the nature of America's idiosyncratic sense of justice, about its racialized political system, and about the enduring consequences involved in circumscribing the access that certain people have to the political community's levers of power.

MOST FOUNDATIONALLY, in this book I argue that it is impossible to understand the racialized waging of the late twentieth-century Wars on Crime and Drugs without reckoning with the shifting nature of local-level policing in the decades before.

Much comment has been made (and rightly so) in recent years about the punitive turn in American politics in the late decades of the last century, and the effects of that turn. This is a matter of critical importance to everyone who lives in the United States, and so the main points are worth reiterating. In the last four decades, the United States has become the global leader in incarcerating its own citizens, with more than 6.8 million people under correctional supervision of some kind, 2.2 million of them in prisons and jails.[8] This punitive extremism challenges our entire value structure, destabilizes families and communities and, as the historian Heather Ann Thompson puts it, "distorts our democracy."[9] It also assaults black and brown communities with a particular aggressiveness. As of this writing, black/white incarceration disparities sit at roughly 5.1:1 nationally, reaching past 11:1 in some states, and have climbed close to 9:1 in Illinois thanks mostly to the imprisonment of black Chicagoans.[10] The divide between our country's demographics and the reality of our criminal justice system is, in fact, so yawning, that the racialized nature of mass incarceration has assumed the moniker of "the New Jim Crow."[11]

Sociologists, policy analysts, legal scholars, and historians have dramatically expanded our understanding of America's path to this point.[12] Some have focused on the recent past, while others have looked at longer historical processes of racial condemnation and historical analogues for the current moment.[13] Collectively, this scholarship has done much to reorient our understandings of American punishment and expose the processes driving America's prison boom. At its best, it has pushed and broken the boxes in which we consider the ideological, temporal, and racialized geneses of mass incarceration.

This book joins that conversation, but my concern lies less with telling (or reinforcing) a broad story of mass incarceration's birth and consequence than with seeking to explain why, when the tumorous growth of mass incarceration *did* begin to metastasize, it developed so suddenly as a full-blown instrument of racial repression. Telling that story involves different questions, different chronologies, and a different focus.

This is an intensely local book. The processes at play here have national implications, and they almost certainly have distinct analogues in most other major American cities. Much of the mass incarceration literature has tended to prioritize federal or state policies over the local context. There are some notable exceptions—especially the work of Ruth Wilson Gilmore, Kelly Lytle Hernández, and Max Felker-Kantor.[14] But all these scholars focus on Los Angeles, and none of them focuses specifically on the intersection of policing and antiblackness in a way that spans America's pre- and post–World War II years. By contrast, this is a book about a particular city, police force, and community historically and over the span of multiple generations. The local context here is essential. The ways that people experience their daily lives, the manner in which they feel served or abused by police within the particularly quotidian contexts of the everyday—these things matter. Police are, for citizens, the most visible agents of the American criminal justice system, if not of the state itself. They are, first and foremost and by occupational definition, the front line of whatever criminal justice initiatives politicians and policymakers decide to push. Regardless of the broad policy at work, virtually all citizen interactions with that system begin with the same, basic step: an encounter between a police officer (or officers) and a citizen (or citizens). And officers are always operating within a particular context. Both their own influence and the influences that shape their actions are, above all else, localized. Without question, federal policies have had significant effects on the contours of policing and the resources available to police departments. But those federal policies are filtered through local networks and play out in different ways depending on the context. More pointedly, those local contexts are not just blank canvases. They also contain their own powers and privileges and ideas—ones deeply rooted in neighborhood- and city-level dynamics and profoundly shaped by class, gender, and, above all else, race.

This book is a history of those powers and privileges—of how they have operated and of those they have disadvantaged. Contrary to traditional approaches in many of the studies of mass incarceration, it takes the Wars on Crime and Drugs (and state-level laws of comparable significance) as relative analytic end points rather than launching pads.[15] Shifting from the national and state level to the local, it takes seriously the ways that policing changed, why it changed, and how it became increasingly racialized in the early and middle parts of the twentieth century. Among its most critical conclusions is this: in terms of the mechanisms and strategies of policing on the ground in urban America, neither the War on Crime nor the War on Drugs actually constituted dramatic reinventions of the wheel. Completely independent of these wars, the local-level policing apparatus became thoroughly racialized, profoundly discriminatory, and deeply punitive. No larger policies were required to make this happen.

Consider, by way of example, the CPD in the year 1970. The War on Crime's central agency, the Law Enforcement Assistance Administration (LEAA), had begun channeling funds to police departments across the country, but did so in comparatively meager ways. In Chicago that year, for example, LEAA funds only made up (at most) about 1 percent of the CPD's annual budget.[16] And yet nearly every identifiable component of today's policing apparatus was already in evidence, in some form or another, on Chicago's black South and West Sides. Contrary to assumptions about the growth of police departments, as measured in the number of officers in its employ, Chicago's police force was actually *larger* than it is today. (Meanwhile, in the fifty years prior, which constitute the core of this study, its size had grown more than 260 percent, at rates *ten times* greater than the growth rate of the overall population.[17]) Black people had always faced disproportionate rates of arrest in comparison to their white neighbors. But now, for the better part of a decade, the disproportion had become so bloated that even the raw totals of black arrests were substantially higher than white ones, the gap growing further apart each year. Stop-and-frisk, long in practice, had been codified into Illinois law, driven first and foremost not by federal policy but by the lobbying influence of CPD officials and Democratic mayor Richard Daley in collaboration with conservative Republicans. The saturation of black neighborhoods with police officers trained to profile so-called hoodlums was a feature of daily life. So, too, were the agonizing consequences of police violence toward black people—most of them unarmed and male. Torture allegations against the police, made by black community members intermittently for most of the century to that point, had been routine for years. Zero-tolerance policing known as "aggressive preventive patrol"—a direct template for the far more famous "broken windows" policies yet to come—had been official police policy in black neighborhoods since the early 1960s. There have been important technological advances in the intervening years, but very little—save for the implementation of computer-driven models of policing and the militarization of police weaponry[18]—that could realistically be called new.

That was one side of the equation. Meanwhile, antigang initiatives by the police were proving totally unsuccessful, in part because they relied on unnecessary force and the exacerbation of hostilities between gangs, as though members of the CPD's Gang Intelligence Unit (GIU) hoped to provoke total war. Police officials identified a code of silence toward officers by young members of the black community—a wall of mistrust based on their and their friends' and families' experiences with the police.[19] At the same time, community members and advocacy groups identified a complete lack of accountability in the ways that the department took officers to task (or, rather, didn't) when they committed acts of misconduct, and a police department that was eminently hostile to change. And through it all, community members continued to live in a heightened state of danger, confronting the rhythms of daily life under a shroud of, to tweak Howard Saffold's phrasing, extreme underprotection.

In sum, by 1970 Chicago's police system worked fundamentally differently for most black communities than it did for most white ones. And it did not work well for the former.

I wish to be clear: I'm not suggesting that the inauguration of the War on Crime and subsequent War on Drugs were insignificant. They were, incredibly so. When measured in social cost and the disruption of human life, these two wars together constitute some of the most significant domestic policies of the post–World War II era. And when measured through a particularly racial lens, they stand in tandem and tension with the Civil and Voting Rights Acts, conjoined at the hips as the federal government's seminal postwar achievements and failures in pursuit of a functioning multiracial democracy. At a moment of supposed racial freedom, these wars invested new moneys and technologies in police departments that already had developed antagonistic relationships to huge swaths of black America. More importantly, they cultivated increasingly harsh sentencing policies, created a political context in which people supported tax-funded carceral construction at the expense of tax-funded schools and other public goods, and invested almost unimaginable amounts of resources in a law-and-order agenda that came increasingly to be accepted as an operational norm, despite its innumerable and profound demerits.

But when it came to policing, the most significant changes and developments in Chicago's story took place before those wars had their most meaningful material impacts. To be sure, arrest numbers in Chicago peaked in the early 1980s, during the opening years of the War on Drugs. But that culminated a decades-long rise that predated that war, and arrests today—total and black—are lower than in 1965. So, rather than asking the question of how we got to where we are today, I ask, *How did we get to such a state by 1970?* This is the guiding question precisely because it is where we should look if we wish to understand mass incarceration's monstrously racialized birth, to understand why mass incarceration is still today as black as it is, and to understand the present state of relationships between the police and African American communities across the country.

THIS BOOK TAKES ITS TITLE from James Baldwin, the great black essayist and novelist, and from his essay "A Report from Occupied Territory," written for the *Nation* in July of 1966. Baldwin wrote from Harlem, and ostensibly in reflection on Truman Nelson's accounting (published as *The Torture of Mothers*) of the "Harlem Six"—six young black men targeted by New York police and erroneously arrested in the murder of a white Hungarian immigrant woman.[20] But that was, in many ways, backdrop. His report sprawled further and cut deeper, carving into the skeletal marrow of northern racism. Deindustrialization, discrimination, segregated education systems, disillusionment—it was all there, bound together as a "hideous state of affairs." But particular focus was reserved for the disastrous treatment that black people received from the police, who beat, chased, tortured, harassed, framed, terrified, and terrorized them. And what was true in Harlem was true everywhere. "What I have said about Harlem," Baldwin wrote, "is true of Chicago, Detroit, Washington, Boston, Philadelphia, Los Angeles and San Francisco—is true of every northern city with a large Negro population. And the police are simply the hired enemies of this population. They are present to keep the Negro in his place and to protect white business interests, and they have no other function. They are, moreover—even in a country which makes the very grave error of equating ignorance with simplicity—quite stunningly ignorant; and, since they know that they are hated, they are always afraid. One cannot possibly arrive at a more surefire formula for cruelty."[21]

Baldwin was far from alone in using the language of occupation to describe what police were doing to black communities. Angela Davis wrote that, "from Birmingham to Harlem to Watts, black ghettos are occupied, patrolled and often attacked by massive deployments of police. The police, domestic caretakers of violence, are the oppressor's emissaries, charged with the task of containing us within the boundaries of our oppression."[22] Huey Newton recruited support for the Black Panther Party (BPP) in its fledgling years by confronting police officers in residential streets and calling black people from their homes to bear witness. "Come on out, black people," Newton said. "Come on out and get to know about these racist dog swine who been controlling our community and occupying our community like a foreign troop."[23] That idiom had local translations in Chicago. There, the relentless police killings of young black men in the late 1960s "confirmed for many people the Panthers' view that the police were licensed thugs, who served as an occupying force in their community," while innumerable citizens described living in terror of and under constant surveillance by the police.[24] And, as we will see later in this book, the sentiment was echoed not just by local black activists, but by allies, independent researchers, and, perhaps improbably, the International Association of Chiefs of Police.

Meanwhile, American cities were going up in flames. Through much of the 1960s, particularly its middle and latter portions, urban rebellions scorched the urban landscape, from Watts to Newark, Milwaukee to Houston, in what Peter Levy has termed "the great uprising."[25] A central catalyst in all of them was the actions of police officers—widely resented across huge sections of black inner cities for the consistent brutality, disrespect, surveillance, and harassment they directed toward black people, as well as for the inefficient services they rendered when black folks actually needed them. As the National Advisory Commission on Civil Disorders (commonly known as the Kerner Commission) famously put it, "To some Negroes police have come to symbolize white power, white racism and white repression. And the fact is that many police do reflect and express these white attitudes. The atmosphere of hostility and cynicism is reinforced by a widespread belief among Negroes in the existence of police brutality and in a 'double standard' of justice and protection—one for Negroes and one for whites."[26]

All these dynamics were deeply shaped by the derogation of black people's political power more broadly. Thus, this is also a book about politics. More particularly, it is about the limits of politics-by-representation, and about the costs of circumscribing the access that marginalized people have in crafting public policy that will better their lives. Chicago was and is one of the meccas of twentieth-century black electoral achievement—it is Oscar De Priest's city, William Dawson's city, Harold Washington's city, Carol Moseley-Braun's city, Barack Obama's city. But when we look at the black community's repeated struggles to receive effective and fair police policies for their neighborhoods, whether in the 1920s or the 1940s or the 1960s (or the 2010s), what we see is little beyond frustration. There were small victories, but they were subsumed beneath a broader systematic neglect. Which begs the question: For all that achievement, what exactly did poor and working-class black Chicagoans get?

Through the lens of policing, we are forced to confront the extraordinary ways that city governments like Chicago's have historically abrogated their obligations to their citizens.[27] When one considers the fact that police protection is a public and not a private resource, the significance of the constellated injustices mapped in this book comes into sharper focus. There are innumerable studies on the challenges black people faced within the context of the housing and employment markets from the First Great Migration through the crest of the Second, and on the vitriolic hatred that many of them faced from their new white neighbors in the city as well. Yet as abhorrent as those sorts of physical, economic, and emotional violence are, the problems black people faced with the police represent something different—something of perhaps less immediate consequence but of a tremendous long-term one. Whereas those other contexts of racism and inequality most often centered around interpersonal interactions and opaque market forces, black experiences with the CPD were confrontations with brute institutional racism within the nominally public realm. Perhaps second only to schools, the police department stood as the most easily identifiable public resource within black neighborhoods. Black taxes helped pay for the police. Black voters helped elect the men (and they have almost all been men) who would ultimately oversee the department's functions and hire its personnel. Police officers swore an oath to serve and protect the public without discrimination or malice. But black people received little in the way of consistently meaningful returns on these promises and investments.

For black people to have their rights to equitable, fair, and nonracist policing undermined in the ways etched on these pages, then, was not simply another form of racism. It was the social compact, undone. It was a derogation of their very rights as citizens—a particular violation of what the social theorist Henri Lefebvre famously called *the right to the city (le droit à la ville).*[28] Having a right to the city implies that one can make claims on the city's public resources, since they are nominally for everyone. (David Harvey is correct in saying that the right to the city is "far more than the individual liberty to access urban resources," but that liberty is nevertheless a core part of it.[29]) Black people saw this right removed when it applied to the police, a fact that lays bare their circumscribed access to the public infrastructure generally, and to one of its key precepts—safety—more particularly.

At various points in time, black people criticized all of this; and as a further reminder of how little their civic voice was valued in the city, their criticisms largely fell on deaf ears. The point was emphasized again and again. And it was reinforced by juxtaposition with the ways that the city and its law enforcement apparatus *did* respond to critiques from other sections of society—particularly those of social and economic elites.

That discordant ability to influence police policy and action would be a recurring theme. This book spins around the relationship between privilege and policing. The central analytic point here is race, although as historians of policing—among them, Sam Mitrani, Christopher Agee, Adam Malka, and Frank Donner—have pointed out, having the ability to place demands on the police has historically been entangled in numerous other social privileges. This is not to argue the value of the public safety tasks that some citizens feel police forces supposedly perform; but it does emphasize that that may not be the *most valued* task they perform from the perspective of city administrators and powerbrokers. In a 1993 interview with the community historian Timuel Black, former CPD superintendent Leroy Martin—the first black person to hold that post in Chicago, after being appointed by

Harold Washington in 1987—was asked to boil down the essence of police work. "What police work does, all over the nation," he replied, "is to try to protect the city's economic interests." Putting it differently, he argued that police work was "basically just trying to contain the problems that occur in a geographical area, trying to make sure that the parts of the city that work continue to work, and in those parts that don't work trying to keep the level of violence down and under control. That's basically it, if you want to really boil it down."[30]

Most public officials aren't so forthcoming about this fact, but that doesn't make the evidence any less clear. The relationship between people's social privilege (racial, economic, or both) and the responsiveness of the police to their demands has been clear from the beginning. Indeed, as the prologue that follows demonstrates, the very origins of the CPD itself lie not in broad and generalized interests in public safety but in the highly specific concerns of Chicago's most monied and elite, who sought to curtail immigrant leisure and contain worker radicalism. Many things have changed about police work since then, but the relationship between police prerogatives and privileged interests is not one of them. In the nineteenth century, the rockiest shoals on which citizens' rights vis-à-vis the police foundered were based on class and ethnicity, in that order. In the twentieth century, those shoals were increasingly structured by race and class.

WHAT FOLLOWS is the origin story of a racially repressive policing system in an American city. This is, of course, but one piece of the puzzle in terms of understanding the repressions of the police and the criminal justice system more broadly. "Every book," Viet Thanh Nguyen reminds us, "has its margins," and I should be clear at the outset about what this one's are.[31] For one thing, this book contains little in the way of gender analysis, and has little to say about how people's identities as cisgender men, cisgender women, and nonbinary people shaped their encounters with the police.[32] For another, it has regrettably little to say about nonblack communities that are also subject to police repression and neglect. The most notable group here would be Chicago's Puerto Rican population, which grew substantially in the postwar years, as well as other Latinx and Indigenous communities.[33] Their experiences with the police deserve and demand their own studies, but they are beyond the scope of this book. For still another, this book has little to say about the experiences of police officers, other than when those experiences are immediately germane. This is mostly because I am interested in what this racialized policing system meant for black citizens and communities, rather than in what it meant for police officers themselves.

It is also, however, because what I am reaching for here is not a rote documentation of individual officers' behavior, but an analysis of a *system*—the component parts of which are less discreetly important.

This book also has little to say about criminal courts (which, at least in the modern era, Nicole Gonzalez Van Cleve has effectively shown to be "central sites of racialized punishment"), sentencing policies, prosecutors, prison construction, or any of the many other gears and cogs that collectively constitute the system.[34] To change metaphors: we might think of the criminal justice system as a network of constellated stars, of which police policy and conduct are but one. What I try to do here is bring that one star into brighter focus, to look at it in a sustained way, animated by the belief that doing so helps us better see and understand the constellation as a whole. In doing so, I hope that we will think harder about how we want the society we live in to be structured, and question the ways that certain sections of our society privilege order for some over justice for all.

I started researching what became this book long before Trayvon Martin and Michael Brown were shot dead in American streets and activists took to those same streets in grief and righteous rage. At the time, the hashtags #BlackLivesMatter and #SayHerName did not exist, and the names of black people shot and killed by the police were not archived with their own personalized hashtags. (This did not mean that black people, adults and children alike, were not being shot and killed by the police.) Ever since the Black Lives Matter movement emerged to force a reckoning with the realities of police violence in the United States, however, when people have discovered what I research, they have routinely asked some variation of the same question: "When did things get so bad?" Readers may enter this book with the same question in mind. Yet, however well-intentioned, embedded in the question is an assumption that "things"—meaning relationships between the police and black folks—were ever some approximation of *fine*. That isn't really true. To be sure, antagonisms and repressions have grown and ebbed, and changed over time. But this book begins at the moment when Chicago began to absorb a critical mass of black people, and it is not a coincidence that that is also the moment at which a racially repressive police system began to take shape in that city. In other words, there is not a time in Chicago's history where the city was home to large percentages of black people, and in which they had a smoothly functioning relationship with the CPD.

When people ask when things got bad, my sense is that they do so in the hope that, if things used to be better, they can somehow be returned to that better state. But to entertain such notions is an act of comfort-seeking detached from historical reality. As the sociologist Alex Vitale has explained, we can't incrementally reform ourselves toward a functional and equitable police system since "the problem is policing itself."[35] Or, as the historian and black studies scholar Keeanga-Yamahtta Taylor writes, "Police violence is a part of the DNA of the United States. . . . There has been no 'golden age' of policing in which violence and racism were not central to the job."[36] I would only expand Taylor's comment: neglect of black interests and disregard of violence meted out on black bodies have been central, too—not for all individual officers, but for the police system *as a system*.

And so, in response to the question and its attending hope, I must simply say that I am of two minds. I am inspired by the activism of recent years, much of it driven by black women and black youth who dare to dream and fight for a better and more just world. Moreover, spending one's professional career studying social movements generally and the black freedom struggle in particular is to constantly be reminded of the world-changing capacities of committed individuals and communities.

At the same time, I also know that police systems—the CPD and many others—not only have by and largely refused to ingenuously engage this new cohort of activists but also have actively denied and sought to delegitimize current grievances and the movements they produce. In this, consciously or not, they echo the hostile dismissals of black grievances that their predecessors in and beyond police departments made throughout the twentieth century. Such intellectual intractability on the part of those in power is worth remembering.

Regardless, what I do know is this: if we don't better understand the depth and genesis of these problems that plague us, we cannot fully engage the process of imagining where we want and need to go. With this book, I am reaching for such an understanding.

Prologue

THE PROMISED LAND AND THE DEVIL'S SANCTUM:
THE RISINGS OF THE CHICAGO POLICE DEPARTMENT
AND BLACK CHICAGO

Chicago's biggest voices have always sung its praises in gray-hued tones. To those who have articulated it best, it is rough-hewn, redolent with brawn and grit. "We are things of dry hours and the involuntary plan / Grayed in, and gray," as Gwendolyn Brooks describes tenants of the city's famous kitchenette apartments in her poem "Kitchenette Building."[1] Nelson Algren loved the place, yet still described it as "an October sort of city even in the Spring . . . the city of all cities most like Man himself—loneliest creation of all this very old poor earth."[2] Studs Terkel once characterized the city as "molded by the muscle rather than the word."[3] Saul Bellow described it as "that center of brutal materialism"; Richard Wright as "this machine-city."[4] Carl Sandburg's description, of course, is probably the most famous—Chicago as his "city of the big shoulders" still endures as a city favorite.[5] His phrasings in turn showed Sandra Cisneros how to, as she put, "sing with syllables"—how to describe her own version of Chicago: Bucktown and Humboldt Park and Pilsen—Mexican homes filled with "bean eaters . . . who live in cramped apartments with shared bathrooms and not enough hot water."[6] To those who best know it, it is a city that grinds more than it glitters.

And yet there is beauty within the brawn. The city looms on the shores of Lake Michigan, the skyline of the Loop announcing itself from dozens of miles away on clear days. The Willis Tower (formerly the Sears), the John Hancock Building, and other skyscrapers pierce the sky. On the ground, Chicago hugs the lake for more than two dozen miles from north to south. The renowned urban planner Daniel Burnham plotted the city's expansion in such a way as to ensure that it took advantage of its natural beauty, with the shoreline reserved for the public and largely occupied by beaches, parks, and nature preserves.[7] Inland, across the city's 234 square miles, stretch seventy-seven officially demarcated community areas (Douglas, Lake View, and so on), which break further into two hundred commonly identifiable neighborhoods (Bronzeville, Boystown). And within those areas, more than two and a half million people live, instilling the city with its vibrancy, and collectively shaping its rhythms.

But spin back in time two hundred years, and none of this existed. The miles on which Chicago now sits were little more than prairie grass and sedge and wild onion, loam and dirt and sand. Rivers ran through it, turning sections of what would later become the city proper into muck and marsh during periods of high rainfall. A series of Indigenous peoples lived off the land for centuries before state-sanctioned settler violence and dispossession drove them out. The first nonnative person to occupy the land was, famously, mulatto—a Haitian immigrant named Jean Baptiste Point du Sable. At the mouth of the Chicago River, du Sable established a trading post in the 1770s. White people came later, first and fitfully at the turn of the century, with construction of Fort Dearborn in 1803, and then with increasing enthusiasm as the American military and government sponsored a series of wars with Indigenous tribes and settler-colonialist projects in the region—culminating in the 1833 Treaty of Chicago, which dispossessed the Potawatomi and encouraged a flood of white settlers into the growing lakeshore town.[8]

As colonization commenced, Chicago was bent into a metropolitan hub with remarkable speed, driven by technological innovation, commercial expansion, and fortunate geography. As the historian William Cronon shows in his classic *Nature's Metropolis*, Chicago's central location allowed entrepreneurs to connect the hinterlands of the Great West and their incredible resources with the markets of the Eastern Seaboard. Driving the budding metropolis were also incredible amounts of human imagination, innovation, resilience, and work. When fire destroyed the city, Chicago rebuilt. When nature stood in its way, humans tamed it. They didn't always succeed, but when they did, they created marvels. (Most famously, when the Chicago River presented sewage drainage and flood problems, Chicagoans embarked on a massive public works project that literally reversed the river's flow so that it drained back outward away from the Lake Michigan water supply and toward the Mississippi River.[9])

And so the city grew. Already by 1854, Chicago industry had grown so much and so quickly that its citizens had begun to worry about the problem of smog, and such growth would only quicken in later decades.[10] First through industries like the McCormick Reaper Works, then on the backs of meatpacking plants, lumber mills, and the steel industry, Chicago muscled its way into national industrial prominence. Railroad lines rolled innumerable products into and out of the city every day of the week. On sites throughout the city, particularly south of the Loop in places like the famous Union Stock Yard—where hundreds of thousands of pairs of hands killed and butchered hundreds of millions of cattle, hogs, and sheep—Chicago embodied America's modern industrial age.[11]

At the center of all of this were, of course, people. From a town of fewer than five thousand in 1840, Chicago registered nearly 1.7 million residents at the dawn of the 1900s. By 1920 it would absorb fully another million people. And if America was a nation of immigrants, Chicago was one of that truth's best microcosms; between the 1870s and the 1910s, roughly four in five Chicagoans were foreign-born or first-generation Americans.[12] They carried traditional customs—languages, clothing, cuisine, cosmologies, and worldviews—and worshipped, ate, drank, sang, and spoke in their own particular manners. They came together at work sites, laboring in Chicago's thousands of blue-collared, big-shouldered industrial jobs, but went home to insular neighborhoods, self-defining the feel and rhythms of their respective communities. They instilled neighborhood social institutions with their tastes and beliefs, and built fraternal and charitable organizations that would respond to their communities' needs.[13] In the twenty-first century, those ethnic barriers have largely faded, although their imprint on the city lingers: in street names, cuisine clusters, church facades, and museums.

"Matters Not Criminal": The Problem of Social Order and the Rise of the CPD

Chicago could never have thrived without those immigrant workers that came to and stayed and worked in the city during the second half of the nineteenth century. Nevertheless, in the early years of city-building, elites worried about them feverishly. City boosters, members of the business community, and elite citizens united in their concern about immigrants' habits, cultures, and politics. They viewed immigrant communities as inherently unruly, constantly drunk, and later, politically suspect. In response, they sought to impress on immigrants certain sets of morals, to restrict their leisure activities, to get them to stop drinking, and to keep them from challenging the socioeconomic status quo.[14]

To do these things, elites used their political power to push for the incorporation of a police force, which was formally founded in 1853. The timing was hardly unique; every major American city implemented a formal police force between the 1840s and the close of the 1880s.[15] As the historian Sam Mitrani writes, the driving forces behind this choice, in Chicago and elsewhere, were fairly clear: "Leading businessmen who dominated both urban economies and their politics pushed city government to build powerful armed institutions that could defend their property and their interests from the new threats that accompanied the development of a wage labor economy."[16] The police department, in other words, was an institution founded by privileged elites in order to protect their interests.

The CPD's activities in its infancy reflected those interests. The city council "made it clear from the outset that it was creating a military-style police department to keep order in the face of the threats posed by a mobile class of wage workers, not to fight crime." It broadly defined police power, to include controlling a certain "class of persons"—working-class immigrants—by a variety of means, including the need to punish them for "matters not criminal" but that would, elites imagined, be damaging to the city's health.[17] Nothing was more important in this respect, early on, than booze. The vast majority of the CPD's early work lay in arresting large numbers of Irish and German immigrants for drinking (despite drinking itself not being criminalized), with only very infrequent attention to more serious crimes.[18] This, in turn, led to deep animosities between those immigrant populations and the police. The most famous of these early conflicts erupted two years after the department's founding when, in the Lager Beer Riot of 1855, a crowd of German immigrants lodged furious protests against Sunday closing laws and the police crackdown on saloonkeepers who violated them, provoking intense conflict between protesters and the police.

As the contours of Chicago's industrial economy took shape in the following decades, radicalism eclipsed the liquor problem in the eyes of elites. Beginning in the 1860s, workers and political radicals organized to try to better the conditions under which laborers worked and improve the wages they earned. They struck for an eight-hour day, fought for improved safety regulations, and demanded better pay. At virtually every turn, they were repelled by the city police force, which overwhelmingly served to defend business interests.

Nonetheless, elites weren't wholly satisfied with the police until the late 1870s, when a general law-and-order consensus coalesced following the

Great Railroad Strike of 1877.[19] As that strike spread across the country, more often than not, police forces—still getting their institutional bearings—were overwhelmed by the workers. In Chicago, however, the police proved fairly adept at crushing the strike's local iteration—most notably, by using extraordinary force and violence. Elites were pleased. Their suspicions of the merit and capabilities of the CPD began to fade, as they turned increasingly to understanding how the police force could be used to their benefit. In the aftermath of the 1877 strike, "Chicago's elite was increasingly organizing itself to make sure the state and municipal governments met its needs. And the single-most important of those needs was the maintenance of order." From that point on, police officers in Chicago, and elsewhere across the industrial North of the United States, "fought to protect the wage labor system from the threat posed by its own wage slaves."[20]

Conflict between police and the working class, and the CPD's repression of dissenters to the wage labor system, reached a culmination in May of 1886. On May 3, in eight-hour-day strikes that brought as many as a hundred thousand workers out on picket lines, strikebreakers at the McCormick Reaper Works met a cordon of furious regular workers. Two hundred CPD officers flowed to the scene to protect the strikebreakers, and in the ensuing melee, police killed four strikers and wounded many more.[21]

The next night, a few thousand people gathered in Chicago's Haymarket Square to protest the killings, and to continue to push the eight-hour-day demand. Heading the rally were the city's leading anarchists, socialists, and political revolutionaries. As the evening wore on, the crowd dissipated, but toward the rally's close, a contingent of 176 officers advanced on those who remained. Police demanded that the crowd disperse, at which point someone in the crowd threw a makeshift bomb that exploded at the feet of the officers. They responded with a torrent of gunfire directed into the crowd, hitting numerous protesters, some of them in the back as they tried to flee. Several members of the rally and seven police officers were killed in the evening's violence.[22]

The repression of radicals that followed—both in formal court and that of public opinion—is well known, but Haymarket also, critically, had the effect of turning public opinion about the police in unprecedentedly favorable directions. Newspapers turned the police into heroes. The *Chicago Tribune* collected funds to erect a monument to the policemen killed in the incident. Private citizens poured money into the police department after the affair in order to demonstrate their support for the officers. The first pension fund for police was established as a result, turning the job of patrolman from one of questionable material benefit to one that would at least guarantee a stable retirement. At the same time, officers insisted—with success—that citizens treat them with greater respect, and the entire affair also "pushed the rhetoric of Chicago's politics far to the right and gave the promoters of law and order increased political power." As a combination of this growing respect for officers and the law-and-order turn, the city government proved willing to channel increased funding toward the CPD for hiring, salaries, and equipment.²³ The department had arrived as an essential element in Chicago's political economy, conjured into being by particular sets of interests, and functioning as a mechanism to protect social hierarchies and the broader status quo.

Other things were changing, too. Nativist hostilities toward German and Irish immigrants began to ease in the late nineteenth and early twentieth centuries, as members of those groups began to, as scholars have said, "become white."²⁴ Members of those groups began to enter into the police department in large numbers, easing the degree to which their respective ethnic groups faced police repression. During the 1880s, the number of Irishmen especially on the police force rose dramatically, while the rates of arrest that Irish people faced plummeted precipitously.²⁵ The status quo, in this regard, was shifting, and not just in reference to the police. By the opening decades of the twentieth century, the sons of immigrants would become some of the most critical players in Chicago's political arena—particularly Irish Americans in the South Side Bridgeport neighborhood. Class would continue to be a critical determinant in citizens' treatment by the police force, but ethnicity became increasingly less correlative to negative treatment from it. Race, rather, would begin to emerge in the late 1910s as the new terrain on which many of the city's social battles would be fought.

The Rise of the Black Metropolis and the Limits of Inclusion

As Chicago built itself and as elites built its police department, black people labored to build a life in the city, too.²⁶ From du Sable's founding of Chicago through the beginning of the twentieth century, the black presence in the city remained comparatively small but reflected many of the larger issues animating the city and nation. Prior to the Civil War, African Americans' rights to basic citizenship in Chicago and the state of Illinois were profoundly derogated. The differences between that northern context and the slave South were, of course, real. But the same racist logics that undergirded the slave regime and upheld its political legitimacy deeply shaped life for black Chicagoans. The Illinois state constitution technically permitted certain forms of slavery. Black men had their voting rights stripped, from a year after Illinois achieved statehood (1818) until ratification of the Fifteenth Amendment in 1870. That disenfranchisement was part of a larger set of Black Codes that banned interracial marriage, "barred black men from serving on juries, testifying against white men, or serving the state militia."[27] In 1853 the state passed black laws that issued heavy fines on anyone who brought a black person into the state. Moreover, any black people who brought *themselves* into the state could be fined and, if unable to pay, "sold to anyone who would pay the fine."[28] Such legislation established the entire system of state jurisprudence as explicitly hostile to black interests. Even when black Chicagoans successfully lobbied for a state civil rights bill in the mid-1880s, the wound of the city's failure to actually enforce the antidiscrimination ordinances was likely salted by the fact that the city mayor, Carter Harrison, had, just a couple of decades before, owned slaves in Kentucky.[29]

The desire to confront such repression ushered in an era of vibrant black political formation, despite the small size of Chicago's African American community. The Great Migrations and the conditions they birthed are the focus of this book, but the twinned issues of repression and struggle certainly precede my chronological brackets. In the late nineteenth century, Ida B. Wells-Barnett, Fannie Barrier Williams, John Jones, and other black women and men worked to challenge the strictures of an intensely racist local context, on everything from inclusion at the 1893 World's Fair to the quotidian aspects of job and housing discrimination. Such powerbrokers waged mighty if ultimately unsuccessful assaults on the contours of Chicago's racial barriers, whether through formal political channels, community self-help, or more militant protest.[30]

Chicago's persistent strains of racism did not crush black freedom dreams, nor did they stem the influx of African Americans into the city.[31] The Negro, as Langston Hughes wrote, may have spoken of rivers. But in the early and middle parts of the twentieth century, she moved in waves. The so-called Great Migration that serves as the backdrop to this book's early chapters began a decades-long process in which America's racial geography would be remapped. In 1910 Chicago's black population stood at roughly 44,000—an impressive number but still relatively small within the broad confines of the city. In the coming two decades, it would double and then double again—to 109,458 in 1920, and then to more than 235,000 by the dawn of the 1930s.[32] Flooding in from points south, people came for opportunities and with hopes for a broad array of freedoms. And they came to escape the wretched horrors of Jim Crow, the Southland's many bitter fruits.[33]

The path for most of these new migrants was wrought from railroad ties, laid out on gravel beds that stretched from the bayous of southern Louisiana into the heart of Chicago's Loop. The Illinois Central was the primary technology by which they journeyed. Like a shadow skirting the river proper, its river of rails wound alongside the east bank of the Mississippi and through the alluvial plains of the Delta, connecting with the Yazoo and Mississippi Valley Railroad in Jackson and Memphis and pulling from tributaries throughout the Southland.

The city to which those rails wound was a promise. Visions of it were emancipatory. Poems and songs of Chicago-bound persons carried titles like "Bound for the Promised Land" and "The Land of Hope" ("Go on, dear brother / you'll ne'er regret; Just trust in God / pray for the best / And at the end You're sure to find / 'Happiness will be thine'").[34] The sociologists St. Clair Drake and Horace Cayton channeled idioms of freedom and emancipation as they interpreted migrants' views of their destination. The rail routes to the city on the lake represented a "flight to freedom."[35] The migration was, to "most Negroes . . . a step toward the economic emancipation of a people" long bound to the exploitations of southern society, the brutalities of its caste system, and its punishing political economy.[36] A group of migrants from Hattiesburg, Mississippi, crossing the Ohio River wept, singing "I done come out of the Land of Egypt with the good news."[37]

If the vision was of freedom, the reality was more mixed. A vast landscape of wonder and wickedness, promise and peril, ambition and anxiety, perhaps more than anything, Chicago was steel and noise. By this point structured around a fully matured industrial economy, the city rushed with a pounding, workmanlike intensity and constant human movement. In contrast to even the busiest of southern locales from which migrants came, by the end of the 1920s, it was estimated that close to two million people poured through the central Loop on an average business day.[38] As a product of Daniel Burnham's singular vision for a magisterial downtown, coupled with the political ambitions of Mayor William "Big Bill" Thompson to see such a vision at least partially realized, the Loop towered and glimmered in architectural magnificence. And while the tallest skyscrapers of the century's second half were still to come, from just beyond the central business district, plumes of industrial smoke jutted high into the air, as if to serve as placeholders awaiting their steel-and-girder descendants. Horses and pushcarts and automobiles lumbered over an expanding grid of both dirt and paved streets. Further to the southwest, from the meatpacking district where many black men were to find their work, emanated the sensory hallmarks of the slaughterhouses—the bellows and cries of livestock, the smells of shit and blood and rendering animal fat.[39] The torrent of smells was overpowering—"a crescendo of coagulated putridity," as an earlier observer robustly put it.[40] And in every direction but the lake, neighborhoods sprawled for miles: German, Italian, Polish, black, and more.[41]

Given the din, migrants could be forgiven their apprehensions. Ida Mae Brandon Gladney, who first caught sight of Chicago in 1937 from the vantage of the Twelfth Street Train Station, gazed onto "a cold, hurrying place of concrete and steel."[42] Langston Hughes novelized it much the same, the young protagonist of his *Not without Laughter* narrating his first impressions of Chicago (via Kansas) as a city colored with "blocks of dirty grey warehouses. . . . He hadn't expected the great city to be monotonous and ugly like this."[43] The writer Richard Wright, who joined the Great Migration's Chicago artery in 1927, recalled a city of similar daunting and bustle. Remembering his first impressions in his 1944 autobiography *Black Boy*, Wright wrote: "My first glimpse of the flat black stretches of Chicago depressed and dismayed me, mocked all my fantasies. Chicago seemed an unreal city whose mythical houses were built of slabs of black coal wreathed in palls of gray smoke, houses whose foundations were sinking slowly into the dank prairie. Flashes of steam showed intermittently on the wide horizon, gleaming translucently in the winter sun. The din of the city entered my consciousness, entered to remain for years to come."[44] Even W. E. B. Du Bois stood in awe: "Chicago scares me: the crowd at State and Madison, the ruthless raggedness and grime of the blazing streets, the brute might of the Thing."[45]

The black center of "the Thing" was the bustling, vibrant, teeming streets of the Southside Black Belt, a narrow stretch of land extending southward from the Loop, centering around State Street. Despite the ongoing repressions that Wells-Barnett and others had fought against in previous decades, the Black Belt and its residents had persevered. Outside of Harlem, Chicago's South Side had become the center of urban African America. The State Street corridor that ran through it— from Twenty-Sixth to Thirty-Ninth and colloquially called "the Stroll"—was home to many of black America's premiere music clubs, theaters, and assorted other entertainments. People flocked there in abundance. The venerable *Chicago Defender*, the most prominent newspaper in black Chicago and perhaps in black America, variously called it "the popular promenade for the masses and classes," a "Mecca for Pleasure," and a "poor man's paradise."[46] From the clubs and theaters on the strip floated the sounds of some of the best musicians in America. From the gambling dens came the sounds of paychecks turned into prayers. And everywhere, a huge mélange of humanity circled about—people of different classes and interests converging on the Stroll, including numerous white Chicagoans seeking pleasures that they could find few other places.

Across Chicago and particularly there on the South Side, black people carved out a vibrant sociocultural life for themselves.[47] They built black businesses, invested in black banks, attended black clubs and theaters, settled in black neighborhoods, and read black publications. They worked in an array of occupations, earned a range of wages, and divided themselves (ideologically, not spatially) along lines of class and social sensibility. They built a black political machine and voted for black politicians and garnered social favors via black-managed patronage networks. They helped raise some of the most brilliant literary minds of the American century (Gwendolyn Brooks, Arna Bontemps), some of its most magnificent visual artists (Margaret Burroughs, Bernard Goss), and some of its most recognizable voices. (A Baptist minister, Edward Coles, migrated to Chicago in the early twenties, bringing with him his four-year-old son Nathaniel. The child grew up, clipped his first name, dropped the s from his last, and went on to have a fairly successful music career under the name Nat King Cole.) Although their white counterparts did not always see them doing so, they helped shape the city, just as the city shaped them.[48]

And yet they had to fight for much of it. In many respects, black people found themselves unwelcome guests in Chicago—the very embodiment of a "stranger in our midst," as the sociologist Thorsten Sellin would put it.[49] As the black population grew in the late 1910s, white powerbrokers, researchers, and opinion-makers constantly depicted their presence in the city, and particularly their *growing* presence in the city, as a problem. They spoke of invasion. The *Tribune*, in 1917, worried over "the sudden and unprecedented influx of southern Negro laborers," who posed "a new problem, demanding early solution."[50] Police and researchers described them as dangerous curiosities—as people with "a very rudimentary idea of sexual morality," who were slothful and mentally broken.[51] The startling vision of black migrants rendered by Judge Andrew A. Bruce, an influential member of Chicago's intellectual and criminal justice communities and the president of the American Institute of Criminal Law and Criminology, is telling: "Thousands of negroes have come to us from the rural centers of the South and have given to us a rapidly increasing population, whose natural home is in the fields and not in the streets and congested quarters of a great city, and who lack the guardianship and advice of their white masters and friends."[52]

The words carried weight. As the tide of black in-migration grew, black folks faced white neighbors who engaged them in a fraught and often furious struggle over individual and collective resources. Indeed, the flip side to the shine of the "Black Metropolis" was the reality of urban segregation—the fact that black people built for themselves separate institutions (not wholly but) in large part because white supremacy stripped their power and options to do otherwise.[53] Mostly confined to the South Side Black Belt—expanding but still rigorously bounded—the majority of black people lived in the city's worst housing. They entered into areas that had already been characterized by dilapidation and delinquency for decades prior to their arrival, when those neighborhoods were the province of European immigrant groups.[54] Due to last-hired, first-fired practices, union discrimination, and occupational skill sets that often were more in rhythm with growing seasons than assembly line speeds, they struggled to find and keep meaningful, safe, and well-compensated work.[55] They sent their children to schools that were often segregated and underresourced.[56] Yes, the Great Migration of which so many black Chicagoans were a part was in many ways emancipatory in its vision and redemptive in its relief from Jim Crow's worst horrors. But it was also, in its brute realities, something in which people's freedom dreams were frequently, punishingly bridled.

Black earning capacities in the formal economy were routinely stunted relative to other groups of workers, and they brought those earnings home to dwellings that were often unsafe. In 1920 and 1921 three black women employed by the Chicago Commission on Race Relations (CCRR) surveyed the living conditions of 274 families living on the South Side. Their notations frequently read like a textbook entry of dilapidation: "Water pipes rotted out; gas pipes leak." "Plastering off; large rat holes all over; paper hanging from ceiling." "Water for drinking and cooking purposes must be carried in; toilet used by four families; asked landlord to turn on water in kitchen; told them to move."[57] The CCRR's summary of the women's findings, in part: "The ordinary conveniences, considered necessities by the average white citizen, are often lacking. Bathrooms are often missing. Gas lighting is common, and electric lighting is a rarity. Heating is commonly done by wood or coal stoves, and furnaces are rather exceptional."[58] And even with such conditions prevailing, there was far too little housing for the number of people flooding into the Black Belt. As early as 1917, only one in thirteen requests filed by black people for help finding housing was being met.[59] With so many people looking for largely nonexistent housing, and with so many of those who did have it struggling to make ends meet, overcrowding followed; multifamily dwellings and the taking in of lodgers became commonplace on the South Side.

Although shunted together spatially, there were nevertheless deep dividing lines of class and sensibility within black Chicago. So-called Old Settlers—people who tended to have been in Chicago prior to the Great Migration, and who self-identified as more refined and of a better moral class— routinely inveighed against the impoverished moral sense of the thousands of new migrants pouring in from the rural South, and implored them to be, simply, *better*. Often guided by particular notions of respectability, these Old Settlers worried over black migrants' ability to comport themselves in public—in streetcars, on sidewalks, and in other public spaces—fearing that through their rural unsophistication they would "[tarnish] the image that Chicago's black community wished to project."[60] But despite Old Settlers' complaints about working-class migrants' public behavior (anything from loud talking to open-air drinking), Chicago's rigid racial-spatial boundaries meant that they could seldom move to areas better suited to their tastes.

Black Chicago's story and that of the CPD began to converge within this context. Even before the Great Migration, police and public policies had specifically channeled vice to, and contained it in, black neighborhoods—knowing that they couldn't eliminate it altogether but wanting to keep it out of white neighborhoods. In the 1890s, for instance, city administrators who had become worried about the proximity of the vice district—known as "the Levee"—to the downtown business district decided not to eradicate the Levee itself but to relocate it farther south into neighborhoods that were beginning to transition into black communities. That situation repeated itself in 1912 when a city-sponsored vice commission recommended a severe crackdown on prostitution in the new Levee, which pushed and scattered vice even deeper into the Black Belt, where sex workers faced far less police harassment.[61] This was not a coincidence. His disparagement of sex workers aside, the words of one former chief of police deftly capture the broader city policy on the matter: "So long as this degenerate group of persons confined their residence [to colored areas] they would not be apprehended."[62] This was a clear symbol of the city's and the department's devaluation of black community stability, even at this early juncture. And it was in some ways a template for how the police would continue to respond to prostitution, drugs, and all manner of vice in the coming decades.

The stories of black Chicago and the CPD intersected in one other crucial way prior to the terrible 1919 race riot—or rather, beginning before the riot and carrying over through its aftermath. This intersection lay in the police response to the growing violence that was a central aspect of Chicago's white supremacist praxis generally, and of the enforcement of residential segregation specifically. As the carrying capacity of the Black Belt strained and buckled under the migration's weight, black Chicagoans with the means to do so tested the rigidity of the Black Belt's invisible boundaries. While racial frictions had arisen intermittently in Chicago for decades—particularly around labor strife and Chicago employers' affections for using African Americans as strikebreakers against labor's demands—it was in black people's search for housing in historically white neighborhoods that white rage crescendoed. Over the course of forty-five months from July 1917 to March 1921, white citizens and neighborhood associations bombed fifty-eight homes—all of them belonging to black people moving to white areas, or to people who had rented to or brokered such deals for blacks. The home of Oscar De Priest, the most powerful black politician in the city at the time, was bombed. So, too, were those of Jesse Binga, a prominent banker and entrepreneur who held one of the largest masses of wealth in black Chicago, and numerous other black Chicagoans.[63]

Chicago's police apparatus did little in response. Even with such high-profile targets and the ubiquity of violence, the police response was negligible. During the entirety of that four-year bombing campaign, police generated exactly one arrest in response to the terrorism.[64] In 1919, prior to the riot, Police Chief John Garrity told an incredulous Ida Wells-Barnett that he "could not put all the police in Chicago on the South Side to protect the homes of colored people," which seemed, in so many ways, as good as saying that the bombs were not his problem.[65] Charles Duke, a prominent member of the black community, bitterly responded that had the racial roles in these bombings been reversed, "a Negro would [not] have been allowed to go unpunished five minutes."[66] So lax was the police response to the bombings that the Chicago branch of the National Association for the Advancement of Colored People (NAACP) took it upon itself (without success) to do the police's job for them; correspondence between local branch executives and national branch assistant secretary Walter White finds the local Citizens' Defense Committee working to "locate and prosecute those behind the bombings."[67] The general stance of the CPD, if unstated, was relatively clear: making much effort to track down white culprits of antiblack terrorism was, simply, not something that they were going to do. Thus, as early as 1917, one of the hallmarks of the black experience with the police was beginning to crystalize. Black people's rights to protection, especially when it involved violence across the color line, was thoroughly undermined.

THIS WAS THE BACKDROP against which the race riot of 1919 would erupt. As black people sought to carve out a space for themselves in the city, the antiblack racism that had long been present became evermore virulent and oftentimes violent. In the face of such challenges, black people struggled to achieve the fundamental perquisites of citizenship and belonging in the city. And within this context, Chicago in 1919 spiraled into racial fury, provoking questions about policing, racism, and justice. A century later, those questions have yet to be fully answered.

CHAPTER 1

Negro Distrust of the Police Increased

MIGRATION, PROHIBITION, AND REGIME-BUILDING IN THE 1920S

Horace Jennings lay in the street as Chicago convulsed. Acrid smoke hung in the air, mingling with the smells of an urban midsummer heat wave: the damp dirt and mud of unpaved streets; the sulfurous odors of manufacturing plants; the animal smells of the packing-houses. Furies raged. Around the city and particularly on the South Side, feet pounded the pavement, echoing hearts beating in chests. The day before, July 27, 1919, the threat of a Red Summer had become Chicago's reality, unleashing one of the worst race riots the United States had yet known. White Chicagoans marauded through black neighborhoods. Black Chicagoans armed themselves. The city seethed.

Blood leaked from Jennings's body, and pooled under his skin, where it would soon turn to bruises. Pain settled into his muscles and bones. He was alive, although with his nerves doubtlessly as racked as his body. A tide wave of racist violence had just cascaded over him, leveled by the hands and feet of a mob of white men.

An officer with the CPD loomed over him. "Where's your gun, you black son a bitch?," the officer growled. "You niggers are raising hell." Before Jennings could respond, his thoughts exploded under a crushing blow that hurled him into unconsciousness. When he woke again at Burnside Hospital, he discovered that the officer had stolen the money from his pockets.[1]

Across town, an unidentified man hurried toward police officers to plead for protection. The officers grabbed the man, searched him, and clubbed him with their blackjacks. Pulling free, the man ran. He didn't get far. An officer leveled his gun and fired, and the man crumpled into a heap under the railroad tracks of an elevated train at Thirty-First and State. Above him, an eerie stillness descended where the trains should usually have clattered—the rage and fear enveloping Chicago had brought rail traffic to a stop.[2] Below the quieted tracks, the officers retrieved the man's body. Finding him still breathing, they took him to a holding cell for processing.[3]

Near the same El stop, William Thornton went looking for his mother, concerned about her well-being as Chicago descended into violence. He couldn't find her. Abandoning his search, he asked a nearby police officer to help him get home and protect him from the white mobs. Instead, the officer escorted him to a police station, where he was tossed in a holding cell.

Another white police officer watched a mob beat and rob John Slovall and his brother. Wellington Dunmore suffered the same indifference—two policemen looked on as white men battered him. On his way to his job at the Union Stock Yards, William Henderson was besieged and badly beaten by a mob as he walked through Canaryville. When police arrived, they arrested Henderson but none of the members of the mob.[4] Joseph Scott, meanwhile, was pummeled on a Chicago streetcar by twenty-five white men. After beating him within an inch of his life, the mob left. As Scott lay on the streetcar floor, a CPD officer peered in and ordered him to get out. The officer told Scott that he wanted to shoot him. He didn't, but he did beat, push, and finally arrest him. Police neither questioned nor arrested any of the white assailants.[5]

Kin Lumpkin, trying to navigate the violence on his way to work at the stockyards, found himself cornered on the El platform at Forty-Seventh Street by still another white mob. The mob beat him ruthlessly, and a nearby police officer followed injury with insult, placing Lumpkin under arrest and charging him with rioting. Lumpkin spent four nights in lockup without contact with the outside world. The historical record doesn't indicate where he was housed, but the options were unpleasant. Many lockups lacked sewage systems other than a floor-length trough through which rivers of piss, shit, and vomit ran. Most lacked toilet paper, and had bad lighting, worse plumbing, and neither beds nor bedding. More than a few were basement firetraps with rickety wooden stairs the only way out.[6] And above all else, Lumpkin and black arrestees like him ran the risk of spending the hot days and humid nights of Chicago's 1919 race war locked in close quarters with white men who loathed them.

It's unlikely that these men knew each other, but history binds them together. The experiences they shared—in holding cells, on city streets, on and under the lines of the El—represent some of the most chilling abuses

Chicago police officers stand over a black victim of the 1919 riot. Chicago History Museum, ICHi-065480; Jun Fujita, photographer.

and the infuriating neglect that black people would experience at the hands of the CPD during those hellish days and nights in the summer of 1919. In an extreme crisis, men and women hoped for some level of kindness (or at least adherence to sworn duty) from the police officers they turned to for protection. All too often, what they received instead was ambivalence, vitriol, or violence.

The 1919 riot is a cornerstone in Chicago's history. It seared the city, leaving psychic scars that lingered in black Chicago's collective consciousness for generations. It mangled beloved things, twisting the familiar into bitter symbols of racial ferocity. For the parents of Dempsey Travis, a community leader, water became freighted with terror. Travis remembered that his mother, stricken by the memory of the riot and its beachfront origins, "never put even a toe into Lake Michigan's water" after that year. His father never wore a swimsuit again.[7] Beyond the individual, it cohered the community. Chicagoan Chester Wilkins looked back on the riot as a moment when the black community realized it was on its own when facing danger. Decades later, he recalled that the riot had brought black Chicago "closer together than they had ever been before," and demonstrated to them their need to arm and protect themselves.[8]

In particular, the riot is critical to the historical relationship between black Chicago and the police department. It was the most pitched interracial conflict that the city has ever known. Many of the black people who experienced it had come to Chicago on the promise of something better than what the Southland they'd left was willing to offer. And within the riot's terrible violence, the police department revealed itself as an institution that would not work well for black people. Members of the CPD repeatedly proved themselves to be defenders of whiteness and the color line, rather than protectors of all life and livelihood. And black Chicagoans would not soon forget. A year after the riot's violence had settled into détente, the *Defender* asked rhetorically: "Who among us does not remember how defenseless men and women of our group, innocent of any thought of wrongdoing, were dragged from their homes and incarcerated in dark and dingy cells?"[9]

The answer, of course, was that everyone remembered. And such memories of a police force unresponsive to black needs and often explicitly hostile to black people would be buttressed and bolstered in the years that followed. This chapter begins with the 1919 riot, but it moves outward through the 1920s, too, tracing several phenomena: police repression within black Chicago, made most acutely manifest in disproportionate arrest rates and grotesque violence; the unsafety black people felt in the face of white violence, with CPD officers frequently operating as racial partisans rather than public servants in moments of interracial conflict; and law enforcement and political operatives actively participating in the undermining of social stability in black neighborhoods by colluding with organized criminal elements.

It also explores the derogation of black people's rights to influence this system, hampered as they were by the mechanisms of patronage politics and suggestive of the limited harvests that black electoral power actually yielded. It is not that the police department could not or would not change. Indeed, by the end of the 1920s, the CPD was proving itself entirely open (at least in theory) to change. But the changes wrought flowed from the activism of white elites trying to guide it toward a more assertive tough-on-crime approach. Black people—those with the most vested interests in seeing the department remolded—were left out in the cold when these conversations took place.

The policing apparatus was not yet a fully formed instrument of antiblack repression. But the baseline represented by 1919 is important. In this moment, black people were not yet a sizable enough population to preoccupy the crafters of police policy, and there was little intentionality that guided public policy toward them. But neither was the police force an instrument that allowed black people fairness or justice. Some black Chicagoans would fume about the police's failure to ensure black safety from racial violence and to eradicate elements from their neighborhoods that they saw as undesirable. Others, beaten by nightsticks or shaken down on the street, would claim discriminatory harassment. Meanwhile, some articulated this as a better age—a hanging moment in time before police-community relationships fell from a precipice. Yet even those in the last camp—who recalled this as a period of general quiescence, as the educator and community historian Timuel Black did—still characterized the relationship as "racial, not brutal."[10] Which is not precisely a ringing endorsement.

Furies and Heat: Chicago's Riot Era

Lake Michigan forms Chicago's gorgeous eastern edge. From the shore, it appears as a seemingly endless, unbroken mass of water. When the sun comes up, it appears to rise from the depths of the water itself. As first light creeps across the lake, on particularly hot days, this combination of moisture and sun creates a haze. Humidity dampens the air and skin becomes sticky; the city shimmers with heat. July 27, 1919, was that kind of day. And under the haze of an ordinary, hot Chicago summer day, the city erupted. The explosion, many people would later lament, was ignited by a policeman who wouldn't do his job.

Police officer Daniel Callahan stood at the Twenty-Ninth Street Beach on Chicago's South Side. By midday, it was unbearably hot, and bodies packed the city's beaches. On such days, the CPD posted officers to the lakefront to ensure that the thousands of swimmers and sunbathers remained orderly. Not all of them were well equipped for the job. Daniel Callahan was a temperamental man, and it's doubtful that standing on the beach in full uniform in hundred-degree heat improved his general mood. He stared out across a mass of people, all white, since Chicago's beaches were segregated— informally, but rigidly.

When it came to beaches, black peoples' "place" was two hundred yards north, just east of where Twenty-Fifth Street dead-ended. That day, seventeen-year-old Eugene Williams and three friends pushed a raft out from the shallows of the "Hot and Cold," a little island just off the shore. Paddling out, the boys hoped to tie up at a post farther out in the lake, where they could dive and swim. But Lake Michigan's currents are unpredictable. The boys' raft got carried south, past the manmade breakwater that marked the northern edge of the white beach. And the sight of a raft of black boys floating into white waters enraged people on Twenty-Ninth Street. A man named George Stauber began hurling rocks—stone after stone raining down on and around

A crowd of black men gathers on the South Side during the 1919 riot. DN-0071297, Chicago Daily News negatives collection, Chicago History Museum.

the raft and the boys clinging to it. Amid the hailstorm, Eugene Williams went under. By the time divers reached him, he was dead.[11]

Williams's friends scrambled to shore, pointing Stauber out to a black policeman, who approached to question him. Officer Callahan intervened, telling his black colleague not to make the arrest, typical of the racial rank-pulling that black officers frequently had to reckon with.[12] Williams's friends pleaded. Crowds gathered. But Callahan refused to see Stauber arrested, and a short while later, he turned around and arrested one of the men shouting for Stauber's arrest. Furious, black citizens swarmed Callahan. A riot, the CCRR noted later, "was under way."[13]

Beyond the sheer horror of Eugene Williams's death, Officer Callahan's actions and inactions in the midst of Williams's killing were the riot's clearest accelerant, so blame churned his way. The *Broad Ax*, one of Chicago's black newspapers, would later write hyperbolically that the situation "would have been ten million times better for all the citizens of Chicago" if Callahan had "discharged his sworn duty and promptly arrested the white person who struck Eugene Williams."[14] The CCRR, in its assessment two years after the riot, wrote that "the drowning and the refusal to arrest, or widely circulated reports of such refusal, must be considered together as marking the inception of the riot. . . . There was every possibility that the clash, without the further stimulus of reports of the policeman's conduct, would have quieted down."[15] That impression was corroborated by Callahan's own police chief, John Garrity, who temporarily suspended Callahan, saying: "If these charges [of refusal to arrest] are true, I believe Callahan is responsible for this outrageous rioting."[16]

For his part, Callahan was perfectly willing to play the villain. Interviewed shortly after being reinstated by the CPD, Callahan was without remorse: "So far as I can learn the black people have since history began despised the white people and have always fought them. . . . It wouldn't take much to start another riot, and most of the white people of this district are resolved to make a clean-up this time. . . . If a Negro should say one word back to me or should say a word to a white woman in the park, there is a crowd of young men of the district, mostly ex-service men, who would procure arms and fight shoulder to shoulder with me if trouble should come from the incident."[17]

Thirty-eight Chicagoans died in the riot, and more than five hundred others suffered injury. Over a thousand more were rendered homeless. Responsibility extended far beyond one man, but the bloodletting began with Callahan.

Outward from the lakefront, the violence exploded across the South Side. Two hours after Eugene Williams's corpse was pulled from Lake Michigan's waters, a policeman's bullet struck down James Crawford, a black man, after Crawford allegedly fired a gun into a mass of police officers. In the black districts near the beach, a handful of white men were beaten. Further west, where black neighborhoods abutted white ones, gangs of white youth mobilized; over the course of six hours, they beat twenty-seven black people, stabbed seven, and shot four.[18]

The geography and patterns of violence would shift to various flash points throughout the coming days, but its intensity never truly subsided until pouring rains and the Illinois National Guard entered the fray four days later. Reports of sniper fire and machine-gun attacks proliferated, as did ones detailing black and white men stabbed, stoned, bludgeoned, or beaten to death. Horror stories abounded. A widely reported but ultimately unsubstantiated story claimed that a black woman had been slashed "to ribbons" by a knife-wielding white mob that subsequently beat her baby to death against a telephone pole.[19]

The riot exposed the deep flaws in city, state, and police department leadership, among them a disregard for black pleas for protection from racist violence in the buildup to the explosion. Black Chicagoans had been begging the city to hire more black officers to police the South Side during the tense

Chicago police officers and a soldier with the Illinois National Guard on a South Side street corner during the 1919 riot. DN-0071298, Chicago Daily News negatives collection, Chicago History Museum.

summer months preceding the riot. They felt—rightly so, it turned out—that they couldn't expect equitable treatment from white officers. Just before the riot, the situation had deteriorated to the point that some citizens suggested that "every white patrolman in the district be replaced by a colored bluecoat."[20]

Once the riot fires started, officials proved ineffective at putting them out. Mayor Bill Thompson was vacationing in Wyoming, and he'd insisted on bringing Police Commissioner John Garrity with him, leaving Chicago without its top law enforcement official when the riot exploded.[21] Illinois governor Frank Lowden, meanwhile, rushed to the city, where he holed up in the Blackstone Hotel and consulted with other officials about how to proceed, occasionally craning his head out his hotel window to take in what was happening.[22] When Thompson returned to the city, he and Lowden (both Republicans, and intense political rivals) locked horns instead of cooperating, arguing over whether or not to muster the National Guard. While they bickered, guardsmen sat in their bunkhouses for days. Finally, four days in, they were formally called out to help quell the riot.

In the meantime, the job fell to city police. The department's plan for curbing the riot called for blanketing the South Side generally with nearly every one of the department's 3,500 officers, and for sending four-fifths of the entire department's force—2,800 officers—into the Black Belt specifically. They swarmed the area, in particular prioritizing its boundaries with white neighborhoods such as the ominous "Dead-Line" of Wentworth Avenue that separated black Douglas and Bronzeville to the east from Irish Bridgeport to the west.[23] Once the saturation of the Black Belt was completed, department policy called for no one to be allowed in or out of it.

The effect was that while black people were functionally quarantined inside the Black Belt, they lay deeply exposed outside of it. White mobs seized the ensuing opportunities. Indeed, while the police focused on containing the Black Belt, far more violence occurred outside of it than within it. Stockyard workers having to commute to work proved especially vulnerable— particularly after the shuttering of the El forced them to travel on foot. Down in the Loop, white rioters roamed through businesses that employed black service workers, pulling them out on the street and beating them.[24] "Those of our group living in other parts of the city," the *Defender* mourned, eulogizing two black men beaten to death in the Loop and criticizing the CPD's approach to the violence, "were left to the mercy of the hoodlum."[25]

Significant, too, was the fact that those hoodlums were extraordinarily well connected within Chicago's convoluted early-century political cauldron and thus often received deference rather than punishment from the police. Most of the deadliest violence in the riot was levied by white mobs, many of them led by youth gangs. The work that social power did in molding different groups' relationships to the police was seldom more evident than in this context. While black people pleaded for protection, white gangs like the Bridgeport-based Ragen's Colts and Hamburg Club marauded through black neighborhoods. (Future mayor Richard Daley was a member of the Hamburg Club during the riot, and would later become its president. Charges that he was involved in the rioting were never substantiated, and Daley himself remained silent on the matter in later years.[26]) And it was they—not black Chicagoans—who had protection from on high, both within and beyond the police department.

Why? On the one hand, the police department at this historical juncture was an organizational and heavily politicized mess. Departmental authority was extraordinarily decentralized (or, perhaps more accurately, *mis*centralized).[27] Police commissioners (the department's highest office) served at the discretion of the mayor, and had little managerial power over daily street-level operations. They lacked job security and were routinely hired and fired with shifting political trade winds. They had to avoid angering their political superiors, which meant doing little in terms of policy-setting without explicit directive from the political operatives and authorities they served. Indeed, they were so tethered to city politics that their offices weren't even attached to police headquarters but sat in city hall adjacent to the mayor's office.

Rather than commissioners and police administrators, then, it was aldermen and political precinct captains (Democrats and Republicans alike) who determined what policing looked like at the street level. Although a Civil Service Commission was nominally responsible for vetting potential city employees, police (and other) jobs were in actuality entangled in ward-level patronage politics, with men who might not otherwise qualify finding work by virtue of who they knew.[28] The relationship was reciprocal. After they got them jobs, party operatives instructed police officers on which lines to toe, which laws to enforce (or not enforce), who to lean on or off of. Officers labored under threat of transfer, or worse, if they failed to bend accordingly.[29] (Little wonder that one of the police department's own commissioners described the department as "a political group."[30])

The ties between those police officers and the youth gangs who marauded through Chicago during the riot were multiple. For one, many CPD officers by this point came from ethnic enclaves like Irish Bridgeport, living in the same neighborhoods as gang members and often knowing them personally. Beyond that and perhaps more important, organizations like the Colts and the Hamburg Club in turn often worked for exactly the same politicians to whom police were responsible. As Adam Cohen and Elizabeth Taylor write of athletic clubs-qua-youth gangs, "most were sponsored by machine politicians, who contributed to their treasuries and took a personal interest in their members. The clubs, for their part, did political work in the neighborhood during election season," and also served as hired muscle when their political patrons needed it.[31] Thus, if ethnic and community solidarity didn't steer officers toward privileging white youth gangs like the Colts, messaging from political benefactors would have.

As a result, when it came to white violence perpetrated by neighborhood gangs against outside groups (particularly black people), there were structural protections in place for the former, at the expense of the latter. During the riot, a local politician reported that police officers were telling whites "to arm themselves, that the blacks were coming and that the cops couldn't stop them."[32] One member of Ragen's Colts reported that the police "had been 'fixed and told to lay off club members,'" while "another claimed that an officer always rode along with a carload of Colts during the riot so he could wave off patrolmen" who might try to pull them over.[33] Still another Colt reported being tipped by police to avoid gang headquarters, because the attorney general's office was running surveillance on it.[34] One white

The Long Arm of the Law

Political cartoonist Cecil Jensen comments on the deep politicization of the CPD. Original source unknown; reprint in *Criminal Justice: Journal of the Chicago Crime Commission* 71 (April 1944).

resident said that white gang members got away with whatever they wanted to get away with, violence included, because they were the sons of neighborhood policemen and thus functioned above the law.[35] Or in the CCRR's more clinical assessment: "Political 'pull' exercised with the police on behalf of [white] rioters has been indicated."[36]

The combination of upper-level policy choices to saturate the Black Belt and white officers' unwillingness to punish white violence dramatically shaped how the police response to the riot looked in the public eye. One report covering criminal arrests during the riot found that of 229 arrestees surveyed, 154 were black, against 75 white. The state's attorney's office reported 81 indictments against blacks, 47 against whites.[37] Such numbers indicated patterns of violence almost entirely inverse to reality: while twice as many blacks than whites had been murdered and injured in the riot, twice as many blacks were arrested and indicted.

As the evidence of blatant discrimination mounted, people balked. The dissonance between arrest stats and riot reality was, in fact, so great that it eventually provoked a near mutiny among members of the grand jury convened to hear riot cases. Disgusted with the state-orchestrated parade of black faces charged with riot-related crime, the grand jury took a nearly unprecedented stand, going on strike until more white people were brought forward for indictment. The jury's blistering statement, in part, said this: "This jury has no apology to offer for its attitude with reference to requesting . . . information of crimes perpetrated by whites against blacks before considering further evidence against blacks. . . . The reason for this attitude arose from a sense of justice on the part of this jury. It is the opinion of this jury that the colored people suffered more at the hands of the white hoodlums than the white people suffered at the hands of the black hoodlums. Notwithstanding this fact, the cases presented to this jury against the blacks far outnumber those against the whites."[38]

State's Attorney Maclay Hoyne quickly agreed. Testifying before the CCRR, he argued that "there is no doubt that a great many police officers were grossly unfair in making arrests. They shut their eyes to offenses committed by white men while they were very vigorous in getting all the colored men they could."[39] An independent coroner's jury echoed the point: "Our attention was called strikingly to the fact that at the time of the race rioting, the arrests made for rioting by the police of colored rioters were far in excess of the arrests made of white rioters. The failure of the police to arrest impartially, at the time of rioting, whether from insufficient effort or otherwise, was a mistake.[40] Illinois attorney general Edward Brundage was even less charitable. Weighing the facts of the riot against the patterns of arrest, he succinctly deemed police conduct "flagrantly neglectful."[41]

"FLAGRANT NEGLECT" by the police was a central black experience during the riot. So, too, were the cascading abuses black people were asked to endure: unwarranted arrests, beatings, abusive comments, and so on. There is no composite record of officer-involved violence during the riot; we are left with the voices of people like Kin Lumpkin, Horace Jennings, and William

Thornton, as well as those of the unnamed—the people whose battered and bruised bodies opened this chapter. Their stories of snarling assaults and brutal abuses haunt, augured by the broad violence of the era, stalked by the unnamed dead men whose stories we still do not know.

It isn't that every interaction black Chicagoans had with police during those seething days was damaging. Some black people did experience the CPD as protectors, just as some reporters offered reports of police officer bravery and fealty to duty.[42] But the cumulative portrait of riot-era policing was ruled primarily by questionable intentions and blatantly discriminatory outcomes.

A City So Corrupt: Prohibition and the Problem of Vice

The chaos of the riot, without question, was unique. But it laid bare core problems of policing for black people: that they may not be properly protected in moments of need; and that police may abuse, harass, and violate them for no reason other than the color of their skin. Those problems powerfully shaped how black people experienced the police from that point forward, including in the Prohibition decade that followed the riot.

Partly as a result of politicians' political calculations, partly because of their corruption, Chicago infamously stood at the center of Prohibition-era battles over morality and criminality. Violence reigned as warring organized crime syndicates sought shares of the underground markets in alcohol and subsidiary economies that attended the liquor trade. As they battled over turf and profit, they stacked bodies by the hundreds in the center of Chicago's neighborhoods.[43] With some exceptions and much to the chagrin of many citizens, these famous and violent Prohibition wars were generally happening not in the city's far removes but in the streets, speakeasies, and alleyways marking the landscape of the city proper. That reflected the broader patterns of how mobsters ran their operations. They frequently rooted themselves in neighborhoods, where they could employ citizens as brewers and distillers, selling to a customer base nearby.[44]

The establishment and sustenance of that geography was possible because of local politicians' and police officers' complicity. From the mayor's office on down, winding through the ranks of law enforcement and city administration, corruption was rampant. In her history of America's war on alcohol, the historian Lisa McGirr writes at length about the ways—both before and during Prohibition—that organized criminals were able to buy off Chicago politicians and police.[45] The relationship was premised on reciprocity: cash and votes flowed to politicians and police; syndicate operatives received favorable treatment and a routine blind eye from local police and courts. Politicians and mobsters attended each other's parties and often seemed to enjoy one another's company. CPD officers rode along on deliveries to prevent theft by rival bootleggers, and were paid for services rendered. One of the city's thousands of illicit liquor joints, located next to a CPD precinct station, benefited from protection to such an extreme degree that precinct policemen literally carried liquor deliveries out to cars waiting on the street.[46]

This corruption had serious effects on the city's poor neighborhoods generally, and on its black ones in particular. Mobsters looked to set up operations in places that the city's political class prioritized less, where police could easily be bribed, and where common citizens lacked both social privilege and access to the levers of power that would help them keep such operations out of their community. And Prohibition-era mobsters already had a model to follow: the police department's practice of shifting Red Light districts such as the infamous Levee into black areas repeatedly in the late 1800s and early 1900s was a perfectly workable template for harnessing race and geography to their own benefit. As a result, for much of Prohibition, the black South Side brimmed with liquor—both in terms of production and consumption. White gangsters did not singularly orchestrate this arrangement: as elsewhere, supply followed demand in jazz clubs and other South Side institutions, and there were certainly economically powerful black members of Chicago's underworld.[47] But the organized crime syndicates dominated by white ethnics were the driving force behind the process. For example, as Al Capone murdered and muscled his way to the top of the organized crime hierarchy, he made the South Side one of his key operational havens because of what he could do with police there. During the Republican mayoral administrations of close Capone affiliate Bill Thompson, city hall ordered police to lay off South Side saloons and vice dens, from which political favors could be gleaned in the form of votes and money.[48] As a result and as a series of exposés in the *Chicago Tribune* and *Chicago Daily Journal* uncovered in 1927 and 1928, the CPD was uniquely tolerant and protective of organized crime and vice on the black South Side.[49] At one point, the papers reported the existence of a veritable "immunity zone" in black Douglas, where police let pretty much anything go at the request of the syndicate.[50]

Not content to trade in liquor alone, mobsters broadened their horizons outward into other forms of vice located in black neighborhoods. Many alcohol entrepreneurs, for instance, tethered their liquor interests to the sex trade. Holding with decades-old city traditions of police and politicians permitting prostitution so long as it was confined to black neighborhoods, white syndicates established brothels on the South Side, often in the middle of black residential neighborhoods.[51] Like saloons and other "animated places" (as the CCRR put it), "white proprietors . . . brought them into the district, and many of them are patronized largely by crowds from other parts of the city. [They] are forced on the colored people."[52] Those proprietors (often syndicate members) had the money to pay the police to refrain from harassing the sex workers in their employ, and the police were by and large willing to cooperate in such an arrangement. "Ineffective policing" in this context, as Khalil Muhammad has put it, "was good public policy" as far as white powerbrokers and politicians were concerned: operations continued to run, votes and money came pouring in.[53]

The story was similar for the flowering of Chicago's drug markets. Cocaine, heroin, and marijuana were all easily available in the Black Belt—not just in covert drug dens but also out on numerous street corners. The police, operating under the containment policies to which they had long adhered, allowed this to happen so that the drug trade would stay out of white neighborhoods.[54] Organized crime operatives running large-scale drug rings set up shop in the Black Belt, responding logically to the fact that police had tacitly accepted other forms of vice to take root there.[55]

As police and public officials deliberately chose to forgo dealing with these problems, they actively abetted the processes by which many black people's quality of life was diminished. The police system was not singularly responsible for creating these circumstances. All their actions and inactions must be interpreted within the broader matrices of white supremacy, material deprivation, intense segregation and overcrowding, and resource decline that black people reckoned with at both the macro and micro levels. Nevertheless, as nominal agents of all citizens, the collusion of politicians and police in driving these processes was a particular affront.

And it was an affront with real consequences. While black Chicago's civil and cultural and artistic lives were incredibly vibrant, all the same, South Side life could be traumatizing for the thousands of citizens who wanted to avoid the loitering, gambling, prostitution, drug use, and drinking that spread as a consequence of city policy and inequality. Most people didn't want to live next door to brothels or speakeasies. Thousands who identified as middle class understandably resented the fact that endemic racism stunted their economic, residential, and social mobility and felt "compelled to be mixed with the undesirable or remain at home in seclusion."[56] Even more seriously, with alcohol and vice dens disproportionately allowed to proliferate on the South Side, private and public violence also escalated, exacerbated by personal frustrations and social congestion. In 1927 alone, for instance, 103 people were murdered in the Black Belt, forty-four of them in the third police district, whether in robberies, brawls, or in acts that the police attributed to "revenge" or "jealousy."[57] Alarmed at both the homicide rate and the various indignities that this arrangement inflicted, many black Chicagoans balked. But this was what Chicago's law enforcement apparatus and the broader systematic inequalities offered them.

Police containment of vice to black neighborhoods had other effects, as well. For one, it reinforced racist perceptions of black people as unfit for urban life. A white observer could walk through the heart of the black vice district, witness innumerable illicit exchanges and activities, and draw their own conclusions about the people living there. Without having any awareness of the broader criminological or social processes at play, white Chicagoans could filter the proliferation of speakeasies, booze houses, brothels, and gambling dens through their inherited racial lenses, interpreting what was happening on the South Side as a natural extension of black people's incapacities for urban life. For people already accustomed to thinking in racial boxes, it was not a hard conclusion to draw.

Nor were such perceptions the lone province of white Chicagoans. Many moralizers in the black community bought into this idea as well, albeit with a classist twist generally and a disdain for city newcomers in particular. They routinely blamed black Chicago's social problems on southern migrants, tacitly granting legitimacy to white racist assumptions as they did. The *Defender*, for instance, crusaded against gambling houses and cabarets consistently throughout the 1920s, singling out gamblers as "cancers" to the community.[58] The antiprostitution investigatory group known as the Committee of Fifteen in 1922 approvingly (and more than a bit self-righteously) noted that "the respectable colored people are expressing hearty approval of the work of the committee."[59] Black journalists and powerbrokers alike slid down a slippery slope of criminalizing the behavior of people they viewed as undesirable presences in their community. They condemned not just actual law-breaking behavior but also what they saw as black idleness. A *Defender* report that "found many loafers hanging around the pool rooms near 31st and 35th on State Street," for instance, quickly turned toward threatening that "those who do not behave themselves will be handled by the proper authorities."[60] At other times, it more generally blasted police negligence in removing "loafers and idlers" from hanging out on South Side corners.[61] An unnamed black alderman took the argument even further, encouraging the closure of poolrooms and vice dens, the forbiddance of loitering on street corners, and passage of a vagrancy law "that will take the idle shiftless and intolerant hoodlum off the streets. *Put the burden of proof on the one so arrested.*"[62]

This twisted vision of justice—a recommendation to literally invert the supposedly bedrock legal principle of presumption of innocence pending proof of guilt—demonstrated just how badly police negligence in black neighborhoods could distort public opinion there. Khalil Muhammad's work in *The Condemnation of Blackness* has shown us how scientists and intellectuals from Reconstruction through the Progressive Era helped construct the idea of black criminality, and some of the ways that police responded to it.[63] By the same token, the police—by making certain allowances and choices in how and on whom they cracked down—actively contributed to those processes of racial condemnation by distorting the reality and perception of crime.

Unequal Justice: Discordant Punishment, "Black Criminality," and the Problem of Violence

None of this is to say that the police did not react *at all* to crime during the 1920s, however. The sensational aspects of the Prohibition decade have led to caricatures portraying it as a time when one could get away with anything. But facing a crime panic as Prohibition violence grew, and needing to address the withering criticism that attended it, public officials in Chicago and elsewhere were compelled to respond.[64] And those responses, too, reflected the larger racisms of the era.

Indeed, the application of the law in Chicago wasn't *absent* so much as it was profoundly *unequal*. The police department's responses to escalating crime demonstrate the degree to which people's access to the benefits of the police and their susceptibility to its repressions were shaped by ethnicity, race, and social class. This was true in the context of liquor: even at peak periods of antiliquor crackdowns, with only a few exceptions, wealthy and middle-class violators of Prohibition laws had little to fear, so long as they kept their violations behind closed doors. So was it true in the world of gambling: gamblers of means, doing their business in hotels and men's clubs, could feel confident that their engagements would pass unmolested. It was even true in the context of driving: the stories are legion of reckless drivers slipping cash to underpaid traffic police, who would let them go with warnings. In other words, law enforcement, with precious few exceptions, as a whole posed little threat to the wealthy and well connected.

Punishment rather fell on the shoulders of the less powerful—immigrants, Catholics, black people, and other socially marginal populations.[65] Differences of class, ethnicity, and religious privileges shaped how, when, and on what constituencies the police levied heavy enforcement. Poor people in particular—regardless of race—were more vulnerable to police harassment and violence than were people of greater means. Many white ethnics, particularly Catholics, faced extraordinarily discriminatory treatment from law enforcement and vigilantes alike within the context of Prohibition enforcement.[66]

And yet in Chicago, more than every other category, race was the most important determinant in distorting patterns of punishment. The city's police force was heavily constituted by immigrants and the sons of immigrants, softening—however modestly—the edge of law enforcement's targeting of immigrant and Catholic communities. Black people did not have the same quarter, and it showed, up and down the lines of Chicago's arrest ledgers. In 1920, Prohibition's opening year and one in which black people made up just over 4 percent of Chicago's total population, they constituted 11.3 percent of the CPD's total arrests. They were overrepresented more than two and a half times in disorderly conduct and vagrancy arrests, and nearly six times over for being inmates of "disorderly houses"—speakeasies, brothels, and the like.[67]

That year was neither an outlier nor a high-water mark. In 1921, according to the contemporary research of E. Franklin Frazier, one in ten black men between seventeen and forty-four years of age living in the dilapidated areas clustered nearest the Loop had spent time in the county jail *that year.*[68] By mid-decade, the *Defender* was lamenting the fact that, particularly in the Black Belt, "the police pick up the just with the unjust and make life [unbearable] for the decent, respectable citizens."[69] By the close of the decade, arrest rates for African Americans were even further misaligned: fully one-quarter of citizens arrested by the CPD in 1929 was black (48,806 out of 194,999), while the African American portion of Chicago's population was less than 7 percent.[70] Black children fared similarly badly. According to the sociologist Earl Moses, by 1930 black children contributed nearly 22 percent of the city's delinquency cases, tripling their representation in the population proper.[71]

Telling, too, were the degrees to which patterns of black arrests splintered from overall arrests, and from those of many white ethnic groups, over the course of the decade. In the main, arrest figures in the twenties fluctuated in accordance with shifts in mayoral stances toward Prohibition. Early in the administration of Democratic reformer and tough-on-crime advocate William Dever (who held office from 1923 to 1927), arrests across racial and ethnic barriers spiked sharply, nearly doubling in the transition from the final year of Republican and wide-open-town advocate Big Bill Thompson's first tenure in 1922 to Dever's first year in office. Arrest rates increased for black people, as well as for most ethnic groups. This was perhaps to be expected. The difference, however, was that black arrest rates mostly plateaued after 1927 (when Thompson seized back the mayor's office), while

overall arrest rates declined significantly and those for white ethnics plummeted.[72] Black arrest rates had begun the decade disproportionately high,
and they ended it even higher. They would never stabilize back toward city
averages.

Why? Contemporaries offered multiple interpretations of this data. Some
characterized it as emblematic of innate, heritable, black deviance. Others
saw those arrest rates and took them as a sign that black crime and delinquency were real problems in Chicago but articulated them as products of
neighborhood ecology and the failed infrastructure that Chicago offered
black people. For instance, pointing to Chicago's patterns of segregation,
"the lack of adequate community facilities," a "lack of non-state institutions" to offer support, and multiple related factors, Earl Moses wrote that
it was "safe to assume that the problem of delinquency among Negroes in
Chicago is not a problem of race" but rather a problem of inequality.[73]

But data showing increasing numbers of black arrests may have demonstrated simply that: heightened rates of arrests disconnected from crimes
committed. Moses's published article on black delinquency failed to fold
stereotypes and racialized policing into the enumerated list of factors that
contributed to data that nominally demonstrated the severity of that delinquency. But in exchanges with the famed and highly influential University
of Chicago sociologist Ernest Burgess, who advised Moses on his master's
thesis and who explicitly (and tellingly[74]) asked if "biological difference" contributed to black delinquency, Moses argued that racist stereotypes of black
people and "the indiscriminate 'picking up' of Negro boys" were worth
considering within the parameters of the question.[75] He wasn't alone. As
the *Defender* put it in a 1921 editorial, "to the white officer, every black face
is a potential criminal," echoing the comments of a criminal court judge
the previous year: "I don't think the police are quite as careful with reference to the rights of the colored man as with reference to the rights of the
white man. I think they hesitate a little longer [to arrest] when a white man
is involved. . . . I am certain that it is so."[76] Meanwhile, Dr. Herman Adler
responded similarly when asked whether it made a difference to a white
policeman if a suspect was white or black: "We all know that it does make
a difference. We know that there is race prejudice. . . . On the whole a policeman is taking fewer chances if he arrests a colored man than if he arrests a
white man. He is not so likely to get into trouble."[77] So widespread were such
opinions that, before dulling the assessment's sharp edges a bit in the report they eventually made public, the CCRR confidentially argued that "the
testimony [of various people within Chicago's law enforcement community]
is practically unanimous that Negroes are much more liable to arrest than
whites since police officers share in the general opinion of the public that

Negroes 'are more criminal than whites,' and also feel that there is little risk in arresting Negroes."[78]

These attitudes, commission members argued, even further reinforced the damaging cycle of racist assumption about black criminality that we have already seen at play. If police complicity in channeling vice to black neighborhoods bolstered associations of black neighborhoods with degeneracy, so did the disproportionate targeting of black people for arrest in moments of crackdown give legitimacy to that messaging. Reflecting on the intersecting crux of racism and law enforcement that would deeply shape American race relations through the entire twentieth century, commission members wrote that "fewer Negroes than whites escape arrest and prosecution. When comparisons are made on the basis of statistics for arrests and convictions, there is presented, unless proper explanations of the statistics are made, an erroneous picture of Negro crime. Thus is kept up the vicious circle: Negroes are arrested more readily because the figures show them as a group to have a high crime rate, and figures are large—showing a high Negro crime rate—because Negroes are more readily arrested.[79] Black criminality, in other words, though built on a bedrock of fictions, became a self-fulfilling prophecy in the broader society's consciousness.

THE RESULTS THAT FLOWED from increasing rates of black arrest anticipated some of the consequences to come for the black community in later generations, although they also differed to important degrees. Black people were more likely than whites to be convicted of crimes of which they were accused, but Chicago's court system during the twenties was so disjointed and overburdened that overall rates of conviction were low, much to the chagrin of tough-on-crime proponents.[80] While arrest was an important event in someone's life, it was not a certain road to conviction, much less incarceration. Additionally, sentencing policies, while stiffening in jurisdictions across the country, came nowhere near the punitive nature that they would eventually assume.[81]

But even if police contact and arrest didn't necessarily lead to jail time or monetary fines (although they frequently did), such encounters could nonetheless have perilous physical consequences for black citizens. Men like Horace Jennings found this out within the context of the 1919 riot, and the decade that followed was an almost unimaginably dark period in the history of police brutality in America, as in Chicago more narrowly. Police work routinely devolved into retribution and violent extraction, both of which became embedded in the culture. The Illinois State Supreme Court heard nine separate cases involving Chicago-based police brutality between

1920 and 1930. Repeatedly, citizens found themselves being clubbed on the street by out-of-control officers. Others faced the horrors of the interrogation room, where they were subjected to what was euphemistically called "giving someone the third degree" but which fits most modern definitions of torture: depriving prisoners of sleep, banging rubber hoses across a suspect's abdomen, placing a box over an individual's head and filling it with tear gas, applying acid to genitals, hanging prisoners upside down by their ankles or beating them with poles to the point of eyeball dislocation and blindness.[82]

Crime reporter Emanuel Lavine crafted a searing portrait of police violence and interrogation methods in his 1930 book *The Third Degree*—a book that endures as a profoundly unsettling depiction of violent excess. Lavine's work primarily focused on New York, although he vacillated between that city and Chicago, and frequently extrapolated his findings outward across the nation. Lavine testified to having borne witness to unspeakable violence heaped on the bodies of citizens by police. Indeed, he often walked away from such witnessing marveling at what the human body could withstand. In one case, he saw police officers strapping a prisoner to a chair, pulling his head back by the hair, and striking his Adam's apple with a blackjack (three times) with such force that "blood spurted half way across the room."[83] In another, Lavine recalled police who were trying to extract a confession taking a suspect on a ride to the office of a dentist who was friendly with the officers. There, after "he was tied more securely and hopelessly than a wild steer at a Madison Square Garden rodeo, the dentist carefully selected an old dull drilling burr and began slowly drilling into the pulp chamber of a lower rear molar in the region of a nerve." The dentist wiggled the drill from side to side as the prisoner writhed in pain. The officers pledged to have him do the same to every last tooth in the suspect's head. The suspect confessed.[84]

Lavine had less firsthand experience with CPD officers' practices, although other observers noted that the city's third degree practices were "highly developed."[85] Nor were these the doings of rogue officers. Top CPD administrators not only condoned the practice but also took an active role. During a successful 1922 lawsuit to have a coerced confession expunged and a conviction vacated, one victim of police torture testified that a cadre of CPD men that included at least two present or future commissioners (Charles Fitzmorris and Michael Hughes) dragged him around by his hair in an interrogation room and beat him with a rubber hose.[86] That same year, after one local judge said that he would no longer allow confessions to be entered as evidence because of concerns over police abuse, one CPD official told reporters that "95 percent of the work of the department will be nullified if the policy is permitted to prevail."[87]

As with so many other police practices, such torture was most commonly inflicted upon Chicago's most vulnerable populations, which once again meant that black people disproportionately bore its weight. As part of the sprawling 1931 National Commission on Law Observance and Enforcement Report (more commonly known as the Wickersham Commission Report), federal investigators examining "lawlessness in law enforcement" noted that several of the cities they studied reported "that third degree practices were particularly harsh in the case of Negroes."[88] Poor people and those without political pull were also uniquely subject to such practices.[89]

Being a child couldn't even keep you safe. In March 1924, a pair of black high school boys, Ivan Glen and Vane Ware, described being taken into an interrogation room at a CPD station house for questioning in an alleged robbery. When Glen said he knew nothing about the robbery, an officer punched him in the gut and knocked him to the floor, while a second beat his head with a rubber hose. One of the officers then pinioned the boy's head to the floor with his boot while others kicked and beat him, hurling strings of racial epithets. The officers threw Glen into a cell, brought Ware to the interrogation room, told him that Glen had confessed, and gave him roughly the same treatment as Glen when Ware said he didn't know anything about the robbery. No witnesses to the robbery could identify the boys, multiple witnesses testified to their having been at a basketball game when the robbery was said to have taken place, and within a couple of days the charges against them had been thrown out. When Ware returned to school four days after the beating, he could hardly walk.[90]

The incident was far from isolated. Three years after the beatings of Ivan Glen and Vane Ware, police reportedly arrested a black suspect, took him into custody, and proceeded to fracture his skull and break two of his ribs using an iron rod. When he passed out from the pain, officers threw water in his face to revive him, and beat him again.[91] Two years later, a South Side woman identifying herself simply as "Mrs. Woods," who lived next door to the police station at 48th and Wabash, described being driven toward a "nervous breakdown from hearing those poor prisoners crying like children" as police officers split their lips, knocked out their teeth, and did any number of other things that could only be left to Woods' imagination. "Why should a man be treated so terribly?," she asked in a letter to the *Defender*'s editor. She answered herself. "I do not see them (white officers) treating their own like that. Maybe because they are only after the colored man. It's a shame, a disgrace to humanity, and it should be stopped now."[92]

It didn't stop. Instead, such violence reached its logical extension, with police killings also disproportionately falling on black people already at this juncture. The data on officer-involved killings for the 1920s is frustratingly

incomplete, but for the years where it's available, African Americans constituted more than 40 percent of people killed by the police in cases that the
courts ruled justifiable or excusable.[93] Relative to the general black population, this was racially disproportionate by a factor of ten. Many black people
looked on in anguish, while sections of the white mainstream cheered. At
decade's close, a furious *Defender* editorial board excoriated the conservative, white-owned *Tribune* for its practice of giving hundred-dollar "bravery"
awards each month to a particular CPD officer, which in the *Defender*'s estimation essentially functioned as a bounty. According to the editors, 70 percent of these awards were given to police officers who had killed someone,
and more than half of these to "killers of black men."[94] A culmination of
sorts came a year later, when a sixteen-year-old black boy accused of breaking a store window was killed in his home in a hail of thirty-five bullets, after
police officers broke into his house without a warrant and started firing. In
response, the famed antilynching activist and longtime Chicago transplant
Ida B. Wells scathingly wrote that "perhaps if the city had recognized [the
consistent killing of black people by police] as a menace to her fair fame and
public sentiment and then sternly demanded the removal of incompetent
heads of the police department, [the boy] might not now be lying cold in
death."[95]

These killings and the violence that attended them shattered black lives,
and they could not have helped but dampen the faith that its victims—as
well as the faith of their familial and social orbits—had in Chicago's promise of racial freedom. It is doubtful that Ivan Glen or Vane Ware ever looked
at police officers the same way. While Horace Jennings's body may have
recovered from his officer-inflicted injuries, he doubtless suffered psychic
scars from the encounter. Mrs. Woods's anxiety-induced insomnia as the
sounds of tortured prisoners drifted through her bedroom window did not,
as her words attest, lead her toward thinking that the police were even marginally evenhanded in how they dealt with black people.

Urban Politics and Police Problems:
Racial Representation and Its Limitations

But despite the problems in the police-community relationship that the riot
era and its aftermath laid bare, black community members possessed almost no ability to meaningfully confront them. Given that the 1920s were
a seminal decade of ascendant black political power in Chicago, this may
seem strange. One of the foremost historians of the black South Side, Christopher Robert Reed, has authored an entire book about the 1920s there,
showing how black people leveraged increased numbers, heightened buying

powers, and growing cultural institutions into expanding political power, giving rise to "Chicago's Black Metropolis."[96] Oscar De Priest organized a formidable black political organization out of the South Side Second Ward, and by the end of the decade, he had grown powerful enough and stitched himself well enough into the Republican Party fabric to capture a seat in the U.S. House of Representatives. Other black men, like Louis Anderson, won city council seats and important committee positions on the council. As the twenties turned over into the thirties, William Dawson found footing to build his own brand and reputation. St. Clair Drake wrote that "if Harlem was [black America's] intellectual capital of the 20's, Chicago was the political capital."[97] For the first time, Chicago had black faces in high places.

Such political ascension opened numerous doors for black citizens, particularly when it came to patronage jobs. Black people moved in larger numbers into professional positions, including as police officers, with the number of black officers creeping up from around 50 in 1915 to 137 in 1930.[98] Those numbers were small (slightly more than 2 percent of the total force[99]), but they were nonetheless significant in that they signaled a certain level of black civic recognition and representation that many black citizens— migrants, especially—had never before seen. As the political scientist Harold Gosnell put it at the time, "In the eyes of many. . . the police officers are the local government. The appointment of Negro policemen was regarded as a sure sign that the race was recognized as a participant in government."[100] Or, as one black man put it, "What colored man's heart does not beat a little faster when he sees a Negro officer go by in his neat uniform of blue."[101]

But representation is not the same thing as power, and the hiring of a few black officers was an ambiguous victory. Black officers were consistently derogated within the context of their work, often by the very institution that employed them. They were sometimes assigned to segregated bunkhouses. Their white colleagues often hated them, sometimes to the point of trying to frame them for misconduct that would get them tossed before a disciplinary board.[102] The department rarely let them police majority-white areas, partly as a result of public refusal to recognize their authority and partly because, as one black CPD lieutenant acknowledged, racism was widespread among the departmental command.[103]

The flagging power to make the CPD into something that would work for black people, then, was attributable to endemic racism on the one hand, and to the politics of city governance that prevailed at the time on the other. Chicago's political system throughout the 1920s was famously a tangled mess of machine politics. Prior to the Democratic Party establishing itself as the city's dominant and enduring force in 1931, Republicans and Democrats worked to gain and hold the allegiances of different ethnic and racial groups. This was a system premised not on ethics, principles, or policies but rather largely on patronage (in the form of jobs, services, and other tangible matters). Theoretically, and absent unique discriminations, this was a system with egalitarian potential. Even many political scientists, guided by pluralist theory, banked on this logic, assuming that this arrangement would lead to meaningful political representation for all sizable ethnic and racial groups, who would trade electoral support for benefits to their respective communities and whose competing interests would keep those of any one group from being either dominant or subsumed.

But those scholars were wrong, and the black experience is the proof. The black faces in high places certainly legitimated machine politics and gave a veneer of representation. But it was symbolic, and came at the expense of meaningful political influence. Critics of pluralist theory have known this for some time—indeed, have articulated the situation black people faced as the exception that most forcefully gives the lie to the merits of machine politics and to the inclusivity of urban pluralism. As the historian James Connolly has written, "The inability of blacks to earn a place as equal partners in the partisan coalitions of big cities highlights the fundamental limitation of the industrial era's urban pluralism," largely because political bosses really only "served the interest of the best-organized, best-connected groups."[104] More particularly, the political scientist Dianne Pinderhughes has shown convincingly that black integration into Chicago's machine politics—in any meaningful way beyond the symbolic—was a fiction. Comparing the experiences of black, Italian, and Polish citizens, she demonstrates the ways in which race was the shoal on which political power foundered—during the Great Migration and beyond.[105] Nor is this just scholarly hindsight at work. The patronage politics that dominated the 1920s were almost always, as the *Defender* put it at the outset of that decade, an exercise in bargaining away "the welfare of all the Colored community . . . for a mess of political pottage."[106]

To effect real change would have required black people being able to seize political power in ways well beyond the realm of the possible at this point in time, given their numbers in the city and the consistent dismissal of their concerns—political and otherwise—by city administrators and many of their fellow citizens. Within the context of inadequate and abusive policing, nothing was more important than the fact that many police officers owed their hiring and continued employment to a combination of their neighborhood affiliations, ethnic ties, and political connections. Because of the ways that politics shaped the CPD, in other words, most officers were buffered from strong disciplinary action except in truly extraordinary circumstances.

(It is perhaps worth recalling here that even Daniel Callahan, infamous for his role in igniting the 1919 riot, didn't end up losing his job because of it.)

Put differently, the rise of the new black political class did not radically alter the fact that black Chicago ranked low on an overwhelming majority of Chicago politicians' priority lists, including of those who actually had power to influence public policy. This translated—directly—into a comparative inability among black people to influence police policy. Consider, for instance, that Democratic officials were able to mobilize CPD officers as a bludgeon of what the *Defender* termed "police terror" a month before the 1927 election, wherein officers arrested a thousand black people on false charges as part of a widespread racist campaign that saw Democrats paint Republicans as friendly to black people, black neighborhoods as filled with "hoodlums," and Chicago as a "white man's town."[107] In the face of such assaults coupled with such civic power, black political efforts, valiant as they were, stood little chance of influencing policy. In 1925 and to some acclaim, Alderman Louis Anderson successfully ousted a CPD officer from the department after the officer brutalized Anderson's son-in-law, but this was mostly a rule-proving exception.[108] Anderson's success was remarkable because it was so unexpected.

And so, despite the many achievements of black Chicagoans during the decade, black people's rights to actual civic power over institutions such as the CPD remained almost nonexistent. This fact was made manifest in different ways for those who felt underprotected by the CPD and for those who felt abused by it, but it hit home for both nonetheless. There is no better example of the frustrations of the former than the aldermanic call, described above, to bend the rules of jurisprudence so severely as to force suspects to prove their innocence rather than have the state prove their guilt. Similarly representative are the *Defender*'s repeated railings against the CPD's failures to keep undesirable activity out of the black community, and its suggestions to criminalize idleness. Others were furious about police abuses—of power, rights, and bodies. Although we don't know the background of someone like Mrs. Woods, we do know that police violence racked her brain to the point of insomnia. Ida B. Wells's furious 1930 comments after the CPD killing of the sixteen-year-old boy (which elicited no reaction from the city administration) were also telling. (And they echoed arguments that she had been making for literally more than a decade about the CPD's disregard for black life.[109]) One of black Chicago's most prominent citizens, the attorney Roy Woods, bridged the gulf between the two positions, railing against the ways that the police harassed even upstanding citizens and embedding that fact intellectually as part of a broader undermining of black rights. Standing before a city night court in 1925 and witnessing a parade of black faces being brought forth for hearing, Woods lashed out at "the tyranny of police rule in this city." He continued: "The time has come when the police of this city must be made to realize that the constitutional rights of the commonest citizen cannot be trampled upon with impunity. The time has come for a redistribution of justice."[110]

But for no one—Old Settler, new migrant, the middle class, the working poor, the deeply impoverished—was such a redistribution in the offing. More common were compounding frustrations with the attenuated access that black people had to force the police department to pay attention to their concerns.

Their frustrations stood in contrast to the successful claims that other groups were able to make on the CPD and the city administration, both exemplifying the role that racial and class privilege played in shaping the police system in this particular moment, and anticipating the ways they would continue to do so going forward. Civic groups dedicated to police reform proliferated across the country during the 1920s, and locally, the most important example was the emergence of the Chicago Crime Commission (CCC)—an influential citizen-activist group pressuring for reform of a wide slate of police and criminal court practices.[111]

Organized in 1919 by members of the Chicago Association of Commerce, the CCC was populated by many of Chicago's most elite white businessmen. Like its counterparts in cities across the country, the CCC grew partially out of a frustrated recognition that the police department didn't perform its duties particularly well.[112] From its inception, its members labored to push the direction of crime-fighting and criminal justice policy in the city aggressively toward increasingly punitive positions.[113] It broke completely with Progressive Era efforts to shape criminal justice policy, in that it, unlike progressive reformers, had no interest in contextualizing crime in behavioral patterns, the built environment, or urban inequality. To CCC members, as the historian Michael Willrich writes, "Crime was what the law said it was. Criminals were morally responsible free agents—rational economic actors like everyone else."[114] The CCC's essential function, then, was to figure out ways to drive the city toward a tougher law-and-order agenda that would reign in such criminals.

Because of its elite makeup and seemingly limitless resources, the commission became influential in Chicago during the twenties, and remained so for decades to come. (It is, in fact, still in existence.) It quickly emerged as a primary driver of public opinion in Chicago surrounding criminal justice policy, particularly the police function. As the CCC grew and matured during the 1920s, commission members published scathing report after angry op-ed, driving civic attitudes further and further toward support for more rigorous crime control, with decreasing concern for the collateral damage that such control would entail.

Although it would be decades before the CCC and members of the black community came to loggerheads in particularly public ways, it's worth noting that black concerns were (perhaps unsurprisingly) not included in the CCC's calculus of what was wrong with the police department. No members of the black community sat on the CCC's board, and none of the board members were in a social position where they would have regularly engaged with black Chicagoans. The CCC may have been interested in hearing black frustrations over lax enforcement in their neighborhoods. But they would not have been interested in black grievances about police harassment, since they didn't believe that such a thing existed. Nor would they have been especially concerned with claims of excessive force, since such claims distracted from the primary goal of reducing crime.

The CCC amassed increasing lobbying influence during the 1920s, and in relatively short order the boundary lines between it and the CPD elite began to blur. Frustrated with what they saw as ineffective crime-related record-keeping by officials at both the local and state levels, commission members launched their own crime database—one that increasing numbers of journalists and, in turn, public officials would come to rely on. They launched extensive investigations into public corruption, what they saw as a failing court system, and an inadequate criminal justice regime in both its broad contours and virtually every one of its particularities.[115] They inaugurated reform efforts that would, in many ways, push the CPD toward major reformation in ways not seen in more than thirty years.

The influence of the CCC over the police department, and the direction of criminal justice in Chicago more generally, crystallized at the end of the twenties. From all sections of Chicago, the CPD faced withering criticism over its failure to deal effectively with Prohibition-era violence and the endemic corruption within departmental ranks. The department was abusive, corrupt, and above all else, ineffective. Critics who gauged the state of the CPD recurrently invoked an idiom of *rot* in doing so: in 1920, it was "rotten from stem to core"; at the other end of the decade, in 1929, it remained "rotten to the core."[116] End-of-decade studies at both the national and local levels would offer ferocious comment on the department's lawlessness, and on its profound failure as an institution of the public good. As a study of the CPD—conducted in 1929 and 1930 and published in 1931, tellingly titled *Chicago Police Problems*—concluded, "Criminal justice in Chicago has come to be a symbol. By common consent it stands as a perfect example of civic failure and official corruption."[117]

That study, perhaps ironically, had grown out of a collaborative investigation by the CCC and CPD Commissioner Michael Hughes into the CPD's problems of disorganization and broken lines of authority. The CPD commissionership changed into the hands of William Russell in the summer of 1928, and in January of 1929, "impressed by the need for better reporting of crime, and feeling the necessity for an increase in the size of the Police Department to cope with current crime conditions," Russell wrote to CCC president Frank Loesch and his affiliates, asking them to conduct an "impartial and unprejudiced study of conditions."[118] A new organization, the Chicago Citizens' Police Committee, was thus convened to conduct that study, and brought together some of Chicago's leading lights in criminology, law, and sociology.[119]

That committee was not predisposed to meaningful racial empathy. Ernest Burgess—the famed figurehead of the University of Chicago School of Sociology who had inquired of Earl Moses as to the role of black biological ineptitude in shaping patterns of criminality, yet who himself possessed an impoverished appreciation of racism's effects—was a powerful force behind the effort. So were numerous colleagues from his own institution and from Northwestern University's School of Law in suburban Evanston. Representing the Northwestern-based Institute of Criminal Law and Criminology was the institute's president, Andrew A. Bruce, the same judge, coincidentally, who earlier that year had framed black migrants to Chicago through a prism of racial mastery: "Thousands of negroes have come to us from the rural centers of the South and have given to us a rapidly increasing population, whose natural home is in the fields and not in the streets and congested quarters of a great city, and who lack the guardianship and advice of their white masters and friends."[120] It was men like these—well-educated, socially elite, and varying degrees of racist—who would become the primary drivers of police reform efforts in Prohibition-era Chicago.

The study they produced was, as promised, a (nearly 300-page) document of so-called police problems. It focused primarily on issues of departmental understaffing, ways to improve the administrative hierarchy, the distribution of personnel, and other matters that, its authors thought, would make the CPD more effective at crime suppression. The study was also devoid of any finding that indicated that those police problems extended to racism, abuse, or harassment. Anything that ran contrary to the CCC's tough-on-crime philosophy was left unexplored. No mentions were made of departmental racism, violence, harassment, or abuse. There was no discussion about how to prevent Ivan Glen and Vane Ware from being beaten, how to rid the department of blatant racists like Daniel Callahan, how to curb the tenfold overrepresentation of black bodies in officer-involved killings, how to realign the fourfold overrepresentation of black arrestees, how to make the department stop allowing vice to proliferate in black neighborhoods, or how to amplify black voices in the conversation over Chicago's police problems. There was, rather, only an imploration to be more effective in dealing with crime, no matter what consequences followed. As we will see, future policymakers in the city, in both the immediate and longer terms, would take those implorations and run with them.

THE PEOPLE WITH THE MOST at stake in these conversations about improving the CPD's functionality were thus left out of those very conversations when they began to happen. While the CCC and other white elites complained about the police's supposed ineffectiveness and used their social power to refashion it, their lived experiences with the police were distant if not nonexistent. On the other end of that experiential spectrum, no other group in Chicago had a more complicated and dysfunctional relationship to the CPD during the 1920s than did black Chicago. But because of black people's marginal social position, and despite the appearance of increasing political influence, they had no way of accessing those levers of influence at this critical juncture.

Thus, the 1920s closed on Chicago with the relationship between the CPD and the black community in a state of profound uncertainty. The idea that the police department was overwhelmingly antagonistic to black concerns and freedom dreams was not yet widely current, as it would later become. But there were, already, glimpses of that future moving inward from the periphery: the outsized arrest rates, the degraded public safety in black neighborhoods, the choked access to the instruments of reform.

And in 1929, Depression came to Chicago, bringing with it new challenges, new radicalisms, and new interpretations of what constituted crime and what that meant. It is to these stories that we now turn.

CHAPTER 2

You Can't Shoot All of Us

RADICAL POLITICS, MACHINE POLITICS, AND
LAW AND ORDER IN THE GREAT DEPRESSION

he Great Depression of the 1930s reaped immeasurable human misery and provoked unprecedented reconfigurations of American political and social life. It birthed the very lexicon of "the American
Dream," a vision given its name by the writer James Truslow Adams,
who framed it both as America's great heritage and unfinished
struggle.[1] It haunted the creative spirits of some of the greatest artists of the
generation that lived through it—searing Woody Guthrie's ballads, Victoria
Spivey's blues, Steinbeck's Joads, and the square-jawed populism of Harburg
and Gorney's "Brother, Can You Spare a Dime?" Chicago transplant Tampa
Red may have put it best: "If I could tell my troubles, it would give my poor
heart ease, but depression has got me, somebody help me please."

As Tampa Red's troubles suggest, Chicago was not immune. Destitution
prevailed in the city by the lake. By October 1931, more than 620,000 workers were unemployed there. Two years later, the manufacturing labor force
had shrunk in half from its 1927 threshold, with payrolls dropping to one-
quarter of previous levels.[2] The historian Arthur Schlesinger Jr. described
a characteristic early Depression-era city scene: "Every night that fall hundreds of men gathered on the lower level of Wacker Drive in Chicago, feeding fires with stray pieces of wood, their coat collars turned up against the
cold, their caps pulled down over their ears, staring without expression at
the black river, while above the automobiles sped comfortably along, bearing well-fed men to warm and well-lit homes."[3] By the winter of 1932–33 in

Chicago, as the labor historian Irving Bernstein put it, "the mood . . . was gloom—unrelieved, despairing gloom." And channeling the literary critic Edmund Wilson, he continued: "'All around . . . there today stretches a sea of misery.'"[4]

Beyond its human toll, that sea of misery harbored deep political implications. Presiding over the city for the first eighteen months of the Depression, Republican mayor Bill Thompson stood accused in the 1931 mayoral election of atrocious mismanagement of the crisis. His Democratic opponent, Anton Cermak, ousted him, setting up the rise of Chicago's Democratic Party to essentially total dominance by the end of the Depression decade. It would thus fall to members of the Democratic machine to deal with the decade's challenges: managing budgets, inflicting austerity, and trying to hold together a political coalition that was fragile in its infancy.

This chapter centers on what those politicians perceived to be a crucial component of the larger crisis: civic disorder. Scholars of policing and crime policy generally haven't paid much attention to Depression-era policies and politics.[5] This is surprising, since Franklin Roosevelt himself articulated New Deal programs of direct relief and job creation as, at least in part, matters of crime control. In 1939 he framed the New Deal as having struck "at the very roots of crime itself," and measured success in part by the fact that "our citizens who have been out of work in the last six years have not needed to steal in order to keep from starving."[6] Even if Roosevelt used social welfare rather than some massive law enforcement apparatus, he was nevertheless aware of how federal policies could advance an anticrime agenda.

The primary arena in which those battles would take place was, however, local, not federal. In Chicago, the Depression-era slate of challenges to civic order—or, at least, what policymakers and police officials *perceived* to be challenges to civic order—was vast. Rates of property crime rose, a robust gambling economy blossomed, and Chicago roiled with radical protests, more ubiquitous and vibrant than anything since Haymarket. Many of the latter actions explicitly challenged the authority of state officers to execute measures of austerity—whether law enforcement officers enforcing evictions, or social welfare agents discriminating against black claimants. Still others were centered on labor militancy and strikes, often against some of the most powerful capital interests in the city, and organized by the ascendant Communist Party (CP) or its affiliates.

Seeing these activities as affronts to public order, politicians and police forces responded. Poverty was routinely criminalized. The CPD founded a new Vagrancy Bureau that, among other things, criminalized destitution and homelessness and turned it into an arrestable offense. Similarly, citizens who turned to petty theft (sometimes literally stealing bread) in order to feed themselves and their families met a police force that responded with inordinate harshness. Meanwhile, after having run for mayor as a tough-on-crime candidate, Anton Cermak turned his police force aggressively against black Chicago, using the CPD as a bludgeon against a community that he saw as morally suspect and politically unuseful. Even when his successor, Ed Kelly, entered into corrupt sweetheart deals with black gambling moguls beginning in 1933, the black poor and working class remained relentless targets of the department under the Democratic regime because arresting them demonstrated police effectiveness without costing much politically. And perhaps more than anything, the Depression saw Chicago's political class dramatically expand the CPD's capacities for surveillance and political repression, coming to rely heavily on the antisubversive "Red Squad" and mustering men out from across the department to suppress citizen dissent.

This was all of a piece with a local Democratic Party platform that took "law and order" as a central operating premise. The phrase "law and order" has often been understood to be an invention of the twentieth century's second half, the fruit of conservative backlash to civil rights and Black Power. While it's undoubtedly true that law-and-order politics developed particularly nasty permutations in and after the 1950 and 1960s, the logics of law and order have been central to ideas about race and to the handling of various social problems for generations, dating back to the abolition of slavery.[7] In Chicago, Ed Kelly began to explicitly invoke the phrase during the Depression, in response to rising tides of radicalism that challenged the social and economic order. (Condemning pickets, he said, "The people of Chicago want law and order, and insist that the laws be obeyed by everyone, regardless of who he is."[8]) Kelly was far more savvy politically than Cermak, excellent as a bridge builder and widely viewed as moderate in temperament and policy. But both he and his predecessor effectively used the capacities of the police and fever dreams of public disorder to build up their own political capital.

Few communities were immune from these processes. When the CPD and the Democratic Party criminalized poverty-induced crime and vice, or when they launched counterrevolutions against the radical protests that financial ruin and governmental austerity conjured, many people bore the weight—black and white, immigrant and native-born.

Nevertheless, the fact that black communities were hit hardest by the Depression, were drawn to radicalism to disproportionate degrees, and were already subject to the racism of fellow citizens and police officers alike meant that they bore a disproportionate share. This was exacerbated by the fact that they were also uniquely marginalized politically. As in subsequent decades, black Chicago appealed to the ascendant Democratic establishment for better treatment, to no avail. Instead, the most powerful machine politicians—all white, some nominally progressive on race—actively used Chicago's police force as a political bludgeon against recalcitrant black voters, a means of repressing radical politics, a way of establishing their law-and-order bona fides, and a mechanism of graft to channel black dollars into the machine.

This history of struggle between citizens and law enforcement in the throes of the Depression raises fundamental questions about policing and the criminal justice system more broadly. The stories told here are in some ways about people trying to survive and in other ways about people rebelling against a system that treated them unjustly. The police, as the criminal justice system's frontline agents, actively did battle to stymie their freedom dreams. As this and the following chapters should make clear, there is an interrogation to be made about what happens when marginalized citizens seek justice and, in so doing, disrupt the status quo. The interrogation almost inevitably leads to a recognition that that criminal justice system is by and large decidedly unconcerned with justice, and rather more invested in protecting whatever status quo exists in that moment.

This chapter takes a hard look at the politics of the Democratic machine as it was consolidating power in the 1930s, and how it shaped policing in Chicago. The relationships between the party and the police department, how they intersected and came to bear on Chicago's social and racial conflicts, will be an important subtext for the remainder of the book. They are also at the heart of this chapter.

"Can You Spare a Dime?": Black Chicago, Depressed

When the Depression hit Chicago, black workers were the canary in the coal mine. Late in January of 1929, nine months before the Black Tuesday market crash, the *Defender*'s editorialists had begun warning readers of an encroaching storm, citing daily reports of black laborers jettisoned out of their jobs. "Something is happening in Chicago," they wrote, "and it should no longer go unnoticed."[9]

That black workers would be hit first by the century's most pronounced crisis of capitalism is not surprising. Scholars of Western political economies have, for decades, interrogated the deep entanglements between racism and capitalism—a relationship that the black radical scholar Cedric Robinson shorthanded *racial capitalism*.[10] As Robinson and a range of scholars following his path have eloquently documented, racism and racial exploitation have long been organizing principles of Western capitalism, with the United States standing as an archetypal example. From the slave labor camps of the antebellum South to twentieth-century real estate profiteering, from the Jim Crow sharecropping fields to Wall Street's colonization of the Caribbean, racial exploitation, in its many permutations, is inextricable from the larger history of American capitalism.[11] So, too, in the industrial centers (like Chicago) of early twentieth-century America, where employers constantly used racism and racial competition to drive wedges between black workers and their white ethnic counterparts in order to suppress labor militancy and further their own capital interests. Indeed, it was precisely this fact that drew leftist theoreticians to interweave anticapitalism and antiracism during the 1920s and 1930s, most notably in the CP's efforts to organize black workers (once the party actually developed a coherent antiracism) in places as diverse as rural Alabama's and Chicago's respective Black Belts.

Within the famed Black Metropolis, a number of black women and men had achieved significant measures of wealth during the 1920s—as business owners, landlords, racketeers, and so on.[12] But in the main, employers and many white workers treated black workers as a surplus population, and the exploitation and abuse of them was one of the economy's pivot points. (This is different from saying that many thousands of white workers did not struggle tremendously, before and during the Depression.) Black women's proscribed occupational roles, as an equal function of their race and gender, were overwhelmingly as low-wage domestic workers or other service jobs. Many black men also labored in service work, and those who found jobs outside the service sector and within Chicago's vast network of industry were often the last to be hired and were constantly relegated to the most menial jobs. They were also first to be fired in lean times, and labor unions that otherwise may have offered quarter from job loss routinely refused to admit black workers. Business owners understood the latter dynamic well. Over and over again, they used black unemployed workers as a bludgeon against the labor movement, bringing them in as strikebreakers to replace white workers when they struck. The handful of interracial solidarities that arose around class identity were important and inspiring, but they were not common before the middle of the 1930s—and even then, they did not usher in a colorblind workers' utopia.[13]

Nor was there much of a safety net that would catch poor and working-class people who needed aid. Well into the 1930s, beyond corporate welfare capitalism, it was largely informal networks, benevolent societies, and religious and ethnic welfare services that had to do the work of feeding the hungry, caring for the sick, and housing the homeless. These support systems were organized at the neighborhood level and were largely insular in their ethnic and racial boundaries: Poles supported Poles, Jews supported Jews, Czechs supported Czechs, and so on. None of these safety nets could fully satisfy the needs of the community they hoped to serve, although their strength varied widely—their quality dependent on the resources at each individual community's disposal. Because Chicago's black communities were more economically depressed, the resources available to help those in need were also lesser.[14]

All of this is to say that when the *Defender* warned in January 1929 that "something [was] happening," it was more prescient than alarmist. The coming months saw more black workers laid off. The Urban League convened the city's black leadership to discuss ways to address the simmering crisis. The *Defender*—after championing the sanctuary of the North for nearly a decade and a half—began to advise aspiring migrants to stay in the South. "Negroes," Drake and Cayton wrote, "were a barometer sensitive to the approaching storm."[15]

The storm proved torrential. In the months and years after the market crash, industrial employers held true to form, cutting jobs from under black workers' feet first and longest. By the winter of 1931, black Chicagoans were overrepresented by fourfold on the unemployment rolls, constituting just 4 percent of the population and 16 percent of the jobless.[16] Those able to keep themselves in work almost invariably found their wages and hours cut. In July of 1930, the centerpiece of the Black Belt's economy—Jesse Binga's bank—shuttered its doors. Within a month, all the other banks there followed suit, wiping out the savings of thousands of depositors, since there was not as of yet any insurance system in place to protect bank accounts.[17] Overnight, thousands of black Chicagoans lost almost all their material wealth, and the effects compounded over time. By 1939, 40 percent of people on the welfare relief rolls were black, while fully half of black families depended on government aid for subsistence to at least some degree.[18] Looking back, Horace Cayton recalled the desperation running through Black Chicago: "hard times had brought real poverty, and they were virtually starving to death."[19]

Cayton's description of real poverty was not hyperbole, and that lived reality conjured a range of responses from Chicago's black citizenry. Some managed to stay in work. Others plugged away in search of employment, picked up odd jobs where possible, and cut costs. They improvised—taking in boarders, standing in bread lines. Some tried to persuade elected officials to intercede on their behalf. Black attorney Earl B. Dickerson, who was voted onto the Chicago City Council at the end of the thirties, recalled that "at almost every meeting of the City Council, delegations came down from the South Side, asking for better relief treatment." Dickerson pleaded with his fellow council members to consider their requests but recalled the council being "grudging and niggardly in its response." One particularly racist

West Side alderman told him that the reason so many black people were on relief was because they were lazy.[20] Laziness of course had nothing to do with it, but with that sort of reception from the political establishment, it isn't surprising that many people cast out of the world of traditional work sought other ways of getting by. Timuel Black recalled: "During that time, none of us had any money. We just hustled as best we could, and somehow we got through it all."[21] The longtime Woodlawn resident Thomas Ellis remembered washing cars, selling papers, and doing other odd jobs to try to make ends meet.[22] Far smaller numbers turned to petty crime in order to get by. Others gambled. Most hoped for a miracle.

"A House for All Peoples?": The Rise of the Machine

As the Depression settled in, Chicagoans went to the polls to elect a mayor. The election of April 1931 pitted three-term Republican incumbent "Big Bill" Thompson against Anton Cermak, a West Side Democrat of Bohemian immigrant stock. Thompson was a familiar face in Chicago. He was brash and full of swagger, but his star had dimmed after eighteen months of hard times. While Cermak was almost punishingly uncharismatic and lacking in political tact and savvy, he had put in years as a Democratic Party precinct captain, state representative, and alderman. In 1928, as county chairman, he had begun building a broad ethnic coalition among Chicago's immigrant communities—"a house for all peoples," he called it—that he hoped would overcome the entrenched support that Thompson had been able to rely on to win three of the previous four mayoral races.[23]

On the campaign trail, Cermak's pitch was twofold. First, he blasted Thompson's miserable response to the Depression, accusing him of failing citizens, of financial mismanagement, and of bankrupting the city. Second, he railed against "Thompsonism"—shorthand for corruption, graft, and softness on public safety. He cast himself as tough on crime—the antidote to the city's declining morals, culture, and safety under Thompsonism.[24]

In the face of these assaults from the foreign-born Cermak, Thompson retreated to ugly xenophobia, publicly taunting his opponent with ethnic slurs. This was an awful idea in a city as immigrant-heavy as Chicago, and Thompson's assaults drove ethnic and immigrant voters hard into Cermak's camp. In the election, Cermak demolished Thompson by nearly two hundred thousand votes.[25]

Cermak's victory marked a sea change in Chicago's politics, bringing about effective single-party rule. A Republican hasn't held the mayor's office since that election—a span of more than eighty-five years. And while

Republicans have won back some offices in city politics, they have remained a minority party, with little ability to meaningfully shape public policy.

Thus, for more than three generations, political operatives associated with the Democratic machine have had almost singular access to shape the city's superstructure.[26] They have controlled the employment rolls for myriad public institutions, and barnacled their political interests to city institutions ranging from the police department to the sanitation crews to the postal service. They have shaped both the mundanities and major processes of urban life, with the understanding that if they could keep the right constituents happy, those constituents would continue to vote for the party. Over time, the machine's growing chokehold on Chicago's electoral politics required less and less responsiveness to an ever-expanding cohort of constituents. But in the beginning, the reciprocity between machine and citizen was very real for numerous communities.

The major exception was black voters. We will return shortly to the particular mechanics of Cermak's administration and what they meant for policing in Chicago, but it is worth taking an aside to think about what Democratic machine control meant and has meant for black Chicagoans historically. Because the reality is that the solidification of Democratic single-party control in the 1930s did very little to improve the lot of most black Chicagoans either in the short or long term. (It is worth being clear that Republican single-party rule, particularly in recent decades, would almost assuredly have been worse.)

In the beginning, Cermak's "house for all peoples" simply wasn't. To be sure, the absence of black people inside the Democrats' "house" was partly because fealty to Republicans as the party of Lincoln still ran deep in black Chicago and because, at the national level, the Democratic Party maintained a lingering and deserved reputation as the party of the lynch mob. But more importantly, as party leader and now mayor, Cermak never imagined that the Democratic Party machine *would* be a place for black people. His 1931 campaign against Thompson trafficked heavily in antiblack racial resentment. He referred to Thompson's administration as "Uncle Tom's Cabin" because of Thompson's support for certain black interests and for elevating black politicians, and placed advertisements that warned whites that "IF THOMPSON IS ELECTED Thousands of Negroes will get Jobs that otherwise go to White Men."[27] Another Democratic Party leaflet, this one more precise about the jobs at stake, bemoaned the litany of positions that black people held on the eve of the election. Among these were Oscar De Priest's place in the United States Congress, a handful of black state representatives, one thousand postal workers, and three hundred police officers.[28] Cermak neither had nor cultivated any meaningful relationships with the black community, seeing it as an indistinguishable and not especially worthwhile bloc.[29] And that impression was reinforced in Cermak's mind when he beat Thompson with very little electoral help from black voters.

White Democratic powerbrokers wouldn't always be so overtly hostile to their black constituents, and indeed, black people *did* migrate en masse into the machine soon enough. Cermak was assassinated in Florida in 1933 by a bullet likely meant for President Franklin Roosevelt, and his successor, Ed Kelly, would modify Cermak's approach to black Chicago in some important ways. A central cog in the growing Democratic machine, Kelly was a second-generation Irish American, raised in Back of the Yards by a mother who oversaw a household of nine children and a CPD officer for a father.[30] More racially moderate than his predecessor, Kelly actively courted the black vote and worked with aspiring black politicians to build a black political submachine. He made numerous symbolic gestures of support to the black community, publicly opposed school and residential segregation, and established a biracial Committee on Race Relations in 1943 to study the problems afflicting black Chicago.[31] As a consequence of Kelly's racial moderation, coupled with national-level political realignments wrought by the New Deal, black voters in Chicago shifted toward the Democratic Party during Kelly's tenure.[32] They have continued to provide Democrats enormous voting margins ever since.

Even so, black Chicagoans found that machine politicians, even the most racially moderate, were unlikely to seriously battle for racial justice. Instead, black Chicago received increased access to certain patronage opportunities and the elevation of some black leaders to elected office. These were not un-important benefits—the problem of jobs in black Chicago was always real, and while patronage opportunities were too small to solve the problem for the community as a whole, they benefited many individuals. Moreover, the elevation of new black politicians helped constituents secure more benefits through machine channels. But more than anything, the machine was orchestrated to reward political fealty and jettison dissenters from the party line, no matter their race or ethnicity. It excelled at channeling black faces into high places, forcing those black politicians into political quiescence, and simultaneously fighting against black challenges to a racially unjust status quo.[33]

As such, with the Democratic Party controlling the city's infrastructure and investments, racial gaps in wealth and opportunity widened over the twentieth century. The machine can't be held solely responsible for engineering what became one of America's most segregated and most unequal cities, but it was undeniably important. Sutured together with immense white resistance to integration, capital and resource flight, and other socioeconomic processes, through its control of public institutions, Democratic machinations worsened an urban arrangement that already profoundly disadvantaged black communities.

And while this long arc of Democratic failures vis-à-vis black Chicago is only fully apparent in hindsight (and will continue to be explored in the remainder of these pages), it began germinating from the moment Anton Cermak first took control of city hall. Emboldened after the 1931 victory, Cermak and his allies sought to solidify power and execute his agenda. In keeping with his campaign promises, when he took the mayor's office, he was fixated on two main things: the budget and the police.

Tackling the first, he appealed to both the state and the federal government for intervention and support, and worked with financial executives in Chicago to secure loans for the city that would stabilize its budget.[34] Meanwhile, in the name of cutting costs, Cermak sought to gut the city's expenditures on public employees, using "mass layoffs, staggered time, payless vacations, the abolition of sick leaves and of the five-day week." By 1932 the city would briefly lay off some of its police officers and firemen because it couldn't afford to pay them.[35] Teachers, meanwhile, were paid with tax warrants in the first couple of years of the Depression until the winter of 1932–33, after which they were paid nothing at all.[36]

Meanwhile, although he had criticized Bill Thompson for using public employment rolls to feed the Republican machine, Cermak similarly abused the perquisites of his office. He appointed lackeys to the Civil Service Commission, which was supposed to ensure that public employees were hired and promoted based on merit alone, and used it as a well of patronage for the Democratic machine. Contemporary police officers recalled that so long as you had the proper political connections, anyone could get a job.[37] Unsurprisingly, under the new patronage regime, black workers suffered. On his first day in office, Cermak fired two thousand public employees—nearly all of them black Republicans who had been hired by Thompson.[38] "Responsible Democrats" who were white eventually replaced them.[39]

Cermak's approach to the police department was part of this larger project of bringing public employees to heel. Almost immediately after assuming office, he consolidated control of the police department inside the mayor's office.[40] Believing that the CPD under Thompson had been woefully inept, Cermak was convinced that the department was full of lazy officers who didn't work hard enough and leeched off of depleted city resources. He would make routine and unannounced trips to police district stations to rake station house captains over the coals for allowing their officers to "[lie] around idle."[41] Under his watch, the department underwent a full reorganization in 1932, much of it in keeping with the recommendations of the Citizens' Police Committee two years prior.[42] Indeed, by the time he was assassinated in 1933, it was estimated that 80 percent of the committee's recommendations had been successfully put in place.[43]

Cermak, along with the Democratic operatives who would succeed him, used the CPD as both a well of patronage jobs and an instrument of social control. Setting a template that would remain intact for decades, Cermak concentrated the department's operations under his direct authority, rendering the commissioner a figurehead while transferring significant levels of power over to district captains.[44] Those captains, in turn, would have to be malleable to the whims of Democratic Party operatives at the ward level if they wanted to keep their posts.[45] Although by tethering police work increasingly to his and his party's agenda, Cermak was further encasing officers and commanders in webs of political influence and graft opportunities, he insisted that Democratic styles of corruption would somehow be less harmful than Republican ones had been.

He was wrong. The Democratic machine's consistent willingness to prioritize self-preservation ahead of effective and democratically responsible governance would over time earn Chicago a reputation as America's most corrupt city. (It retains the title to this day.[46]) While Cermak had framed his seizure of the CPD as an effort to *divorce* the police from politics, binding the department to the machine encouraged police to be more loyal to party officials and their own pocketbooks than to the nominal obligations of their jobs. The effects of this were worsened by poor pay, especially during the cuts of the Depression, heightening the appeal to officers of earning extra money from side jobs—even illicit ones. A culture of corruption that had already taken root in the CPD was thus strengthened during the 1930s.

This would have important consequences over the long term, precisely because Chicago's Democratic machine was so uniquely powerful and durable. More than its counterparts elsewhere, the machine tightly controlled the police department from this point forward, and blocked reforms of it for decades.[47] To be sure, the machine's power over the CPD was not totalizing, and sections of the CPD would prove very difficult to reign in at times. But the machine's influence was nevertheless strong enough to etch deep consequences into the nature of policing in Chicago over both the short and long terms.

This politicization of the department served to undercut the functionality of the CPD and eviscerate its legitimacy in the eyes of many Chicagoans; it also made it harder for police officers who honestly wished and worked to do their jobs in an ethical way. I am up front about the fact that this book does not dig deeply into the experiences of police officers themselves, except to the degree to which those experiences came to bear on the lives of black Chicagoans. That is a book that someone should write, but this is not that book. Yet it's worth knowing that by doing nothing about the crimes of "the bad cop," the department and the political machine of which it was an adjunct created crises for "the good cop" (as *Collier's* magazine put it in an article series years later).[48] Scandal after scandal would rock the department from the 1930s forward until serious reform efforts began in the sixties, and even then corruption was too deeply embedded to fully root out. For those who believed themselves to be good police, the effect was powerfully demoralizing. And in the immediate sense, it was exacerbated by the fact that police work was profoundly dangerous because of the Prohibition wars, and by the fact that the man who was the police officers' boss—Mayor Cermak—publicly ridiculed them for laziness, fired their friends to save money, and gutted their salaries.

All of this would morph and evolve over the coming years, although it didn't take long for the results to begin to crystallize. Two years before Kelly reached the end of his term as mayor, the *Tribune* published a prominent, weeks-long, and excruciating series on the problems of police corruption and the consequences of political influence on the department.[49] The problem was so bad that, by 1945, CPD commissioner James Allman and the man who succeeded him, the chief of the CPD's Uniformed Force John Prendergast, issued a department-wide order to all personnel decrying the "lack of discipline, slovenly appearance, discourteous treatment of the public, and lack of enforcement of all laws and inspection" within the CPD. Officers spent too much time hanging out in bars and taking bribes, and lacked both supervision and personal responsibility.[50] The lament might have been framed as an order to improve, but it was also an admission that Allman and Prendergast had little ability to control the people at their command. This was the machine at work.

Crime, Policy, and Crime Policy: The Machine Gets to Work

Although Cermak only lived long enough to serve for about twenty months, he presided over what were arguably the most difficult and unruly years of the Depression. As such, during his tenure, he sought to make the police more aggressive than ever before. Crime was spiking, vice was booming, and radical protest was exploding. Cermak believed that public order needed to be maintained at all costs—a vision that Ed Kelly would inherit. This shared belief would shape Chicago's social and political landscape in crucial ways in the coming years.

One piece of the two mayors' concern lay in the fact of crime. A caution: measuring the early Depression's impact on crime with any precision is difficult. Beyond the standard problems, biases, and imperfections that mar *all* crime reporting into the present day, gauging crime from a particular locality in the late 1920s and early 1930s means leaning on anecdata and highly incomplete police department statistics.[51] Not until 1931 did the CPD implement an official Bureau of Crime Statistics, meaning that drawing comparisons between that year and any of the ones before it is complicated.[52] Indeed, for the first two years of the Depression, the CPD didn't even log (or, at least, didn't make publicly available) what are called "offenses known to the police"—essentially, reported crime. As such, the only measures we have from the Depression's early years are arrests made and charges brought—both of which say as much about police activity as they do about crime itself, and are thus best taken with multiple grains of salt.[53] Nevertheless, if we are to trust them even marginally, it is clear that Cermak inherited a social situation in which crime was spiking. From 1929 to 1931, larceny charges in Chicago rose by 11 percent, felony burglary charges by 47 percent, and robbery charges by 60 percent. The one category of "offenses known" that the CPD *did* make public, auto theft, skyrocketed more than threefold in those three years, from around ten thousand in 1929 to more than thirty-three thousand in 1931.[54]

Cermak's solution to the problem was to ramp up policing. Indeed, beyond shoring up the machine's political fortunes, many of his efforts relative to the CPD were intended to free up more police officers to go out patrolling the streets to put an end to property crime. Internal departmental reports emphasize the need to cut administrative and service work and redirect officers to foot patrols, in keeping with the recommendations of Citizens' Police Committee members who had emphasized the value of a "patrolling force" as a preventative measure.[55] In his first year in office, Cermak oversaw the implementation of a new offense-reporting system, as well as the Division of Stolen Autos in order to address the problem of auto theft.[56] Those restructuring efforts continued under Kelly, whose CPD continued to search for greater efficiency by extracting greater man-hours from beat cops, improving communication, and bolstering the public image of the police through public relations campaigns.

The choice to foreground the police in city hall's responses to the Great Depression's assorted crises had real, material human consequences. Thousands of people were arrested annually on charges of petty crime during the Depression. But the numbers cloud the human face. Imagine the plight of the fourteen-year-old Chicago boy, shot in the leg by a storeowner and subsequently arrested by CPD officers after he was caught trying to steal something to eat.[57] Or that of the black fifteen-year-old arrested by CPD officers for stealing warm clothes out of a parked car in the Loop; the officers stripped him to his underwear before releasing him into the December night.[58] Or those arrested by agents of the CPD's new Vagrancy Bureau for being jobless and homeless in a historical moment in which joblessness and homelessness skyrocketed. In the face of the Depression's ravages, Chicago criminalized human misery. And that criminalization happened, variously, with the tacit acceptance of the Democratic Party machinery or under its explicit direction.

The general drive against crime was one thing, but Cermak as functional orchestrator of police policy channeled his greatest focus elsewhere: toward the Black Belt–centered gambling economy known as *policy*.[59] The general outlines of the game were simple: players placed bets as low as a penny on a particular number (or set of numbers) in the hopes they would win one of the daily drawings. Bets were generally low-stakes, but with the ubiquity of gaming stations throughout the area and with multiple drawings per day at some stations, it was possible for a player to spend a lot of money quickly. Many members of black Chicago criticized the game's immorality, but its popularity only grew as tens of thousands of people looked to it as a diversion with a chance, however fleeting, to strike it rich.

By the time Cermak became mayor, the game had become an institution. It grew to such prolific proportions, funneled so much money, enchanted so many people, and employed so many workers that to call it an "underground" economy doesn't seem to get it quite right. One observer of Chicago politics writes that, by the 1930s, policy had become a multibillion-dollar industry, and "the chief source of capital within Bronzeville."[60] In the hundreds of gaming wheels spread through the Black Belt, thousands of black people worked and made a living. The policy enterprise kept legitimate businesses alive, charities open, and pride intact in the possibility of black autonomy, since most elite policy wheel owners (commonly known simply as policy kings or kingpins) proved willing to reinvest their windfall profits back into the community.[61] (Indeed, as just one of many signs of how embedded policy was as a community institution, Mitch Duneier reports that the famous Jones brothers, policy kingpins, helped fund the research that became Horace Cayton and St. Clair Drake's seminal *Black Metropolis*.[62])

Be that as it may, Cermak loathed it. Policy wheel operators and other moguls in black Chicago's vice economies had cast their lot with the Republicans, and Cermak saw the policy industry as among the worst manifestations of Thompsonism. After effectively taking control of the CPD, he ordered the creation of a special vice and gambling unit that operated essentially under his supervision.[63] He transferred the famously hardened police captain John Stege to the Black Belt, ordering him to "raise all the hell you can with the policy gang."[64] Stege's men arrested hundreds of people per day in the Black Belt on gambling charges, "cramming them into jail cells so tightly that no one could sit down."[65] Although cloaked in a veil of shoring up public safety and morality, in reality, the raids were retributive and explicitly political: Cermak's primary concern was to use the police force to bludgeon black Chicagoans into political obedience and give up their long-held loyalty to the Republican Party. As a Republican ward committeeman remembered, recalling the overflow of black people in police stations on weekends after Cermak's gambling raids: "When the [black] aldermen would try to intercede for them, they would be told, 'The minute you people find out there's something besides the Republican Party, come back and talk to us.'"[66] Thwarting standard assumptions about machine politicians exchanging favors for votes, Cermak's approach to black Chicago relied on sticks, not carrots. And he charged CPD officers with carrying the sticks.

The policy moguls lawyered up, but it was the impoverished and working-class players who felt the worst of the wrath. Prefiguring practices that will sound very familiar to modern observers, Stege's officers stopped and searched cars at random and busted down the doors of private residences throughout the South Side's black neighborhoods. They had racially selective law enforcement down to a practical science: 87 percent of police raids conducted that year took place within the Black Belt.[67] And all told, well over half of all those arrested in the city on gambling charges of some kind were black—in a city where black people were still less than 5 percent of the population.[68]

If Chicago's tradition of confining vice to black and other undesirable neighborhoods had posed challenges to the community in the past, the sudden, massive, and discriminatory criminalization of it at unprecedented levels was just as bad. The raids earned CPD officers the derogatory moniker "Cossacks" from black citizens and newspaper writers, who drew parallels with the forces of Soviet repression. After all, in a city where fewer than one in twenty residents were black, it was remarkable how many African Americans were being arrested under the new Democratic regime for petty gambling. Indeed, on the eve of the Depression, Chicago's gambling worlds were widely known to be a diverse milieu.[69] But it was black people who felt, by far, the sharpest burden of antivice enforcement under Cermak.

After Cermak's assassination, Ed Kelly reversed pieces of his predecessor's war on gambling but left important parts intact as well. On the one hand, the policy kings would now supply the Democratic machine with money and votes in exchange for a blind eye from the police.[70] Kelly and other machine operatives filled their political coffers with contributions from the policy syndicate, in a reciprocal exchange that worked to the advantage of both the machine and the policy wheel owners. Players, on the other hand, found no quarter. Instead, the CPD's vice police were, under

Kelly, even more aggressive toward low-level players than they had been under Cermak. From 1934 to 1937, the raw numbers of gambling arrests increased nearly fivefold; by 1944 they were roughly 700 percent higher than they had been a decade prior.[71] No disaggregation of these statistics by race appears to exist for these years, but if 1931 statistics (the last year during this period that the CPD reported stats by race) are any indication, there can be little doubt that they skewed overwhelmingly against black Chicagoans.

Couple this story with the waging of the Progressive Era war on prostitution and the Prohibition-era war on alcohol, and it isn't hard to understand the pattern. Across the early twentieth century, there was never a time when the policing of vice in Chicago was *not* racially distorted. While the story of the machine's rise and influence is important and while Cermak's utilization of vice policing as a political bludgeon is especially notable, it may be that an equally important takeaway is that it didn't matter *who* was calling the shots regarding police policy. The targeting of black people, even for completely victimless crimes, was embedded in the culture.

"You Can't Shoot All of Us": Law and Order, Radicalism, and Repression in the Depression Decade

Attacking black vice was one thing, but for Cermak and Kelly, a much larger threat loomed in the rise of radical politics. The Depression era, as historians have long acknowledged, was a high point of radical struggle and labor militancy in America. The Depression roused many Americans to action as their lives crashed around them. For others, particularly those on the far left, the financial collapse proved the imminent demise of capitalism and spurred them to organize within its void. With its vast population of blue-collar workers and deep tradition of labor and political radicalism, Chicago predictably emerged as one of the nation's hotbeds of the new militancy. And the earliest driver of that militancy was the Communist Party.

Chicago had, in fact, been the American CP's midwife and first home. Although founded there in 1919, the party's local influence had never truly gelled during its first decade of existence.[72] When the Depression hit, however, that changed. As the economy collapsed, the CP offered itself as a radical alternative to an American capitalist system that was obviously, visibly failing people every single day. More importantly, the party *did* things, in contrast to the inertia of mainstream political organizations. Chicago's labor unions were also important within this milieu, but the CP's vision and plan of action was much broader, focusing not only on workplace rights but also on larger bread-and-butter issues such as unemployment, evictions, homelessness, and hunger. With the party promising to confront these social plagues, official local membership grew from less than seven hundred in 1930 to nearly six thousand in 1938.[73] And given the high rate of turnover from year to year, as well as the number of people who never officially joined the party but attended its actions and supported its mission, those official single-year figures always dramatically understated the party's actual influence.[74]

During its early years, foreign-born immigrants made up the party's base in Chicago, and its relationship to black Chicago was not especially meaningful. According to the historian Glenda Gilmore, the CP's organizers garnered some modest support from black Chicagoans by helping them fight exploitative landlords, and by establishing the American Negro Labor Council to challenge labor market exploitation and racist violence.[75] But throughout the twenties, the CP as a whole wasn't quite sure what to do with black members. In her study of the CP "at the grassroots" in Chicago, Randi Storch notes that white party members before the Depression had little understanding of how race and class intersected and not much appreciation for the unique aspects of black workers' plight.[76]

The CP's racial analysis became more sophisticated over time, however (even if racism among party members remained a problem), and as it did, the party began sharpening its appeal to black communities. As a result, during the Depression Chicago's black neighborhoods emerged as the party's most important base. By 1931 the South Side's majority-black First Congressional District was home to the nation's largest population of black Communists. People came to the party partly because of activisms beyond Chicago, like the CP's famous legal defense of the "Scottsboro Boys"—nine young black men erroneously arrested in Alabama and facing the death penalty for allegedly gang-raping two white women. They also were attracted to its strident interracialism, both nationally (the party ran a white/black presidential ticket in 1932) and locally (black people assumed prominent leadership roles in the local party).

But the most important factors driving black attraction to the CP were pragmatic and tangible. Communist-affiliated organizers—both those inside the formal party and those working on behalf of satellite organizations like the Unemployed Councils (UCs)—challenged the terrible burdens of racial capitalism in Chicago in ways that no one else at the time was doing. By the Depression, the Communist party line on American racism was that it was a compounding factor making the lives of black workers and the black unemployed even more precarious than those of their white counterparts. Furthermore, party leaders understood that racism and the stoking of racial fury between workers served to buttress capitalist interests by making it harder for interracial groups of workers to trust each other and organize. As such, they labored to challenge not just capitalism but also white supremacy.

In so doing, they launched the decade's most assertive efforts to better the lives of the black poor and working class. Their plan of action covered a host of issues. Working through the UCs—which sought to organize the unemployed for purposes of mass action—organizers held demonstrations to demand a more robust relief structure for starving and desperate citizens and to attack racism in the administration of welfare relief. They turned people's gas and water back on when those utilities were shut off for lack of payment. In one well-known incident in 1930, black unemployed workers allied with a UC, angry at a Black Belt streetcar project that employed only white unionized labor, marched to project job sites, literally took the tools out of white workers' hands, and demanded jobs for black people.[77]

The party's most sustained actions in the Depression's early years, however, and the most formative in establishing the contours of their relationship with the CPD, focused on evictions. These actions, too, were concentrated in the South Side Black Belt. As we saw in the last chapter, black Chicagoans had been exploited within the housing economy for years, with the joined processes of migration, segregation, and ghettoization meaning high rents and low-quality housing. The Depression made things worse. Very few people in the Black Belt owned their homes outright when the market crashed, opening them up to crippling insecurity in housing, should they lose their ability to pay their rent.

Once the Depression gutted incomes and savings, swaths of black Chicago faced a full-blown eviction crisis. Beginning in 1930 and escalating during 1931, the sight of landlords with law enforcement accompaniments serving eviction warrants and putting black people out of their homes became commonplace. But so, too, did community resistance. When authorities executed an eviction warrant, they would go to the evictee's house and remove all personal effects from the home, piling them in the front yard or on nearby streets or sidewalks. To resisters, the most obvious course of action was to reverse the process. As the eviction crisis deepened, groups of black citizens formed squads that would dispatch themselves to the homes of evicted residents and, once authorities left, move their belongings back in. In doing so, they were explicit in articulating their actions as a matter of community defense.[78] And it did not go unnoticed that they were rejecting the authority of the police and sheriff's officers to actually enforce the eviction.

Because of that rejection, the threat of violence always hovered around these campaigns. This was to be expected since CPD officials and officers had, since the department's first days, seen violence as a rational response to civic protest.[79] Horace Cayton recalled being at one representative scene in which black South Siders gathered to protest an eviction and were met with a wall of police officers, with "night sticks playing a tattoo on black heads." The protesters were not deterred; Cayton also recalled a young anti-eviction activist who stared down guns-drawn police, shouting at them, "You can't shoot all of us so you might as well shoot me. I'd as soon die now as any time."[80] In this instance, as in the eviction fights more broadly, the lines were fiercely drawn.

As the frequency and boldness of the anti-eviction campaigns built, so did a counterrevolution which demanded that the city and the CPD stop them. Landlords led the charge. When we talk about racial exploitation and economic plunder within the context of black history and racial capitalism, a common assumption is that we are invariably talking about the transfer of black money into white hands.[81] The assumption holds true in many of its historic contours, but as the historian Nathan Connolly points out, it misses the fact that greed knows no particular skin color. In his study of how early and mid-twentieth-century real estate markets in South Florida were molded by racial and economic exploitation, Connolly shows the vulturous way that landlords, black and white alike, dealt with their tenants—neglecting to maintain apartments and buildings, gouging renters, and trying to jettison tenants who protested their exploitation. This was especially the case with black renters, who lacked sufficient economic, political, and social capital to take legal recourse.[82]

The same held true in Chicago. The South Side was a gold mine for many landlords, including some of the city's most prominent black people. The most famous among them was the U.S. congressman Oscar De Priest, who at that time was the most powerful black man in Chicago. He was a millionaire, the first African American to hold a U.S. congressional seat since Reconstruction, and the first ever to do so outside the South. He was one of the prides of the South Side. But he was also a landlord. He hated the anti-eviction protests, and perhaps more loudly than anyone, prevailed on the instruments of law and order to stop them. This was telling. Thinking about black politics and radicalism through a lens of class is not a perfect optic, but De Priest's and other landlords' choices to demonize and criminalize anti-eviction protests does emphasize how intraracial class fissures could play out in terms of policing at this and other junctures. Despite the CPD's inconsistent relationship to black life and livelihood in previous years, wealthy elites like De Priest continued to perceive the police as a resource that could be claimed to their benefit.

So it was that in early August of 1931, De Priest, fusing capital interests with his own political influence, led a group of landlords in demanding that the CPD "take more severe measures to stop the anti-eviction activity."[83]

Two days later, fueled by his demands, the deadliest Depression-era conflict between police and citizens until the 1937 Memorial Day Massacre erupted.

Under an afternoon sun in front of a Dearborn Street flat, septuagenarian Dianna Gross's belongings lay strewn. Bed, couch, table, chairs, books, and things less replaceable—photographs, clothes hemmed with memories, gifts from the seventy-two-year-old widow's late husband—all sat on yard and sidewalk. Gross was being evicted. A real estate agent stood nearby, joined by two Municipal Court bailiffs and two CPD officers stationed there to maintain order. Channeled by a vast web of communication, word of the eviction was quickly delivered to protesters nearby who were marching to demand better social relief. When word got to them, they diverted toward the Dearborn Street address, their numbers swelling as large as five thousand by the time they arrived. Word had also spread along other communication lines: CPD district commanders, sensing trouble, ordered reinforcement officers to the scene. When those reinforcements arrived, they found a crowd of people moving Gross's furniture back into the flat.[84]

The reports of what happened next are difficult to parse. The *Defender* reported that one officer admitted to firing a shot into the air to get the crowd to disperse, at which point hell broke loose.[85] The *Tribune* claimed the crowd attacked the police, who acted in self-defense.[86] Harry Haywood, a legendary black Communist organizer, recalled the police simply "open[ing] fire" when people tried to move Gross's belongings back into her house.[87] CP organizer Bill Gebert later wrote to national party leader Earl Browder that a handful of protesters, including a black man named Abe Grey, "had disarmed and beaten three policemen, causing other police to attack and fatally shoot Grey."[88]

Regardless of how it started, it ended in blood. Abe Grey, John O'Neil (spelled *O'Neal* in some accounts), and Frank Armstrong—all of them black members of the southern diaspora—died from police bullets. Some witnesses alleged that police had killed Armstrong execution-style in nearby Washington Park, although those reports were never confirmed.[89] Many others were injured, some of them seriously, including more than a dozen police officers.

The three men died in the middle of the afternoon. Beginning that night and continuing for the following week, the CP convened nightly meetings in Washington Park, each consisting of five to ten thousand people "listening, questioning, and cheering as Communists and others struck verbal blows against the capitalist state, racism, and police violence." Organizers also arranged a massive public funeral for Grey, O'Neil, and Armstrong.[90] Fifty thousand leaflets were distributed throughout the Black Belt before the funeral, demanding the death penalty for the police officers who had killed them.[91] Sixty thousand people marched in the funeral procession itself, the majority of whom were black. They walked through throngs of forty thousand more onlookers—90 percent of them black—who offered money to help pay the men's funeral expenses.[92] Later that fall, the CP held a mock trial of Cermak for "complicity in promoting what the Communists regarded as police terror."[93]

The violence and protest forced Cermak to temporarily halt evictions on the South Side. Although the landlords hated the eviction freeze and tried to argue against it, it was a good thing in the context of the Depression—one of the very few reprieves that Cermak extended to struggling black families during his mayoralty.

At the same time, however, the mayor labored to delegitimize the protests. Invoking a trope common among anti-Communists, he ridiculed radical activity as the fault of "outside agitators," rather than the organic response of angry and desperate people. And he harnessed the police to help him in this effort. He huddled with CPD Commissioner John Alcock and subordinates, after which Alcock announced a plan to pursue deportation options for those involved, claiming without substantiation that most dissidents were foreign-born and thus alien threats.[94] Meanwhile, members of the CPD's "Red Squad"—the nickname for its secretive antisubversive unit—raided Communist headquarters in the Pilsen neighborhood, where they discovered the handbills calling for the death penalty for the officers who had killed the three men.[95]

The appearance of the Red Squad at party headquarters isn't surprising. Indeed, although the historical record isn't clear about which police units were involved in what Harry Haywood called the "Chicago Massacre," it is impossible to believe that the Red Squad didn't play a critical role. By this point in time, the Red Squad had become the central cog in Chicago's war on radicalism. Under the leadership of a Russian émigré named Make (pronounced Mak-ee) Mills, the squad was seemingly omnipresent—opening surveillance files on thousands of organizations and individuals and watching over hundreds of demonstrations. And Mills's squad was ruthless, its tactics for harassing and intimidating suspected radicals boundless. They disrupted the daily activities of dissident groups either by surveilling or breaking up political meetings. They tried to incite violence so as to undermine radicals' credibility and give proper cover for police repression. (For example, one of Mills's agents infiltrated the Industrial Workers of the World, and was subsequently outed as a police agent after he tried to convince striking workers to plant a bomb in their boss's car.[96]) And, of course, they were themselves violent. Squad officers routinely drove police cars into assemblages of people, committed rampant brutality, and, simply, shot people.[97] Anyone participating in direct action protests had to always be prepared for violence.[98]

The squad in many ways reflected its leader. Mills was a man of tremendously ill temper and a loose moral compass. While he believed firmly in the mission of social control and antiradicalism, he also frequently used his position to further his own self-interest. He brazenly took bribes from businesses in exchange for using police powers against organized labor: infiltrating unions and UCs, attacking workers on picket lines, arresting and beating labor leaders, and supplying information to newspapers hostile to organized labor.[99] He was corrupt, angry, and violent, and one of the most powerful law enforcement officers in Chicago.

He was also an inveterate racist. Among black community members, Mills became known for his bad temper and flagrant use of the word *nigger*. (Though he did claim to have many "nigger friends.") He also hated white antiracists and deemed interracial activity innately suspicious. In 1934 his unit arrested three white University of Chicago students for demonstrating against police brutality in the Black Belt, and in a subsequent interview with an interracial student group, went on a tirade in which he blasted interracial protest gatherings as unwise and unlawful and pledged to stop them as part of his law enforcement mission. He turned his wrath especially on the white members: "Any time you go into a nigger district you'll get hit with a [police] club. You've got no right to parade with niggers. . . . You've no right to go into any nigger neighborhood."[100]

The *Defender* ran a partial reprint of Mills's comments, alongside an editorial recalling black Americans' rights to equal treatment before the law *as Americans*, and accusing the police unit of intentionally creating interracial antagonisms. Braiding Mills's comments together with larger observations about the Red Squad's work, its writers surmised that "it is the duty of [the Red Squad] to cruise around the city in search of 'Reds' as evidenced by a group in which black and white people are found together as friends and not fighting each other. Whenever these squads find such gatherings, they immediately pounce upon the offenders, beat men and women over their heads with clubs, haul them off to stations and put them through 'the works'. . . . This is not Russia; this is America: black men fought, gave up their lives that such people as 'Make' Mills might leave a country of cruelty and brutality and become police officials in a free country."[101]

Mills's attitude did not mark him as an outlier; what was unique was his position at the top of an elite police unit. And while a dearth of source material prevents us from knowing much about his subordinates' attitudes on their mission, as Mills (with the CPD's and thus city administration's blessings) called on his men to crack down on black and interracial activism,

there is no evidence that they wavered. In the winter of 1932, squad officers used clubs and night sticks to beat protesters outside Oscar De Priest's
State Street office when they gathered to ask him to do more to help his
constituents in the throes of the Depression.[102] In November 1935, the unit
led a larger police detail in breaking up an interracial assemblage at Forty-
Seventh and Prairie who had gathered to peacefully protest fascist Italy's
invasion of Ethiopia. Police beat both demonstrators and bystanders and
arrested some five hundred people.[103] When the National Negro Congress
(NNC) held its inaugural national meeting in Chicago in February of 1936, rumors abounded that the Red Squad was bent on raiding and disrupting it.[104]

The Red Squad's drives against black activists and Communist radicals
were prelude and accompaniment to larger disruptions of human rights
protests in Chicago. In the coming years, squad members arrested demonstrators at labor pickets, removed speechmakers from school board meetings who demanded reinvestment in public schools, and suppressed protests by Works Progress Administration employees who tried to strike for a
living wage.[105] These labors culminated most infamously in a South Chicago
field in 1937, when CPD officers killed ten unarmed striking workers at a
Memorial Day picnic.[106] That event, known as the Memorial Day Massacre,
is deservedly remembered as a singularly violent moment in the history of
Chicago's political activism and police repression. But it was preceded by
years of sustained conflict elsewhere in the city—especially in the parks,
streets, and sidewalks of the South Side, with black Chicagoans bearing
the brunt.

Mills and the Red Squad might now strike us as unsavory, but the CPD's
leadership and the city's political machinery saw both squad and leader as invaluable. At the end of 1935, Mills was nearly forced off the CPD because he'd
reached the department's mandatory retirement age. But when word of his
forced retirement spread through department and community, numerous
people—including from "several patriotic organizations"—recommended
that Mills be given special treatment so that the CPD could retain his services.[107] The protests worked; Mills was given a special designation that attached him directly to the commissioner's office, allowing him to stay on
the police force.[108]

The adoration Mills and the Red Squad enjoyed ensured that the squad
would survive its own controversies, and signposted a departmental embrace of surveillance and repression that would grow increasingly severe
over time. Because the Red Squad's files between the 1930s and mid-1940s
are essentially gone (destroyed or lost), it's impossible to gauge its activities
with much certainty.[109] But from evidence in the files that survive, it is clear
just how extensively the department used the squad to invade the lives of

Chicagoans—following them to political meetings, monitoring their mail, and so on. Those actions were historically specific, but also seemingly out of time. Indeed, while it's rare for historians to successfully draw straight lines between different time periods, it isn't especially difficult to see how the Red Squad's escalating power and boldness in the 1930s and 1940s prefigured its relentless and illegal responses in the 1960s and 1970s to civil rights and leftist protests—a story we will return to in later chapters.

Yet for all the scale and depth of police repression, it never succeeded in crushing activists' spirits. The scars from "rough handling by the police" on the face of David Poindexter, one of Chicago's black Communist leaders, provided physical proof of his dedication to the struggles against racism and capitalism.[110] Claude Lightfoot, another local black leader, remembered the moment on a speaker's soapbox in Washington Park that catalyzed him into the vanguard of black Chicago's Left: "After having gotten up on the soapbox and cursing out the police and then marching away triumphantly with the workers, well, from that day on I was a man." He liked the whispers that followed him after that: "There goes Claude Lightfoot. He's the one that cursed out the police the other day, you know."[111] Or consider the fact that when police brutally beat black women who were striking from their jobs at the Sopkins & Sons Apron Factory, demanding better wages and working conditions, nearly all sectors of black Chicago—from the *Defender* to Oscar De Priest to William Dawson to the Brotherhood of Sleeping Car Porters—rallied in their defense.[112] Or think back to the hundred thousand mostly black citizens who crammed the streets of the South Side to pay their respects to the three men killed in the Chicago Massacre. Weekly if not daily during the worst throes of the Depression, black Chicagoans confronted a rapacious economic order, a racist relief system, and relentless city-sanctioned police violence, and they refused to be broken by it.

Moreover, what becomes clear in light of the vast numbers of black Chicagoans who turned out in support of leftist activists like those killed in the Chicago Massacre is that when dissidents criticized and struggled against the CPD, they were preaching to a choir of receptive ears. City politicians and mainstream media outlets—including within black Chicago—frequently castigated Communists and other Depression-era dissidents as troublemakers and outsiders. This would prove to be a recurring theme throughout the course of Chicago's radical politics. Whether black Communists in the 1930s or the Black Panthers in the 1960s and 1970s or Black Lives Matter activists in the 2010s, mainstream opinion-makers have consistently tried to discredit criticisms of the police and the larger socioeconomic system that they protect as hovering at the extreme intellectual and political margins. But then as now, what those activists were doing was not so much telling people *what* to think about the police as they were channeling opinions that large sections of the community already held.

The Limits of Redress: Coalitional Challenges in the Face of Police Power

But not all sections, of course, for black Chicago was hardly a monolith. On the one hand, some black Chicagoans were thoroughly invested in the system as it stood. One needn't look further than Oscar De Priest calling the police on black renters to see that, but it is worth remembering that De Priest was far from the only black man or woman on the South Side who believed in the gospel of capitalism. And it actually seems unlikely that most of the people who participated in Communist-led or Communist-affiliated actions on the South Side did so because of the party's radical theoretics. There is no evidence that a critical mass of black people sought the actual overthrow of capitalism itself, so much as they sought a way to live with some modicum of stability and comfort.

Relatedly, plenty of black Chicagoans joined their countrymen in opposing anything that hinted at radicalism. If the pull of radical protest was strong among the black unemployed and working class, so, too, did the patriotic anti-Communism that permeated the United States exercise its own strong influence. The local NAACP is a classic example. The organization constantly sought to distance itself from radical action, whether because they knew that getting too close risked castigation as anti-American or because they actually hated the Communists. (It is worth noting too that the 1930s NAACP took a zero-sum outlook on black politics: either they would lead the fight for black rights, or the Communists would.[113]) For instance, in the immediate aftermath of the Chicago Massacre, local branch president Herbert Turner sent a frantic telegram to national headquarters in which he rejected the idea that activists' aims were for racial justice, attempting to preempt the NAACP from getting dragged into what he viewed as a potential political quagmire. By Turner's calculus, the police had been "extremely lenient" and were not to be blamed, and he emphatically stated that what had happened constituted "nothing discriminatory" and was "not racial but radical."[114] This stance aligned Turner and the branch as being firmly opposed to the tidal waves of grassroots anti-eviction activism then swelling; in their characterization, evictions—although one of the central concerns of black Chicago—were "primarily social and economic in nature and not a legal and civil rights problem."[115] Turner's argument so infuriated the families of the three men killed outside Dianna Gross's flat that after Turner was selected to serve on the coroner's inquest jury investigating their deaths, the families had him removed from the jury as a hostile presence.[116]

In the 1930s, the Chicago NAACP did pursue some piecemeal legal campaigns in the face of police abuse of black people. But its vision was as narrow as its popularity.[117] The Communists articulated police violence and harassment as systematic, and laid it at the feet of the city and the larger structural forces of American racism and capitalism. The NAACP instead campaigned against police violence only on a case-by-case basis, and only when that violence was meted out to nominally respectable members of the community in general, and business owners in particular.[118] If the Communists' point was that the police system was part of a larger repressive apparatus, the association's was that police officers should know the distinction between upstanding and troublesome members of the community.

The inability to see these problems as civil rights issues showed the hand of the NAACP's contemporary conservatism, but the organization was hardly alone in laboring to distance themselves from political radicalism. The *Defender*'s editors, for example, who routinely castigated the CPD and city officials for their treatment of black citizens and unresponsiveness to black needs, offered far more negative opinions about "the Reds"—functionally shorthand for all radicalism—than they did positive ones. And although William Dawson and Oscar De Priest—the two most prominent politicians in black Chicago—could be on hand to demand justice for black women whom police manhandled on the picket line, they were never going to come to the defense of Communists.

As a consequence, despite the severity of the early Depression's weight on black Chicago and the level of repression that arose when they tried to cast off the yoke, few among black Chicago's foremost powerbrokers hitched their wagons to the CP, whether within the context of protesting police repression or otherwise. It is well known that, in the context of the late 1940s and early 1950s Cold War, feverish anti-Communism across American politics had a chilling effect on coalition-building in service of black rights.[119] On a micro level, the same dynamic was at play in early Depression-era Chicago. Although the CP, the NAACP, the *Defender*, and myriad other institutions and individuals all had some particular vision for trying to help Chicago's black community, a deep bifurcation cut the heart of the political landscape. And the one organization that did the most in terms of tangible activism— the CP—was so politically toxic for nonradicals to associate with during the Depression's early and worst years that hardly any of them ever did.

If ideological cross-pollination proved elusive in the early Depression, prospects for it were better in the second half of the 1930s and into the 1940s, with the rise of the Popular Front. During that time, a coalition of radical and liberal leftist groups arose that "united to expand New Deal reforms and beat back what they saw as an alarming growth of fascism, both at home and abroad."[120] During this period, the CP worked more closely with organizations like the Chicago-based Brotherhood of Sleeping Car Porters and other labor unions. At the same time, the NAACP and other black elites on the one hand and the CP on the other, relaxed their shared hostility.[121] This new Popular Front meant new opportunities for interracial solidarities, new labor and civil rights militancies, and, potentially, the bettering of black Americans' lot in the process.

Chicago was one of the new movement's epicenters, especially because of the emergence of the Congress of Industrial Organizations (CIO) in 1935, which made critical inroads among Chicago's vast numbers of steelworkers, packinghouse workers, and auto workers during the late 1930s and onward to World War II.[122] Through local organizations like the Packinghouse Workers Organizing Committee (PWOC), the Steel Workers Organizing Committee (SWOC), and the Back-of-the-Yards Neighborhood Council, labor organizers worked to bring black and white workers together across deeply entrenched racial lines, under slogans such as "Negro and White, Unite and Fight!" Meanwhile, the NNC, which the historian Erik Gellman identifies as "the black vanguard" of the movement, bound together the fate of "the Race" and larger questions of labor justice, emerging as a critical presence in Chicago from the time the NNC's first national conference was held on the South Side in February of 1936.[123] (The NNC floundered under external anticommunist pressure and internal discord in the aftermath of the CP's signing of the Hitler-Stalin Non-Aggression Pact in 1939, but it nevertheless remained active in Chicago well into the 1940s.)

The Popular Front offered up unique opportunities for coalition politics, especially in pursuit of economic power for workers. The PWOC, for example, successfully organized thousands of black and white workers in Chicago's stockyards during the late 1930s, and by 1940 its Local 347 won exclusive rights to bargain with the massive Armour Packing Company, among other packinghouses across the city. This in turn allowed them to secure a contract that guaranteed seniority rights, weekly hourly guarantees, and equal pay for equal work, among other things.[124] Similarly, the SWOC bound together black and white steel workers, with interracial solidarity serving as a crucial bulwark in the face of extreme antiunionism from steel corporations.

Because it was so closely identified with the CIO and other labor initiatives, Chicago's Popular Front has mostly been seen as a movement first and foremost for economic justice. And while that framing has merit,

Popular Front–affiliated organizations didn't uniformly avoid larger social issues—including problems with Chicago's police. United Packing Workers of America (formerly the PWOC) Local 347, for instance, "involved itself in virtually every civil rights campaign in the city" during the war years, including initiating its own campaign against police brutality in 1943, provoked by an incident in which an unarmed sixteen-year-old was shot by police.[125] The NNC, meanwhile, crafted an agenda within its first year that promised campaigns against police brutality in Chicago, defended a white plainclothes officer in 1944 when he was arrested by other CPD officers for intervening on the side of a black streetcar motorman being harassed by white youth, and, not coincidentally, eventually folded into the Civil Rights Congress—perhaps the organization that was most overtly condemnatory of America's police until the late 1960s.[126]

Nevertheless, when black Chicagoans encountered the police within the context of Popular Front activism, it was mostly to the degree to which they were part of larger black-white labor coalitions. The most famous case here is the Memorial Day Massacre in 1937, in which Chicago police—who had been provided lodging, food, and weapons by the Republic Steel Company—killed ten labor demonstrators outside Republic's South Chicago plant during the SWOC "Little Steel Strike" at mills across the Midwest. Thanks to the organizing work of the SWOC and its dedicated racial bridge-building, more than four thousand black workers were out on strike at Republic at the time of the massacre; one black man, Lee Tisdale, was among those killed in the unprovoked CPD attack.[127]

The fact that such violence unfolded within Popular Front labor struggles shaped how workers responded, for better or worse. The death of Tisdale, who had been shot in the back and died from infected bullet wounds after police left him to fester in a jail cell for days after the incident without medical treatment, provoked an uproar among other striking black steelworkers. Some of them suggested "get[ting] our guns" in response to his killing, showing the inclination they felt toward militancy in the face of police terror. What happened instead was that black labor leaders like SWOC's Joe Cook convinced them to channel their energy toward keeping the picket going. "Men," he told them, referring to a picket sign, "this is our gun. So long as you keep our ranks united, they can't beat us—so hold that line!"[128]

The SWOC did hold the line, but it lost that particular war. The CPD killings in South Chicago were followed several weeks later by similar police violence in Massillon, Ohio, at the scene of the SWOC Little Steel strike there, which witnessed three men killed and untold numbers injured in a hail of police bullets. State repression accompanied by employer intransigence crippled the strike. By the middle of July of that year, it had essentially fizzled out.[129]

Be that as it may, the police violence in South Chicago ironically provoked some important long-term victories for workers. While the CPD's initial response to the Memorial Day Massacre was to obfuscate, arguing that they had only fired on the strikers in self-defense when video footage plainly showed otherwise, word spread within Chicago's working-class communities about what had really happened.[130] As it did, Mayor Ed Kelly found himself saddled with "an unsavory antilabor reputation"—an untenable situation for someone seeking votes from the masses of blue collar workers in the city.[131] As a consequence, when the Union Stockyards and Transit Company battled with the PWOC in 1938, including calling in the CPD to remove the union's bargaining agents from its offices and locking out the union, Kelly, looking to shore up his bona fides with the working class, stepped in on the side of the union. Using the power of the purse, Kelly threated to dramatically raise the price of water—an essential resource for the stockyards—if the Union Stockyards didn't deal fairly with the PWOC. The company caved.[132]

Despite Kelly siding with the PWOC in that confrontation, the victory failed to serve as a true turning point in the CPD's relationship to labor. As protests for economic and job justice continued in the late 1930s and through the war years, activists continued to find themselves contending not just with reticent employers but also with police officers and officials working in service of those employers' interests. Police were routinely dispatched to the sites of CIO pickets to monitor picketers' actions, and to prevent them from interfering with strikebreakers' entry to job sites.[133] By December of 1945, large-scale arrests of CIO picketers brought union leaders into conference with Kelly, CPD Commissioner James Allman, and Red Squad leader George Barnes, where the mayor and police officials used the ongoing threat of arrests to secure a pledge by the CIO to keep more "orderly" pickets.[134] The CPD's allegiance to employers continued after Kelly's departure from office, as well, when the openly probusiness Martin Kennelly took the mayor's office and gave the Red Squad free reign to attack picket lines with "batons and brass knuckles" and arrest activists handing out leaflets.[135]

Nor was the repression only confined to Popular Front–affiliated groups. Consider, for instance, the case of the Negro Labor Relations League (NLRL), which in the late 1930s "pursued an agenda of aggressive economic nationalism" through "race conscious job campaigns as a method of community development."[136] Formed by William Dawson and other members of black Chicago's elite and middle-class ranks and intimately connected with the

Urban League, the NLRL was far afield ideologically from the working-class radicalism of the CP and the CIO, and was focused on race-specific economic gains rather than interracial solidarity. Nevertheless, its focus on economic power echoed Popular Front activism in important ways. The NLRL waged numerous campaigns that got black Chicagoans hired and promoted in a range of jobs: from newspaper carriers to theater operators to delivery drivers to telephone repairmen.[137] These labors won the league numerous enemies among white South Side businessmen, who exerted pressure on Kelly and the state's attorney to investigate the group, and their activism drew them into clashes with the police on picket lines in the same way that the CPD faced off with CIO campaigns.[138]

In this way, police repression and police violence continued to shape Chicago's larger political culture throughout the late 1930s and well into the 1940s. Despite this, a cohesive and durable campaign *against* that repression didn't emerge at the time. That fact stemmed not from activists' lack of concern with repression; activists during the Popular Front era were, for their time, deeply concerned with matters of social justice, and the late 1930s and early 1940s represented an important moment of possibility for interracial organizing and activism. Rather, the simple fact of the matter was that Popular Front organizations, as well as organizations like the NLRL that were unaffiliated with the Popular Front but shared its emphasis on economic justice, largely kept their eye on the prize of working-class power and job justice. It was, then, the pursuit of such power that preoccupied their activism.

The fact that no cohesive campaign arose in response to rising police repression during a Depression-era moment that seemed rife with possibility meant that violations of black rights by the CPD continued more or less unabated, other than in extraordinary situations. And those violations were frequent, stretching beyond the conflicts and invasions already sketched out here.

On the one hand, Anton Cermak fought passionately for the expansion of a police practice then known as stop-and-seizure. The precursor to the infamous practice of stop-and-frisk, stop-and-seizure had first been implemented during Prohibition. The original intent behind the statute implementing it had been to lay out the parameters by which liquor licenses (for medicinal, religious, and manufacturing purposes) would be granted; to establish record-keeping guidelines for carriers of such products; and, importantly, to establish an operating system where police could enter into places that served, sold, or made illegal liquor, search the premises and people there, seize illicit products, and make arrests.[139] But as Prohibition had plodded onward, police officials had broadened stop-and-seizure's meaning and application, increasingly using it as a means for targeting *suspected* criminals on the street.[140] By blurring whatever specificity stop-and-seizure laws had previously possessed, this new application wedged open doors that would later prove difficult to close. Even in the 1920s, legal fights erupted over the constitutionality of such application, and police officials guarded it jealously as an important weapon in their arsenal. CPD Commissioner William Russell, for instance, brushed off questions about whether or not his officers would quit using stop-and-seizure, saying that the department would keep stopping and seizing "no matter what the state's attorney or the judges do about it."[141]

In the Depression—particularly under Cermak and the ascendant Democratic machine—stop-and-seizure's use against Prohibition violations diminished, as political and criminal justice priorities shifted. Instead, it morphed into a policy that increasingly opened up black cars, persons, and homes to invasive searches by the police. Already in 1931, the NAACP Legal Redress Committee argued that, in their efforts to eradicate policy gambling, "police officers have taken upon themselves to break into homes, beat up citizens and search people on the streets without probable cause or legal process."[142] This predilection to search people without cause was echoed in reports of officers randomly stopping and searching cars in the Black Belt; as the Associated Negro Press reported, "'Drive to the curb' has been the command given to many citizens [on the Southside] and their cars searched without warrants and the owners subjected to abusive language and in some cases to arrest."[143] Officers' tendency to target black people for stop-and-seizure operations was also reflected in contemporary *Tribune* reportage showing that, in both 1931 and 1932, a third of citizens interrogated and arrested by the police in Chicago in firearms seizures were black.[144] (This despite the fact that less than 10 percent of Chicago's population was black, that stop-and-seizure's ostensible purpose was to cut down on white-dominated Prohibition violence, and that no evidence existed suggesting higher rates of firearms possession among African Americans.) Yet it was clear that what the NAACP was angriest about in its condemnations of illegal searches was not that it was a violation of *everyone's* civil rights. They continued to support strong antivice measures, after all. The problem was that such searches were being used against respectable members of the community who didn't deserve such treatment.

Even on the most serious issue of all—police violence—black organizations could not transcend their differences. Consider, for example, that at the exact moment when Herbert Turner actively dismissed the Chicago Massacre as not a civil rights issue, he and the branch he headed had been fighting police violence (against respectable community members) for more than a decade. Just the previous year, correspondence between the national NAACP, Turner's Chicago office, and the branch office in Detroit had called for "a thorough investigation" into a "ruthless killing" by the CPD.[145] In December of 1931, the association challenged CPD officers' savage beating of a black bakery owner named Ernest Draine, although they characteristically emphasized Draine's role as a business owner and a man who wouldn't "voluntarily enter into a controversy with the police."[146] Similarly, around the same time as Draine's beating, protest in black Chicago erupted after a police officer beat a black woman over the head with a flashlight.[147] Following that incident, Turner and other community leaders utilized their station to warn Cermak and Police Commissioner James Allman that failing to reign in abusive officers risked reprising the 1919 riot.[148] Against that backdrop of rampant police violence, thinking of Abe Grey and others differently may have been politically convenient, but it wasn't intellectually consistent.

And the stakes were high. Under Cermak, commenters in the black community began deploying the language of terrorism to talk about the CPD's treatment of black Chicagoans—an evocation that would continue during Kelly's administration and onward into the postwar era.[149] In 1932 a white South Side realtor and landlord, Melville Kolliner, wrote an impassioned warning to Cermak (furnishing a copy to the *Defender*, as well) after one of his janitors was beaten and robbed by two CPD officers. His employee was hesitant to speak out for fear of retribution, so Kolliner harnessed his own racial and social capital to speak for him. When he did, he framed brutality as far more expansive than the immediate case. Kolliner wasn't specific in naming cases but might have had any number in mind. Perhaps he remembered Hattie Shaw, who was verbally assaulted at Forty-Second and Indiana by a drunken police officer while waiting for a streetcar two months prior, with the officer threatening to beat her or have her arrested if she didn't get off the street and out of his sight. Or maybe he was remembering the charges against Patrolman James Kerrigan, who, reportedly while drunk, assaulted one man on the South Side and attempted to rob a newsboy.[150] Or perhaps he was reflecting on a drugstore porter who was passing out advertisements on the Far South Side when a white police officer called him a nigger and told him to get out of the area. When the porter protested, the officer reached for his gun and warned the man not to give him any attitude or he would "give you something" in return.[151]

Whatever evidence guided him, what Kolliner was angling toward in his letter to Cermak was a rendering of police abuse as systemic. And the consequence, he wrote, "is breeding among the people of the South side not only a very great and strong animosity toward the police department, but also a very great disrespect and lack of regard for police power. That is but natural."[152] The "great disrespect" and "lack of regard" and "strong animosity" with which he colored community attitudes toward the police were birthed not by one incident but by the totality of the situation—by fear and anxiety and anger about the ongoing humiliations and violence to which black Chicagoans were finding themselves subjected. Two months later, the *Defender* editorial board called without success for the state's attorney to "at least investigate some of the killings committed by police officers under the guise of law enforcement."[153] And they reiterated the call several months later in an angry comment on killings of black people by CPD officers—"men who think that their badge and gun give them the right to kill citizens at will." Echoing the power of such ubiquitous violence to turn public opinion against the police, the editorialists wrote that "the marauding type of policeman who patrols his beat with his finger on the trigger is responsible for the disrepute in which the department of police is now held by the public."[154]

IN LATE SEPTEMBER of 1939, a headline in the *Defender* read: "CHICAGO POLICE VS. THE SOUTH SIDE." "Chicago police," the lede ran, "have never been slow about performing impromptu surgical operations upon Race citizens who happen to fall into their clutches." Conjuring once again the telling language of *terrorism*, it continued: "Third degree torture and wholesale police terrorism of Race neighborhoods have earned 'Chicago's finest' one of the bloodiest reputations borne by any group of officers in the country." Furthermore, the editorial went on to note, "the several hundred policemen stationed in this community wear their blue uniforms as ornaments," but did precisely nothing to safeguard the community. Lamenting concentrated crime and poverty in some pockets of the South Side, and appealing to the guarantees of civic protection of "life and property in the American constitution," the editorialist(s) suggested that it was time to oust Police Commissioner James Allman from office if he wouldn't work to remedy the problems.[155]

What the Depression decade had done was further embed the idea among larger numbers of black Chicagoans that the police department was not only uninterested in but perhaps actively aligned against the community's greater interests. The point could hardly be made more clearly than it was by one of the most important newspapers in black America deploying *vs.* in order to frame the relationship between police and public as explicitly adversarial.

The criminalization of human misery, the rise of what later became racially specific stop-and-frisk, and other Depression-era police practices are significant pieces of that story, to be sure. But probably the most important pieces, understood with the benefit of historical hindsight, are the ways that the city (now under the control of the Democratic machine) and the police department labored to frustrate social and political movements seeking greater forms of social justice in Chicago. Particularly in the conflicts that erupted surrounding radical protest and police repression, the rhythms and tensions of the decade had laid bare the inherent dichotomies between order and justice, law and rights that lay at the heart of the relationship between police and citizens. Those conflicts were not in and of themselves new, but the Depression decade changed the calculus in terms of their frequency and explosiveness. All the time, month after month, especially during the early years of the Depression, radical activists challenged the status quo with direct action protests, whether in the name of civil rights or labor rights or poor people's rights or all of them at once.

Prefiguring the contours of protest movements and police and political responses ever since, the CPD and the Democratic machine responded in the name of law and order. For forty more years, the Red Squad would lead the city's effort to surveil, curtail, and terrorize social movements in the city. Shrouded in darkness, ruthless in its methods, and antidemocratic almost by definition, the squad would shape the prospects and tenor of freedom dreams in ways that even radical dissidents themselves could not have fully known. And when the Red Squad was finally abolished in the 1970s, those guiding suspicions and impulses did not magically vanish with it. Rather, its central logics were simply absorbed into other corners of the department.

In the coming years, a wide range of left-wing protest movements—all of them, really—would feel the costs of police repression that the CPD carried out in the name of order and antisubversion. Queer activists came under surveillance when they tried to demand basic equalities and decent representation in the realms of civic rights and the public sphere in Chicago.[156] The Puerto Rican Young Lords, the white Young Patriots, the Chicago Peace Council, Students for a Democratic Society, the Latin American Defense Organization, the Jobs or Income Now Community Union—all of them had to struggle through tide waves of police repression as they sought to bring about what they saw as a better Chicago and a better America.[157] Many more organizations dealt with the same—hundreds more, at least, and thousands of individuals from all across Chicago. Disclosing information from the Red Squad files is complicated for researchers like myself because of the legalese associated with the lawsuit that ended it, so I have chosen in this book to focus narrowly on some of its specific targets rather than broadly across its range. But anyone who doubts the pervasiveness of what it did and how deeply it disrupted Chicago's various freedom struggles over time need only travel to Chicago, take the bus or train to Clark and North, get a free pass to the Chicago History Museum archives, and sign the requisite forms to look at the squad's files. The sheer volume of materials is overwhelming. The paranoia and darkness contained within them is even more so.

All of that said, because their freedom struggles started earlier, were more public, and were more intimately bound up in the larger mechanics of the city's politics, no single blanket demographic in Chicago dealt with police repression of social protest more than did black Chicago. The Black Panthers would become the public face of that repression and the resistance to it, but dozens of other community organizations would align themselves with the Panthers or wage their own struggles. The ensuing conflicts are central to the remainder of this book.

So, too, is the power of the Democratic machine to shape the nature of policing in Chicago. The influence of politicians on the police apparatus would not always be as direct as in the early years of the Depression, but it always lurked. This would have important consequences going forward, into and after the Second World War. The war ushered in a new wave of changes in Chicago, a new wave of black migration to it, and a profound explosion of violence from white Chicagoans who felt under siege as a result. These things would present new tests of how much the police and politicians valued order over all else, as had long been the presumed case.

CHAPTER 3

Whose Police?

RACE, PRIVILEGE, AND POLICING
IN POSTWAR CHICAGO

n August of 1953, a constituent letter landed on Chicago Mayor Martin Kennelly's desk. Cramped, single-spaced, riddled with underlines and furious all caps, the letter was signed by a man named Joseph Beauharnais—an American Nazi Party affiliate and founder of a Chicago-based hate group called the White Circle League of America. For years, Beauharnais had watched despondently as black migration to Chicago had ticked upward, and as the boundaries of Chicago's traditionally white communities had been pushed. He hated black people, hated integration, and saw it as a legitimate and necessary political project for white people to violently expel black people from their neighborhoods.

What inspired Beauharnais's letter was the city's use of CPD officers to protect black in-migrants to the Trumbull Park housing project in the South Deering neighborhood from the wrath of white mobs. Writing to the mayor, he railed against a law enforcement apparatus that wouldn't let whites expel this "plague," and claimed that whites in South Deering were living in a police state. Black integrators being afforded police protection was both absurdity and abomination. "The negro's intrusion into the intimate community life of white people," he wrote, "is an ACT OF WAR and when an impotent, flabby, anti-white government uses the POLICE POWER to forcibly infiltrate the negro into the very blood stream of white community life, you strike at the FIRST LAW OF LIFE, THE LAW OF SELF-PRESERVATION."[1] Dispatching the police to protect black people from white violence was, he felt, an act of white genocide.

Beauharnais was an extremist, but his underlying logic was common enough. Across Chicago during and after World War II, thousands of whites sought to resist the potential weakening of the city's segregated walls. What was happening in Trumbull Park followed a familiar script. Over and over, black families and individuals would try to move into an all-white neighborhood and white residents would gather to terrorize them back out, through words and threats and violence, in actions deserving the label of *riot*. They overturned cars, assaulted innocents, destroyed property, and threatened lives.

And as they did so, much like Beauharnais, they variously expressed disbelief or anger at police officers protecting their targets. They condemned officers who arrested white men, tried (with some success) to collude with white officers, invoked their privilege, and often explicitly assumed that the officers could not possibly have *wanted* to do what they were doing. (One investigator with the Chicago Commission on Human Relations [CCHR] recorded the following dialogue between two white men: "These cops would like to let us go in their [*sic*] and break their [*sic*] backs of [expletive] niggers." "Yeah, sure they would. They don't like this any more than we do."[2]) To them, it was unimaginable that white police officers would stand opposed to them in the race war they sought.

On the other side, many black Chicagoans figured that white rioters' assumptions about police officers' racial sympathies were largely correct. They excoriated the police response to white terrorism as wildly uneven; despite Beauharnais's ravings, it was actually not especially common for police to stand up meaningfully to white criminal violence directed against blacks. Sometimes they did. Sometimes they didn't. And sometimes they actively advised white rioters on avoiding discovery and arrest. To black people seeking equality of freedom and opportunity in the city, that unevenness was a violation. Their taxes helped pay for the police department, yet their ability to make use of its resources was circumscribed, over and over again. And that fact begat larger, fundamental questions about who could expect what from the police. After all, if black people couldn't get the CPD to protect their bodies from public, racially motivated, violent assault, what *could* they get from it?

This chapter explores the claims that white and black Chicagoans made on police resources during battles over space and belonging between the early 1940s and the end of the 1950s. It overlaps with the chapter that follows, which explores the politics of Chicago's racialized post–World War II punitive turn. The two are in close dialogue with one another, while asking different questions. Among other things, this chapter pays much closer attention to white citizens and white racial terrorism.

As various groups of white and black citizens tried to establish what the CPD could and would do for them, most of them—black and white—agreed that they wanted a police force that would keep people safe from violence and serious crime. But beyond that, their visions splintered. Some white progressives, including from some of the city's various interfaith groups, promoted integration and fought alongside black citizens for an open city. Yet they were frequently drowned out in a chorus of louder white voices raging against the compromising of neighborhood racial integrity. The latter group saw the ejection of black people from white neighborhoods as a legitimate, inviolable prerogative. Others, whose neighborhoods *did* racially transition, feared that migrating black people would bring crime and deteriorating neighborhoods. In response, they sought a more muscular police force that would control troublesome and threatening black people.

Black citizens tried to make multifaceted and often conflicting claims of their own on police resources. The desire for police protection from white violence was widely shared at this juncture. But some sought to harness police power to protect their rights to safe and orderly neighborhoods, while others saw the police as reinforcing a fundamentally racist social arrangement. Although such black intraracial disagreements were important, neither side possessed sufficient political capital to meaningfully shape police policy and bring about the changes they sought—a fact that highlights the chapter's animating question.

And that question is this: *Whose police force was it?* This question has shaped the city—in the postwar era, and today—to a degree not yet fully appreciated. Social and racial capital colored how it was asked and molded how it was answered, in ways that resonate with longer patterns of inequality.[3]

The notion of the police as a finite civic resource, the benefits of which are unevenly distributed across the city landscape, might be unsettling to some readers. But it's not a new idea. As the historian Robert Fogelson put it long ago, "The big-city police have always done more than just enforce law, keep the peace, and serve the public. *They have also decided, or at least helped to decide, which laws to enforce, whose peace to keep, and which public to serve.*"[4] In other words, the police have never been a resource equitably claimable and equally controllable, and the benefits of police protection have never been evenly distributed. Indeed, as we saw in the prologue, the earliest iterations of police forces in major American cities were forged by social elites to protect capital interests and tame immigrant immorality and radicalism. And as we saw in the last chapter, the desire to use the police to contain political radicalism and maintain an unequal social order disadvantaged many people during the Depression. From the 1940s onward, the primary purpose of the police was to control supposedly unruly and dangerous racial minorities and to keep crime out of white neighborhoods.

It was in performing this latter function that the police gradually began to solidify their standing in the eyes of the majority population. The police in twenty-first-century America rank among the institutions that citizens trust and value most, according to recent polls and despite (or perhaps because of) the intense criticisms that black activists and allies have lodged against police.[5] But well into the 1950s, police forces in America were not especially well esteemed. Doing police work was often dangerous and never lucrative, and Americans generally viewed it as something that people did because they lacked the skills to do something else. The bad reputation was partly self-inflicted, shaped by evidence of corruption and incompetence, and partly a result of Americans' inability to pin down exactly what the social utility of the police really was.[6]

In the long postwar moment, however, the social function of the police began to clarify. It took time, of course, but by the middle and late 1960s, studies showed that public opinion on the police was that they were generally doing a pretty good job.[7] By the same token, however, black people were three times more likely to think that the police were doing a bad job, and by the early 1970s, one reputable poll found a twenty-four-point gap between blacks and whites on the favorability rating of the police.[8] There were many reasons for this. For one, police organizations (the precursor to unions) and police administrators, in Chicago and elsewhere, ran public relations campaigns with the explicit purpose of bolstering the police image.[9] The most famous example might have come out of Los Angeles, where, in 1952, Police Chief William Parker launched a television series called *The Thin Blue Line*, which was meant to push back against "current attempts to undermine public confidence in the Police Department."[10] The show was a boring commercial flop that the studio canceled after five months. But it signaled the sorts of measures that police officials would take to boost the police image, while also implanting the idea of the police as a "thin blue line" separating civilization and anarchy in the public consciousness.[11] Moreover, first in the context of the early Cold War and fears of juvenile delinquency, and later in the 1960s amid the civil rights and sexual revolutions, Black Power, and antiwar protests, a belief took hold among conservatives (and many white liberals) that the police could be a central force in restoring traditional versions of social order and containing chaos. That belief would become especially pronounced in the wake of the urban uprisings of the mid- and late sixties, when urban America was shaken to its core by explosive protests.

Yet, just as it would be a mistake to consider those uprisings in isolation from their longer historical contexts (as Thomas Sugrue, Heather Ann Thompson, and others have shown[12]), so, too, with white desires to bring the police department to bear in their struggle for city space, racial privilege, and neighborhood integrity. As cities like Chicago got blacker during the second Great Migration and black people encroached on white neighborhoods, white anxieties grew. Such fear of blackness was, of course, not new.[13] But whereas the black population had previously been a small if significant minority, warranting concern but not outright panic, the second Great Migration changed the math. With that latest black influx, old imperatives for sections of white Chicago to keep black people away from their homes and social spaces, and to maintain a social order that they imagined black people naturally threatened, were reignited and lent greater urgency. The first of these was premised on illegality, in that they hoped that the police would look the other way as they tried to push and intimidate black people out. The second was the stuff of history—they hoped for (and impressed on) the police to expand their power and further racially hone its application. The CPD more or less obliged in both respects—sometimes reluctantly and always unevenly responding to white-on-black racial terrorism and expanding the long-term practice of overpolicing black bodies and communities.

The answer to the question *Whose police department is this?*, in other words, became more fully realized over the course of the postwar era. It was, first and very much foremost, for white Chicago, and for its middle and upper classes especially. Increasingly, police policies and attitudes benefited white Chicagoans as both individuals and communities but did not benefit black Chicagoans as either. Women and men like Joseph Beauharnais and others who wanted the police to help maintain Chicago's segregated housing didn't get exactly what they wanted, but neither did Chicago experience meaningful widespread shifts toward open housing. White residents in racially transitioning neighborhoods would be able to bend the ears of city and police officials when they requested more, and more aggressive, police as their neighborhoods got blacker. When their neighborhoods reached a racial tipping point, however, they left anyway. Black Chicagoans ultimately would have the most to lose or gain by transforming the ways that the police operated in their neighborhoods and across the city, and yet it was their claims that police officials and individual officers alike were least receptive to hearing.

So degraded were black rights vis-à-vis the CPD that, by the spring of 1958, one of the city's black newspapers would conjure the ghosts of Dred Scott and Roger Taney and the language of anticitizenship to describe them: "In the eyes of the police," its editors wrote, "no Negro has any rights that a policeman is bound to respect."[14] That invocation, as much as anything else in this book, warrants a reckoning.

Remapping Chicago: Residential Succession, White Violence, and Negligent Policing

When Joseph Beauharnais wrote to Martin Kennelly in 1953, it was in the midst of a demographic sea change in Chicago. As in most urban centers across the northern United States, the Second Great Migration of black southerners profoundly altered Chicago's racial makeup. Once again drawn by the promise of jobs and greater freedom, between 1940 and 1960, Chicago's black population grew nearly threefold, from roughly 280,000 to more than 812,000, and from 8.2 percent of the city's population to just under 23 percent.[15]

For generations, the South Side had been black Chicago's anchor and hub. Yet the sheer number of black people hemmed into confined areas there had long been unsustainable, and with the new migration underway, new migrants and displaced South Siders looked elsewhere across the city for places to live. Their aspirations for spatial mobility led them to Black Belt–adjacent neighborhoods on the South and Southwest Sides, as well as toward sections of the West Side—Lawndale, Austin, and Garfield Park, especially.

White Chicagoans had long fought against this sort of incursion. Their motives were part racist, part economic. During the 1930s and into the 1940s, the federal government, through the Home Owners' Loan Corporation (HOLC) had begun systematically assessing the value of American homes based on the neighborhoods in which they were located, for purposes of determining risk value in offering home loans. They assigned neighborhoods an A, B, C, or D rating, in order of what were considered good to bad neighborhoods. Banks used those grades to determine which neighborhoods were safe to lend to and which ones were not—a practice reinforced by the weight of the Federal Housing Administration (FHA), which used the seeming stability of the federal government to effectively "insure long-term mortgage loans made by private lenders for home construction and sale."[16] The problem was that these government agencies stamped into federal housing policy the racism that white Americans had long harbored about living next to black people. The HOLC constantly gave black urban neighborhoods D ratings, coloring them in red when drawing the maps of cities. Following that lead, the FHA consistently drew red lines around those same neighborhoods (redlining them), marking them as high-risk and unsuitable for federally insured loans. It similarly treated neighborhoods that were racially mixed or transitioning as high-risk, slapping them with C ratings and forecasting that they would soon be downgraded to the bottom.[17]

These pieces of housing policy are central to understanding why white Chicagoans resisted black migration so vociferously during the 1940s and 1950s. When black people moved into white neighborhoods, the official rating of those communities almost instantly dropped, which depreciated the value of white homes in the open market. Knowing this, usurious real estate agents engaged in panic selling and blockbusting—wherein they would figuratively (or sometimes literally) whisper to white homeowners that black people were about to move into their neighborhood or onto their block—and urged them to sell their houses at cut rates before they lost even more value. What resulted was a potent mixture of racial hatred and economic fear, emanating from white communities and directed at black in-migrants.

What had held the racial purity of white neighborhoods for so long in Chicago were legal contracts known as restrictive covenants. The covenants forbade the sale of houses to certain undesirable populations—mostly black people but also sometimes Jews and other minorities. The FHA explicitly encouraged white homeowners to use the covenants, warning them that "if a neighborhood is to retain stability, it is necessary that properties shall continue to be occupied by the same social and racial classes."[18] These mechanisms were largely responsible for the rigidity of Chicago's segregation from the 1920s to the 1940s, keeping black people out of white neighborhoods and weakening the infrastructure of black communities because of overcrowding and depleted resources.

Black Chicagoans challenged this system, but whites fought back tenaciously. In May of 1943, black lawmakers in Springfield introduced a bill to the state legislature that sought to eliminate racial covenants in Illinois. White property owners, neighborhood "improvement associations," and newspapers in Black Belt–adjacent neighborhoods like Oakland-Kenwood responded with a vengeance. The Oakland-Kenwood Property Association (OKPA) argued that the bill would mean the demise of the neighborhoods, and accused its authors of attempting to "stir racial controversy" (rather than demanding basic human rights)—both claims that were endorsed and reprinted in the community newspaper serving the area.[19] The OKPA and affiliated improvement associations bombarded Springfield with demands to bury the bill, and succeeded after less than a month.[20] And they continued to wage a proactive war to save covenants over the coming years. As the Black Belt bulged against its eastern edge, pushing toward the lake where blacks could find houses without covenants built into the deeds, improvement organizations like the OKPA labored to get more and more white residents to bind themselves into covenants.[21]

But in 1948, the bottom fell out from underneath them. That year, the United States Supreme Court upheld a lower court's ruling in *Shelley v.*

Kraemer which rendered restrictive covenants unenforceable.[22] That ruling involved rearguard action (they did not prevent whites from writing covenants, but only said that they had no legal footing if they ended up being sued), but it nevertheless signaled the beginning of the end of the covenant system. The next year, the FHA said that it would no longer back mortgages that had covenants attached to them. The legal scaffolding on which Chicago's racial segregation had been erected thus began to crumble.

Violence helped prop it back up. The conflict in Trumbull Park that sent Beauharnais into fits was hardly an aberration, nor was he alone in thinking of black expulsion as a legitimate prerogative of white communities. Particularly in white ethnic enclaves on the South and Southwest Sides, which were among those most likely to transition, violent antiblackness threaded deep through the neighborhood's marrow. As a white Oakland-Kenwood resident named Alton Baird put it, "I've been living here nigh on 12 years and now I got nigger neighbors on the north and on the south of me. . . . Bombing don't do no good. We—er—they bombed and burned the niggers on Michigan Boulevard and they bombed 'em and burned 'em on Grand, and now the niggers are there anyway."[23]

Baird's talk of bombs wasn't idle. He and his neighbors turned the borderlands of black and white neighborhoods into minefields. In October of 1944, a recently discharged black war veteran had a stench bomb thrown into a home he'd recently purchased on the Near West Side.[24] In May 1945, the home of a black minister was bombed.[25] In November of the same year, whites smashed windows and vandalized a property in Woodlawn after black tenants moved in.[26] Opponents of black encroachment into white neighborhoods unleashed a string of at least twenty-seven bombings of black homes between 1945 and 1946, while the NAACP put the number at fifty-nine.[27] White terrorists smashed black peoples' windows and doors, and on some occasions shot into their homes.[28] They marauded neighborhoods in which blacks (and Jews and other minorities) lived, issuing threats and lobbing racist insults.[29] Most famously, a series of particularly furious mob actions, that I here call by the proper name *riots*, erupted over the span of a little more than a decade, from roughly 1946 to 1957, around community areas like Fernwood Park, Park Manor, Englewood, and Calumet Park. Trumbull Park, described in brief earlier, was the largest of these incidents, but the pattern there held in broad strokes: facing black integration, white resisters overturned cars, threatened violence, threw rocks, and beat African Americans and white sympathizers.[30]

The extraordinary (and extraordinarily *public*) violence of white rioters challenged Chicago's political and law enforcement leadership to make choices about how to respond. During his mayoralty, Ed Kelly had tried to be proactive. In 1943, at the behest of the Chicago Industrial Union Council, Kelly had established the biracial Mayor's Committee on Race Relations as race riots rocked Detroit and Harlem, hoping to head such an eruption in Chicago off at the pass.[31] Fundamentally liberal in nature, the committee held numerous conferences over the course of the late 1940s and 1950s that drew together white and black scholars and community leaders from across the city and beyond in order to formulate suggestions for future action. Kelly charged the committee first and foremost with investigating Black Belt housing inadequacies and ending racial discrimination in employment, although the committee lacked enforcement power and mostly was only able to make recommendations. Therefore, how much the committee actually accomplished is unclear, but the fact that it cultivated a close alliance with the NAACP, coupled with the fact that Chicago steered clear of widespread rioting that year, reinforced Kelly's reputation as a deft manager of so-called race relations.[32] The committee went through a series of various iterations over the remainder of the 1940s and 1950s, reassigned first as the Mayor's Commission on Human Relations (MCHR) and then as the Chicago Commission on Human Relations.

In 1945 a permanent Subcommittee on Law and Order was established under the committee's auspices. It included prominent members of black Chicago like Alderman Earl Dickerson and Urban League Executive Secretary A. L. Foster, some of the leading lights of Chicago's liberal white Left, including the attorney (and future antimachine alderman) Leon Despres and members of the Cook County public defender's office and Juvenile Court.[33] Whereas in the past, law and order had typically been invoked in the context of labor and left radical protest, the subcommittee reclaimed it, taking as its primary mission the eradication of white violence against African Americans and the training of police in the fields of human and race relations. Subcommittee members kept in close contact with CPD Commissioner James Allman and Chief of the Uniformed Police John Prendergast, both of whom they praised as being cooperative partners in the committee's efforts, and in 1945 the subcommittee seemed relatively optimistic about the CPD's ability to effectively handle white terrorism.[34]

The following year, however, that terrorism began to erupt with greater force and frequency. Whereas previous moments of white violence earlier in the 1940s had been largely individualized, they now became both collectivized and markedly more dangerous. The CPD wasn't keeping up, either. In 1947 white crowds rioted in the Fernwood Park neighborhood when black people tried to move in, and after the police failed almost completely in preventing them from doing so, Prendergast, who had assumed the commissionership after Allman's retirement, constructed a plan specifically targeted toward dealing with mass disorder. Codenamed "Plan Five" and prefiguring how the police would try to respond to 1960s civil unrest, the plan was organized to systematically coordinate fast arrival times for large numbers of squad cars to the scene of civil disturbances. It was reevaluated and reinforced twice more in 1949: once when an emergency regiment was established that could get battalions of hundreds of officers to city flash points in a hurry; and again when the department implemented a more aggressive "dispersal policy" that would break up "crowds gathered to express . . . antagonism against a person or his property because of his race."[35]

The new plan was an almost unqualified failure. (Indeed, the most prolonged and vicious antiblack protests, such as those in Trumbull Park and Calumet Park, unfolded in the decade *after* its innovation.) For the most part, this was because of the actions not of administrators but of the officers who were actually dispatched to the scene. As Arnold Hirsch wrote in his classic study of the midcentury making of Chicago's "second ghetto," policy reforms like Plan Five "were not sufficient in themselves to ensure the effective control of racial disturbances. True, the police now had the intelligence to deploy officers with foresight, the skill to dispatch quickly, and plans to use them effectively. But the most glaring weaknesses in law enforcement, the point at which all the reforms broke down, was neither institutional nor tactical. The failure was individual."[36]

The reasons for these individual failures were not hard to discern. In some ways, not a lot had changed since 1919, when racial fealty governed officer conduct more than the oaths they'd sworn. In the housing riots, many officers wore their sympathies and racism on their sleeves, and engaged in conduct at riot scenes that the *Chicago Sun-Times* succinctly labeled "provocative."[37] As a letter-writer to the *Chicago Daily News* (perhaps St. Clair Drake) put it, too often in these cases of violence "the police have stood by, disappeared, or actually egged on the criminals or hoodlums."[38] Examples were legion. The MCHR relayed a story from May 1949 in which a black man complained to a CPD officer, in the presence of a white neighbor, that someone had tried to set his garage on fire the previous night. The white neighbor hurled a racial slur at him, "put his hands in his pocket, and said he would blow my brains out." The officer did nothing.[39] Meanwhile, black reporter Vernon Jarrett was on the scene at a set of white riots at the Airport Homes projects, one of the first major explosions of the postwar housing riots. Years later, he recalled sitting inside the home of a black integrator there as white mobs outside "threatened to 'barbecue all of you niggers and nigger lovers,'" agonizing as they waited in vain for police to come help.[40] An officer responding to a 1951 riot in Bridgeport reportedly instructed young white rioters to "hold your rocks until night comes" if they were smart.

Some of his colleagues, meanwhile, watched a white man sympathetic to integration get beaten on the street before promptly arresting the beaten man.[41] As the *Sun-Times* put it, "The fact seems to be that in this case the sympathies of the police were very largely with the mob."[42]

In Trumbull Park, Donald Howard, whose move into the projects had incited the violence, complained that police "seemed more intent upon protecting white families from contact with us than in protecting my family from . . . white mobsters."[43] In 1957 the *Sun-Times* again excoriated the police after rioting exploded in the wake of white attacks on black picnickers in Calumet Park: "One of the reasons for the outbreaks is police inefficiency and the undisguised sympathy of some policemen for the race-haters who are stirring up antagonism and kindling passion at every turn."[44] Undisguised sympathy, indeed: observers of the post–Calumet Park trials of white assailants reported that the officer who had arrested the accused white rioters "was observed shaking hands with the defendants and joking with the defense attorney. He stated he did not want to get anyone in trouble, that he had lived in that neighborhood and had gone to school with a number of the 'boys.'" He hadn't even wanted to testify but had felt pressured into doing so by a superior officer.[45]

As these officers abrogated their professional responsibilities, they sent clear and important signals about who they served. Robert Fogelson's point that the police choose which laws to enforce and which publics to serve bears reiterating here, because there are few clearer examples of that dynamic in play. For, above all else, the white terrorism directed at black integrators must first be understood as a blatant violation of the law. Throwing bombs through windows, smashing windows, overturning cars—all were criminal acts of property destruction and threats against black life, livelihood, and basic civil rights. And yet officers on the ground routinely refused to actually criminalize such acts.

Causes Legitimate and Not: Politics, Police, and the Critique of Freedom Dreams

Even if those rank-and-file officers who shirked their responsibilities deserve a large part of the blame for not forthrightly addressing white violence, they don't deserve it all. After all, police departments are purposefully organized in a hierarchical structure, where there are supposed to be consequences to subordinates for not doing their jobs. But in the Chicago of the mid-1940s and the 1950s, that structure remained badly muddled as a consequence of the Democratic machine's politicization of the department. Recall, again, that a fundamental tenet of the machine's approach to the police was to invest district-level CPD captains with unusual amounts of power, and arrange them into a political relationship with party ward bosses. In the context of the housing riots, this meant that a party boss representing an all-white, rabidly antiblack neighborhood that was in danger of integrating could pressure the district captain to do everything in his power to ensure that integration would *not* succeed. Machine control, once again, was attended by steep costs to the city's social fabric.

This was compounded by the fact that after Ed Kelly left the mayor's office in 1947, top city officials gave almost no signals to the CPD that they were particularly invested in seeing neighborhood integration succeed. The reason, as always, was political. As mayor, Kelly had been vocal about his support for integration, which had won him significant praise from the black community despite his other shortcomings. But it hadn't played well with white voters. In 1946 the Republican Party had made significant gains at the county level, capturing congressional seats and a number of local positions as well. Democrats found themselves in the weakest political position that they'd been in since before Anton Cermak's mayoral victory in 1931. Machine operatives canvassed members of its most sizable white ethnic constituencies—Germans, Irish, and Poles—and found that they "shared one thing in common—an opposition to Kelly's stand on open housing." Seeing that Kelly's public stance on integration was such a nonstarter for so many white voters, machine powerbrokers asked him not to seek reelection.[46] They handed city hall to Martin Kennelly, who would not make similar waves.

Very few white politicians wanted to touch the issue of segregation even before Kelly's ouster. Afterward, it was practically radioactive. Routine mass violence was bad for the city's image and worse for its social fabric, but black citizens were not a valuable enough constituency to make white politicians press the matter. The black scholar Chandler Owen highlighted the relationship between politics, integration, and riots in his 1954 assessment of Trumbull Park: "Whether Republicans or Democrats, the leaders feel that the white residents are generally opposed to Negro residential invasion. These politicians are not going to take a course which they fear will retire them to private life."[47] Kennelly and his successor, Richard Daley, used different methods in how they approached black constituents, with Daley in particular relying heavily on black voters early in his mayoralty. Nevertheless, both men were bound together by an extreme reticence to speak against white vigilantes. This was partly political: as Owen suspected, the two mayors stayed mostly silent on the violence for fear of alienating blocs of white ethnic voters. (Indeed, both at times explicitly tried to deny that segregation even *existed* in Chicago, let alone as an issue of political significance.[48]) It was also personal: both came from Bridgeport, whose white residents were themselves fiercely resistant to integration. And while we know less about Kennelly in this regard, it bears remembering that as a kid, Daley had been a member, then leader, of one of the gangs that terrorized black South Siders before, during, and after the 1919 race riot.

Their reluctance to speak out against white rioters extended also to a refusal to criticize police negligence in dealing with the terrorism. The Bridgeport community that both men came from channeled thousands of police officers onto the CPD's employment rolls. Daley and his wife had multiple family members on the force, and he sympathized deeply with policemen's dangerous work and low pay. As one of his biographers summarized the consequences of these personal entanglements, "The mayor's extensive connections to the police department made it easy for him to overlook the shortcomings of some of its members."[49] Kennelly's relationship to neighborhood police families is less clear, but the same general silence on police neglect of black safety prevailed.

Moreover, police administrators delivered repeated messaging to the public that black efforts to integrate Chicago were bad for the city because they undermined the CPD's ability to perform its other (presumably more important) functions. Called before a Committee on Racial Tensions in Housing Projects in 1953, with Trumbull Park raging in the background, the new CPD commissioner Timothy O'Connor did not suggest new police policies to deal with the violence or new disciplinary systems to get officers to be more assertive in its face. Nor did he lay blame for what was happening at the feet of violent white terrorists. Instead, he suggested that, at least for the time being, integration should stop because it would be a threat to the city to have more black people move into white areas before the ongoing Trumbull Park "situation" "was completely settled." Doing so, he testified, "could mean great difficulties for the police department in meeting their other responsibilities; traffic, crime and general policing, if they had to allocate too much of their force to racial problems."[50]

This appeared to pass without significant comment at the time, but it was an important rhetorical move. It may have been true that the CPD was struggling to keep up with other duties because it was constantly trying to put out white supremacists' literal and figurative fires. But framing black attempts to desegregate Chicago as imperiling the rest of the city advanced a message that resonated with already-extant white resentments. Police service, through this prism, was a zero-sum affair; if black people were getting it, white people were not. O'Connor's formulation articulated a hierarchy of claims on police resources, within which protecting black people from white violence existed somewhere further down the ladder of legitimate and necessary police functions than did others he enumerated. Moreover, through his logic, the burden of stopping white racial terror was intellectually shifted *away* from white rioters and law enforcement, and heaped on the shoulders of black neighborhood integrators and their allies. In doing so, he set a precedent that future police officials would echo—most notably when Daley slapped Martin Luther King Jr. and the Chicago Freedom Movement (CFM) with a movement-crippling injunction in 1966, claiming that their street demonstrations required so much police protection that they were endangering the rest of the city.[51]

The cumulative effect of all of this was that anti-integration forces won the day in most of the areas where these housing riots broke out. A couple of dozen black families moved into Trumbull Park against the backdrop of the chaos there, but the amount of courage such a choice entailed was substantial. And it was, generally speaking, an aberration. Absent decent police protection, threats, intimidation, and violence served as a crucial factor in the reification of the segregation of Chicago. It would be unfair and inaccurate to fully lay the blame for all of this at the police department's feet; economic deprivation, urban renewal, housing policies, and the legacies of restrictive covenants were all significant.[52] But as an instrument of public safety and order—one that black people like those seeking to move into Trumbull Park and other areas helped fund, no less—its role in ensuring segregation's durability was a different sort of violation. Through public statements like O'Connor's suggestion that supporting integration imperiled the rest of the city, administrative failures to craft policies that would better protect integrators, and the inability or unwillingness of individual officers to prioritize black rights and safety over white racial prerogatives, the police department sent avalanching messages that it was not invested in the opening up of the city.

What happened in those moments of police laxity is also worth thinking about relative to longer historical trends. Less than a decade after the last of these white riots, Chicago's black West Side would erupt in multiple large-scale uprisings against urban disinvestment, resource extraction, police violence, and political disenfranchisement. Those uprisings (called *riots* by city officials who would not have thought to apply the same label to white violence) would be *severely* punished by the CPD and the city, both at the individual and institutional levels. The differences between the two phenomena were significant in terms of their particularities and objectives but were not at all meaningfully different in terms of the degree to which they violated public order. In fact, the black uprisings in the sixties rarely targeted other people for violent reprisal; by contrast, the white violence of the forties and fifties took the targeting of other people as gospel and point of entry. The criminalization of black property violence in the sixties, compared with the failure to assertively criminalize white interpersonal violence in the fifties, is worth remembering.

The Fight for Freedom: Black Chicago Responds

While the city and CPD stalled in repelling white violence, black Chicago's activist machinery ramped up. Their ensuing fights against mob terrorism and police apathy mobilized an important but sometimes overlooked civil rights coalition during the postwar era.

Policing and police abuse were central to early civil rights initiatives. The most famous document tethering policing discrimination and abuse to the larger plight of black Americans may be the Black Panther Party's Ten Point Program, released in 1966. But in 1951 the Civil Rights Congress (CRC) delivered a petition to the United Nations Genocide Convention, under the title *We Charge Genocide: The Historic Petition to the United Nations for Relief from a Crime of the United States Government against the Negro People*. The document gathered evidence of the murders of American blacks and the abuse, harassment, and terror unleashed on them in the years since World War II. It framed America's racial injustices as systematic, its racist violence as endemic, and its overall structure as functionally destructive of black life. Central to its indictment was police brutality and the refusal by police forces to protect black citizens from white racist terrorism. "Once the classic method of lynching was the rope," activists wrote. "Now it is the policeman's bullet. To many an American the police are the government, certainly its most visible representative. We submit that the evidence suggests that the killing of Negroes has become police policy in the United States and that police policy is the most practical expression of government policy."[53]

We Charge Genocide was national in scope, but some of its most cutting data points emanated from the Windy City. As evidence of police violence, the report cited the case of nineteen-year-old Andrew Johnson, who died in a CPD holding cell from a lacerated liver after being assaulted by two officers. As evidence of officer harassment, it cited the case of another nineteen-year-old, Robert Kirkendoll, who was reportedly sentenced to a seventy-five-year prison sentence after he refused to pay a five-dollar bribe to CPD officers. As evidence of officers' refusal to protect black people from white violence, the report listed the fifty-nine "arson-bombings and other acts of terror committed against Negro households between May 1944 and July 1946"; the 1949 assault on Roscoe Johnson's home by two thousand whites hoping to drive him out of the neighborhood into which he'd moved; and the weeklong "reign of terror" toward blacks and white allies later that same year on the Southwest Side.[54]

As the CRC sought to lay America's human rights violations bare before an international audience, local mobilizations were underway, too. Paralleling the CRC's campaigns against police violence, for instance, activists and attorneys flooded the South Side with leaflets in the early 1950s in order to try to coax community members forward with information about abusive officers and bring them to justice. The handbills lent a searingly personal face to the issue of police violence, showing a series of black men staring into the camera or bent over in pain to showcase their wounds. World War II veteran Tommy Melson, gazing forward in a suit just a little too big, having survived a bullet from CPD Officer Walter Green a few nights after Christmas in 1951. Joseph Clay, with nattily coiffed hair and a sharp leather jacket and a hint of a smile on his face—also having been fortunate to survive a gunshot from Officer Green at the corner of Forty-Third and South Parkway. Joseph Murray, a young railroad worker, his downward-turned face not hiding how swollen and disfigured it was, bandages covering the cuts and bald spots on his scalp where batons and hands had worn away the skin and hair during an incident in July 1952.[55]

Police negligence and hostility to black rights and well-being also animated local activism in other ways. In 1946 the *Defender* conjured the image of Hitlerism—the most resonant example possible at that time of the perils of exclusionary citizenship—to ask if antiblack white terrorist bombers would "have free reign until it is too late? The Chicago Police Department," it concluded, "should have an answer for that question that haunts some 400,000 Negro citizens of this community."[56] The following year, when the decade-long barrage of more or less sustained violence began, black leaders turned to Martin Kennelly for answers. Three months after Kennelly took office, members of the NAACP, the local American Civil Liberties Union (ACLU), and other organizations met with him and Police Commissioner John Prendergast concerning white violence against black people. They noted nineteen separate white attacks on black neighborhood integrators already in the first half of that year. They accused the police of unprofessional conduct and of "openly siding with mob elements in many cases," and urged the mayor to push for better training for police officers in such situations.[57] In 1949 black citizens in Park Manor again appealed for police protection in response to a two-year-long harassment campaign against black residents, with the CRC's Chicago office railing against Kennelly and Prendergast for failing to "point the finger of authority at the criminal instigators of racist force and violence."[58] As early as July 1949, black residents reportedly began holding

This man was shot

Did you see it happen ?

On Tuesday, September 9, 1952, at about 10:15 in the evening, on the southeast corner of 43rd and South Parkway, Joseph Clay, an employee of Swift and Company, was shot by Police Officer Walter Green.

Persons having knowledge of the facts and circumstances surrounding the shooting are requested to communicate with either of the following: Joseph Clay, 4327 South Parkway, BO 8-6168, or Attorney Charles Liebman, 39 South La Salle Street, ST 2-1776.

1952 handbill distributed in Chicago seeking information on an incident of police violence against Joseph Clay. American Civil Liberties Union, Illinois Division, Records, box 565, folder 4, Special Collections Research Center, University of Chicago Library.

meetings to debate the merits of taking up arms in self-defense "if the police fail to provide adequate protection."[59] Later that same year, after mob violence on Peoria Street, black leaders and CCHR personnel reported "on visiting Negro homes lately finding people armed and ready to repel persons whom they presume to be invading their rights."[60] Kennelly and Prendergast promised to do better. Police made a few arrests. The assaults continued.

This man was shot

Did you see it happen ?

On Saturday, December 29, 1951, at about 3:30 in the morning, in the drug store on the southeast corner of 43rd and South Parkway, Tommy Melson, a wounded war veteran, was shot by Police Officer Walter Green.

Persons having knowledge of the facts and circumstances surrounding the shooting are requested to communicate with either of the following: Tommy Melson, 5601 South Michigan, FA 4-6661, or Attorney Charles Liebman, 39 South La Salle Street, ST 2-1776.

1952 handbill distributed in Chicago seeking information on an incident of police violence against Tommy Melson. American Civil Liberties Union, Illinois Division, Records, box 565, folder 4, Special Collections Research Center, University of Chicago Library.

Chicago's wider liberal and progressive Left joined with black Chicago in condemning the city for its failures. The CCHR, despite being an official instrument of the city administration, routinely found police responses to violence lacking. Though its public statements were tempered, their investigations painted a damning portrait. The ACLU was even more pointedly critical, perhaps best seen in a scathing letter that chairman Edgar Bernhard

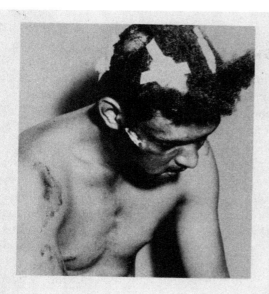

This man was beaten

Did you see it happen ?

On Wednesday, July 2, 1952, at about 4:15 in the afternoon, on the northwest corner of 61st and Indiana, Joseph Murray, an employee of the Chicago and Northwestern Railroad, was severely beaten by police officers.

Persons having knowledge of the facts and circumstances surrounding the beating are requested to communicate with either of the following: Joseph Murray, 4635 South Wabash, OA 4-1676, or Attorney Charles Liebman, 39 South La Salle Street, ST 2-1776.

1952 handbill distributed in Chicago seeking information on an incident of police violence against Joseph Murray. American Civil Liberties Union, Illinois Division, Records, box 565, folder 4, Special Collections Research Center, University of Chicago Library.

delivered to Kennelly: "During the course of your administration there has been vacillation and on the whole unsatisfactory implementation of police power in the areas where violence has broken out. . . . Concrete and detailed plans for handling mobs bent on violence have been presented to you and your Police Commissioner by experts in the field of human relations. . . . When [those suggestions] have been accepted and sincerely executed, these plans have proved remarkably effective, but all too often can the work of the Police Department be characterized as too little, too late and too half-hearted."[61] The American Jewish Conference took out a full-page ad in the *Sun-Times* similarly calling out the administration, and the newspaper itself issued an editorial suggesting that "in the [police] commissioner's office there seems to be no recognition of the need for changing the attitude of policemen toward racial conflicts."[62] An article in the *Nation*, meanwhile, written by local Unitarian minister Homer Jack, blamed egregious police misconduct for what he labeled as "Chicago's Violent Armistice."[63]

It was this barrage of criticism that led CPD Commissioner John Prendergast to revisit and bolster the CPD's mob control protocols late in 1949; but as we have seen, the bolstering didn't work.[64] And as the white violence escalated and the 1940s gave way to the 1950s, perhaps the most famous of these explosions of white riotous violence was still looming on the horizon.

It came in August of 1953, with the violence at the Trumbull Park housing projects. For a decade and a half, the Chicago Housing Authority (CHA) had adhered to unwritten but rigid policies that only allowed white residents to move into housing projects in white neighborhoods like South Deering. In July of that summer, however, Betty and Donald Howard had slipped through their screening process because of Betty's exceptionally light complexion.[65] When white residents in Trumbull Park discovered that a black family had moved in, the projects erupted. Over the next few years, Trumbull Park became arguably the most important and heated referendum on racial integration in Chicago that had ever taken place. Racists in the projects and their supporters outside them demanded that the CHA remove the Howards and restore racial purity. Progressive activists encouraged the agency to instead see their mistake as an opportunity to further advance integration in Chicago. When the CHA bent itself to the latter group and allowed a handful of other black families to move into Trumbull Park, Chicago's Far South Side twisted into a simmering cauldron of racist violence.[66]

As it became clear that the police department would not adequately protect black families in Trumbull Park, Chicago's black activist network, led by the NAACP, mobilized in much more formidable ways. In early 1954, the organization announced a new campaign called "The Fight for Freedom," assembled under the clarion call for "full freedom by 1963"—the hundredth anniversary of emancipation. To association leaders, the many struggles still to come in order to secure "the achievement of the unfinished tasks of emancipation" was the need to protect "every American" from police abuse and white terrorism.[67] "Daily," the organization wrote in its newsletter's pages, "Negroes meet humiliation and insult—at work and at play, in his home town or while traveling, in sickness and in health. He is the frequent subject of mob violence and police brutality. He is denied freedom of residence."[68]

By the spring of that year, a coalition of community organizations voted to present Kennelly with an ultimatum, calling for a grand jury investigation into the ongoing violence in Trumbull Park. The ultimatum would include examinations of "the responsibility and possible malfeasance of office by the Mayor, city officials, and the police department," with the expectation that those officials and officers found responsible would be indicted. In the absence of such measures, activists pledged massive marches on city hall and "continuous demonstration until these objectives are obtained."[69] Days later, they also met with Police Commissioner Timothy O'Connor (who had since succeeded Prendergast) to present him with evidence of his department's failure both to stop the violence and to treat black citizens fairly and with dignity.[70] O'Connor was receptive at the meeting and appeared eager to cooperate, according to the NAACP. But little changed. Two weeks later, Kennelly issued a public statement that activists widely interpreted as tepid and unsatisfactory.[71]

As tensions mounted, some black citizens made good on earlier promises to take up arms to defend themselves.[72] In April of 1954, Donald Howard, whose family's move into Trumbull Park had touched off the violence, chased off attackers by brandishing a gun.[73] When three white women signed statements that Howard had *fired* the gun at a pair of white teenagers, CPD officers arrested Howard and charged him with assault with a deadly weapon, discharging a firearm in the city, and disorderly conduct.[74] The following month, the CPD arrested two other black men, Herman King and Staddie Edwards, for carrying weapons as they led an "armed convoy" to a local grocery store in order to safely get supplies back to Trumbull Park.[75] And while black revolutionary violence rarely materialized in the streets of Chicago during the 1940s and 1950s, these hints of its potential during the postwar years are suggestive in part of why black organizations promoting self-defense and armed protection during the 1960s in Chicago—whether it was the Deacons for Defense or the Black Panthers—found strong support in certain sections of the black community. Logically if not tactically, such sixties-era impulses toward community protection were not just born from the depths of violence current at the time but also drawn from traditional wells of self-protection.

In the moment, however, the affront of black men being arrested for defending themselves, while thousands of CPD officers funneled to Trumbull Park watched languorously as whites terrorized blacks, was a bridge too far. As activists came to the realization that public and political appeals were not enough to force the CPD to act, they turned toward more assertive legal action. In August of 1954, the NAACP announced a series of civil suits that would be brought not just against white rioters in Trumbull Park but also and more notably against members of the CPD for dereliction of duty and "improper . . . action."[76] The particular impetus for these lawsuits was the CPD's "false arrest and malicious prosecution" of Herman King on weapons charges, stemming from his arrest in May. In its press release, the NAACP announced that it was also preparing "an indefinite number of additional suits against rioters and policemen . . . for later filing."[77]

The conflation of "rioters and policemen" was telling. In both the activist networks and black press treatments of what was happening in Trumbull Park, white rioters and white policemen became increasingly indistinguishable as the conflict dragged on. At the same time as the NAACP's announcement of legal action, the *Defender* published an excoriating overview of events so far in Trumbull Park, highlighting the fact that "police assigned to the area . . . seemed from the first to be sympathetic to the hoodlums and, even they at times have been accused of abusing and insulting the Negro families that they were 'Ordered' to protect."[78] While the paper credited black police with making most of the major arrests that had been undertaken during the riot, the police department as a whole appeared through many black eyes to be an agency supportive of white supremacists' larger mission in Trumbull Park. Black lives and freedoms did not appear to matter much.

Trumbull Park was an important turning point in black challenges to the CPD. More so than ever before, the mainstream of Chicago's black politics turned toward aggressively challenging a police apparatus that suddenly seemed to be failing in almost all measures. Most prominently, the NAACP, after years of chaos, dysfunction, and infighting (the national office at one point discussed putting the Chicago branch into receivership) came under the leadership of Cora Patton and Willoughby Abner, who steered the association in new and more responsive directions. Abner, an ardently leftist black trade unionist, was an especially powerful force, and for a few years, he and Patton turned the local branch into a protest vehicle with a far more progressive agenda than it had ever had before.[79] That agenda included all manner of things meant to challenge white supremacy and convince city hall to better deal with racist violence. But it should be remembered that *dealing with* the violence there ultimately boiled down to protecting black life from white violence. Policing, in this sense, was fundamentally a civil rights issue.

The following year, that local story fused together with the larger black freedom struggle in America, sparked by one of the most infamous racist killings in the history of the United States. In August of 1955, two white men, J. W. Milam and Roy Bryant, tortured and lynched fourteen-year-old Emmett Till, a Chicago resident visiting family in Mississippi, for allegedly making sexually suggestive comments toward Bryant's wife Carolyn. The two men kidnapped Till from his uncle's home in the dead of night, tortured him mercilessly, put a bullet in his brain, tied a cotton gin around his neck, and dumped his body in the nearby Tallahatchie River. Till was far from the first to be murdered so brutally; indeed, the rivers and woods of Mississippi were burial grounds for hundreds of victims of Jim Crow violence. But what made his case exceptional was the choice made by Till's mother, Mamie Bradley, to defy local officials in Mississippi, smuggle Till's body back to Chicago, and invite the black press in to photograph and publicize what had been done to her child.[80]

The historian Adam Green has described the Till lynching as a "moment of simultaneity" for black Chicago and African America.[81] It was a reminder of black America's collective vulnerability. But it was also an organizing moment—one credited with helping launch the civil rights movement. Young movement activists took to describing themselves as the "Till genera-tion," and black leaders and citizens from the Mississippi Delta to Madison Square Garden used the case as an opportunity to rally for the overthrow of white supremacy.[82] Closer to home, the Chicago NAACP called for the federal government to occupy the state of Mississippi "to halt the wave of terror, intimidation and lynching of Negroes who refuse to bow to the Jim Crow system."[83]

Activists understood racial terror in Mississippi to be intimately con-nected to racial terror in Chicago. After Till's lynching, Chicago activists noted that "Trumbull Park stands out as Chicago's 'Little Mississippi,'" and announced a "mass picket demonstration at City Hall," "in view of the failure of the Mayor and other City officials and the Police department to meet their responsibility."[84] Further, they submitted an eleven-point set of recommen-dations to newly minted Mayor Daley concerning Trumbull Park, the first of which contained directives for Daley to issue to the police department, affirming black people's freedom of movement and rights to protection.[85]

These linkages between the local and national culminated at a massive South Side memorial rally for Till in late September of 1955, where ten thou-sand people gathered to hear speeches from Mamie Bradley, her lawyer, and local NAACP activists.[86] When it was his turn to speak, Willoughby Abner stepped to the pulpit, and the broken body of Emmett Till, the murders of civil rights workers George Lee and Lamar Smith, and the hundreds of other racist killings in the state of Mississippi over the previous decades became his starting point. He offered up a "graphic survey" of violence and racism in the South generally, and Mississippi in particular, and declared that the NAACP would "spotlight the Mississippi situation throughout America and the world so that we may get the kind of Federal intervention needed to halt the wave of terror and murder against Negroes who demand their rights as American citizens."[87]

But Abner soon pivoted to Chicago, where Daley had issued condemnations of the Till lynching. These Abner framed as convenient evasions of the mayor's complicity in racism in Chicago. Though pleased to know that Daley "protested and demanded action in the slaying of Emmett," Abner demanded to know what were his "responsibilities in the Trumbull Park situation here at home?" Citing the NAACP's eleven-point plan demanding better police action in Trumbull Park, Abner noted that Daley had failed to ever respond to it, and that "the time is now long overdue for him to act."[88] Tellingly, the NAACP adopted two resolutions by the end of the meeting. One called for the federal government to crush mob terror and Jim Crow in the South. The other demanded that Daley "immediately take action" on the association's eleven-point program. If he didn't, they warned, daily pickets of city hall would begin.[89] And though the daily pickets didn't come to pass, campaigns to effect better policing would continue.

In the summer of 1957, racial violence ripped Chicago again—this time in Calumet Park, where white mobs assaulted black picnickers. In response, the Coordinating Council for Citizens' Rights held a rally in Washington Park, with fliers urging attendees to "Remember Calumet Park" and "Demand Strict and Impartial Police Protection."[90] At the rally, a platform of action read on Abner's behalf called for the City Council to hold a public hearing on racial violence in Chicago, where black citizens "could tell their shocking stories of racial brutality and police ineptitude."[91] It also called for Daley to implement a campaign to "Make Chicago More Democratic" (riffing off the mayor's antilittering "Make Chicago Clean" campaign) that would unqualifiedly declare the mayor's support for open occupancy and integration, including the commitment of "the police and all law enforcement agencies of the city to the full protection of all citizens."[92]

Similarly, Calumet Park inspired the Chicago Urban League's (CUL) executive director Edwin Berry to pen a request to Daley that he "make it unmistakably clear to all police officers from top to bottom that Negro citizens and all citizens are to be protected to the fullest extent of the law."[93] The CUL's Research Department, meanwhile, convened a study of racial violence across 1956 and 1957, which listed a stunning 166 separate incidents of such violence—two-thirds of them in racially transitioning neighborhoods, and three-quarters of them committed by whites against blacks. The data set was alarming in itself. But, the CUL warned, the city's negligent response to white terrorism was also beginning to inspire reprisal attacks by blacks. In his preface to the report, St. Clair Drake lingered on this point, noting that the only reason Chicago had not yet exploded into a redux of 1919 was because "the Negro people have exercised a degree of restraint in the face of repeated provocations which is amazing and for which the city should be grateful." But such luck, he noted, was bound to run out. In order to create a lasting peace, he wrote, "The city administration needs to make up its mind that this type of violence will not be tolerated in the city; that when it occurs the full resources of the detective forces will be used to find the culprits; that arrests are going to be made; that policemen who evade their duty will be punished by something more than a slap on the wrist; and that the governmental attorneys will prosecute vigorously."[94] What Chicago needed, in other words, was for the law enforcement community to take white antiblack crime seriously.

The stories of these campaigns are important in their own right, for they highlight the depth of concern that citizens seeking to democratize the city had about the police. The fights for police reform surrounding police inaction in Trumbull Park and Calumet Park, and at other sites of white violence, were important crucibles in early civil rights campaigns. Moreover, combined with the willingness of police officers to arrest Donald Howard for defending himself and similar affronts to black rights, these were important hallmarks of the ways that "law and order" in postwar Chicago meant particular kinds of law and narrow visions of order.

But it's important to understand why these fifties-era police reform efforts failed. One reason is that the CPD had few mechanisms that would make officers do their job in these situations. White racial fealty was a powerful drug, and if the primary level at which police protection of black rights broke down was at the individual, there was no oversight system preventing that from happening. The department had no meaningful internal investigations unit. In human rights conferences and commission reports throughout the postwar era, leading experts and observers of the department talked about the various ways that police officers harassed black people and the fact that "no policeman pays the penalty in any respects, if he doesn't actually believe that the Negro is equal to the white."[95] In other words, even if police officials like Timothy O'Connor *had* wanted to prioritize black protection (there isn't much evidence that he did), it was a challenging proposition to carry out.

The other major reason for these failures was the lack of political will on the part of city politicians. Neither Daley nor Kennelly was meaningfully invested in integration personally, and neither was going to use the power of his office to demand policies that would protect integrators and thus risk alienating white voters. The failure, in other words, was not just a product of the CPD's conduct and policies. It was also a function of political calculation and white Chicagoans' near-total access to influence public policy.

Fighting for an Open City: The Police and the
Battle to Desegregate Public Places

Housing was the most notable site of conflict where the CPD was entangled in Chicago's integration battles, but it was not the only one. Just as the CPD's failure to criminalize antiblack violence emboldened segregation's agents, so, too, did officers' frequent refusal to uphold both state and local antidiscrimination laws governing public accommodations, and their willingness to arrest challengers *to* segregation, reinforce segregation's strength.

For decades, numerous businesses in Chicago had operated under an extralegal de facto system of segregation. In the 1950s activists began aggressively targeting such businesses to force them to overturn illegal and racist practices, but it was activists, not business owners, who found their actions routinely criminalized by the police. In one such case, an interracial assemblage gathered at Jennie's Café in East Chatham one night, where the restaurant refused them service under the pretext that, among other things, it was a private club and thus could limit access. According to NAACP reports, whites in the group were called "nigger-lovers," and management organized employees and customers alike to physically throw them out. When police arrived, they arrested the group on charges of disorderly conduct, and courts affixed steep fines as penalty.[96]

More striking still was a 1950 incident at the South Side Trianon Ballroom, where a group of eleven young people that included at least three African Americans—Elizabeth Hicklin, Dennis Banks, and Gladys Burke—entered the ballroom lobby together one night to protest its whites-only policy. Inside, they met a surge of CPD officers who literally threw them back out on the street, then arrested them on charges of unlawful assembly and intent to incite a riot. Among the police personnel there was Timothy O'Connor, then-deputy CPD commissioner who would soon ascend to the department's commissionership. Gerald Bullock, executive director of the local branch of the Congress of Racial Equality (CORE), was on the scene and was especially taken aback watching O'Connor look on as officers under his command manhandled the activists. Bullock was particularly struck by the treatment of young Elizabeth Hicklin. "I had seen that young girl," he recalled, "pitched contemptuously out into the snow-covered street while a score of Chicago's 'finest' under command of a deputy commissioner looked placidly on and could take no action except to arrest the stricken child and her friends, drag them to a filthy lock-up, subject them to torture of hours of stupid inquisition by the official representatives of the State's chief local law enforcement officer who must have previously been ordered to the scene for this very purpose, and charge them with serious violations of city and state statutes."[97]

Similar to the mobilizations of civil rights activists over the housing riots, in the coming months, Bullock, CORE's national chairman James Farmer, local ACLU chairman Edgar Bernhard, and a slew of other activists and lawyers swapped communiqués about the so-called Trianon Incident. CORE forged ahead with plans to further publicize and protest what had happened, organizing a meeting of community groups and activists to determine a path forward. In his call for the meeting, Bullock raised a string of questions about the conduct of the police that night. Among them were these: "Why was Deputy Commissioner O'Connor present? And being present, why did he stand mutely and quietly by while assault was being committed in his presence? Why didn't he perform his duty and inform officials of the Trianon that to refuse admittance to this public hall to anyone because of race or color is a violation of the civil rights law of the State of Illinois?" "Why," given the steep fines levied against the activists, "is the State's Attorney's Office so interested in maintaining a policy of racial discrimination at the Trianon?" To that one, he ventured an answer: "Could it be that the [Democratic] machine did not want an incident which would focus attention on the race problem in this area and so thought that by getting tough with these kids they would be able to put down this rebellion against the social mores and avert the very type of incident official rashness precipitated?" Referring back to the light punishments to violent white rioters, compared to nonviolent black protesters: "Why were the charges so different in this case than in the 56th and Peoria St. arrests when [white] hoodlums of the lowest criminal stature were charged with disorderly conduct, freed on $10 bonds and virtually commended for their conduct by a sympathetic judge? Who is so interested in convicting of serious charges any Negro or white person who protests violations of human rights in Chicago?"[98]

Bullock, however, left his most important question for last. In issuing a call-to-arms for his fellow citizens to join him in protest, he asked, finally: "Who stands to benefit by these official acts?"[99]

Black and Blue: The Question of Black Police

As antiblack animosity crescendoed in the postwar years and the police force constantly failed to protect black people adequately, one of the solutions that black activists and liberal reformers alike constantly proposed was the hiring of more black men to the police force. Black Chicago had made the argument for black police repeatedly and for years.[100] But the immediate case of the housing riots reinforced that argument's core logic: If it was racism that made white officers unwilling to protect black life and property, black officers would have to be hired in greater numbers to do the work white officers wouldn't.

This calculation was correct in some respects; on balance, black officers were less likely to carry severe antiblack racism with them to the job site. They were *of* black Chicago, so why not let them *serve* black Chicago? They knew the community, and had meaningful relationships with people there. Black officers routinely won praise from the *Defender* and other outlets for service to the community, and served as a source of pride for community members. Moreover, they would emerge as a crucible of community activism for police reform by the late 1960s.

But executing this solution wasn't so simple. Until very late in the 1950s, CPD administrators flatly refused to even consider hiring more black officers. With the number of black police stalled in the low hundreds, as white violence escalated in the second half of the 1940s, the number of black officers actually declined.[101] Moreover, white Chicagoans struggled with the reality of black officers' authority. In 1952, for instance, one white man asked a white officer to take him in rather than his black colleague, since he'd "just die if a 'Nigger' cop arrested me."[102]

Most importantly, however, there is little guarantee that black police officers would have been better for the community, even if they had been hired. Black officers' attitudes toward black communities weren't studied in any meaningful way until the 1960s and 1970s. Even so, there is a powerful anecdotal cautionary tale in the story of the most famous black police officer in Chicago's history, known in South Side lore as "Two-Gun Pete."

Properly named Sylvester Washington, Two-Gun Pete was an enigmatic stockyard-worker-turned-CPD-officer, who had moved to Chicago from tiny Terry, Mississippi, at the age of fourteen. He bounced from job to job before landing a position with the CPD in 1934, at which point he joined the small ranks of black officers and was dispatched to the South Side.

Over the course of his career, Washington cultivated a complicated reputation as both a ruthless fighter of crime and a compulsively violent man. In a recent retrospective on Washington, the *Tribune* described his career arc thus: "Two-Gun started as an anonymous bluecoat walking a beat, but he ended up as a ghetto superstar—a flamboyant, crooked, braggadocios, womanizing, hard-drinking, foul-mouthed police detective."[103] Toward the end of his career, he claimed to have made more than twenty thousand arrests during his time on the force. It was rumored that some criminal suspects feared him so much that he could simply order them to turn themselves in at the police station, and they would comply.

Their fear was justified, for Washington's entire persona was couched in a dark, mean bloodthirst. His third wife described him as "the meanest, cruelest person that I have ever seen in my entire life," and the bodies he stacked suggested the same.[104] Within six months on the force, Washington had killed a twenty-seven-year-old robber with a hail of bullets. After that incident, he came to the nickname "Two-Gun" after the twin .357 Magnums that he wore on the beat. He supplemented those weapons, frequently, with his nightstick and fists—big, meaty paws that he was happy to put to violence. By his career's end, he proudly declared that he had killed eleven or twelve men. As former deputy CPD superintendent Rudy Nimocks recalled, Washington "kind of epitomized the worst of policing, where police officers were totally brutal and had no regard whatsoever for some of the professionalism that people demand now. You'd crack a guy, you'd smack some guy in the mouth. You'd knock them down the second they disrespected you."[105]

Washington's profile steadily rose, almost entirely on the back of his own meanness. He was the kind of black cop, the historian Marvin Dulaney writes, that "the police department and the white public had in mind when they referred to a 'good colored cop,' because he 'kept the niggers in line.'"[106] By 1950 *Ebony* magazine gave him significant page-and-ink space to publicize his own legend to its readers. There, Washington argued that his methods were the only reasonable response to a dangerous job and a troubled society. "Chicago," he said, "wasn't a place for a policeman to call for help with a pencil and arrest book in hand. If you wanted respect—and wanted to stay alive—the best thing to do was go in with your guns drawn, cocked, and ready to back up your words."[107]

After leaving the CPD amid allegations of corruption, Washington opened a dive bar called the HillTop Lounge. Behind the bar, his decorations included a cigar box filled with bullet fragments that had been pulled from his victims, most of whom were black, as well as a sawed-off shotgun and a billy club.[108] In retirement, he served as a teacher to other police: public lore alleges that the HillTop was a haven for police officers to swing in and glean wisdom from Washington on his methods and success.[109]

Nor was Pete unique on the force. In 1953 an unidentified informant for the Chicago Crime Commission working within the CPD described the actions one night of a black officer named Marion Byrd. Byrd pulled over a black man for having no license plates, essentially demanding money from the man and his friends under threat of arrest. Byrd, the whistleblower wrote, "was abusive and threatening, once more bearing out my contention that the Negro policemen are tougher on their own people than white officers."[110] Indeed, many years later, Timuel Black speculated that the violence of black police toward African Americans was partly to blame for emboldening white officers to act in kind.[111]

Two-Gun Pete, Marion Byrd, and others didn't reflect the attitudes and practices of all or even most black police officers. Even so, they present a cautionary note about the limits of merely changing the skin color of the person in the uniform. Pete reified a view of black Chicago that was becoming increasingly commonplace among many police officers and white citizens alike—one that saw it as irretrievably destitute and morally decayed, and in need of control by violence if necessary. By word and deed, he amplified the impression that there was something *wrong* with black communities, and added to the narrative that there were immense swaths of black Chicagoans that needed to be forcibly contained. That narrative was different in its particulars from what white racists in Trumbull Park and elsewhere would say. But it wasn't different by much.

AS THE CASE OF Chicago demonstrates, social and racial capital were deeply implicated in the ways that American policing systems were being constructed and constituted during the postwar years. The social arrangement that Chicago police officers were protecting was one that was governed by white interests. That arrangement was met by legitimate black challenges—both by everyday citizens trying to live their lives and move where they wanted to move and by activists seeking to forthrightly challenge the larger and fundamentally racist social order. The response by the city's politicians and police to such freedom dreams was sometimes hostile, sometimes ambivalent, and almost never supportive. In this way, the increasingly, distinctively racialized policing regime that prevails to this day began to take shape: one that is responsive to and operates to the benefit of only certain sections of the city.

Gerald Bullock's question to his colleagues and countrymen, leveled in the heart of black Chicago in 1950, resonates: "Who stands to benefit by these official acts?" The answer to the question in the specific context that Bullock posed it was that white citizens, business owners, and other opponents of integration stood to benefit. But more generally, the question hovered over the entirety of the postwar years, reverberating out into many more social arenas. For elsewhere, white individuals and organizations,

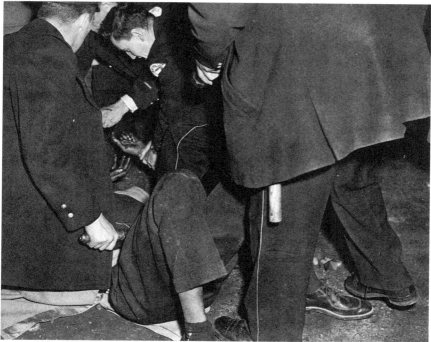

CPD officers arrest and beat a black Chicago man, 1958. American Civil Liberties Union, Illinois Division, Records, box 534, folder 4, Special Collections Research Center, University of Chicago Library.

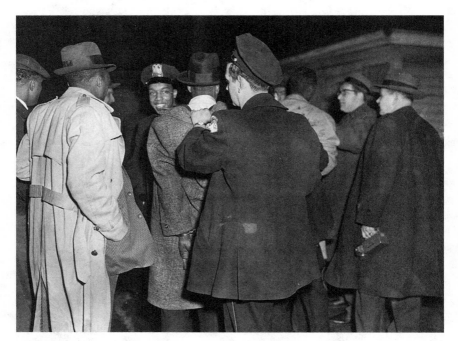

CPD officers arrest a black Chicago man, 1958. American Civil Liberties Union, Illinois Division, Records, box 534, folder 4, Special Collections Research Center, University of Chicago Library.

fearful of supposed black criminality and joined by some black people themselves, began to demand an enhanced police presence on the streets of Chicago—not to address violent white racism but to deal with the supposed criminal and moral threats posed by the black presence. In doing so, they sent Chicago careening toward a punitive future.

The Law Has a Bad Opinion of Me

CHICAGO'S PUNITIVE TURN

n January of 1945, with Chicago in a deep freeze, a fictionalized dialogic story entitled "Simple and the Law" by the writer Langston Hughes appeared inside the pages of the *Defender*. Hughes had been writing such pieces—known as the Simple stories—for some time, the titular character of which (full name, Jesse B. Semple) he imagined as the voice of a workaday black man, a speaker for the proverbial folk. For Hughes, Simple was a vehicle: through him, Hughes ruminated on everything from divorce to love, structural racism to cultural folkways, white people's use of *nigger* to black people's use of *motherfucker*.

In "Simple and the Law," he turned his attention to the police and the larger justice system, sketching a conversation between Simple and a middle-class narrator. Simple was, as he told his conversational companion, scared of "the Law," which "beats my head" and "will give a white man one year, and give me ten." Police officers were loose with racist epithets, and thought "all Negroes are in the criminal class." They were never there to offer protection when it was needed but would stop Simple on the street for no reason and shake him down "as they will any old weed-headed hustler or two-bit rounder." When Simple's companion suggested that Simple must be talking about southern police, Simple retorted that North or South—it made no difference. The same with black and white police; indeed, Simple suggested that black police were worse than white ones, since they couldn't punish or hit white people and thus treated black people twice as bad. When his companion suggested that Simple had no respect for the police, he responded that "the Law has no respect for me, you mean." And when his companion suggested that there were shades of gray to the matter, telling Simple that he saw "everything in terms of black and white," Simple retorted: "So does the law. White is right—and black ain't—to them."[1]

"Simple and the Law" was not among the most famous of the Simple stories, but it is remarkable in hindsight for the many elements of the police-community dynamic that it captured in so short a space: fear of the police, failures of protection, racial slurs, racial condemnation, harassment, brutality, the hope and disappointment that black cops would somehow be better. It was all there—a laundry list of grievances. Not only that, but, published in 1945, it was remarkably prescient. Although Hughes couldn't have known it for sure at the time, things were going to get worse, not better—and soon.

This chapter explains why. It takes as its central unit of analysis what I call Chicago's postwar punitive turn. While the previous chapter situated the police inside the city's battles over integration, this one turns more assertively back toward public policy, its central narrative being this: in the postwar years, Chicago witnessed a massive growth in police power, both numerically and in terms of influence. In the span of two decades, from 1945 to 1965, the CPD's budget allotment from the city quadrupled, and its sworn personnel doubled. The ambit of those officers' powers grew, too. Beginning in 1946, the CPD assembled "roving squad" units that would target certain neighborhoods to generate as many arrests as possible. A decade later, they were institutionalized and made permanent under the aegis of a task force, which relied heavily on stop-and-frisk, racial profiling, and neighborhood saturation. Simultaneously, the department followed vice policing patterns of the past, heavily targeting black drug users and low-level dealers. The template for modern policing of black communities was falling into place.

This punitive turn was profoundly and sometimes explicitly racialized. From the immediate postwar years through the 1970s, the police presence and function were refashioned—by forces both internal and external—in lockstep with the influx of African Americans to the city. For a range of reasons and by a variety of mechanisms, as cities like Chicago got blacker, police officials constructed systems of invasive, hyperaggressive, and racially specific surveillance, and worked to implant them as sanctioned public policy. Over time, black districts were earmarked as "areas of selective enforcement," and within them, officers' efficiency ratings were tethered directly to the number of stops and arrests they made. Timuel Black described this extended postwar moment to me as a time in which police officers shifted from being "our protectors" to "our attackers"—a framing that glosses the severity of earlier problems but nonetheless is telling.[2]

The common rendering of the carceral state in this country suggests, among other things, that when federal investment through Lyndon Johnson's War on Crime began flowing into metropolitan centers in 1965, it fundamentally altered the nature and contours of urban policing.[3] This isn't true. Police administrators were of course happy to take federal monies and attach them to existing or aspirational projects. But those departments were hardly cash-starved, disorganized, and weak before that point. Quite the contrary: they were sprawling in both reach and power, and had achieved a social and financial position that other city institutions would have envied. By the mid-1960s, the CPD was supported politically by members of both major parties, was flush with cash, and possessed extraordinary power and autonomy. When the federal crime and drug wars began, then, they did not recruit unwilling or naive police departments into a punitive federal project of which those departments wanted no part, nor did they reinvent what police departments did or wanted to do. Instead, those wars simply offered new opportunities for departments like the CPD to boost the aggressive pivot that they had been making for years. And because that pivot had been so deeply shaped by racialized policies and outcomes in the years prior to 1965, when the crime and drug wars were grafted onto local initiatives and as they collectively birthed mass incarceration in America, they produced a system that was laden with demonstrably racist outcomes from root to bloom.

It took many people and many impulses to produce this: reformist advocates warring against police and political corruption; Democratic politicians who saw crime, policing, and public safety as politically salient campaign material; police officials seeking professionalization and modernization; and white citizens who feared that the black postwar migration would inalterably change their city for the worse. Because of the way that social power and political capital work and were made manifest, those were the most important drivers of the new punitive policies and investments.

Black people wanted safe streets, too. Crime did increase, and because of the city's intense segregation, black people did bear most of the burden when it did. Nevertheless, people understood this to be a product of an indefensible social contract—something best salved by investment and opportunity, rather than punishment. As Drake and Cayton lamented in their 1962 reprise to *Black Metropolis*, while "the [black] middle classes insist upon police protection, [they] . . . realize that arrest and punishment solve no problems. There is a general feeling that all social work efforts are merely 'holding operations' until complete job equality and adequate housing provide a new physical and economic framework of existence and new incentives for young people."[4]

As history shows us, those frameworks never arrived. Punishment, however, did.

Crisis and Crime: The Punitive Turn Begins

The years during and after the Second World War molded metropolitan Chicago in ways still recognizable today. Three main and interrelated processes drove that refashioning. First was the Second Great Migration, detailed in the last chapter, and the attending flight to the suburbs of many white Chicagoans.[5] Second, massive urban development—beginning especially under the progrowth Daley administration in the second half of the 1950s—shifted increasing amounts of resources toward the Loop and its surroundings at the expense of outlying neighborhoods, dramatically exacerbating urban inequality.[6] Third, relatedly, and most importantly for the purposes here, was the onset of what scholars now call the urban crisis, in which white and capital flight, deindustrialization, and economic retrenchment crippled the economic and resource infrastructure of black neighborhoods on the margins.[7]

To be sure, the war years and those that followed were halcyon days for some black Chicagoans. When Drake and Cayton updated *Black Metropolis* in 1962, they were encouraged to note that "an Era of Integration" was opening and that "Negroes have shared in the prosperity."[8] Black people were entering new jobs, and a more robust black middle class was coalescing. Similarly, in William Julius Wilson's classic 1996 study *When Work Disappears*, Wilson's benchmark for how bad things were for black Chicagoans in the 1990s was how comparatively good they had been in the 1950s and into the 1960s.[9]

But for those on the margins, getting by remained an everyday challenge. Thousands of black children fell behind in schools that were increasingly underfunded and overcrowded.[10] Inequality prevailed in employment, too. A racial job ceiling remained intact in many economic sectors, and numerous employers began leaving urban areas that were easily accessible to black workers on foot or by public transit, in favor of cheaper real estate and lower taxes on the outskirts that were more accessible to white suburbanites. Opportunities to hold down a decent living wage became increasingly scarce for black workers. Even in 1960, only about one-third of nonwhite workers in Chicago worked in skilled or semiskilled work, while two-thirds of white workers did.[11] And Drake and Cayton reported that, by 1966, 20 percent of black workers labored in jobs that still left them living below the poverty line.[12] Those numbers would only worsen further over time.

The consequences were etched into the city's facades and fabrics. (They still are.) The interconnections of racial discrimination, eroding work opportunities, and declining urban infrastructure produced "persistent, concentrated, racialized poverty" in ways that were unprecedented in American urban life.[13] And the process was self-reinforcing. As the economic integrity of impacted neighborhoods collapsed, so did their tax bases. When tax bases collapsed, political capital diminished and governmental investment became even stingier. As neighborhoods became further dilapidated, as schools within them became more overcrowded and underresourced, as work opportunities in them dried up further, those with the means to do so simply left—weakening tax bases, political capital, and governmental investment still further. In sum, what the sociologist Robert Sampson has called the "cumulative disadvantage" afflicting many of black Chicago's neighborhoods in the twenty-first century began assuming its coherence in this postwar moment.[14] The city could have chosen to combat the effects. The Democratic machine, under Richard Daley especially, had its hands on so many different levers of power that it could have worked harder to stave off the effects of crisis. That it didn't (and doesn't) is a product of politicians' priorities and political will, and of how they viewed the importance of some communities relative to others.

The contours and consequences of the urban crisis are important in their own right, but of particular significance here is how it affected crime and perceptions of it. The distinction between the two is important. On the one hand, the concentration of poverty and the erosion of opportunities in geographically specific areas was attended by the increasing concentration of reported crime. After undergoing an immediate postwar surge, from the late 1940s to the late 1950s, major crimes in Chicago stayed relatively stable relative to population fluctuations. But those crimes were heavily clustered: first on the black South Side, where a 1946 report by the CCC noted that the Fifth Police District was responsible for one-fifth of the city's reported murders, one-ninth of its robberies, and one-quarter of its rapes; and, over time, migrating to West Side neighborhoods that were becoming simultaneously blacker and more underresourced in the midst of migration and crisis.[15]

Chicago's segregation ensured that victims of these crimes were almost always black. Then as now, people committed crimes where they lived, and black and white people didn't usually live in the same neighborhoods. While the only offense for which the CPD broke down the race of both victim and perpetrator together was murder, what this shows is that black people killed black people and white people killed white people.[16] There is no reason to think that those dynamics can't be extrapolated outward to crime more generally, and there were plenty of reasons why some black Chicagoans began pushing for more attentive policing of their neighborhoods in this moment.

Be that as it may, what drove Chicago's punitive turn was not the experiences of black people. Instead, and despite crime's inherently segregated nature, it was primarily driven by white fixations on the specter of black crime, especially as black in-migration to the city escalated. The widely discussed 1946 report by the CCC analyzing crime conditions in the black South Side Fifth Police District was especially significant as both example and launch point. While for two and a half decades, the CCC had waged war on lenient sentencing policies, police corruption, and other matters that they thought depressed the state of law and order in Chicago and damaged its reputation as a commercial center, race had rarely been an important intellectual component of the organization's work. But in 1945, a spike in alleged holdups of delivery drivers passing through the black Fifth District spurred it to investigate conditions and determine "the underlying reasons for the high incidence of crime" there.[17]

The CCC report's explanations for high crime incidences in the Fifth District revolved around three key problems. The first was environmental: that residential segregation and its attending overcrowding and social disruptions yielded juvenile delinquency and stress-bred violence and criminality. The second was behavioral: while the CCC insisted that race and crime should be intellectually decoupled and that there was no such thing as racial ineptitude, they failed to properly decouple the two themselves—treading in tropes of black immorality, laziness, wildness, and hypersexuality. (The CCC argued, for instance, that the South Side's extreme overcrowding led to widespread extramarital sex once people were forced to share apartments. They also speculated that black Fifth District residents who worked in factories "many miles away" from their homes had "no incentive to return home following working hours" and thus "would stop in taverns and other places of amusement," which "resulted in immorality and other delinquent acts.")[18] These first two points rendered the commission's hypotheses on crime's root causes a mixed bag of sober reportage and racist nonsense. Despite the commission's enumeration of the challenges facing the black working poor and despite its assurances that "race itself has no significance," it would take mental contortions to not see how notions about black inferiority wormed their way into the report, even if they lay beneath the surface.[19]

The report's third point, meanwhile, was ultimately even more consequential than the others: that crime was high in the Fifth District because "law enforcement conditions" there were "totally unsatisfactory." According to the report, numerous district residents "complained that a police officer is rarely seen on the streets" and "expressed that patrolmen should be walking beats and that the number of squad cars patrolling the area should be materially increased." Such patrolmen of course needed to be honest and competent; interviewees accused most officers in the district of being neither. But the quantity of police mattered at least as much as the quality, since "almost everyone interviewed expressed the opinion that the police protection for the district has been inadequate for many years" and, as one "very prominent political leader" put it, "Chicago is a 1945 city with a 1919 police department." Thus, ultimately, the CCC's foremost prescriptive measure for curbing South Side crime was to dramatically increase the police presence there.[20]

Members of the crime commission were skilled in the art of publicity, and rather than simply delivering the report to city hall, they dispatched it to the city's newspapers. It landed like a bombshell. Indeed, what was most significant about the report was not even necessarily what it said but what it produced in terms of public opinion and public policy. After its release, commenters outside the black community mostly elided the report's notes on the poor conditions in which huge swaths of black Chicagoans were living. And none of them, at least that the historical record discloses, made any meaningful pitch to alleviate systemic inequality and the structures of white supremacy as a means of crime control. Instead, they focused in on the report's underlying argument that the CPD was failing to keep the city safe, and highlighted the fact that police corruption was corroding public safety. Only weeks after the report landed, the *Tribune* launched a twelve-part series in coordination with the CCC that detailed just how badly politicized and corrupt the department had become.[21]

All of this sent CPD administrators and commanders scrambling to defend themselves against accusations of corruption and inefficiency.[22] Facing a barrage of bad press, CPD Commissioner Prendergast announced that three new "special squads" of officers would be assigned to the Fifth District to help suppress crime there.[23] Responding to a CCC suggestion that more black officers be involved in policing black districts, the squads reported to Sargent Robert Harness, who was black, and were headed by Julius Tillman, Joseph Geeter, and "Two-Gun Pete" Washington, all of whom were black.[24] Working exclusively in black neighborhoods and led by black policemen, the officers' essential mission nonetheless was little more than to generate as many arrests as possible. Granted extraordinary discretion, they targeted people they found to be suspicious, routinely subjected them to searches for weapons and other contraband, and generally engaged in newly aggressive forms of racially specific harassment.

Although they arrested dozens of people and harassed many more, the new squads' general effectiveness was minimal. The crime commission hired informants within the CPD to evaluate the department's efficiency, one of whom reported that squad members were just as corrupt as other officers— routinely taking bribes from citizens who could pay for their freedom and targeting for arrest those who could not.[25] Moreover, there is no causal data showing that crime in the Fifth District meaningfully dropped on the strength of the squad's actions.

Nevertheless, their creation was an important innovation in police policy with significant impacts in the long view. At their root, the squads' imple-mentation and guiding logics represented the beginning of a shift away from beat-patrol policing, a transition from a police system built on general familiarity between patrolling officers and citizens (despite some mutual animosities embedded within that familiarity) and toward one that priori-tized rapid responses and legitimated blanket assumptions about the crimi-nality of local residents. And because they earmarked black neighborhoods exclusively as zones for special police attention and action, the squads were the first institutionalization of police power in ways that were systematically unique to black communities.

While Prendergast's special squads constituted a very small portion of police work during the mid-1940s, they nevertheless set the template for much more aggressive and selective police policies in future years. As we will see in later pages, there is a distinct lineage that runs from these squads forward to more expansive police powers that came down the pike. Most no-tably, Prendergast's successor, Timothy O'Connor, formalized the squads' concept in his development of the CPD's infamous task force in the mid-1950s. And the task force, in turn, was the laboratory in which police admin-istrators germinated aggressive and repressive police policies such as stop-and-frisk, arrest quotas, and neighborhood saturation during the late 1950s.

Merriam vs. the Machine: The Crime Politics of Reform

In the more immediate sense, the creation of the special squads was part of a larger postwar growth in investment in the police department from city hall. From 1945 to 1946 alone, the city's appropriation to the CPD jumped $5 million—a significant budgetary allotment at that time, which was used primarily to hire new officers to the force.[26] The department also began to invest in new technology that would increase its mobility across Chicago; between 1946 and 1953, the CPD more than doubled the number of vehicles at its disposal, established a crime laboratory, and implemented narcotics and crowd control units that would modernize the department and increase its reach across the city.[27]

The most explosive growth of police power would not come until the mid-1950s, however, and when it did, it was predictably spurred most significantly by political battles in the city. The most important stage in that drama was an internecine battle between machine and reformist Democrats, and its most important actors were Richard J. Daley, the career politician and entrenched head of the Cook County Democratic machine, and Robert Merriam, a young and charismatic Democratic city councilman from Hyde Park who led an antimachine reform bloc within the party. Merriam's pedigree was impressive. The son of famed University of Chicago professor and political reformer Charles Merriam, the younger Merriam had earned widespread praise as a World War II war hero after having survived the Battle of the Bulge. After the war, he'd authored a book about his wartime experiences that elevated his star still further, and had then taken up a career in public service, first as director of Chicago's Metropolitan Housing Council, and then, beginning in 1947, through a seat on the city council, where he cosponsored the council's first serious effort to eliminate discriminatory housing and undertook a range of other legislative initiatives that bucked the general policies of the machine.[28]

Merriam disliked the machine in a general sense, of course, but a core component of that dislike was how it corrupted Chicago's public safety. He literally broadcast the failings of the police department to the public through his television show *Spotlight on Chicago*, where he enhanced his bona fides as both crime-fighter and reformer by exposing corruption and crime cases to as wide an audience as owned televisions in Chicago at the time.[29] He also employed informants inside the CPD, who detailed incessant collusion between politicians, police officers, and criminal interests and solidified Merriam's understanding of Chicago's police system as one that was awash in graft and corruption. (In the words of one of his informants, the entire police function had basically become "one big racket and shakedown proposition."[30]) In 1952, after a Republican ward committeeman named Charles Gross was assassinated near Humboldt Park, Merriam convened an Emergency Committee on Crime to investigate, further publicize, and hopefully finally sever the links between organized crime, police, and politics.[31] It didn't go well. With the committee under attack from CPD rank-and-file and Democratic machine partisans, the *Tribune* characterized it as having "an angry but futile existence."[32] It also suffered from numerous attempts to undermine it from above, according to Merriam, including efforts by Timothy O'Connor to disparage and discredit its most important investigator, former FBI Agent Aaron Kohn.[33] (Merriam eventually became so disgusted with O'Connor that he sought his indictment for dereliction of duty.[34])

Merriam's war was symptomatic of a larger pattern that understood police corruption and inefficiency to be both widespread across the United States and particularly acute in Chicago. In 1950 the U.S. Senate convened a special committee on organized crime and interstate commerce, known as the Kefauver Committee, that focused especially on police complicity in aiding and abetting organized crime, and singled out the Windy City for the "deplorable laxity" of some of its police officers.[35] A few years later, *Collier's* magazine published a series of articles on "the police problem," the first of which, "The Plight of the Honest Cop," explored how police corruption was "shaming our nation" and putting "honest cops" in a hopeless situation.[36] In that piece, its author, Albert Deutsch, focused heavily on Chicago, exploring a litany of "shady practices attributed to local cops," which included "framing businessmen and other citizens for the purpose of extorting bribes; shaking down gamblers, prostitutes, lawbreaking tavern keepers, narcotics peddlers and traffic violators; extorting money from ex-convicts under threat of arrest; indiscriminately harassing slum-area residents; beating up and blackjacking suspects; harassing private citizens on behalf of favored politicians or hoodlums." In the final analysis, Deutsch wrote, "I am fully prepared to accept the widely held opinion that the Chicago police force is by far the most demoralized, graft-ridden and inefficient among our larger cities."[37]

Ongoing investigations and continuing press coverage—whether in the newspapers, on the radio, or on Merriam's television show—drew wide attention to the failure and corruption of the CPD throughout the late 1940s and the first half of the 1950s. And while the links between corruption, political influence, and organized crime captured the greatest attention, these arguments also helped to construct a larger narrative about police inefficiency and public unsafety. For part of what Merriam and others like him were doing was relentlessly framing the CPD as a public liability—one that was leaving Chicago unsafe and robbing it of services to which it was entitled. (Merriam's message was not, it is worth emphasizing, antipolice. Having long argued for more police and more robust enforcement of law, he was opposed to police corruption and police impotence, not to police themselves.[38])

Frustrated by Chicago's punishing inertia on the subject of meaningful political reform, Merriam eventually upped the stakes. Rather than continuing to work from the political system's lesser offices, in the runup to the 1955 mayoral election, he entered into what the *Tribune* bitterly called "obviously and shamelessly a marriage of convenience" with the Republican Party, which recruited Merriam to represent it and hopefully breathe new life into a party that was effectively moribund at the local level.[39] Although Merriam had always been firmly in the liberal bloc of the Democratic camp, he now shed his formal Democratic affiliation, recast himself as a Republican, and announced that he would run for the mayor's office as someone who could effectively oppose the machine and rehabilitate the city's degraded political system.

Merriam positioned himself against a Democratic machine that was itself in a state of flux. In preceding years, incumbent mayor Martin Kennelly had been increasingly at odds with the machine leaders who had helped install him in power, and the machine camp was nonplussed when Kennelly announced his reelection campaign in December 1954. Daley in particular possessed extraordinary power over what the machine's official slate would look like in the coming elections, and he quickly maneuvered to oust Kennelly. The slating committee that Daley appointed dropped its support for Kennelly, stripping him of the expansive political benefits that accompanied a machine candidacy. To no one's surprise, Daley then entered the race backed by the machine instead. In the ensuing primary, Daley beat Kennelly and Cook County state's attorney Benjamin Adamowski, based largely on the strength of machine turnout, which included huge numbers of black votes that flowed in as part of William Dawson's famed black submachine.[40]

From the beginning of the ensuing campaign, Merriam made the state of Chicago's law enforcement apparatus into one of the election's core issues. On the campaign trail, he excoriated machine corruption and tethered it to the dysfunctions and failures of the police department. In particular, he suggested that Daley—as his electoral opponent but also as the machine's conductor—would never get tough on crime or give the department the political space to do its job impartially. Indeed, he accused Daley of wanting to make Chicago back into a "'wide open city' for syndicate gambling and other illegal activities."[41] Those attacks struck a political nerve. Seeking to bolster his credentials on public safety in the face of Merriam's onslaught, candidate Daley made a hard pivot toward trying to appear tough on crime—most notably by making the expansion of the CPD into a signature piece of his campaign. Indeed, by midcampaign, in speech after speech, Daley began hammering away on the public safety issue and pledging to hire two thousand new CPD officers in order to ensure it. (Internal campaign memos were explicit about the influence of Merriam's attacks in generating this approach.[42])

In the end, Daley's gambit worked. Merriam's battle was always going to be an uphill climb against a machine opponent in a machine-controlled city. Although the race was surely closer than Daley would have preferred, reliably machine-voting wards in the city generally continued to be reliably machine-voting. Meanwhile, Merriam, known as "the WASP Prince of Chi-cago," struggled to connect with many of the city's blue-collar ethnic com-munities, particularly those that had benefited from machine patronage over the years.[43] For his part, Daley also benefited from talking out of both sides of his mouth across the color line. On the campaign trail, he spent time with black voters and political operatives on the South Side, telling them that he supported their freedom dreams and eventually earning the *Defender*'s crucial endorsement. Meanwhile, he was simultaneously assur-ing white racists that he would "hold the line on integration"—a pledge believable enough for him to earn the endorsement of the South Deering Improvement Association, which was leading the ongoing antiblack terror-ism still raging in Trumbull Park.[44] Although Merriam put up a stiff fight, he lost.

What Merriam accomplished, despite his electoral defeat, was to firmly inject police expansion into the heart of Daley's campaign pledge, which subsequently rolled over into the new mayor's administrative platform. As we have already seen in brief, Daley had long been positively inclined toward the police. He came from the Irish neighborhood of Bridgeport, home to thousands of retired and acting police officers. He and his wife both had po-lice officers in their family tree, and Daley had had good relationships with political bosses and local police alike ever since he was a teenager. But the 1955 mayoral victory showed Daley, and by extension the machine and other politicians, that casting their lot with the police was also good politics. In a city in the midst of extraordinary demographic change, expanding the power and influence of the police department proved to be a useful policy point with broad swaths of the electorate. And, in his first couple of years after taking office, Daley successfully got the two thousand new officers he had pledged on the campaign trail.

That was only the beginning. Once departmental expansion began, it did not roll back. Under the Daley regime, by 1965, on the eve of the federal War on Crime, Chicago had fully doubled its number of sworn police personnel from where it had stood in 1945.[45] This expansion cost the city an incredible amount of money and constituted a dramatic reimagining of priorities. Be-tween 1945 and 1965, the budgetary allotment from the city to the CPD more than quadrupled, and spiked even higher after that point. By 1970 the CPD's budget was more than 900 percent larger than in 1945, approaching $200 million per year. By the mid-seventies, the city was spending one-quarter of its budget on its police.[46]

It bears knowing that it was over the course of that same period that the urban crisis began to wreak further havoc on black Chicago's educational infrastructure, housing markets, and employment sectors, hurling citizens on the margins into deeper states of deprivation and desperation. And it is surely worth considering that as that happened, the one major investment that Daley and the city council made in those neighborhoods was to send in more police.

At the Grassroots: Community Concerns and Community Power

These city-level political debates over the nature, size, and power of the police force did not, of course, take place in a vacuum. Nor was the CPD's changing role and function in society simply a top-down process driven by well-known political operatives.

Indeed, the changing police force was also a consequence of grassroots pressure and political activism by white citizens, particularly those belonging to neighborhood organizations that worried over the changing demographics of their city, neighborhood, and block. For instance, in 1950s Hyde Park and Kenwood, white residents went into hysterics about an imagined "crime wave" as black Chicagoans began to push into the area. Organized into block clubs, residents of those neighborhoods "banded together to petition for extra protection [from the CPD] against a wave of 'purse snatchings and burglaries.'" The CPD complied, sending additional patrols to the petitioning blocks, even though it was eventually discovered that block club members' fears had been stoked to eruption by "one local resident's rumor-mongering," and had no basis in fact.[47]

The CPD's responsiveness was not always so direct, but it was real nevertheless. And it was perhaps most readily visible on the West Side, which experienced postwar Chicago's most rapid and concentrated racial transition. The case of North Lawndale is a useful example. By the 1950s, North Lawndale was undergoing rapid racial succession, resource flight, and creeping blight. As the area transitioned (in 1940 it was less than 1 percent black; in 1960, more than 90 percent[48]), a group of Lawndale residents—interracial, but mostly white—organized themselves as the Greater Lawndale Conservation Commission (GLCC) in order to "stem physical deterioration of real estate" in the neighborhood.[49] Like many neighborhood conservation commissions, the GLCC's stated goals at the outset centered around getting the neighborhood designated as an urban renewal site (it never got such a designation) and attacking blight. Prominently funded by the Sears, Roebuck and Company that, until 1974, was located in the neighborhood, the GLCC was deeply aligned with corporate interests in these fights—a fact that did not help its responsiveness to the many low-income black residents moving into the area. Even as the 1950s progressed and as more black people came into the leadership of the GLCC, racial and class fissures contoured its programming and stunted its reception by working-poor black sections of the community.[50]

As an accompaniment to fighting blight and pushing for urban renewal, one of the GLCC's primary concerns was to increase the police presence in the district and elevate the power of officers.[51] Both through and outside the GLCC, Lawndalers proved successful at harnessing influence over the CPD. The organization held community meetings, sent innumerable communications to local police officials trying to draw attention to the area, and parlayed their influence into meetings with city officials—all the way up to the mayor—to push for a more robust police presence.[52] In 1954 local rabbi and Chicago Rabbinical Council leader Leonard Mishkin pressured Mayor Kennelly to hire one thousand new officers to deal with rising crime. (Tellingly, he framed this argument in part around Timothy O'Connor's hierarchical vision of legitimate causes, complaining about the "immobilization" of three hundred officers because of Trumbull Park as he lodged his own request for more officers.[53]) The CPD responded by doubling the number of patrol cars in Lawndale during the overnight hours, and adding thirty-five additional patrols to the neighborhood.[54] Shortly after Daley's election in 1955, meanwhile, the GLCC enrolled their local alderman, Sidney Deutsch, to push the new mayor for more intensive police patrols and support Daley's campaign plan to hire thousands of new officers.[55] Daley obliged on both counts. For the rest of the decade, block clubs in Lawndale—autonomous entities but, by most appearances, operating under the auspices of the GLCC—filed petition after petition with city officials, consistently trying to achieve "intensified patrolling" of the neighborhood, especially after dark.[56] Indeed, so effective was Lawndalers' lobbying that in 1956, GLCC members claimed to have spurred CPD commissioner Timothy O'Connor to implement a massive new task force—modeled after John Prendergast's flying squads of a decade earlier but dramatically expanded and reimagined in terms of what they could be.[57] We will explore this latter development further momentarily, but suffice it to say that this was citizen activism with real impacts on the city and the CPD.

There was nothing innately malicious about these campaigns. Unlike in some other parts of the city, the problem of rising crime in Lawndale was real, according to anecdotes and crime statistics. And even though most black people in the neighborhood never aligned with the GLCC, some did, and still many others were doubtlessly worried about crime.

But it is instructive to note how much race mattered in that story. While much of the GLCC's operations maintained an outward veneer of race neutrality, it's difficult to ignore how that neutrality faded when it came to issues of crime. By decade's close, groups of white Lawndalers repeatedly lodged their appeals to police not as citizens generally but as white people in particular. The most striking examples are found in the years-long correspondence between law enforcement, the GLCC, and four white families who clung to their homes on an otherwise all-black block in the neighborhood. Echoing the vagueness that contoured much white fear of black criminality, beginning in 1958, this series of exchanges shows the families and the GLCC making demands for police protection against "general harassment by Negro teenagers and young Negro adults."[58] Sympathetic to their plight, the CPD responded by assigning an extra patrolman to the block for round-the-clock service.[59] The following year, GLCC members met with a CPD official to complain about continuing problems on the block; after they had presented their case, the official reportedly told them that he was "aware of the difficulties that the white families on this block" had been facing.[60] Members of the CCHR were afforded direct hearings with Commissioner O'Connor multiple times about the plight of these four families, and their reports emphasize the families' Caucasian-ness over and over again.[61] As late as 1960, white families in the neighborhood were meeting in private, their black neighbors uninvited, to discuss crime and communicate their concerns with members of the CPD.[62]

It seems unlikely, from everything else we know about the workings of political and racial capital, that the GLCC would have had anything remotely like the success it had if it were an all-black organization. In other words, even for those blacks on the commission who agreed with its larger mission concerning police expansion both at the micro level and citywide, it is impossible to imagine them succeeding without having white voices helping lift theirs up. This is, again, how racial privilege worked and works. And it was racial privilege that shaped the contours and rhythms of policing in ways both deep and lasting.

"Dope Must Go": Black Chicago, Chicago's War on Drugs, and the Ambit of Police Power

The proof is in the counterpoint.

Throughout the postwar years, black individuals and organizations fought a parallel fight against crime in their neighborhoods, but without the same success as their white counterparts. There is a mythos, grounded in no evidence, that black Americans are quick to condemn police violence but slow to comment about crimes committed by black people against other black people. This is as much a fiction historically as it is now. Indeed, if the 1946 crime commission report on the Fifth District had helped goad the city and CPD down the path toward a more expansive and powerful police department, it happened in spite of, not because of, black demands for better protection. To wit, even before the CCC report went public, the local NAACP had gone to then–CPD commissioner John Prendergast requesting the department's help in dealing with burgeoning crime in black neighborhoods. According to the branch's executive secretary, Prendergast literally responded with a shrug, and attributed the problem of crime not to structural inequalities or stretched police resources, or even, as a popular mythology went, to new southern migrants unfamiliar with the rhythms of the city. Rather, in a classically racist take on the problem, he chalked it up to "a spirit of restlessness with you people."[63] And once the report *did* become public, scandalizing the city in the process, Irene McCoy Gaines, president of the Chicago Council of Negro Organizations, pointed out that "many Negro groups, for years, had been going to the offices of the chief of police and state's attorney" begging for relief from pressing crime problems.[64]

What distinguished black communities' approaches to crime suppression in these early years (and since) was that whereas most white citizens and white politicians turned mainly to the police to fix the problem, black Chicagoans sought amelioration for poverty and inequality and the root causes of crime in addition to attentive law enforcement. In his study of black tough-on-crime advocacy in 1970s Washington, DC, the legal scholar James Forman Jr. found that most black people living in the majority-black city understood crime to be a function of the deeply racialized and systemic inequalities that molded urban life. As such, they called for an "all-of-the-above" approach to fighting crime, in which more rigorous policing and tougher sentencing would be coupled with community uplift and infrastructural investment. As Forman writes, they "wanted more law enforcement, but they didn't want *only* law enforcement."[65]

So, too, in the immediate postwar years in Chicago. In a radio address in the fall of 1945, the black attorney and politician Christopher Wimbish probed the roots of crime, and America's approach to it in an age of global war: "*Can we adults* of the 20th Century," he asked, "who spend *billions of dollars* to wage a war to *kill*, and have not spent a fraction of such amount to provide a wholesome environment to the living—hold the criminal responsible for our social negligence? . . . Crime springing from misery and poverty, disillusionment and frustration, is a condition for which *society is responsible*, although we hold the criminal accountable. We must strike at the cause—the roots—the source of the thing—if we are to have a real and lasting solution to the problem of CRIME PREVENTION."[66] St. Clair Drake and Horace Cayton found similar attitudes a decade and a half later, when they wrote that the black middle class understood that "arrest and punishment" were "merely 'holding operations'" for crime prevention, until real social and economic justice came.[67]

In this view, whatever problems of crime existed within black neighborhoods were at their root fundamentally problems of white supremacy, capitalism, and exclusion. And even if the fullest articulations of that view wouldn't cohere until the civil rights and Black Power revolutions, they were already emerging in fragmented fashion in this moment. Readers of the *Defender* would have found multiple variations on a theme advanced by J. Hamilton Johnson in the newspaper's pages, where he bundled together crime rates with segregation and, above all else, with the effects of the "great lie"—"white supremacy."[68] Denton Brooks, an assistant editor-in-chief at the *Defender*, noted that "south side crime . . . is a part of the whole pattern of ghetto conditions existing there. . . . It's not just a police job, it's a social job."[69] Meanwhile, as publicity about so-called "Negro crime" increased, the Chicago NAACP worried over whites concluding "that the high crime rate was the cause of the negro as a class," rather than something attributable to the actual causes of it—"housing, policing, recreation, sanitation, etc."[70]

Meanwhile, and in contrast to the negotiated lobbying of the GLCC or the block clubs in Hyde Park and Kenwood, the police presence and power expanded heavily in black Chicago during the late 1940s and throughout the 1950s, but without meaningful engagement with the community as to the terms of that expansion. The first turning point involved Prendergast's flying squads, born in 1946 and dramatically expanded by O'Connor ten years later—a story we will return to shortly. The second took place in the interim, however, and it revolved around the explosion of an acute public health crisis in black Chicago.

SCHOLARS OF OPIATES in the United States have repeatedly pointed to World War II as an important rupture and turning point in the American drug trade. The war, they argue, sent the supply of drugs into a period of sustained freefall when it brought international shipping blockades and disruptions in global economies, including the ones in drugs. Postwar peace brought with it the reopening of traditional smuggling networks and the resuscitation of the drug trade.[71]

When the trade resumed, its locus had shifted. The composite portrait of an American heroin user had previously vacillated between white women and Chinese immigrants, and in the years immediately preceding the war, had been a white urban dweller. In postwar Chicago, however, heroin's primary habitat relocated into the heart of the black South Side. The shift wasn't a minor one. Even as late as the 1930s, the overwhelming majority of the city's addicts were still white or of Asian descent, whereas 17 percent were black. By 1957, however, according to official accounts, more than three-quarters of addicts were black. The city's African American population had roughly tripled, but its share of the reported addict population had quintupled.[72] Most of them were poor, and most of them were young. (Roughly one-third of them were under the age of twenty-one; in the early 1930s, only 2 percent of local addicts had been that young.[73]) Because of the city's patterns of segregation and marginalization, most of them spent their days in overcrowded schools, went home to dilapidated neighborhoods, and searched for things to do in their defined stretches of the city that often contained few parks or recreational facilities. Many of them described being drawn to elders and peers they met on the street or in clubs, and how their curiosity was piqued by descriptions of how heroin made those elders and peers feel.[74] Already in 1947, Federal Bureau of Narcotics (FBN) agents on the ground in Chicago were stunned by the new patterns of addiction emerging in front of them. As the local FBN supervisor R. W. Artis reported back to his boss in Washington, Harry Anslinger, "This is the only territory in which I have worked where young boys from fourteen years old to the very early twenties are addicted to the use of narcotic drugs."[75] Drug markets often abutted kids' primary daily orbits, particularly schools. In some cases, such as that of DuSable High School, the schools themselves operated as a marketplace of information on heroin and where to get it. Students who gleaned such information and were so inclined could then walk a short distance to known drug markets on Forty-Seventh Street, five minutes from the school.[76]

Community members on the South Side tried to fend off heroin's assault. Most notably, they launched a vigorous "Dope Must Go" campaign that involved literature drops throughout the community and an array of educational measures in an attempt to coordinate with law enforcement in order to crack down on the supply.[77] Those efforts, sadly, proved insufficient. By 1951 the *Defender* identified one South Side drug market as being so flagrant and destructive that the newspaper labeled it "Dopeville, USA."[78] The article copy ran amid a photograph collage of track-marked arms, violently ill addicts suffering heroin shivers, and drug paraphernalia. This miserable scene appeared as the heart of Chicago's drug problem. Local residents were furious at the brashness with which dealers dealt, and bristled at the fact that the larger processes of racial exclusion and ghettoization sequestered hundreds of thousands of people into the same spaces as dope addicts and peddlers.[79]

The city's official response to the trade illustrates the inability of black communities to attract city resources and sharpens the outline of the punitive turn. Initially, officials suggested medical treatment as a means of dealing with the heroin crisis. In late fall of 1949, State's Attorney John Boyle announced that he would seek counsel from the Chicago Board of Health, affiliates of the American Medical Association, and other health experts to try to find medical solutions.[80] But the institutional imperatives at levels above him simply weren't there. Fighting the heroin deluge through ameliorative means would doubtlessly have been costly, and since black communities were being hit the hardest, it was impossible to pull substantial public resources into the fight. Many of the people tasked with leading the fight had terrible opinions about black people to begin with, and those opinions carried over into how they approached drug addiction in the black community. Examples abound. It is, for instance, worth remembering CPD commissioner John Prendergast's comment a couple of years earlier about black people being animated by "a spirit of restlessness." But the dynamic is perhaps best seen in a memo from Artis to Anslinger, in which he wrote, "As you know, by nature the great majority of these individuals [black people] are inclined to anything that they believe exciting or easy living, which makes them susceptible to drug addiction."[81] This suggested not just that black communities were facing a crisis but that the crisis was brought into being by innate black deficiency.

Thus, as the heroin wave continued to pummel the South Side, no treatment facilities or other ameliorative measures appeared. The situation on this front was so bad that even among the small number of addicts who *did* receive treatment, most had to do so within the confines of the city jail. For those who managed to kick the habit, there was no support system for them upon their return to the community—particularly unfortunate, since they came back to the very same communities where the drug and temptation were concentrated. Rates of recidivism were off the charts. When Boyle suggested that he would look into getting support from professional medical associations, Prendergast wasn't optimistic that he could, or that it would even do much good. Boyle wasn't optimistic either. "If the medical profession can't end the dope habit," he told reporters for the *Chicago Tribune*, "we'll have to consider locking up these unfortunate people for life, as a crime prevention measure."[82]

As treatment support failed to materialize and crimes ascribed to addicts crept upward, the response from the city grew increasingly punitive. While scholars have long noted that the federal government turned toward punitive antidrug policies in the early 1950s (most notably the 1951 Boggs Act and 1956 Narcotic Control Act), local authorities in Chicago beat them to the punch. Because they lacked confidence that they could get resources to pursue treatment, at the same time they were advocating for such measures,

Boyle and Prendergast were seeking ways of waging a "war on drugs" (the *Tribune*'s words).[83] Whether this would mean expanding the CPD's attention to narcotics, getting help from federal agencies in order to wage it, or a combination of the two, the language of war signaled what was to come.

Already by 1949 the police department had become the primary institutional force fighting against the heroin deluge. In the Fifth District alone, from March through December of that year, an aggressive drive against narcotics resulted in more than eleven hundred adults and sixty-two juveniles being arrested on drug use charges.[84] The outcome of such charges was rarely innocuous—many of those so arrested were hit with monetary fines, while still many others received jail time. By April of 1951, the chief justice of Chicago's municipal court, Edward Scheffler, ordered the creation of a special narcotics court in order to manage the exploding caseload of people that police had arrested in cases "in which narcotics are in any way involved."[85] The court was equipped with a psychiatrist and a social worker, suggesting a social component to the whole arrangement. Be that as it may, because addiction was now primarily being addressed through the police and court system, the matter of addiction was now, first and foremost, criminal in its nature.

That criminalization was institutionalized permanently inside the CPD, as well. On his way out of office in the fall of 1950, Prendergast announced a new narcotics detail based out of the CPD detective bureau that he anticipated would be more effective at controlling the sale and spread of drugs on the South Side.[86] His successor, Timothy O'Connor, made his support for an even further expansion of the new unit an early feature of his commissionership after taking over the department.[87] That newly established narcotics section would prove proficient at increasing police-civilian contact and logging arrests. The problem was that such arrests did nothing to curb drug addiction, in part because patterns of arrest mirrored the patterns of arrest that had *always* governed vice policing in black Chicago: drug users and low-level pushers faced arrest; wealthy suppliers did not.

Those patterns didn't help citizens' trust in the department. Echoing the accusations that were frequently lodged against police officers in the context of other vice economies, black journalists accused CPD officers of being on the take from dealers, who would pay them to look the other way when they were going about their business.[88] That accusation is impossible to confirm, but it does accord comfortably with historical patterns of corruption in Chicago. Adding to the cloud of suspicion under which the department operated was a public belief that perhaps the department didn't *want* to stop drug addiction in black communities. Even Milton Deas, one of the most decorated and respected black police officers in Chicago's history, seemed to tacitly endorse this understanding, when in a later interview he recalled his role in trying to suppress the drug trade. A son of Englewood who knew many of the men involved in the heroin trade, Deas told his superiors that he could probably do something to curb it if given the chance. Instead, he quickly found himself transferred far away from the district. As a consequence, he remembered, "what was going on was no longer in my district, and there was nothing more I could do."[89]

In the background, influential white experts and local organizations continued to offer comment on the addiction problem, study the present and future of the city's response to it, and in turn shape how policymakers thought about it. Their conversations generally reinforced the notion that punishment was the best way forward. Some argued explicitly for the total criminalization of drug addiction.[90] One study, conducted by the Illinois Institute for Juvenile Justice and the Chicago Area Project (which originated in the University of Chicago's Department of Sociology) was particularly noteworthy, because the conclusions that its analysts arrived at on the matter of drugs and public policy were so influential. Citing the punishment-heavy emphasis of the CPD's criminalization policy, they quite accurately described it as "consist[ing] of the frequent arrest of heroin addicts[,] and their short-term commitment to city and county jails[,] occasionally tempered by referral to out-patient clinics or by arranging to send the person to a Federal Narcotics Hospital." In an artful understatement, they estimated that police "were probably more vigorous in arresting drug law violators during the recent period than they were ten years ago."[91]

The description was not condemnation. Some people, in their minds, *deserved* to be locked up. The conceptual move they made in order to determine precisely *who* was so deserving was to differentiate Chicago's postwar addict population into a hierarchy of salvageable peoples. The intellectual starting point for their assessment was that virtually all addicts were criminals, and that they were addicts *because* they were criminals *first*. In their words, "Delinquency is not a result of their addiction to heroin, but is a reflection of the same interests and problems which lead to addiction." Older addicts were dismissed as pariahs whose prospects for eventually living better lives were negligible; they were deemed to be an irretrievably criminal element, and the report's crafters advocated that they be treated as such. Analysts purported to take a more nuanced approach to young users, but even there, they saw a mass of kids who were "unmotivated" enough to ascend into a life of the "conventional adult male," and who would instead lead an adult life governed by "criminality." Above them was an apparently smaller group who would naturally transition themselves out of addiction and into "conventional" life, though by precisely what mechanisms remained unclear.[92]

These findings aligned with larger belief systems inside the FBN and CPD (or pockets of both, at least) which posited that the problems of the young black heroin addict had less to do with the "heroin addict" part than with the "young black" one. In its final estimation, this group of analysts—comprising some of the most influential minds and antidelinquency organizations in the city—said that the most effective way to deal with the problem was not through an attack on the supply or through a comprehensive treatment program. Rather, it was to attack what they perceived as a *cultural problem among black people.* The only way to fight addiction, as they saw it, was by "altering the character of the adolescent street culture of the city's disorganized areas"—a euphemism, by that time, for primarily black Chicago.[93]

These sorts of findings reflected and reinforced ongoing law enforcement imperatives. By 1955 the police department's attention to the drug trade had grown monumentally. That year, the increasingly robust narcotics section preferred narcotics charges against 7,454 people—more than 97 percent of them for possession. The larger department around that section arrested still many thousands more on the same charges. And the police department's own data set demonstrates the profound degree to which drug enforcement was almost exclusively confined to black neighborhoods, with 86.6 percent of preferred charges listed as having been against "colored" persons.[94]

White Crimes Disappear: Honing in on Black Crime in the Punitive Turn

Chicago's early War on Drugs prefigured the drug war of the late twentieth century. Yet it was also illustrative of race and racism's operative role in the punitive turn that was taking place. It is true that the postwar heroin crisis in black Chicago was precisely that—a crisis. But for the first time, the city undertook widespread criminalization of drug addiction now that it was seen as a predominantly black problem. And even despite the fact that the heroin epidemic hit black neighborhoods the hardest, it is exceedingly difficult to look at arrest statistics and think that 87 percent of the city's drug users were black. (Similarly reflective of vice policing's racialization, that same year in which the CPD preferred 86.6 of its drug charges against "colored" persons, 84.5 of those arrested on gambling charges were black, too.[95])

In other words, what was significant was not so much the criminalization of drug addiction and other personal behaviors in the main. Instead, it was the degree to which selective enforcement was coming to govern how the CPD *approached* these personal behaviors. Or, to beg the question, is it possible that in an overwhelmingly majority-white city, white people were only 15 percent of the population that partook in gambling and drugs? As Khalil Muhammad asks in a different chronological context, "Where did all the white criminals go?"[96]

Where indeed? From the early 1950s to the early 1960s, the numbers of black arrests in the city grew by more than 150 percent. To be sure, part of that escalation was a product of demographic growth: it makes sense that as Chicago got blacker, arrest rolls did, too. But they still remained stunningly disproportionate; and just as significantly, white arrests began a slow disappearing act in the late 1950s. Indeed, consider this: although they went through periods of upward and downward flux, from their high point in 1953 to 2010, white arrest numbers in Chicago plummeted in the aggregate by a stunning 88 percent. Incredibly, the CPD only logs about fourteen thousand arrests of white people these days, meaning that while huge numbers of Chicago's black population are saddled with criminal records, it is extraordinarily difficult to be arrested while white in the Windy City.[97] While those decreases, too, flowed partly from demographic shifts (white people moved out to the suburbs in droves beginning in the 1950s), white flight doesn't get very far as an explanatory mechanism. To wit: late in the 1970s, white arrests were less than half of what they had been just twenty years earlier, which does not at all mirror population trends. Nor is it plausible to think that white Chicagoans magically decided to stop committing crimes.

Instead, what drove the racial divergence in arrests more than anything else was an increasing concentration by the CPD on black neighborhoods and on so-called black crime, which came at the expense of deemphasizing quality-of-life arrests in white neighborhoods. These patterns will become clearer in the next chapter, and they did not, of course, congeal overnight. It took time, and those emphases would be stabilized more in the 1960s and 1970s than they were in the 1950s. Nevertheless, they were central to the postwar punitive turn.

Beyond the drug war, much of this escalation took place in the second half of the 1950s, after Richard Daley's election. Although Timothy O'Connor had held a pretty miserable record as CPD commissioner during the final years of Martin Kennelly's mayoralty, when Daley took office in 1955, he somewhat inexplicably kept O'Connor on. This was an unusual move in a city where the police commissioner was a political appointee who had always served at the pleasure (or mercy) of the mayor. Most previous occupants of city hall had brought in their own police head. It seems likely that Daley kept O'Connor around because he felt that O'Connor—who had been appointed by another machine mayor and who appreciated the machine's workings—would be particularly pliable to the new mayor's demands and open to his visions for the CPD. And indeed, when Daley finally replaced O'Connor in 1960 because of a massive scandal within the CPD, a fiercely independent CPD detective named Jack Muller argued that O'Connor was "a commissioner in name only," with Daley ultimately overseeing the department.[98]

Regardless of why Daley kept O'Connor, together they undertook the process of dramatically expanding the power of the CPD. It wasn't just the thousands of new officers that Daley hired; nor was it O'Connor's relocation of officers to certain blocks and neighborhoods in response to the pleas of white constituents. It could also be seen in new policies and modes of social control. Sometimes this shift was so incremental as to be almost invisible for what it was. One example was the growing effort to control young Chicagoans, both in the CPD's expansion of its Juvenile Unit beginning two months after Daley took office, and in the expansion (which police encouraged) of the city's curfew laws to keep everyone under eighteen off the streets during the late-night and overnight hours.[99] These measures were seemingly banal to most observers at the time, but they had the effect of further embedding police control and surveillance of individuals' behavior—even behavior that was not in and of itself damaging. For a second-offense curfew violation, minors and their parents would be forced to appear in Family Court. And over time, some kids in the city's most disadvantaged neighborhoods amassed long criminal records comprised mostly of curfew violations, not crimes per se.[100]

Even more significant was the increasing amounts of power and discretion with which officers were invested. As Christopher Agee and others have noted, the late 1950s saw the issue of police discretion assume increasing prominence in discussions about the future of policing in America's cities, as officers acquired greater latitude to judge which laws to enforce and in what contexts.[101] Indeed, by the 1960s, criminologists and legal scholars were debating the appropriateness of such discretion, pointing out that, for better or worse, police officers were not simply *executors* of public policy but *crafters of it.*[102] Regardless, by the early 1960s, such discretion was commonplace in police departments in nearly all major locales across America.

Not until 1960 would that discretion be explicitly formulated as police policy in Chicago, but new inventions and methods in the second half of the 1950s were early predictors of what was coming. The most important piece of that story was O'Connor's implementation of the task force in 1956 (the new rapid-response team for which the GLCC had taken credit). The task force was the elaboration of Prendergast's special squads of the 1940s but expanded dramatically. It comprised a set of squads, eleven officers in each. One officer patrolled on a three-wheeled motorcycle. Nine more walked beats covering just three to six blocks each. And one designated sergeant commanded every ten-person squad. Rather than three individual squads, there were instead twenty, and a police captain and four lieutenants were charged with overseeing the whole enterprise. All told, the new unit comprised 225 members, who were detailed night after night to augment normal forces in "high crime" areas, with orders to "fight crime until it is knocked out."[103] Members of the task force shifted between different neighborhoods on any given night, bolstering the strength of regular patrols there on the ground. And it was black neighborhoods that they saturated, often paying particular attention to areas in which black people predominated but where whites still lived and exercised their political voice. An analysis by the police department in April 1958—reported on to much comment in the *Defender*—showed that black districts like Englewood, Woodlawn, Fillmore, and Lawndale had received task force visits at a rate twenty to twenty-eight times that of white neighborhoods.[104]

This was a fundamental shift in policing methods, and represented a transformed relationship between police and community. Despite tremendous friction between the police and the black community in recent years, police officers working the beats in black neighborhoods had previously at least generally become familiar with community members and various neighborhoods' social rhythms. Some black citizens, without question, saw officers as a repressive force, but at least they were knowable. Members of the task force, meanwhile, had no acclimation period to a neighborhood and no intimate knowledge of the people and place, instead policing citizens with whom they had no relationships whatsoever.

And they policed them in new and more aggressive ways. Constituting an opening wedge that would soon define much of the patrol work done in minority neighborhoods across Chicago, task force officers were invested with wide discretionary leeway: the nature of their assignments meant that the department expected them to decide for themselves who to target and how intensively. The most vital evidence of this was the task force's reliance on stop-and-seizure, soon to be rebranded as stop-and-frisk. Under their mandate from the department, task force officers assigned to cover neighborhoods like Lawndale would, on any particular night, set up a series of traffic stops in order to ensnare the greatest number of people passing through. When a vehicle would arrive at the stop, officers could direct the driver and any passengers to get out of the car, after which occupants would be frisked for weapons or drugs, and the cars would be searched. Passersby on the sidewalk were subject to receive the same treatment—stopped, frisked, and ultimately arrested if officers found anything illicit on their person.

Black Chicagoans recoiled in anger as these operations became standard practice in their neighborhoods. This was hardly the first time that black Chicagoans would accuse the police of racial harassment, but the new system amplified the intensity of such accusations exponentially. This was a law enforcement matter that galvanized an unusual cross-section of the black community across lines of class and social standing, for even black elites began to quickly appreciate, through bitter experience, the fact that their social station wouldn't shelter them from police harassment. Within weeks of the task force's formal implementation, the black-owned *Crusader* newspaper was offering to sponsor attorneys for black readers whose rights had been violated by the task force. "Our community is for good law enforcement," its editors wrote, "but for the life of us we can't see why policemen who are being paid out of the taxpayer's money must run roughshod over Negroes. Cars are stopped regardless of who you are [in black neighborhoods], lights flashed in the driver's face, he and his car is searched without a warrant. This is in violation of his or her rights."[105] Making few distinctions in terms of who they stopped, questioned, and searched—from preachers to panhandlers—task force missions, as a local attorney unguardedly put it, constituted "a definite violation of basic civil rights."[106]

It didn't matter. Even black elites and politicians were unable to meaningfully challenge these practices, illustrating once again the unresponsiveness of the police force and the broader political framework to black influences on the CPD. By early 1958, a black alderman, Sidney Jones, was receiving such strong pressure from his constituents concerning the task force's stop-and-seizure methods that he introduced an ordinance to the city council to stop the task force's "illegal searches." In defending Jones's ultimately doomed effort, members of the black press deployed the idiom of terrorism to talk about task force actions in the community. In an editorial published under the title "The task force Terrorists," for instance, the *Defender* compared Timothy O'Connor to a Soviet police chief, citing, among other things, that he "ignores the question of rights of citizenship and speaks only of the 'effectiveness' of the illegal searches." "The terroristic tactics of the task force," the editorial board continued, "particularly the public searching of a citizen who has been stopped for a minor traffic violation, represent a basic infringement on the right of citizenship and a threat to individual liberty. The object of curbing crime, as laudable as it is, does not justify such means, not in a democracy anyway."[107]

Despite accusations of terrorism, these methods would be deployed more and more expansively, well beyond the confines of the task force, within a few short years. They would bind tightly together, for black people, the experience of being *both* underprotected *and* overpoliced. Black middle-class individuals and even wealthy black professionals would increasingly find out that their class would not save them from a police department that took blackness of any sort as a signifier of suspicion. Increasing discretion brought increasing repression and did virtually nothing for protection.

A Question of Torture: Discretion, Detention, and the Third Degree

The problems with deferring to the discretion of individual police officers as they patrolled black streets were compounded by the fact that the department *still* had no ability to reign in illegal and unethical behavior by individual officers. Brutality and arbitrary harassment, of course, had been rampant for decades, and certainly continued. But, beginning in the late 1950s, Chicagoans began to confront a new problem, as the police department interpreted its discretionary latitude on a greater and greater scale. That problem was widespread illegal detention by the police.

Officially, Illinois state law required that prisoners be taken before a judge as soon as possible following their arrest by police. Yet under O'Connor, the CPD jettisoned any adherence to that law. Officers routinely detained people without charges for grueling periods under extraordinary duress. Arrestees faced multiday ordeals of being held incommunicado—no charges, no contact with the outside world. In 1957 alone, the Illinois ACLU reported that more than twenty thousand Chicagoans arrested annually were held in such circumstances for more than seventeen hours.[108] The situation was especially bad over weekends, when people would be brought in on Friday but wouldn't face a judge until the following Monday or Tuesday. Once they were arrested, their families had no way of knowing if their loved ones were alive, let alone where they were. It was entirely possible for people to be picked up by the police on their way home from work, and for their families to spend days and nights wondering what had happened to them. And it was, predictably, the poorest, blackest, and least politically connected members of society who had to deal with such practices most consistently.[109]

Beyond the psychological violence inherent in such practices, physical violence also frequently governed people's experiences while in police detention. Consider the case, for instance, of Jessie Mae Robinson, a black woman who owned the New South Park Record Store, whose story was recently recovered by the organizer and scholar Mariame Kaba. In 1959, Kaba writes, Robinson "was arrested, along with nearly fifty others, during a warrantless police raid of a party at a private home." CPD officers stole the beer from the party and took Robinson and the other party attendees to a station house in Englewood. There, while drinking the stolen beer, they subjected Robinson and the other women among the partygoers to "indignities" that included physical assaults so severe that they left Robinson hospitalized. No officers were disciplined.[110]

In the case of Robinson and the other women that officers assaulted that night, detention gave officers access to black women for purposes of either sexual gratification or, at the very least, the fulfillment of some other violent desire. In other cases, holding people in a state of prolonged detention served the more direct purpose of giving police extended access to suspects in order to extract confessions. This often meant physical and psychological abuse so severe that it essentially amounted to torture.

Beyond the terrifying ordeal of Jessie Mae Robinson and her compatriots, two high-profile cases at nearly opposite ends of the 1950s illustrate that point. In January 1952, Oscar Walden Jr., a twenty-one-year-old ironworker and minister, was accused of raping a white woman on the South Side. When police arrested him, they brought him in for three days' worth of illegal detention and interrogation, which included being threatened with rubber hoses and a hanging rope in the style of a lynching noose, and having the fingers on his hand bent so far back that, sixty years later, the physical damage to his hands still showed.[111] Walden was prosecuted on the basis of his own coerced confession that resulted from such treatment, and was sentenced to seventy-five years of incarceration. He subsequently appealed for a new trial on the basis of the physical and psychological terror that underpinned his confession, but the appeal was denied. Walden was sent downstate to the penitentiary and spent fourteen years behind bars before being paroled. Sixty years after the fact, in 2012, he finally received restitution from the city for the hardships he endured, to the tune of $950,000.[112]

Meanwhile, in the autumn of 1958, CPD officers raided the home of James Monroe in the dead of night. Led by Deputy Chief of Detectives Frank Pape (pronounced pap-AY), an officer infamous for his temper and violence, a cadre of officers broke down the family's front door, forced parents and children from their beds, and made them huddle in the living room (the adults both naked) while they searched the house. Pape slugged Monroe repeatedly in the stomach with his flashlight, hurling racial epithets at him. Other officers reportedly manhandled and kicked at least three of the children. They had no warrants, and refused requests to contact an attorney. Instead, they hauled Monroe to a district station, held him without access to lawyers for ten hours, and beat and interrogated him as a murder suspect in a case in which a white woman in the midst of an extramarital affair had killed her husband and told police that a black man had broken in and done it. (She and her lover would subsequently recant their story about a black man having been the killer, admitting that they'd done it to try to collect the husband's life insurance.)[113]

Monroe eventually sued the officers and the city of Chicago, seeking $200,000 in restitution for the various violations of the family's rights—his own wrongful arrest, the extensive time in lockup without contact with the outside world, the brutality and humiliation. His lawsuit was initially rebuffed on procedural grounds, with Chicago's corporation counsel arguing that "unlawful search and seizure, unjustified batteries, and unjustified secret detention" did not constitute a violation of the 1871 Civil Rights Act under which Monroe sought redress, and that he was therefore not entitled to file suit.[114] Undeterred, Monroe appealed all the way to the United States Supreme Court, where he won his case, *Monroe v. Pape* enshrining into law a citizen's rights to sue state agents like police officers (although the court denied Monroe's right to sue the city of Chicago itself).[115]

Even after James Monroe sued Pape, the twinned practices of illegal detention and torture continued to shape police practice in Chicago. In a 1960 exposé by John Bartlow Martin in the *Saturday Evening Post* investigating illegal detention and torture across the country, Martin pointed to Chicago as a place where the nexus of the two was particularly ferocious.[116] Based on information provided by the Chicago ACLU, Martin wrote that "the police, while holding [prisoners] incommunicado, extracted confessions from them by touching their genitals with an electric prodder, a metal rod which emits an electric shock and was devised for herding cattle."[117]

THROUGH THE CONSTRUCTION of this evermore racialized and evermore punitive police apparatus, as the 1950s closed, relationships between black Chicagoans and the police force around them had grown strained to the breaking point. Continuous warnings of brewing tensions were infused throughout late-1950s comments about the wages police abuse was reaping in the city's black neighborhoods. Prior to World War II, community opinions on matters of failing protection on the one hand, and overly punitive or aggressive policing on the other, had rarely occupied the same intellectual and experiential spheres. But during the 1940s and 1950s, that began to change, as black Chicagoans across lines of class came to understand that unsafe neighborhoods and police violence and abuse (of both bodies and power) were two sides of the same coin.

Combined with the tacit decriminalization of white antiblack violence, by the end of the fifties, who the police department best served was readily apparent. These facts placed black Chicagoans in the difficult position of wishing for more effective police protection, while at the same time knowing that expanding police power carried with it the risk of greater abuse. As the ACLU wrote in early 1959, "often police abuses are tacitly condoned because of general dissatisfaction with ineffective law enforcement," but increasingly and for wider cross-sections of black Chicago, the assessment of cost and reward was shifting away from such condoning.[118]

As for the police department itself, it exited the 1950s both bigger and substantially more powerful than it had been fifteen years earlier. Built on the back of political pressures, racial fears, reformist impulses, grassroots activism, and increasing discretion, Chicago's police politics turned increasingly punitive over the course of the late 1940s and, especially, during the 1950s. By the middle of the 1950s, black arrest figures began to jump sharply upward. In 1956 alone, the first year that the task force was put into place and the first full year of Daley's mayoralty, black arrests spiked by more than 31 percent, sparking an upward trajectory that remained largely uninterrupted for decades thereafter. Meanwhile, at roughly the same time, white arrests crested and began to fall, as the CPD shifted its focus to black areas and to policing black behavior more aggressively and single-mindedly. The results of these processes would take time to be borne out. But what the total picture shows is that the punitive turn began to unfold well before the 1960s, and that racial dissonance was its essence.

It thus likely struck black Chicago as a cruel irony that what undid the police regime that oversaw this turn was not any sort of racially abusive practice, but was instead the abject corruption of the CPD. At the outset of 1960, an embarrassing scandal of epic proportions hammered the department. In the autumn of 1959, a young man named Richard Morrison, the self-proclaimed greatest burglar in the world who had committed a string of extraordinary robberies in Chicago, was arrested by CPD officers and interrogated as to how he had managed to pull off so many heists of such great value. The answer was that he had been joined in his schemes by eight members of the police department operating out of the North Side Summerdale district, who would serve as lookouts before helping Morrison carry away contraband and cash, to later be divvied up between them. Morrison spilled his story to investigators in August 1959, but word of the "Summerdale scandal," as it came to be called, didn't hit the newsstands until January of the following year. When it did, it scandalized the city, and served as the last nail in Timothy O'Connor's professional coffin.[119]

How much of this was truly news to many Chicagoans is an open question, given police corruption's place as a Chicago tradition by this point. But to many black people, there would have been no great shock value in the revelations. Plenty of African Americans had been facing constant shakedowns—what amounted to petty robbery—by police officers stationed in their neighborhoods for years. The fact of widespread corruption and dereliction of duty, for innumerable reasons, would have come as no surprise.

But more insidiously, the contours of the Summerdale scandal were innocuous in comparison to what African Americans had been forced to contend with during recent years. In the coming decade, famous black writers and revolutionaries would begin to invoke the language of colonialism and occupation to describe the policing of black communities in America. But many black people had already arrived at that conclusion by the end of the fifties. The postwar CPD had been steeped in a departmental lineage that, as the *Defender* described it, considered "the Negro public," to be "separate and apart from the body politic."[120] It treated them in kind, adhering to an old ethic, dating back decades, that perceived African Americans as a suspect population. In particular, as the CPD's chief executive, O'Connor, the *Defender* wrote, "has won the unwelcome reputation of being generally hostile to Negroes, to programs to benefit them and dedicated to the proposition that all a Negro is good for is to be locked up wherever found."[121] Paraphrasing Langston Hughes from fifteen years earlier, the law had a bad opinion of black people.

This was the racial legacy of the punitive turn in Chicago, one that the CPD carried into the 1960s. The consequences of the turn would not become clear for years afterward, but it is impossible to understand what came next without understanding what transpired in this extended postwar moment. It was not for this reason that O'Connor was asked to resign his post, but handling an increasingly volatile relationship with the black community would presumably be a central component of his successor's job. And the coming decade, too, would be volatile.

CHAPTER 5

Occupied Territory

REFORM AND RACIALIZATION

rlando Wilson was a legend—one of the most respected criminologists and policing experts in American history. Bespectacled, pro-
fessorial, and gray-haired by the dawn of 1960, for several years he
had served as the dean of the School of Criminology at the University of California, Berkeley. The deanship was the culmination of
an illustrious career. He had previously headed the police departments of
Fullerton, California, and Wichita, Kansas, helped with the de-Nazification
of German police forces after World War II, and consulted on police reorganization efforts in more than a dozen cities. His textbooks on policing were
canonical in the field.[1] His star in criminal justice circles had risen so high
that he was rumored to be on the short list to replace J. Edgar Hoover as
head of the Federal Bureau of Investigation if ever Hoover vacated his post.[2]

In the early winter of 1960, Wilson came to Chicago as a well-paid consultant to help stabilize a reeling police department. Throughout the 1950s,
while the CPD stumbled from scandal to scandal, policing elsewhere had
been changing, spurred by criminologists like Wilson, new urban political leadership, and good-government reform movements. Though Robert
Merriam and other police reformers in Chicago had been stymied by the
Democratic machine and a recalcitrant CPD, most fifties-era criminologists
and reformers elsewhere across the country had talked incessantly of *professionalization* and *modernization*, and policymakers had listened. From
San Francisco to Milwaukee, mayors and city councils had begun to bend
police departments into something more befitting a twentieth-century city.

Richard Daley had held out for as long as he could—until Summerdale. Though hardly an aberration in the long arc of police corruption in Chicago, the new scandal was such a *public* embarrassment that changes to the department became unavoidable. Daley was forced to go along with a plan to seek out new leadership for the CPD, and to abide by the decisions of that new leadership. In January of 1960, he assembled a headhunting committee to find a new CPD commissioner, which hired Wilson as an expert consultant.[3] The committee spent most of February debating its options, but when none of their candidates impressed, Wilson himself began to look like the man for the job to the rest of the committee. After negotiating a hefty salary and securing Daley's agreement that he would have the freedom and flexibility to reform the department without mayoral interference, he agreed. His appointment was announced on February 23, and on March 2, he became the CPD's superintendent. (The city had to rename the position in order to get around residency requirements that were tied to the commissioner title.)[4]

Wilson would spend seven years heading the CPD. His administration was arguably the most significant in the department's history. Policing in Chicago got more professional, more sophisticated, more centralized, less politicized, and more disciplined under his leadership. Whereas most police officials in Chicago, especially in the post-1945 era, left office with a record full of black marks, Wilson not only was celebrated by much of Chicago upon his retirement but continued to be held up as a paragon of success for decades afterward. It is no exaggeration to say that Wilson changed policing in Chicago—fundamentally and permanently.

At the same time, Wilson's tenure was terrible for black Chicago. Though he emphasized the need to treat all citizens with respect, and implemented significant projects to improve community relations with racially marginalized communities, intentions mattered less than effects. Wilson was a stern law-and-order proponent who viewed police efficiency almost obsessively through prisms of citizen contact and arrest. Under his administration, the CPD formalized a program of "aggressive preventive patrol," taking some of the most invasive practices then in use in the CPD (most notably on the task force) and expanding them across patrol forces that worked minority neighborhoods. He also personally lobbied for a state law enshrining police officers' rights to stop-and-frisk; gave officers complete assurance that department resources would back them in illegal arrest accusations; expanded practices of neighborhood saturation; wrote numerous articles about police prerogatives and civil liberties that shaped the national and legal discourse in ways preferential to police; and more generally labored to expand the ambit of police powers. What all of this meant in practice

was the targeting of "high crime" and almost inevitably nonwhite neighborhoods for increasing police attention, and that the police who worked such
neighborhoods would focus on citizen contact and arrest, even for nonse-
rious offenses. Little of this was explicitly racial, but then again, it didn't
have to be. In the final analysis, Wilson's innovations systematically turned
previously informal police repression of the black community into *formal*
police department policy.

Wilson's regime coincided with two other transformative events in Chicago. One was the assortment of freedom struggles that coalesced there
over the course of the early and mid-1960s. Spearheaded by local activists
and later amplified by the work of national leaders and organizations like
Martin Luther King Jr. and his Southern Christian Leadership Conference
(SCLC), civil rights activists labored to try to improve black neighborhood
schools, win open housing, and improve the overall infrastructure of black
community areas. Meanwhile, more militant groups like the Deacons for
Defense served as early progenitors of Black Power politics that would take
center stage in the city by the end of the decade. And black protest exploded
in the form of two urban rebellions, as well—both fueled by frustration
and anger at chasmic social inequalities and eroding opportunities for a
decent life. In all their iterations, these freedom dreams challenged the police department's priorities and prerogatives. And at the same time, they
produced blowback from a law-and-order apparatus that sought to contain
and curtail them.

The other, and related, major process undergirding this part of the story
was the growth of youth gangs amid Chicago's full-blown urban crisis.
While the city budget for policing increased almost exponentially, resources
continued to erode for schools and other social goods. By the early 1960s,
gangs were becoming a feature of the environment in black neighborhoods,
drawing membership from young people who faced second-tier educational
opportunities and even worse career prospects. The geneses and goals of
those gangs took many forms, but by the end of the decade they were routinely embroiled in violence against one another. Small conflicts were amplified: a kid who feared violence in his neighborhood joined a gang because
it might help protect him from that violence, thus fueling a spiraling cycle of
recruitment and violence that in the 1970s and 1980s would claim the lives
of thousands of young black and brown men and women on the West and
South Sides. The only response offered by the city and nation was to send
in more and more and more police, but those officers were rarely able to do
much about actual public safety concerns.

The latter parts of that story will return in the final chapters of this book,
but they have important antecedents in the Wilson years. Most importantly,

in this moment, the entanglement of underprotection and overpolicing in black Chicago came to full fruition. As we have seen, those threads had long run through black Chicago's experience but were not truly systematized until the 1960s. During this decade, deeply punitive and heavily racialized policing became fully and explicitly institutionalized in Chicago. It has never left. And while Orlando Wilson is remembered for his dogged reformism and brilliant mind, this, too, is his legacy.

Promise and Peril: Reform, Power, and Race in the 1960s

Orlando Wilson arrived in Chicago to great fanfare, and black Chicago's leadership and media joined the celebration. Urban League Executive Secretary Edwin "Bill" Berry heralded Wilson's hiring as "the greatest thing for Chicago since the discovery of Lake Michigan"—a statement that, for all its strange hyperbole, was not unrepresentative.[5] The *Defender* went so far as to evoke the language of democratic renewal, seeing in Wilson's administration the coming of "a new deal . . . for Chicago and its law enforcement agency."[6]

   The effusiveness wouldn't last, but it was understandable. After the miserable relationships that black Chicago had had with Timothy O'Connor's department, it's likely that *any* new administrative blood would have signaled an improvement. Moreover, Wilson appealed to black Chicago by laboring to make the CPD more racially representative and a less hostile place for black people to work. Under Wilson's leadership, the department placed recruitment ads in the *Defender*; "enlisted black businessmen . . . to put recruiting posters in their windows; and provided assistance to black men in filling out applications to the department."[7] In his first two years alone, Wilson hired five hundred new black patrolmen, bringing their total number to 1,200—still underrepresented but nearly double previous numbers.[8] He also pushed for integrated patrol squads and sought to distribute black personnel across the city—an important symbolic demonstration of black officers' rights to police white people.

   Wilson also sought to bring police and community into closer dialogue. Black intellectuals and activists across the country spent the 1960s describing police departments as occupying forces within black communities; perhaps the most famous of those articulations came at the end of the decade from Black Power acolytes and radical intellectuals like Angela Davis and Huey Newton, but James Baldwin and other writers made that same case even earlier. Wilson understood that police–black community dynamics were riven with mistrust and frustration, and he hoped to counteract the impression of police officers as aloof, disconnected, and abusive. Most

famously, he oversaw the implementation of the "Officers Friendly" program, in which neighborhood police officers were tasked with being liaisons
to schoolchildren in order to cultivate a vision of the police as fundamentally good and sympathetic allies.[9] He similarly established Community
Relations Workshops, which were intended to be spaces in which police
and citizens could discuss pressing matters and engage one another in dialogue.[10] He also bolstered the police academy's civil rights training, working
in collaboration with the CCHR and the National Conference of Christians
and Jews to train officers on the "psychology of prejudice," "myths about
race," and the various problems of racism in Chicago.[11] Such moves were
intended to strengthen bonds of trust between department and community,
in the hopes that doing so would make for more cooperative publics and
easier work for officers. They were gestures at community engagement that
no previous administration had even thought to attempt.

Such efforts were only a sliver of Wilson's wider agenda. He tried to make
police hiring and promotions more merit-based, and convinced Daley to
implement a nonpartisan police board to oversee major administrative
changes within the department.[12] A strong believer in technology's benefits,
he utilized innovative new communications and intelligence methods, and
expanded officers' report-writing and organizational expectations. He expanded radio capacities, citing the steep reduction of what had once been
two- to three-hour delays in police response time because of radio-induced
backlogs.[13] All these things, in theory, would make the CPD more effective
and responsive to the public.

At the same time, Wilson also looked to further expand police powers.
This was an uphill climb, in some respects. During the first half of the 1960s,
Earl Warren's Supreme Court offered several key decisions that expanded the
rights of criminal suspects and, by extension, seemed to curtail the power
that police officers had over those suspects. In 1961 the court established in
Mapp v. Ohio that evidence obtained via unreasonable search and seizure
was inadmissible to state court proceedings. (It was already inadmissible at
the federal level.) Three years later, it enshrined suspects' rights to counsel
during police interrogations in *Escobedo v. Illinois*—a case that originated
with Chicago police officers repeatedly denying counsel to a murder suspect
and interrogating him for fourteen and a half hours until he implicated
himself. And two years later, the 1966 *Miranda v. Arizona* decision established the requirement that police officers inform suspects of their rights to
an attorney, and to remain silent in order to avoid self-incrimination.

For his part, Wilson loathed these decisions, routinely and publicly laying
out defenses of more, not less, expansive police power. In a 1960 article published in the *Journal of Criminal Law and Criminology* under the unsubtle

title "Police Arrest Privileges in a Free Society: A Plea for Modernization," Wilson urged the "liberalization" of "police arrest privileges," arguing that expanding police power was a boon for American liberty because it would counteract supposedly rising rates of crime that were making people unsafe. He called for legislation that would legalize "common police practices" like stop-and-frisk, and for enhanced police prerogatives to detain without formal arrest anyone who was "unable or unwilling to explain satisfactorily the reasons for his presence and actions" if an officer deemed either "suspicious."[14]

Over the next few years, Wilson repeated and expanded this view. In November of 1962, he delivered an address to a conference of police officials, lawyers, and legislators at Northwestern University that was subsequently reprinted in its entirety in the *Journal of Criminal Law and Criminology*. There, he lodged an even stronger condemnation of the judiciary's turn toward civil liberties protections and enforcement of the exclusionary rule in prior years. "I plead only for the rule of reason," he concluded. "Let the police have the authority to do what the public expects them to do in suppressing crime."[15] He repeated the argument many times in public addresses and local and national media interviews alike.[16] The rights of crime victims should be paramount, police prerogatives should be protected, and the "philosophy of excuse" by which the Warren Court and the ACLU washed away the sins of sinners was an ethically dubious burden holding law enforcement back.

More expansive police power was, then, the sine qua non to Wilson's vision of a properly functioning society. As in his public writings, in private meetings with his central staff, he lamented "the restrictions that [had] been placed on the police in recent years," and strategized ways to work around them.[17] At the center of his philosophy on this front was implementing what was known as "aggressive preventive patrol." Described by Wilson as the "largest manpower investment" of the CPD by the mid-1960s, aggressive preventive patrol's goal was to provide "constant surveillance of every corner of the city," and its guiding principle lay in "putting the police officer in the location and at the time the criminal is most likely to be there."[18] The city was divided by need into large numbers of small beats, each of which would be worked by a patrol car. In high-crime neighborhoods, that presence was augmented by plainclothes police in unmarked cars, patrolling officers walking on foot, and the ever-growing number of officers employed on the task force.

Arrests were the strategy's entire point, at least in the short term en route to long-term public safety. Internal CPD communications made clear that success was measurable most clearly in the number of arrests officers made.

Whereas police departments, in Chicago and elsewhere, have long denied the existence of quota systems for arrests, the contradictory evidence is fairly clear. In 1961 Wilson and his administrative circle discussed measuring patrolmen's effectiveness based on the number of stops and arrests they made.[19] And three years later, his chief of patrol, fed up with officers "dragging their heels," reported the development of a new "arrest report by star number and it is hoped that this will have an effect in increasing the number of arrests that are made."[20]

These arrest quotas were implemented in predictably uneven ways. The CPD explicitly identified certain areas "of selective enforcement" and confined its arrests-as-success metrics to them, the premise being that interacting with more people in high-risk areas would lead to less crime there.[21] The actual criminal inclinations of the people with whom they interacted were of no apparent consequence. Whereas officers on foot patrol in the Loop were there "to answer questions, furnish directions, and keep automobile and foot traffic flowing in an orderly fashion," the officers in areas like that around Sixty-Third and Stony Island in black Woodlawn were there more "because of the nature of its habitués than because of the value of the property."[22] This was, in other words, a difference in policing styles that was so fundamental as to be almost occupational. And as theories about "the nature of . . . habitués" in black neighborhoods suggested, race determined the difference.

Part and parcel to this was the practice of stop-and-frisk. In the early sixties, the practice sat in legal limbo at both the state and federal levels, but this was of no consequence to Wilson. In May 1961, he visited the Woodlawn police station to instruct patrolmen there to get more "aggressive" in what was then still being called "stop and search."[23] He was there principally because some officers had expressed reservations about the practice because they feared legal repercussions for using it. Wilson reassured them, and instructed them to continue to conduct intensive field interrogations, stop and search "suspicious persons," and make on-view arrests for even minor infractions.[24] If citizens sued, Wilson promised that officers would have the department's full resources backing them.[25]

He also pressed to resolve the legal questions surrounding the practice. It's a misconception that police simply enforce laws as they are; rather, they routinely define the very nature and word of those laws. During his tenure, Wilson lobbied on multiple fronts to get stop-and-frisk codified into law. In 1963 he went before the Illinois State and Chicago Bar Associations to make his case, and by the 1965 biennial legislative session, he had recruited Daley, drawing the Democratic kingmaker into alignment with conservative Republicans from Chicago's white North Shore, the Fraternal Order of

Police (FOP), and the Police Benevolent and Protective Association.[26] The bill passed both legislative chambers, only to be vetoed by the liberal governor Otto Kerner (future head and namesake of the Kerner Commission on Civil Disorders) on the grounds that it was unconstitutional.

In his lobbying, Wilson framed stop-and-frisk as a commonsense measure with minimal social costs but said little about the intrusions into personal space and bodily integrity that are its essence. Examples of the violation are legion: Milton Davis, running to his car one night in Chatham when three plainclothes CPD officers yelled for him to stop and searched him and two friends under pretense of "looking for contraband." The officers found nothing, hauled them to a police station anyway, and wrote Davis a ticket for driving with out-of-state license plates.[27] Or consider M. Zimbalist Hayes III, who officers stopped on the street in February 1966. The officers refused to say why they were stopping him, other than that he fit the description of someone who had "robbed a store in the area." When he declined to give his name and address, officers brought him to the station without explanation.[28] White social justice worker Mike James, stopped and threatened with a beating by Uptown police officers, was asked whether he wanted his "mother to fuck for niggers."[29] Montgomery Williams and Karen Herter, a black man and white woman, were stopped together and searched on charges that made no sense by CPD officers who verbally and physically abused them.[30] Williams recalled that the officers clearly loathed the interracial couple.

Understanding the damage and risk that stop-and-frisk promised, black Chicago balked at Wilson's efforts to codify it into law. As a South Side saleswoman told the *Defender*, "If this proposal ever became the law in Illinois, it would lead to infringements of the rights of individuals and would result in the practice of shaking down innocent people."[31] Another commenter to the *Defender* asked: "Can anyone imagine Sen. Percy or Sen. Dirksen [both white supporters of the bill] being stopped and frisked? Solid citizens of the black community are constantly undergoing this experience. The proposed laws are simply seeking to legalize these procedures before they are challenged in court."[32] Similarly, every member of the state legislature's black caucus voted against stop-and-frisk. House member and future Chicago mayor Harold Washington commented, "One thing that most of our white friends do not understand is that measures like 'stop and frisk' in practice are seldom applied in the larger white communities. They are used only against Negroes, Puerto Ricans, Appalachian whites, the uneducated and uninformed."[33] The ACLU agreed, noting that those most likely to be affected by stop-and-frisk were people living in "the south and west side ghettos, the Division Street Latin-American area and the uptown Southern-white area."[34]

But Wilson was undaunted. In contravention of Kerner's 1965 veto, Wilson issued a formal directive for CPD officers to continue to use stop-and-frisk, as did district commanders "until the Supreme Court declared it illegal." Wilson and Daley continued to push, and the measure passed the legislature again in 1967 before Kerner once more vetoed it. But in 1968, Kerner moved on to a federal post. The political groundswell of support for stop-and-frisk won out, and Kerner's successor, Samuel Shapiro, signed it into law soon after taking office.[35] The same year, the United States Supreme Court settled the question for the time being anyway, validating stop-and-frisk as constitutional in *Terry v. Ohio*.

On Liberty: The Harm Principle and the Mendacity of Crime Stats

Wilson's body of work in Chicago was part of a larger shift across the country, in which reformers sought to modernize and professionalize police departments, bending them into more effective public resources. One piece of that shift was the turn by politicians and police administrators toward organizing policing practices around what's known as the *harm principle*. The concept comes from the philosopher John Stuart Mill's *On Liberty*, in which, describing a framework for behavioral regulation and punishment, Mill wrote that "the only purpose for which power can be rightfully exercised over any member of a civilized community, against his will, is to prevent harm to others."[36] Applied to the police, this meant that officers should deemphasize crimes without victims, and focus instead on crimes that bore real jeopardy toward others.[37]

Wilson was at the vanguard of most midcentury policing innovations, but he saw little merit to harm principle policing in "at-risk" black and brown neighborhoods, where every infraction could be seen as an opening wedge to something worse. To be sure, Wilson understood the economic and social plights confronting black Chicago. But accepting causal explanations for even minor crimes in his mind only ensured that "crime will continue to rise."[38] Directly anticipating by two decades the infamous "broken windows" theory of policing popularized in the 1980s by James Q. Wilson and George Kelling, Wilson argued by act, if not always by word, that the way to deal with crime at the neighborhood level was to aggressively police any and all infractions, no matter how small.[39] Where the harm principle effectively recommended that police officers nullify laws that they deemed harmless, aggressive preventive patrol—practically unique to black and brown neighborhoods in these years—demanded that officers pursue heavy punishment.

This aggressive (and racially selective) crime control policy was justified on the basis of exploding crime rates. But the explosion was more chimerical than real. When he took over the CPD, Wilson revolutionized the collecting and reporting of crime statistics—most importantly, by reporting *attempted* crimes rather than simply *executed* crimes. Intellectually, this made sense; citizens were likely interested in crimes attempted as well as crimes successfully completed—particularly those of a serious nature. But even Wilson acknowledged that that shift produced a crime panic. At the beginning of 1961, the *Tribune* reported that 1960 crime rates had jumped by 90 percent from the previous year.[40] And while the paper emphasized that this was due to new reporting metrics, the public was nevertheless alarmed. Speaking before the American Society of Criminology at the end of 1961, Wilson admitted that while the spiking crime rates were "due only to accurate crime reporting . . . one still has the problem of convincing the public that this is so."[41]

Wilson wasn't prone to intentionally provoking or exploiting public fear about crime. That said, it worked to his advantage to have artificially inflated crime rates as a baseline from which to build support for his new programs. On the one hand, when citizens *thought* crime was rising, they were more likely to support and demand strong police action. This was what happened in places like Kenwood and Hyde Park during the 1950s, and it increasingly unfolded on the citywide level, too. On the other hand, when Wilson's CPD chipped away at those inflated statistics, bringing the crime rate down incrementally from unnaturally high rates, it implied that his strategies were working. Indeed, when the *Tribune* reported dropping crime rates throughout the autumn months of 1961, Wilson expressed deep satisfaction in the effectiveness of his programs.[42]

Crime stats and the police response thus entered a feedback loop. Wilson reinvented the methodology of crime reportage, creating an artificial spike in crime rates. Public fears of crime crested, causing support for police action. Such police action, here in the form of aggressive preventive patrol, was implemented simultaneously with the new crime reportage systems. In turn, because the crime statistics were inflated to begin with, once they began falling, they appeared to prove the effectiveness of that police action.

And although Wilson was outwardly racially moderate, the explicitly racist logic of these policies is seared into the historical record. Given the larger racial dynamics at play in 1960s Chicago, the CPD trod cautiously, and there was little public talk among the police of blackness as innately problematic. Internally, it was a different matter. The vague talk of targeting suspicious persons, and the specific locations where newly aggressive patrol methods were implemented, were two barely concealed examples. But the clearest one was found in a confidential memorandum that circulated within the CPD in late 1964 or early 1965. Ostensibly a scientific forecasting of crime rates for the remainder of the decade, the memo was a testament to how theories about race and criminality remained operative in this new reform age. Jammed with charts and graphs, the long memo interwove crime statistics and predictive population forecasts to argue that Chicago was on the verge of a crime crisis. While superficially concerned with three racial demographic groups—blacks, Puerto Ricans, and Appalachian whites—the report dispatched with analysis of the latter two almost immediately. In a police worldview that was literally rendered in black and white, it noted that Puerto Ricans' effect on crime was "vague and inconclusive because their identity is submerged in the general white race category" for both population counts and crime statistics. Instead, the memo focused on the demographic group that the CPD *could* pick out statistically—"Negroes."[43]

Its premise was this: between 1964 and 1970, the combination of a growing black population and declining white one would produce major spikes in "criminal activity trends." Although crime rates across Chicago had been falling up to this point, the authors looked to rising crime rates in black neighborhoods and extrapolated. This was the feedback loop in action, and it had profound effects on policy. The report concluded that the rising tide of black people—young black people, especially—would yield "an increase of 20.2% in major crimes from 1964 to 1970. An equal increase in minor offenses can be anticipated." Those forecasts served as the basis for the department to request still more muscular surveillance and punishment. Claiming that the police had "nearly exhausted every resource of supervision and management in containing present criminal activity," the report concluded that only a 20 percent "augmentation" of the department's current strength would give Chicago a chance of weathering the coming criminal storm.[44]

Chicago's political class complied with gusto. Following the CPD's recommendation of a 20 percent increase in its strength, from 1965 to 1970, the department's total personnel grew by 19.89 percent, from slightly over 13,300 to slightly less than 16,000. The number of patrolling officers—on the frontlines of aggressive preventive patrol—increased by a full 25 percent, from just more than 7,000 to just over 9,000.[45] But even those numbers paled in comparison to the city's newfound financial investment in the department. Over those same years—in half a decade—the police department's budget appropriation from the city fully *doubled*, growing from slightly over $90 million in 1965 to more than $190 million in 1970.[46] Thus, while the urban crisis wreaked havoc on black Chicago's educational infrastructure, housing markets, and employment sectors, the one major investment that Daley and the city council continued to make into those neighborhoods was to send in more police.

This resonated with larger crime control politics nationwide. At the local level, city police budgets exploded across the United States throughout the 1960s and 1970s much like Chicago's had.[47] And at the federal level, under the presidential administrations of John F. Kennedy and Lyndon Johnson, the federal crime control apparatus expanded rapidly, setting in motion programs and policies that profoundly altered Washington's entanglements with state and local carceral systems. This was especially true of Johnson, who in 1965 famously declared a "War on Crime" that, the historian Elizabeth Hinton persuasively argues, set the United States on track to being the world's leading incarcerator. Through the Law Enforcement Assistance Administration (LEAA), the federal government began providing direct aid to states and cities to bolster their law enforcement efforts, personnel, and technology. When Richard Nixon won the White House in 1968 on the back of calls for law and order, he dramatically expanded the amount of money flowing into the LEAA, and by the time of his impeachment in 1974, the agency's budget was more than $871 million.[48] Against that backdrop, it's not at all surprising that Chicago began dumping increasing resources into policing. Although Johnson had envisioned the War on Crime as an accompaniment to his War on Poverty, it was becoming clear by the end of the 1960s that the national political temperature was tilting steeply toward punishment.

But pointing out that the sharp increase in the CPD's personnel and budget coincided with the launch of the War on Crime doesn't mean it happened *because of* it. Indeed, the immediate impacts of LEAA funds on the CPD were actually fairly small. The information here is fragmented, but for the two-year period from July 1969 to June 1971, for example, total LEAA grants to the city of Chicago amounted to a little more than $7.6 million, or an average of $3.8 million annually.[49] Certainly less than all of that was directed toward the CPD, since LEAA monies also went toward facilities construction and other projects. But even if every dime of those dollars went to the CPD, it still would have represented less than 2 percent of the CPD's total budget. And while federal block grants to cities would become exponentially more important during the mid-1970s, even those could not account for the department's budgetary growth.

The point is not that the invention of the LEAA didn't matter. It did. The point, rather, is that the advent of the War on Crime and the federal punitive turn don't explain what was happening at the local level. Chicago had been on an increasingly racialized punitive trajectory for years by the time the War on Crime began. And when it *did* begin, the CPD was already doing all the things that people generally think of when they think of police repression: indiscriminate (and, at the same time, discriminatory) stopping of people of color, invasive searches, neighborhood saturation, aggressive quality-of-life policing (in opposition to the harm principle), and so on. It is, in other words, hard to make a case that the War on Crime made policing demonstrably worse for black Chicago, even though it did shape a larger punitive context in which sentencing policies and judicial practices would send people to prison for less and for longer.

Meanwhile, as the CPD escalated its own war on crime, virtually the only thing that it accomplished was the steep amplification of black arrest figures—not the prevention of crime. Between 1958 (the last year prior to Wilson's arrival for which data is available) and 1967, black arrests rose nearly 65 percent, increasing by more than fifty thousand in less than a decade. Over that same period, disorderly conduct arrests, a catchall misdemeanor charge that roped in many of those arrested for minor public order infractions, ballooned by nearly 165 percent.[50]

Moreover, from the start of Wilson's term until 1965, even the police department acknowledged that serious crime was *declining* in the Windy City, at the same time that it was enacting tougher policies and seeking expanded power.[51] Statistics from the time, in fact, offer precisely no causal relationship between escalating arrests and safer streets; indeed, any statistical relationship that existed at all was a negative one. In 1965 Wilson trumpeted to Daley that aggressive preventive patrol was finally blanketing the street to unprecedented levels.[52] And it was that year that violent crime began to rise in Chicago, after having held roughly steady from 1958 to 1965. In Wilson's final years in office, when aggressive preventive patrol and all its attending invasions and violations were firmly in place, murders jumped by nearly 40 percent in Chicago, with black neighborhoods experiencing most of the terror.[53] When black citizens talked about being both overpoliced and underprotected, this is what they meant.

Orlando Wilson's War: The Rank-and-File Revolt

Despite Wilson's successful efforts to empower the officers under his command in their day-to-day operations, his relationship to his subordinates was a strange one. When he took over the department, he acknowledged both publicly and privately that it was a mess, at one point calling the task of fixing the Chicago police "the greatest job facing law enforcement in the United States and perhaps in the world today," and telling the Illinois State

Legislature that many people thought the job was "impossible without divine guidance."[54] In a surprisingly candid interview the summer after his hiring, he told reporters that the CPD's "quality of personnel" was a major concern, and estimated that there were enough bad police in Chicago that it would be "a generation" before the city had "the department that it deserves."[55]

He thus undertook a sweeping reformation of the department's personnel structure, as part of his larger reform effort. As a symbolic gesture in acknowledgment of the problematic optics, he relocated the superintendent's office out of its home adjacent to the mayor's office in city hall, and into police headquarters. He extricated (or tried to extricate) the department from its decades-long entanglement with the Democratic Party machine by redrawing police district lines so they no longer conformed with political boundaries, and by forcing district commanders to report directly to him, rather than to local aldermen and party committeemen.[56] He also cut the number of districts substantially and recalibrated lines of communication to make the system more hierarchical, lamenting that previously, the city had had something closer to thirty-nine individual police departments because of the number and organization of the districts.[57] He fired all seven of Tim O'Connor's deputy commissioners, and called for new promotional exams to try to bring new blood into the higher ranks. And most controversially in terms of the department's internal dynamics, he established an Internal Investigations Division (IID) to root out police misconduct and corruption, removing that task from the purview of the Civil Service Commission, where it had always floundered.

What these reforms amounted to was an effort on Wilson's part to bring greater accountability to the department. Shortly after taking over, he made his first big introduction to the rank and file at two massive gatherings of CPD personnel at the Chicago Amphitheater (half the department personnel at a morning gathering, half at an evening one). He delivered a long speech in which he declared his intentions to "increase the effectiveness of the Chicago Police Department as a great crime fighting machine" and "increase its effectiveness in providing services to the general public." But he also told them, memories of Summerdale doubtlessly bouncing off the room's walls, that "a little reflection on your part will make it clearly apparent that the real reason that I am here is to deal with the small number of elements within the department who have brought disgrace to this great police force." He appealed to their pride, making repeated references to the public shame associated with being a CPD officer in that moment. And he spurned the department's traditional efforts "to cover up, to excuse, to deal with these recalcitrant [officers] in a manner dissimilar to the manner in which the offender would be dealt with were he a private citizen. When the police do not deal forthrightly with recalcitrant members in their own midst, the public reaches the conclusion that the police condone the act."[58]

The reception was frosty. Wilson's arguments doubtlessly appealed to many CPD officers; but those complicit in organized crime, or who frequently took bribes and shook down citizens, had clear investments in the old order. Even those who labored within the confines of the law were accustomed to a particular status quo and a way of doing police work that Wilson's massive overhaul threatened. Many had grown comfortable within the CPD's established culture, and resented Wilson for his actions, tone, and outsider standing. The solidarities between officers and the department's punishing insularity (the famous "blue curtain") were designed to protect "against inquiry by anyone who did not himself rise through the ranks"—which Wilson, the bookish California transplant, had not.[59] Given that context, as the crime commission's Virgil Peterson put it, "Anyone familiar with local conditions knew at the outset that *any* reorganization program would be fought tooth and nail by a large number of officers on the force."[60]

And fight they would. The 1960s are justifiably famous for conflict between the forces of law and order on the one hand and social dissidents on the other. But in Chicago, there was also tremendous upheaval *inside* the police department. Indeed, the staunchest challenge to Wilson's policies in the first few years of his administration actually came not from activist citizens or civil liberties groups but from within his own department.

The revolt started within weeks of Wilson's hiring, and was led by the Chicago Patrolmen's Association (CPA). The largest of Chicago's police organizations at the time (they would not formally unionize until later), the CPA had long served primarily as an advocate for better pay and benefits for CPD officers. But during the early 1960s, it recast itself as a fierce opponent of oversight and accountability. The CPA's assault on Wilson's reforms was fronted by the organization's president, Frank Carey—a beefy, bespectacled man with twenty-five years of service under his belt. Carey loathed Wilson, ridiculing the superintendent incessantly on everything from his bookishness to his outsider status.

But nothing bothered Carey and those he represented quite like the implementation of the IID. As even Wilson's top subordinates admitted, officers were unaccustomed to entertaining questions about their authority, and the idea of a powerful review system chafed.[61] It suggested a lack of faith in officers from the department's top brass, as well as an infringement on their professional prerogatives. Throughout Wilson's first year in office, the CPA launched rhetorical grenades against Wilson and the IID, with the conflict finally boiling over in the spring of 1961 when CPA members literally

threw a mayoral representative out of a rally when he tried to speak in support of the IID. Afterward, Carey refused to submit to questioning from superiors about the incident. Instead, he sharply criticized Wilson in front of
television cameras that broadcast those criticisms across Chicago. He also
covertly traveled to Wichita, Kansas, to try to drum up dirt on Wilson from
his time heading that city's police department.[62]

Carey had a particularly intense personal hatred for Wilson, but he was
no rogue agent. If anything, he was significantly more popular than the
superintendent among the rank and file. A month after the CPA's expulsion
of the mayor's representative from the IID meeting, Carey was brought to
trial before the Civil Service Commission on charges of insubordination
and conduct unbecoming an officer. In response, his supporters mobilized,
gathering nine thousand signatures from police officers and their spouses
supporting Carey, while the CPA flirted with the idea of holding a massive
rally in the Loop on his behalf. The *Tribune* said that the conflict gave "the
impression that the Chicago police force is close to mutiny."[63] Meanwhile,
at his trial, Carey's CPA-funded attorney called Wilson as an adverse witness, unsuccessfully tried to goad him into making a truce with Carey from
the witness stand, and in closing arguments described him as "tyrannical."
Carey lost the trial and was suspended for sixty days. His response was to
call for Wilson's resignation.[64] Tellingly, a year later, he was reelected as CPA
president. His supporters literally hoisted him onto their shoulders triumphantly after the votes were counted.[65]

Wilson generally prevailed in the setting of policy, despite such resistance,
but that did not make these conflicts a footnote. Beyond what they indicated
about officers' reticence to be held accountable, they more broadly represented police organizations' growing power to resist reformation—even internally, even from the uppermost echelons.[66] In recent years, police unions'
power to resist reform and oversight has come under increasing scrutiny
from journalists and activists, with authors in the *Atlantic*, the *New York
Times*, and elsewhere exploring the negative social impacts of police unions'
reactionary self-protectionism.[67] As the headline of one such column reads,
this from the *New Yorker*, "Why are police unions blocking reform?"[68] But
the logic of that question is muddied by the fact that blocking reform has
been a part of police unions' DNA for decades. The CPD's rank and file would
not officially unionize until 1980, in part because of ambivalence about official union standing from many officers, and in part because unionization
efforts faced strong resistance from city policymakers and departmental
administrators (Orlando Wilson and Richard Daley among them).[69] But after
spending the 1950s as generally weak entities that bent to the will of city
hall, in the 1960s and 1970s, the antecedents to official unions sought not

only to improve officers' pay and benefits but also to preserve or expand officers' autonomy, public standing, and power.

This trend wasn't confined to the CPA, either. Indeed, during the 1960s and 1970s, a number of police organizations fought each other for membership, and the CPA lost significant ground—first to the Chicago Confederation of Police (COP), and then to the Fraternal Order of Police (FOP), which is today the primary police union in Chicago.[70] And all of them, despite their disagreements, hated police oversight. They likened internal investigatory units to Orwell's "Big Brother," employed the ACLU to defend officers' due process rights in internal investigation cases (an unlikely alliance given the ACLU's record fighting police harassment and violence), and joined the CPD's upper administration in rejecting out of hand a civilian review board that would have investigatory powers over brutality cases.[71]

In the 1960s the matter they were most concerned with, however, was the IID. It had been Frank Carey's obsession, and rank-and-file members had loved him for it. The obsession was more philosophical than practical, however; from the outset, the IID was so ineffective as to make officers have little to fear. Nominally organized to investigate corrupt police officers in a famously corrupt police department, its investigators failed to discover a single instance of corruption during the first five months of its existence. Wilson publicly interpreted this as a signal of the decline of malfeasance.[72] But even if he believed it at the time, it would soon be evident even to him that the system wasn't working. In the early 1960s, Chicago's FBI office routinely cataloged information on police officers who maintained affiliations with organized crime syndicates. Vincent Inserra, who worked in the field office for years, recalled that, in 1963, Wilson had a chance meeting with United States Attorney General Robert Kennedy, who informed him that the bureau had compiled serious and compromising information on several dozen officers inside Wilson's department. Wilson requested a fuller report, which "listed twenty-nine police officers reportedly on the payroll of the Chicago mob," including a number of high-ranking CPD officials. Wilson showed the document to Daley, who dismissed it as "gossip, rumor, and innuendos" and "pretty vicious."[73] Wilson enjoyed more autonomy from Daley than his predecessor or successor, but such a response meant that the report was going nowhere.

Indeed, although Wilson's reputation as a maverick crime crusader has persisted in Chicago's public mind, the steep level of corruption within the CPD eventually wore him down. *Life* magazine published a profile of the CPD and Wilson shortly after his retirement which made it clear that, between the 1963 FBI report and other evidence that came to the fore during his tenure, Wilson simply had to concede that he couldn't fully control the people under his command.[74] The profile highlighted a joint raid by

FBI and Red Squad officers on a South Side gambling operation's headquarters that produced, among other things, a list of 469 CPD officers who had taken bribes. That number was stunning, but it was of a piece with the larger pattern of corruptions that Wilson was powerless to stop. By his own and other accounts, he left office proud of most of his record, but officer discipline and accountability remained elusive. As *Life* reported, "Leaving Chicago, Wilson spoke about his inability to cope with the crime syndicate. . . . Nor, he added, had he been able to eradicate corruption on the police force."[75]

The primary reason it wasn't working, various activists and organizations argued, was because police couldn't be relied on to investigate—and punish, if necessary—other police. Bernard Weisberg of the ACLU wrote to Wilson in 1965 that the public was naturally suspicious of the IID "because the situation is one in which the accused (police officers) investigate themselves (i.e. through other police officers). Such natural suspicions could be allayed only if the public were given some means of ascertaining for itself that investigations of brutality complaints are in fact conducted with impartiality."[76] Indeed, the general consensus was that the IID was more concerned with optics and public impressions than police misconduct. According to black CPD sergeant Earl Davis, an IID officer for five years, the IID's entire model was shaped by "purposeful and deliberate malfeasance." The division, he reported, devoted "75% of the effort and time to window dressing which protects the police image in the eyes of the public." For all intents and purposes, the IID served as "an eyewash operation not vitally concerned with changing improper police behavior or serving the public interest." Researchers from the University of Chicago–based Center for Studies in Criminal Justice concurred.[77] So, too, did the ACLU, whose independent reviews of IID practices showed IID officers essentially bending over backward to look past evidence of officer guilt, to rule in favor of acquittal.[78]

Thus, in the public mind, while the IID existed on paper, its raison d'être seemed to be placating the public by sheer fact of its being, not to do anything about officer misconduct. And even though Wilson seemed to privately understand that it wasn't effective, he adhered to the common thought among law enforcement officials that the public couldn't be trusted to oversee police conduct.

"Nigger, I Will Kill You": Race and the Problem of Police Violence

Black Chicagoans had the most to lose when accountability mechanisms failed. The policy of aggressive preventive patrol encouraged officers to view the public with intense suspicion in the neighborhoods where it was

implemented; and recognizing the inversion of normative law, citizens remarked that "the police treat suspects as guilty until proven innocent."[79]
Aggressive preventive patrol unleashed a police regime premised in hypersurveillance and constant contact with citizens, and the failure of the IID
meant that there was no corresponding policy mechanism in place to ensure that expanded power was coupled with expanded accountability.

This was a problem for many reasons, not least of them the fact that police officers' opinions about black people were demonstrably retrograde by
the 1960s. We can see the legacies of racist logics about black criminality
in the CPD's crime forecasts and budget requests, of course, but they were
also there in even plainer view. Hard data on racial attitudes is always complicated, and it's nonexistent for the first part of the 1960s, even though in
1961 the CCHR reported serious "hostile attitudes toward Negroes" among
police recruits.[80] The picture clarifies later in the decade, however. Working under a federal grant and in coordination with Wilson in Chicago and
police heads in Boston and Washington, DC, University of Michigan social
scientist Albert Reiss conducted several studies in the mid-1960s on community attitudes toward the police and police attitudes toward the community.
The results of the latter were particularly notable. Of the 510 white police officers that Reiss and his colleagues interviewed and observed, *72 percent* of
them admitted to or displayed attitudes that the researchers characterized
as "highly prejudiced, extremely anti-Negro" (38 percent) or "prejudiced,
anti-Negro" (34 percent). Meanwhile, of the ninety-four black officers they
observed or interviewed, 18 percent also demonstrated some level of disdain
for black people.[81]

Police brutality was the most potent issue on which these questions of
racism and accountability collided. As we have seen already, police violence
had plagued members of the black community for years, and now, under
Wilson, both the power and presence of the police in black neighborhoods
were escalating. For community members, that growing power was not only
an affront in that it heightened the chances of being stopped and frisked
and treated like a criminal; it was also legitimately dangerous when decoupled from meaningful oversight and accountability. If, as Earl Davis put
it, the IID was only there to serve as an "eyewash operation," what hope was
there of curtailing police violence?

The answer to the question depended on who you asked. For police officials and their supporters, the fundamental premise of the question was
illegitimate. Wilson, crime commission members, and others repeatedly
claimed that brutality was either a dead letter or was becoming so.[82] In the
summer of 1963, for example, CPD officers brutalized civil rights demonstrators when they picketed for better schooling opportunities for black

children, drawing criticisms from the black press as conjuring "shadows of Mississippi."[83] Wilson responded by issuing a stern press release suggesting that officers were just doing their jobs and that claims of brutality had no validity.[84] Meanwhile, at the same time that police organizations rebelled against Wilson's reform efforts, they agreed that brutality was not a real issue.[85]

Early on, several watchdog groups concurred. In 1961 the federal Commission on Civil Rights "lauded the diminished brutality by Chicago policemen under Wilson's administration," while the ACLU reported a decline in brutality incidents.[86] But others were slower to praise. The attorney George Leighton, chairman of the Chicago NAACP's Legal Redress Committee, tersely rejoined the ACLU's declaration of brutality's decline, noting that his office had actually witnessed a marked *increase* in it.[87] And while Wilson, Daley, and law-and-order supporters maintained a line of public denial, over time, black citizens, community organizations, and civil libertarians grew increasingly assertive in pushing back against their narrative. In 1963 Leighton observed that, in his sixteen years as a lawyer, he'd never seen as many cases of police brutality as he had in recent months, while the following year, Southside alderman Leon Despres wrote, "I am sorry to say that my files are now filled with documented cases of police brutality upon arrest."[88]

Meanwhile, the ACLU was assembling compendious case files that testified to the ubiquity of police violence. They read like a new red record[89]: Samuel Wallace was stopped and searched by two white officers on his way to work. Officers beat him with fists and nightsticks on the street, in their squad car, and in the officers' locker room at the station, one of them screaming "Nigger, I will kill you."[90] Regina Spikes, sixteen years old, threw herself between her father and a gun-wielding police officer who proceeded to club her on the head and push her down a flight of stairs before arresting both her and her father.[91] John Johnson Jr. was handcuffed to the back end of his car by a CPD officer who bashed his face into the car's rear deck while his wife and young children watched.[92] Stanley Reed watched police shoot his son, handcuffed after being stopped on a traffic violation, in the back. Reed could do nothing but watch as his son cried "Dad" twice with his last breaths as he died.[93] Ralph Bush, twenty-three, was arrested for loitering and reportedly stealing a bottle of whiskey.[94] He was taken into police custody and never made it out alive, suffering fatal head injuries from a beating delivered by police. The city settled a civil suit with Bush's family for $20,000.[95] And on and on.

The CPD itself knew more about the raw realities of brutality than it publicly let on, particularly after 1963 as complaints avalanched. The case of Ralph Bush—the twenty-three-year-old who went into police custody alive and came out dead—is illuminating, as one of the few instances in which a record survives of CPD internal discussions surrounding police brutality. At a meeting Wilson convened with his division heads in December of 1963, the superintendent used Bush's case as an example of "evidence of brutality within the department," and suggested that an inability to *prove* such abuse might be less a function of its nonexistence than of "inadequacies in [IID] investigations." After all, given the circumstances surrounding Bush's death, Wilson said, "there is no other logical explanation" than that he died from injuries sustained while in custody.[96] Meanwhile, in June 1964, the superintendent circulated an internal memorandum to all CPD personnel instructing them to "avoid any semblance of brutality, rough treatment, or discourtesy." "Brutality is wrong," he offered, "both morally and legally. When practiced by police officers it is cowardly and inexcusable." Even here Wilson leaned toward dismissing most claims of brutality as incidents where "the complainant has resisted arrest, thus necessitating the use of force." But he also emphasized to those under his command that the department wasn't above reproach, and would suffer worsening relations with the community until it was.[97]

Ralph Bush's death especially sparked inquiry into whether CPD officers were actively engaged in torture. The most famous torture cases in Chicago's police history—those committed by CPD detective Jon Burge and the men under his command in the 1970s and 1980s—were still to come.[98] But those cases must be read inside a longer history of the violence embedded within CPD culture, and, indeed, while recent mainstream revelations of police torture in Chicago, including the Burge cases, have tended to frame torture as a tool wielded only by the worst of a small crop of bad apples, the frequency with which it arises in the historical record of the CPD suggests something far more commonplace and endemic to the culture. The killing of Ralph Bush was a case in point. At the meeting in which Wilson discussed Bush's death in police lockup, he also explored larger accusations of torture: charges that officers had beaten prisoners with paper bags over their heads, shocked them with cattle prods and electric probes, and simulated drowning by dunking their heads in slop sinks. Some of those present at the meeting with Wilson, either unaware or dismissive of the CPD's long record of torture, shrugged off the accusations as self-interested or inconceivable. Nevertheless, they seriously discussed tossing officers' lockers in search of torture devices.[99]

And Wilson had good reason to take it seriously. Earlier that year, a letter had arrived on his desk from a man too scared to sign his name, who testified that during his stint in a police lockup, "every night" men would be brought in "who were beat up so badly they required medical treatment." Suspects were chained to radiators and beaten. Their heads were dunked in ice baths. The letter-writer claimed to have been kicked in the stomach until his ribs broke.[100] A year later, further accusations of torture splashed across the *Defender*'s pages after an alleged drug dealer accused two police officers, one of them notoriously brutal, of forcing his head into a water-filled bathtub and robbing him of $1,400.[101]

Stories like this played out repeatedly in 1960s Chicago. And each incident is important in its own right. These brutalities were done to *people*—individuals with lives and loved ones, and the violence committed against them would be something they would carry for the rest of their lives. But, moreover, when considered together, when brutality's portrait is drawn as a composite rather than fragments, it becomes easier to understand how such recurring instances of police violence yielded sharp opposition among black Chicagoans to any further expansion of law enforcement powers. As news reportage, anecdotes, and family histories of police brutality surged through black Chicago, they clarified the risks involved in even the most quotidian points of contact with the police. John Johnson's kids surely learned lessons from watching their father's face being bashed into the rear bumper of the family car during a routine traffic stop. If Regina Spikes ever had kids of her own, she surely would have passed on her own experiences getting thrown down a flight of stairs. And $20,000 may have bought the Bush family's quiescence on the matter of the civil suit, but it would not have bought forgiveness, nor silence as they told Ralph's story. These stories thus heightened people's awareness of how quickly things could escalate in dealings with police. And they understood that by imparting further power and legal shelter to police, aggressive preventive patrol, stop-and-frisk, and the general expansion of police power posed legitimate physical dangers by putting them in contact with potentially abusive officers.

"Living a Severe Life": Oppression and the Problem of Community Violence

And none of this—not the expanding surveillance net nor increased police-citizen contact, and certainly not the brutality—yielded better public safety anyway. For in the second half of the 1960s, crime *did* increase—terribly. The CPD's 1964 predictive modeling of growing crime through the end of the decade was racist in premise and faulty in method. But it did nevertheless inadvertently stumble on one truth: Chicago was about to get more dangerous for those citizens already living on the margins.

Endemic poverty and systemic inequality, not imagined racial characteristics, were the reason. The conditions in impoverished black neighborhoods that had long been bad and on the brink had deteriorated rapidly in

the 1960s under the strain of the urban crisis and rapacious capital interests. While a sizable black middle class had coalesced in metropolitan Chicago, hundreds of thousands had been left behind in glaring poverty and
with few options. Nor would the process abate; over a twenty-year period
beginning in 1967, Chicago lost a staggering 60 percent of its manufacturing
jobs—the sort of well-paying work that black men especially had often relied on for stability.[102] Simultaneously, housing conditions and city services
eroded precipitously, particularly on the West Side and driven by exploitative real estate practices and corrosive public policies.[103] Schools continued
to face crises both of funding and overcrowding. The collapse of the industrial economy, the decline of other job opportunities, and the flight of the
black middle class to the suburbs decimated the already perilous economic
condition of majority-black areas.

   Although crime rates in Chicago (as elsewhere) grew far less than the panic
surrounding *perceived* crime did, by the late 1960s and onward through the
next two decades, criminal incidences undeniably proliferated. As an influential study by Judith and Peter Blau demonstrated, criminal violence in the
nation's 125 largest metropolises (including Chicago) was tethered deeply to
those cities' rates of racial and economic inequalities—both from "lack of
advantages" and, even more so, "being taken advantage of."[104] The Kerner
Commission's report of 1968 noted that some neighborhoods in Chicago,
black and at the bottom of the economic stratum, had serious crime rates
that ran thirty-five times that of upper-class white neighborhoods.[105] And,
worst of all, the number of homicides began to increase at an alarming rate
beginning in 1966.[106]

   The main drivers of that violence were gangs. By the early and mid-sixties,
thousands of black youths found themselves shut off from standard avenues
to material success and alienated from traditional institutions of upward
mobility (resource-depleted schools being the most obvious). As that happened, many of them were drawn into affiliations with youth gangs that had
begun to pop up on the South and West Sides at the end of the 1950s and into
the 1960s. Inside and out, people talked of the gangs as having been forged
in the fires of a punishing socioeconomic system—a product of young men
and women feeling the pain of circumscribed choices and plans, and of the
city's failure to keep them safe and give them chances. At a gathering with
civil rights activists in the summer of 1966, gang leaders talked about wanting to help their members turn toward more stable and socially productive
lives, including "set[ting] up our own agencies for jobs, health, information
and recreation" and "tell[ing] our younger members how important it is to
remain in school."[107] One 1968 magazine feature, meanwhile, explained that

people in Woodlawn who supported the Blackstone Rangers did so because they believed that "the schools, the welfare centers, the political clubs, and all the other cogs of the machinery powered at city hall are designed to keep ghetto blacks poor, dependent, and powerless. That is a severe judgment; it is the result of living a severe life."[108]

The gangs' imprint on Chicago was complicated, their presence enigmatic. They were often aggressively expansionist, making "block-by-block conquests of 'turf'" and "growing from small sets to large 'nations' with leadership cadres and dues-paying members."[109] As the historian Andrew Diamond writes, by late in the sixties, Chicago's black youth gangs "had developed within a logic that placed a premium on autonomy and the control of turf, and they followed a code by which one never allowed a physical attack to go unchallenged."[110]

To a certain extent, this emphasis on autonomy and hyperlocal protectionism predisposed some gang leaders and members of the rank and file to revolutionary politics, linking them especially with emergent strains of Black Power. Some of the major gangs, the Rangers and Gangster Disciples included, for a time self-styled—both rhetorically and programmatically—as instruments of community uplift. As early as 1966, Jeff Fort, the leader of the Rangers, used his platform not only to challenge police repression and criticize structural inequality but also to instill in black South Side youth the self-perception of them all as "princes." That vision spread like wildfire among South Side youth, with graffitied versions of the word *prince* spreading across building walls all across the neighborhood.[111] More concretely, the Rangers collaborated with the Saul Alinksy–affiliated Woodlawn Organization to harness better opportunities for their members and the community. They aimed to provide job training to South Side youth—with or without gang affiliations, and even (along with the Disciples) got a grant from Lyndon Johnson's Office of Economic Opportunity to do precisely that, under the auspices of the War on Poverty.[112] (Daley was nonplussed.) They also established cultural programs in churches and ramshackle community centers in Woodlawn; accounts of the social life at such centers are filled with descriptions of children coming in and out, having found a rare safe space to play and hang out in a neighborhood often lacking such places.[113]

Perhaps the culmination of the gangs' activist work in the community came at the end of the 1960s, when in the summer of 1969 gangs entered into the Coalition for United Community Action (CUCA)—a coalition of more than sixty-one church, community, and civil rights organizations.[114] Working within CUCA, black Chicago's three most significant gangs—the Conservative Vice Lords, the Black P. Stone Nation (formerly the Rangers), and the Disciples—"sought to transform themselves into agents of economic renewal for poor black neighborhoods," most notably by engaging in direct action protests to demand jobs for black men.[115] Their most important target was the construction industry, especially federal construction sites totaling more than $80,000,000 that gang-led CUCA activism successfully shut down while demanding that building contractors end discriminatory hiring practices that kept black men out of work on those projects. By January of 1970, their activism, coupled with an ugly public backlash from white workers and their unions, forced Mayor Daley to convene a meeting at city hall that brought representatives of the building trades together with CUCA representatives, including members of all three major gangs, to negotiate a solution. The so-called Chicago Plan established a thousand jobs immediately for minority journeymen workers, job training for one thousand young aspiring minority workers, and the exemption from craft exams of one thousand more.[116] The Chicago Plan ended up falling far short of its goals, but it nevertheless demonstrated gang members' willingness to fight for community betterment.

Yet the gangs' community commitments—whether it be their involvement in civil rights, revolutionary politics, or other forms of community betterment—were inconsistent. And violent factionalism between them ultimately undermined their social function and cultivated increasing amounts of chaos. Indeed, while Michael Shane of the Disciples hailed the gangs' collaboration in CUCA as evidence that "three youth nations could come together peacefully," and that it would "alleviate much of the gang warfare," what was happening in the background indicated otherwise.[117] From 1966 onward, spiking especially after 1968, turf wars between the gangs produced higher and higher body counts. During the first four and a half months of 1968 alone, the *Tribune* attributed twenty-nine shooting deaths to South Side gang violence, mostly a result of the Rangers' battles with their rivals over turf.[118] All told, from 1965 to 1970, homicides increased by a horrifying 104 percent, from 396 to 810, before peaking at 970 in 1974.[119] In the Second Police District, where the Rangers made their home, murder statistics were 30 percent higher than the next highest district—which, not coincidentally, was the district covering an Englewood neighborhood also heavily wracked by gang violence.

That violence, as the escalating murder rate testified, was self-perpetuating. Teenagers (and younger kids) who constituted the gangs' main membership saw violence in their daily lives—even before they joined themselves. As they became more exposed to such violence, it pushed them to seek protection. The bad best-case scenario in that situation was to seek protection under cover of a gang, where at least they had someone looking out for them when they were outside the confines of their home. As a *Presbyterian Life* feature on the Rangers put it, "the world [people living in Woodlawn] see is, in any perspective, a place of violence. . . . Children in such neighborhoods are interested in protection, and they form gangs at a tender age to get it."[120] The same held true in Englewood and pockets of the West Side, too.

The next chapter explores more fully the CPD's response to gang violence—which was rooted most notably in the implementation of a controversial Gang Intelligence Unit in Wilson's final months that his successor would inherit and shape. But it's worth pausing to appreciate that spiraling gang violence happened *after* Wilson's new and more aggressive policing regime was in place. A common misconception is that harsh policing was historically a response to rising serious crime. It's a sequence that makes ontological sense, but it isn't true. Wilson's reforms were largely rooted in concepts and ideas of what policing should look like, not material conditions on the ground in Chicago. What this meant was that, as policing became *more aggressive* in Chicago, it correlated with the city becoming *less safe*.

Correlation is not necessarily causation, of course. There is no clear and decisive evidence showing that more aggressive policing *precipitated* a spike in violent crime. But a few things bear remembering. For one, members of the GIU often intentionally exacerbated conflict between the gangs. As we will see, this is a matter of historical record, not of conspiracy theory. For another, the GIU also intentionally disrupted efforts by the Rangers and Disciples to bring job placement and vocational training to their communities—the very things that could potentially help address, however incrementally, Chicago's embedded economic and opportunity inequalities. And it also bears remembering that the CPD's antigang practices destabilized young people's lives through frequent stop-and-frisks and arrests, and in so doing undermined public confidence in the police. Police complained constantly of a lack of cooperation from the public, but it was a self-made problem. By decade's end, researchers described police officers in black districts as working "in an environment where the code of silence prevails. This code of silence reflects the people's fear within the community. Very few residents cooperate with the police; and any assistance given the police, they must have earned."[121] In other words, the public offered the police little assistance because they couldn't trust them. And as a result, as black policeman Harrold Saffold lamented, "the police department was the greatest gang recruiting tool in Chicago because they treated everybody as if they were gangbangers anyway."[122]

To Remake the City: Revolution and Counterrevolution in Civil Rights–Era Chicago

In the midst of rising gang tensions and the growth of a repressive police apparatus, Martin Luther King came to Chicago. Late in 1965, King and the SCLC had convened to debate the next battlefields in the struggle for civil and human rights. Among them was a plan to go north, to address the yawning inequalities endemic to most major cities there. After evaluating five possible cities, they settled on Chicago.[123]

While his spotlight was always bound to burn exceedingly bright, King didn't create the civil rights movement in Chicago. (Nor did he create it elsewhere, for that matter.) As we have seen, civil rights activism had been ongoing if erratic in Chicago for years, but it had coalesced as the Chicago Freedom Movement in 1963, organized most notably around fighting educational inequalities.

Whether before King's arrival or after, the police were not that movement's central concern. But they were important all the same. For one thing, matters of police violence and harassment directly drove numerous protest actions and demands. In 1964 the local executive committee of the Congress of Racial Equality (CORE) discussed the viability of using police brutality as an organizing issue.[124] In the first week of 1965, when a CPD officer killed a black man named Richard Garner, the Student Nonviolent Coordinating Committee (SNCC) held a rally to demand justice, at which fliers condemned the officer as "a killer-cop, with a gun in his hand. He has killed your brother and *the city is still paying him* to 'protect' you!"[125] Four months later, SCLC held a demonstration in Englewood over police brutality in general, and in particular concerning the reinstatement of the notoriously brutal CPD captain Frank Pape (of *Monroe v. Pape* infamy) after he'd left the force following the Supreme Court's concurrence in the case finding him guilty of gross brutality.[126] At another march a week later, a SNCC flier enumerated their demands concerning the CPD's relationship to the black community, including "an end to all forms of police harassment and brutality," an end to "false arrest of poorer citizens without warrant or case," integration of all squad cars, putting officers back on foot rather than in cars so that they and the public would know each other better, and a civilian review board to investigate citizens' complaints.[127]

The CPD also helped shape the freedom movement by virtue of how it responded to movement activism. During the Great Depression eviction protests, the distinction between *justice* on the one hand (represented in the pursuits of Communist and Popular Front organizers) and *order* on the other (witnessed in the police and politicians' responses) had been drawn in sharp relief. So, too, with the freedom movement, whose direct action protests in pursuit of social and racial justice intentionally disrupted the status quo, as activists sought to heighten public consciousness and provoke political action from the city. Despite movement activists' noble goals, their actions put them at loggerheads with Orlando Wilson's obsessive vision of order. The point is not that Wilson opposed the movement's end goals, intellectually or morally. There is no evidence this was the case, and he repeatedly affirmed activists' rights to picket peacefully. But what mattered was that whatever his personal feelings on civil rights and racial equality, they were submerged beneath his interest in preserving law and order.

This meant that over the course of the first few years of the movement, as in its more famous southern iterations, activists faced constant arrest by the police. If citizens wanted to picket outside city hall, according to Wilson, they could. (Even though Daley hated the movement and tried to smear it as "Communistic."[128]) But if they blocked traffic, chained themselves to fences, or did anything else that violated the strict rule of law, the CPD reacted. On top of that, a rejuvenated Red Squad conducted constant, relentless surveillance on all aspects of the freedom movement—infiltrating organizations, attending meetings under cover, hiring informants, and manipulating press coverage in an effort to delegitimize it.[129]

This was, generally, the story of the police department's engagement with the freedom struggle leading up to 1966, and that year, King came to town. Wilson and Daley knew that he would bring high publicity with him, and they initially worked hard to demonstrate their philosophical support for what he was trying to do. When King announced the Chicago campaign, Wilson personally invited him to the table to discuss his plan, and afterward, both men expressed satisfaction with the cordiality and tenor of the meeting. For King especially, his meeting with Wilson seemed promising after so many years dealing with the Bull Connors and Jim Clarks of the South; indeed, he called it the first time that he had been able "to engage in a dialogue [with police] in good faith."[130]

But détente was almost inevitably going to be short-lived. From the outset, King had warned Wilson of the likelihood of civil disobedience, telling him and other CPD officials that "it might be necessary to break a particular law to reach the higher law of brotherhood and justice."[131] In keeping with his opinions on harm principle policing and civil libertarianism, the very notion of civil disobedience was anathema to Wilson's entire worldview. It signaled lawlessness and a disrespect for public order. There was little middle ground between the two men's philosophies on the matter, and this set the superintendent and King on a collision course.

The collision came when the movement escalated in the summer of 1966. That July, King led a rally at Soldier Field of some thirty thousand Chicagoans that served as a formal launch point for a summer of action. After the rally, five thousand people marched to city hall, where King taped a list of the CFM's demands to the front door. The slate of demands included open housing, equitable access to quality education, and approval of a civilian review board to oversee the CPD.[132] The following day, King, the Chicago teacher and CFM leader Al Raby, and others met with a contingent of city officials that included both Daley and Wilson. The primary focus was, again, on open housing, but King also reiterated the movement's vision and demands for the police department to be more accountable and responsible to the people. Reflexively distrustful of public influence on police functions, Wilson was unmoved by the activists' arguments—the civilian review board, especially. He explained that such a board would muck up his efforts to root out abusive and bad officers through formal police channels. This set off Raby, who pushed the issue and told the superintendent that he personally knew of "at least fifteen men who contribute to the bad image of the department." Wilson responded defensively that he was "sure there are more than fifteen and I am trying to rid the department of these men."[133]

And so things stalemated. As activists emphasized the need for official action on their entire slate of issues, no one from the city would make commitments. Political maneuvering was Daley's forte, and King saw the mayor's skillful evasiveness on full display in those July negotiations. King threatened to amplify the movement's street protests, "which included the possibility of staging sit-ins on the Dan Ryan Expressway," the busy eight-lane highway cutting southward from the Loop through Chicago's South Side. In the end, he left the meeting frustrated, telling reporters later that day that the movement would have to "escalate."[134]

Conditions beyond the activists' control, however, escalated things for them. The day after that meeting, violence exploded on the Near West Side beginning with a confrontation between the CPD and black residents. The West Side had been a cauldron of tension for years, and had exploded into an urban rebellion in Garfield Park the summer before after an out-of-control city fire truck knocked over a street sign and killed a black woman in the process. Furies had not meaningfully eased since that time. Now, in a stretch of scorching summer heat, they exploded once again. It was the fifth day in a row with temperatures spiking above ninety degrees, and black kids, seeking a reprieve from the heat, opened up a city fire hydrant to play in the water—a Chicago tradition, and an act so banal that even Daley admitted to having done it when he was young. CPD officers passing by took issue with the violation, however, and closed the hydrant. When the children reopened it, officers again closed it, and they were soon met with a hostile crowd who resented the police's infringement on so mundane a

CPD officers gather in Garfield Park during the urban rebellion of 1965. Chicago History Museum, ICHi-077900; Declan Haun, photographer.

civic privilege. Bricks and bottles flew as residents and officers exchanged harsh words, pushes, and shoves. A swarm of CPD officers flooded the scene, but the entire neighborhood was soon erupting. For several days, pockets of the Near West Side and the neighboring communities of Lawndale and East and West Garfield Park simmered, conjuring fears of "another Watts." Arson fires and scattered looting rocked the area. The police made frequent use of their nightsticks and guns in their quest to restore order.[135] After days of violence, two people lay dead, hundreds had been arrested, and millions of dollars of property damage incurred.

In Watts the previous summer, King had famously remarked that the so-called riots there were "the language of the unheard." He took a similar philosophical approach to Chicago's 1966 West Side uprising, noting that while he thought they were counterproductive because they "intensify white fears and relieve their guilt," they nevertheless demonstrated in dramatic fashion the moment's urgency. In his eyes, the movement needed to respond to the uprising by "mov[ing] on with our positive program to make Chicago an open city. We have dual housing, a dual school system, dual everything."[136] And although many of the local activists disagreed with King's particular focus on open housing (and many chafed at his hogging the limelight and decision-making to begin with), shortly thereafter the movement

CPD officers occupy a Chicago street corner. Chicago History Museum, ICHi-075526;
Declan Haun, photographer.

launched aggressive open housing campaigns to try to challenge Chicago's
still-rigid segregation.

By this point, after years of battling to strip legalized Jim Crow from southern law books and win the right to vote, King had honed the tactics of nonviolent protest. Coupled equally with intense and localized grassroots organizing
by thousands of black and white activists across the South, the southern movement had succeeded by undertaking mass direct action campaigns that had
conjured such terrible reactions from white racists (including ones in law enforcement) that the government was forced to respond. In Chicago, the same
essential idea held. In the wake of the West Side uprising, the movement's
strategists plotted marches through some of the city's most infamously racist
neighborhoods, where they assumed that the viciousness of residents would
force the city to condemn racist violence and enforce open housing.

The racists didn't disappoint. They threw rocks and bottles and cherry
bombs at the marchers, carried signs advocating White Power, and chanted
such invectives as "I'd like to be an Alabama trooper / That is what I'd really
like to be / For if I were an Alabama trooper / Then I could hang a nigger
legally."[137] In one march, a thrown brick struck King in the head, sending
him crumpling down onto one knee. He was able to get up and continue
the march but afterward commented to reporters: "I have seen many

CPD officers handle crowd control as racists gather to oppose the Chicago Freedom Movement. Chicago History Museum, ICHi-077640; Declan Haun, photographer.

demonstrations in the South, but I have never seen anything so hostile and so hateful as I've seen here today."[138] The CPD's response in these situations was uneven. Activists frequently found cause to praise the police's work holding the violent mobs at bay; other times, they found the police effort less impressive.[139] And while Wilson firmly believed in people's right to peaceful protest, he didn't like the chaos that ensued when they did—no matter the fact that it was racist counterdemonstrators, not antiracist protesters, who were at fault.

In any event, as the movement and its counterinsurgency convulsed Chicago, they put Daley in a bad position. For the mayor, the political optics were a minefield. He had made a name for himself nationwide as a Democratic Party powerbroker, had helped secure the White House for John F. Kennedy in 1960 and Lyndon Johnson in 1964, and was considered one of the most powerful politicians in the country because of Chicago's importance to Illinois and Illinois's position as a swing state in national elections. With the national Democratic Party having officially become the major party most aligned with the civil rights movement (however uneasily and reluctantly it had been dragged to that position), Daley couldn't afford to be publicly hostile to the movement, no matter how deep his resentment toward it. On the other hand, huge contingents of white voters hated that movement, and when the CPD was deployed to white ethnic neighborhoods to defend civil rights marchers, citizens responded with the political equivalent of their 1950s riots, turning in droves away from Daley and toward the Republican Party.[140]

Wilson, too, was in an awkward position as the movement dragged on. He seemed to admire King personally, and harbored no opposition to the movement's goals in and of themselves. The CPD issued formal statements and fliers stating that it wouldn't tolerate racist violence against protesters, and if Wilson had had his way, it's likely that his officers would have done a more uniformly satisfactory job of protecting activists from white violence.[141] But at the same time, Wilson continued to disagree philosophically with the entire premise of direct action protest, saw sit-ins on highways and streets as illegitimate and illegal forms of expression, and was therefore fundamentally at odds with the movement tactically.

As they found themselves between these rocks and hard places, Daley and Wilson sought ways out. When movement opponents responded to its work with reactionary violence, it emphasized the movement's moral righteousness, and in so doing, breathed more life into it. Spectacle was important, but it wasn't what city administrators wanted. Echoing the complaints of his predecessors, Wilson publicly warned about the drains on departmental resources caused by protecting movement activists. In mid-August of 1966, he pointed to a 30 percent spike in the one-month crime rate from the year before, and blamed it on the freedom movement having taken hundreds of police officers off their normal beats. Taking a hard-line stance against the continuation of the demonstrations, Wilson braided the freedom movement's activities with dangerousness, recklessness, and disregard for the greater good of Chicago; the high crime rate, he concluded, "can be expected to continue as long as we have these demonstrations."[142] In other words, the movement was making the city less safe.

That rhetorical move gave Daley the firepower he needed to shut the movement down. Shortly thereafter and in consultation with Wilson, Daley hit the freedom movement with an injunction to force an end to its street demonstrations. Bringing to a head the logics that Timothy O'Connor had advanced fifteen years earlier, Daley told Chicago that the injunction was necessary in order "to end that kind of street demonstrations which have adversely affected the rights of all people by making it impossible for the police department to adequately protect the lives and property of every citizen."[143] Daley explained that while he "hated" injunctions, he was being forced to choose between one group's right to petition versus the entire city's right to adequate police protection.[144] Once again, black freedom was less important than law and order.

The injunction jolted King and the freedom movement, and for most intents and purposes, had its desired effect. Legally denied access to the streets, the injunction forced the movement to the bargaining table, which was where Daley thrived. Activists met with the mayor and came away with an array of promises about city-supported open housing. King couldn't have felt great about how things had gone but expressed public satisfaction with the mayor's pledges. More militant leaders in Chicago derided them as empty, which more closely resembled the reality. Chicago remained profoundly segregated. Once again, civil rights died at the altar of public order.

But the core problems undergirding the movement's demands didn't vanish, and these included demands for reformation of the police department and police policy in a way that would work better for black people. During the freedom movement, King and others had pitched the idea of a civilian review board, which would give Chicagoans greater and more direct oversight of police officers who broke the rules. They had challenged the ethics of the CPD reinstating demonstrably bad officers like Frank Pape. They had marched to demand justice for victims of police violence. They had sought to reestablish more personalized relationships between the police and the public in the form of beat patrols. None of these were radical suggestions. The city and the CPD stonewalled them at every turn all the same. In so doing, they set the table for far more assertive challenges to the status quo, coming soon down the line.

ORLANDO WILSON retired abruptly, announcing it early in the summer of 1967. According to the legendary journalist Mike Royko, rumors swirled long afterward that Daley had forced him out, frustrated that Wilson wasn't sufficiently pliable to his demands and wanting someone who would be much tougher on dissidents.[145] It could have been that he was sick of battling rank-and-file leaders like Frank Carey. It could have been that he was worn down from trying to navigate Chicago's civil rights era as the head of the city's police. It could have been that he was just tired. Wilson was sixty-seven and had given nearly five decades of his life to his profession and passion.

Either way, when he stepped down, many in Chicago mourned. Wilson had inherited a department that was dysfunctional and corrupt and had been both those things for most of its existence. Facing resistance from the rank and file, he had nevertheless pulled the department forward to a place where it was presumed to be among the finest in the country. By reconstituting the CPD's organizational arrangement from the ground up, making greater use of new technology and communications, and wrenching the department from some of its entanglements with the Democratic Party machine, Wilson had proved to be the astute and modernizing mind that many people had hoped he would be back in 1960.

But racially selective—and ultimately racially repressive—measures were part of this modernizing bundle, as well. One cannot talk about the positive changes that Orlando Wilson brought to the department without acknowledging that things like invasive patrol, jettisoning of the harm principle in racially selective contexts, stop-and-frisk, racist metrics for crime prediction, and freedom movement subversion came right along with them. Despite his own nominal racial liberalism, when Wilson was reimagining a new day for the police force, he was doing so with a vision focused most keenly on the maintenance of law and order. Modernization and professionalism on the one hand, and racial repression and punitive policing on the other, were thus joined at the hip. And this bears remembering, for when people, now and across time, call for police reform, they should know that the period of the most successful police reform in Chicago's history was accompanied by the institutionalization of its greatest racial repressions.

Early in this chapter, we heard Urban League Executive Secretary Edwin Berry call Orlando Wilson's hiring "the greatest thing for Chicago since the discovery of Lake Michigan." We will close with Berry, too. On Thanksgiving Eve of 1966, Berry testified before the Citizens' Committee to Study Police-Community Relations, and argued that while some things between the police and the community had improved since Wilson took office, intractable problems persisted. Quoting a Harris poll from that summer, Berry began from the fact that, in urban centers across the country, including Chicago, 49 percent of black people "felt uneasy about the operations of their local police force." That sort of deep mistrust, he offered, didn't happen accidentally. Rather, it indicated "that something is wrong with the way in which the police have been carrying out the law enforcement function when Negroes are involved."[146]

The Committee to Study Police-Community Relations had advanced a premise that "the causes of the mistrust, low esteem, and lack of confidence ... [were] the result of misunderstanding or unfamiliarity of the Negro community with their responsibilities in the maintenance of law and order." Berry shredded the argument. Instead, he offered, the community's mistrust of the police had "two very real roots. First, in a society without racial justice, the police bear the burden of policing an unjust order. And second, the way in which the police have operated within Negro neighborhoods, the brutality with which Negroes have been handled by the police, and the separate standards of law application and enforcement that have been used in the ghetto, have all left indelible marks in the Negro community."[147]

In other words, after segregating, underresourcing, and saddling black Chicago with the wages of a punishingly unequal system, after choosing to invest little in infrastructure to help impoverished black neighborhoods— after all of that, Chicago threw money at the CPD hand over fist and asked it to deal with the problems in the community. This wasn't an enviable position for the police to be in, but they in turn did not handle it well. They applied different sets of standards to the people living in "the ghetto" than they applied to those living outside of it, and the operative set in black neighborhoods wasn't an enviable system for people to have to live with. Although one other Wilsonian reform had been to emblazon CPD squad cars with the slogan "We Protect and Serve," that bifurcated set of standards ensured the pledge's failure when it came to marginalized neighborhoods that were, in reality, neither meaningfully protected nor responsibly served. Underprotected and overpoliced by the CPD, wildly underserved by the city, and scorned by many of their countrymen in other parts of the city, huge swaths of black Chicago fumed.

CHAPTER 6

Shoot to Kill

REBELLION AND RETRENCHMENT IN
POST–CIVIL RIGHTS CHICAGO

The Democratic National Convention (DNC) of August 1968 was supposed to be a triumph for Richard Daley—a showcase for the city of Chicago, and affirmation of the mayor as political powerbroker. Instead, it proved disastrous and has lingered in the public consciousness as one of the most iconic moments of police repression in American history.

In the week leading up to the convention, Chicago was on edge. Antiwar demonstrators and leftist dissidents nationwide were descending on the city—most to protest the Democratic Party's complicity in the war in Vietnam, some with more abstract countercultural goals.[1] Chicago readied its police force, and imported thousands of National Guard troops to help with crowd control. Violence seemed imminent. Todd Gitlin of Students for a Democratic Society wrote a piece for the underground *San Francisco Express Times*, headlined "If you're going to Chicago, be sure to wear armor in your hair."[2] Some of Gitlin's colleagues didn't care for such prophecies of violence. He was, however, right.

The chaos that ensued is infamous. In brief strokes: the weekend before the convention's opening, demonstrators began assembling in Lincoln Park, and by that Sunday night, as many as five thousand people were there, using the park for music and speeches, and as a staging ground for marches down into the Loop past the hotels housing most of the DNC delegates. By Sunday evening, confrontations between demonstrators and the CPD simmered as the police cleared protesters from the park, scattering them into Old Town and down onto the northern part of Michigan Avenue. Reporters and cameramen captured repeated incidents in which police used unnecessary and sometimes brutal force in performing this task. The next two nights saw similar patterns, but amplified.

By Wednesday, August 28, the center of the protests had moved to Grant Park, sandwiched between Chicago's famous Magnificent Mile to the west and Lake Michigan to the east. Ten thousand people gathered there that day. In the middle of the afternoon, a young protester walked to the flagpole near the Grant Park band shell and began to lower the American flag to half-mast. Police rushed in and arrested him. Other demonstrators swarmed in and lowered the flag entirely. The police advanced. The crowd pelted them with various objects. Police threw a smoke bomb, and like a battle scene, assumed formation under billowing plumes and advanced on the demonstrators.

When the former reached the latter—bedlam. The police line broke apart and individual officers waded into the crowd, clubbing and macing people indiscriminately. As demonstrators poured out of Grant Park, they first tried to march northward back in the direction of Lincoln Park, but police and guardsmen rebuffed them. At the corner of Columbus and Balbo, machine guns sat poised and menacing, guardsmen at the ready to use them. The Jackson Street artery remained open, however, and many protesters poured through it, linking up with other demonstrators and continuing down Michigan Avenue. A huge number of people assembled outside the Hilton Hotel across from the park's southern portion, where police continued to club and mace them and began making sweeping arrests. Television cameras captured it all. Protesters chanted, to global audiences: "The whole world is watching." The whole world watched the next day, too: more protests, more beatings, more tear gas, more arrests.[3]

The whole world has, in some ways, continued to watch ever since. What a government report subsequently labeled the "police riot" at the 1968 DNC stands as an archetype of sixties cultural conflict and excessive state violence. The journalist Haynes Johnson, who was there in Chicago, wrote in a fortieth anniversary retrospective that "the 1968 Chicago convention became a lacerating event, a distillation of a year of heartbreak, assassinations, riots, and a breakdown in law and order that made it seem as if the country were coming apart. . . . No one who was there, or who watched it on television, could escape the memory of what took place before their eyes."[4]

The 1968 DNC was, yes, a "lacerating event," in many respects. It was incredibly politically important then, and remains historically significant to this day. But it has also lingered as perhaps *the* iconic symbol of a supposedly unhinged, out-of-control police force in late-sixties Chicago. And that is an almost entirely wrong interpretation.

The late 1960s were awash in police violence in Chicago, almost all of it more serious than what happened at the DNC. For all the violence that Chicago police reigned down upon protesters at the DNC, no one was killed or severely injured. And yet it has loomed so large in sixties iconography that it has fully eclipsed for most people the routine police violence and constant fear that defined everyday life for many Chicagoans, especially on the black South and West Sides. Indeed, five months before the DNC police riot, an uprising on the black West Side in the aftermath of Martin Luther King's assassination resulted in the deaths of nearly a dozen black people at the hands of the CPD—some of whom appeared to have essentially been executed by the police. Several months before *that* violence, a Ku Klux Klan cell was found to be operating and recruiting within the police department, including a CPD patrolman who also doubled as the Illinois Klan's grand dragon and was plotting mass death in the city and beyond. In the two years *after* the DNC riot, the CPD killed at least fifty-eight black people, the overwhelming majority of whom were not, at least based on police evidence, armed. Included within this terrible statistic were Fred Hampton and Mark Clark, young leaders of the Black Panthers, who the CPD assassinated while they slept. To bear witness to community members' testimony on police violence and harassment, a core aspect of being black in late-sixties and early-seventies Chicago was to live in unrelenting fear that anyone at any time might fall victim to perhaps-fatal police violence.

That violence and fear was an extension of the everyday workings of the police system. In the wake of the DNC police riot, local civil rights leader Al Raby argued that it showed that "the police are not only against blacks. They are against anybody who messes with their thing."[5] The journalist John Schultz argued in his book about the riot that, as the police beat protesters and observers alike without particular distinction, the experience forged common understandings of the stakes and extent of police violence: "The cops did us a great favor by putting us all in the same boat. A few upper-middle-class white men said they now had some idea of what it meant to be on the other end of the law in the ghetto."[6]

This may sound superficially logical, but if one approaches the DNC police riot from the perspective of black Chicagoans, one could also see the police actions there as an example of comparative restraint. Contrary to Schultz's claim, upper-middle-class white men—even those with nightstick bruises—had essentially *no* idea of what it meant to be subject to police power and violence in "the ghetto." To wit, Schultz titled his memoir *No One*

Was Killed—which was true of neither black experiences in the King riots nor within the quotidian contexts of daily life. Indeed, the fact that Chicago police violence gathered widespread national media attention only at that point, when it was groups of primarily (though certainly not exclusively) young white people experiencing it, reminds us of black freedom activist Ella Baker's famous axiom about America's varying valuations of "black mothers' sons" and "white mothers' sons."[7] The reality is that if one wants to understand the history of policing in Chicago, the DNC riot actually tells us very little. Instead, we must look to the more prosaic aspects of policing, and what it was like to be black in that extended late-1960s and early-1970s moment.

That moment constituted the beginning of a nadir in police–black community relations that lasted for the duration of the twentieth century and onward into the twenty-first. Officer-involved killings skyrocketed. Brutality became so widespread that even the conservative *Tribune* offered condemnations of it. The expansion of vehicular patrol further eradicated familiarities between police and community, exacerbating the sense that black people lived in occupied zones.[8] One researcher in 1968 described police as "a 'foreigner' who all too often fails to stop the ever-growing crime problems and insults the citizen's dignity. . . . This 'foreign' policeman is all too easily transformed into the symbol of White authority."[9] And the International Association of Chiefs of Police, studying Chicago in 1970, wrote that there was a "substantial separation of the department from . . . the community, which reduces the effectiveness of the department and the quality of life in Chicago. . . . [In] some areas, the police have all the outward appearances of an occupational force."[10] That impression, in many respects, remains intact to this day.

The 1968 report by the Kerner Commission, impaneled to study the wave of urban uprisings in 1967, famously observed that the United States was "moving toward two societies, one black, one white—separate and unequal."[11] The tacit and incorrect implication that the country hadn't *long been* two unequal societies notwithstanding, Chicago was a distillation of the thesis. This was true of material stability and opportunity access. But it was also true of law enforcement—primarily in the sense that, as Bill Berry had suggested in his late-1966 testimony to the Citizens' Committee to Study Police-Community Relations, law enforcement in black communities was administered in totally different ways than it was in white ones. Indeed, it operated under a different set of principles altogether.

This fact had clarified in the early Daley-era punitive turn and crystallized under Orlando Wilson. Policing in black communities had become explicitly more aggressive, intrusive, and punitive. Many community members would have said that it had also become more abusive and racist. Wilson had orchestrated this through his efforts to expand police power both systematically and individually.

At the same time, however, Wilson had tried hard to make police officers be more accountable for their actions. This didn't mean that the department had worked well for black Chicagoans, but what had kept police-community dynamics from full implosion may have been the fact that the racially repressive apparatus that the CPD had become at a macro, policy level was overseen by a man who was deeply averse to police abuse at the individual level. This wasn't much, but it was something.

But the modest control that Wilson had held over the rank and file melted away once he retired and headed back to California. Corruption, violence, and unabashed racism from the white rank and file exploded again. Already in 1969, a CPD officer wrote directly to Daley, warning the mayor that what had been gained under Wilson was being lost under his replacement, Jim Conlisk.[12] In 1972 one of Wilson's old confidants on the force wrote a long and brutal excoriation of the department's "giant strides to the rear" that had begun almost immediately after Wilson's departure.[13] Around the same time, another wrote that corruption on the force was "even more of a problem today than it was during Summerdale," but that "the most troublesome long range problem remains the police attitudes toward the black community."[14] And *attitudes* weren't even the half of it.

The chapter that follows this one—this book's last—explores the rising tides of civic activism for police reform and semi-abolition that crested simultaneously and in response to those problems, in the late 1960s and early 1970s. But in order to understand those movements, we must understand their context and the deep anger and despair that animated them. That is the purpose of this chapter.

"Law and Order": New Regimes, Old Ideas

The journalist Mike Royko loved to portray James Conlisk Jr. as a hack and yes man. Richard Daley had known Conlisk since the latter's childhood. Born into a police family, Conlisk's father and Daley had been close friends, and James Sr. had been a top administrator in the CPD until 1960, at which point he was axed during Orlando Wilson's overhaul of administrative personnel. While his father's star fell, however, James Jr.'s rose. Shortly after Wilson fired his father, the superintendent named the younger Conlisk chief of the CPD's Traffic Division, and shortly thereafter, bumped him all the way up to deputy superintendent for field services, making him the department's second-in-command.[15] When Wilson retired in 1967, Conlisk took his place as superintendent. Daley's political opponents suggested that James Jr.'s career arc had been orchestrated from on high, implying that Daley had forced Wilson into promoting him as compensation for James Sr.'s firing.[16]

Regardless of how he'd come into the position, Conlisk was indeed a Daley lackey. Royko, never subtle, suggested that Conlisk was nothing more than a rubber stamp.[17] In an arrangement that recalls the long-standing tradition of machine meddling in the police, local judge Keith Wilson described Conlisk as the CPD's second-in-command, to Daley.[18] Years later, when Conlisk was being deposed in connection with killings committed by CPD officers, he launched into effusive, unsolicited praise for Daley, before his attorneys directed him to stick to the questions.[19] Whereas Wilson had worked tirelessly to disentangle the department from political influence, Conlisk's administration effectively ceded control of the CPD back to the mayor's office.

That happened at a moment when Daley's politics were becoming increasingly hard-line, resentful, and impatient. Royko once described Daley, prodigal son of Irish Bridgeport, as embodying both the best and worst of ethnic Chicago's rigid traditionalism and cloistered insularity. "Daley was a product of the neighborhoods," Royko wrote, "and he reflected it in many good ways—loyalty to the family, neighbors, old buddies, the corner grocer. . . . But there are other sides to Chicago's neighborhoods—suspicion of outsiders, intolerance toward the unconventional, bigotry, and bullying. That was Daley, too."[20] Year after year in the sixties, the mayor's politics and public face tracked more toward those worst inclinations.

He was not unique in this. The social activism that agitated the decade stirred a deep backlash, in Chicago and elsewhere. The fissures revolved around familiar touchstones—the war in Vietnam, civil rights and Black Power, hippies and the counterculture. Daley and his ideological compatriots saw a culture coming undone. The evidence was everywhere: in the subversion of traditional dress and music, casual drug use, the sexual revolution, the loud demands for radical democracy, and the growing opposition to American foreign policy. People who self-identified as traditionalists hated it all. "I'm getting to feel," one Chicago ad salesman told *Time* magazine in 1968, "like I'd actually enjoy going out and shooting some of these people. I'm just so goddamned mad. They're trying to destroy everything I've worked for—for myself, my wife, and my children."[21]

Subversive threats seemed everywhere at once. But few of them, save perhaps the protests against the Vietnam War, scandalized more than the decade's black insurgencies—especially Black Power politics and the torrent of urban rebellions/riots in places like Watts, Detroit, Baltimore, and New-ark.[22] The backlash was deep and intense, especially in white northern com-munities. Chicago was a case in point. There, segregation's deep cut into the city fabric, in almost all facets of life, kept many white citizens from seeing black activisms and grievances with any nuance at all. People who lived on the Gold Coast or in River North didn't go to Lawndale or Englewood (most still don't), and had no frame of reference to understand life and living con-ditions in those places. Meanwhile, white citizens who lived in close proxim-ity to black neighborhoods—like Daley's Bridgeport—largely despised that proximity and rejected the idea that blacks had much to complain about. When the local civil rights movement launched, they were enraged by ef-forts to crash the gates of white schools and neighborhoods; "This is not civil rights," as one white Chicago man, angry with black demands for open housing, put it.[23]

That visceral resentment and empathetic detachment consumed how people thought about race and crime. While law and order had been invoked in the past to counter black claims on freedom, in the sixties it became a loud racial dog whistle. In 1964 Republican presidential candidate Barry Goldwater made law and order the center of his campaign, calculating that it would yield a bumper crop of white votes.[24] He lost but set a useful tem-plate for other conservative politicians. In the 1968 campaign, both Repub-lican Richard Nixon and Independent George Wallace used the rhetoric of law and order to court white voters. Indeed, they jockeyed with one another repeatedly on that issue, trying to outmaneuver each other to be the tough-est law-and-order candidate.[25]

But liberals stoked the law-and-order fire, too. In 1968 Democratic presi-dential candidate Hubert Humphrey explored ways of keeping pace with Wallace and Nixon on the law-and-order front, even as he tried to reject the underlying racism. The chairman of the Democratic National Committee emphasized that Humphrey and the DNC were "intensely interested in pre-serving law and order," while Humphrey's chief opinion analyst conceded that law and order was "the major issue, no doubt."[26] Humphrey disavowed "the politics of fear and despair," in his words, but he nevertheless bent himself to the political pressure to address law and order. To do so, he ar-gued that social justice and greater investment in America's most poverty-stricken communities would be the key to unlocking a safer America. Like Lyndon Johnson had done in pitching the War on Poverty, Humphrey ar-gued that a more robust social welfare system would help curb criminality and radicalism. And like Johnson had done in pitching the War on Crime, Humphrey "relentlessly advocated federal assistance to local [police] de-partments," seeking to boost departments' material and technological resources.[27] Johnson, Humphrey, Goldwater, and Nixon, despite their differences, all saw the merit in reinforcing and monetarily supporting the nation's police apparatuses.

So, too, with Daley. He dismissed Humphrey's arguments about social welfare as a means of crime control, and had long been suspicious of the War on Poverty.[28] But he was in full alignment with his political peers in advocating for a stronger police force. This was especially true within the context of what he saw as collapsing law and order in a black community with which he had grown increasingly adversarial. Despite his public cordiality with Martin Luther King, Daley had viewed the CFM negatively, and resented arguments that Chicago was a racist city. He viewed the poverty of the city's black neighborhoods less as a product of endemic disadvantage than a function of personal and collective black failure. And he thought that the CPD under Wilson had done too much to coddle dissenters and dissidents. Daley wanted someone who would go further. He had that man in James Conlisk.

AS THE DOMINANT political temperature in America leaned toward law and order, whatever fetters existed on police departments began to fall off. At the federal level, the government began pumping increasing millions into the War on Crime, gifting police departments with more money for everything from technology and weapons to salaries and research programs. The Warren Court retreated from its early-decade rulings that expanded the rights of citizens and criminal suspects in the face of police power, most notably with its decision in *Terry v. Ohio* ruling stop-and-frisk to be constitutional. Elsewhere, the Attica Prison revolt in 1971 yielded severe blowback from various wings of the criminal justice apparatus, including propelling the Rockefeller Drug Laws in New York State, which established the mandatory minimum sentencing that would later come into vogue across the country.[29] Even being a recipient of welfare increasingly risked criminalization.[30]

State and local dynamics contributed to the change. Governor Sam Shapiro signed stop-and-frisk into Illinois law in 1968. Through federal block grants, Illinois began to use War on Crime funds to obtain helicopters for police use, alongside other measures to expand the technological and surveillance base. Meanwhile, James Conlisk began to rapidly dismantle the accountability mechanisms that his predecessor had put in place, stripping away the things that had caused so much of the rank and file to hate Wilson in the first place.

Among the first things to go were screening examinations for police officers, which had been used to gauge recruits' emotional stability and fitness for duty. In 1966 Wilson, understanding that better screening for recruits was needed and working with a grant from the LEAA, had commissioned University of Chicago experts to craft a screening program for the CPD that would weed out emotionally unfit applicants. In 1970, just as the program was about to go live after four years of construction, Conlisk killed it, calling the program redundant and claiming that it offered no new benefits to the department above its existing programs.[31] Taking it a step further, Conlisk then also *cut* the existing screening programs that he claimed the new ones duplicated. According to the *Tribune*, the programs were "screening out many recruits sponsored by city politicians," which was why they had to go.[32]

The result was the complete rejection of Wilson's goal of only employing people who were mentally and behaviorally sound. CPD critics had long argued that officers were insufficiently vetted prior to employment. The best system before had only monitored officers during their probationary periods, and had offered no meaningful filters for mental instability or prejudicial biases.[33] Now, new officers were joining the force after going through no screening whatsoever. A 1979 *Chicago Tribune Magazine* article on officer stress included a psychological analysis that police work "attracts three times as many persons with marked (psycho) pathology as one would expect by chance," and detailed a litany of cases of officers going "berserk." This included Michael Winfield, an officer flagged as a problem applicant by the University of Chicago screening process during its testing phase, who the CPD hired anyway. Winfield received fifteen complaints from citizens in his first fourteen months on the job during the early 1970s, and was eventually fired after he pistol-whipped a woman without cause and hit her pregnant daughter in the abdomen with his revolver, causing the baby to be born prematurely and permanently deformed. The city settled with the woman in 1974 for $131,000. Other cases involved officers kidnapping citizens, terrorizing innocent people without provocation, and one officer who killed his wife in a murder-suicide.[34]

Conlisk not only took aim at the screening system but also further undermined the functionality of the Internal Affairs Division (IAD, a rebrand of the Internal Investigations Division). In public testimony in 1972 about police violence against minority communities, police sergeant Arthur Lindsay testified to a "marked decline in the quality of [IAD] investigation" under Conlisk's watch.[35] The concluding report from those hearings excoriated the IAD and the CPD for working more as an operation to protect officers than functioning as an actual tool of discovery, and for taking far more seriously breaches of internal departmental decorum than violations of citizens' rights. The report cited a range of problems that were inherent in the system: "procedural defects," the veil of secrecy that surrounded investigations, the fact that the department self-investigated, and, above all else, "police attitudes."[36]

In time, that ineffectiveness would prove to be Conlisk's undoing, as stories of police corruption exploded back into Chicago's newspapers in the early 1970s and forced him to resign late in 1973. But meanwhile, it had extreme consequences for many Chicagoans in the short term. As police accountability mechanisms eroded, the use of aggressive preventive patrol grew, with the decoupling of power from accountability effectively meaning that officers were not just free but tacitly *encouraged* to be more aggressive, without fear of pushback.

Black Chicago would feel the effects most pointedly. Wilson had made it a matter of departmental gospel that aggressive preventive patrol would primarily be visited on black communities. But Daley wasn't satisfied, viewing the black community primarily as a problem in need of containment. As Royko wrote concerning the transition from Wilson to Conlisk, "The police sensed what Daley wanted and began pushing blacks harder."[37]

"Pushing blacks" meant, first and foremost, increasing still further the amount of police-black civilian contact and generating more black arrests. On the whole, the police drove the number of citizen arrests upward from around 250,000 in the mid-1960s to a mid-1970s peak of more than 330,000 before it settled and spiked again in the early 1980s.[38] Meanwhile, the number of black arrests in Chicago climbed by 56 percent—surpassing two hundred thousand, and averaging more than one arrest annually for every five black citizens.[39] At the same time, like a magic trick, white arrests continued the disappearing act that had begun during the 1950s. Despite the fact that officers had incentives to generate as many arrests as they could, and despite studies showing that officers were more likely to find arrest-worthy evidence when they stopped white suspects in comparison to black ones, police-white community contact and arrest continued its decline.[40] In 1968, Conlisk's first full year governing the department, black arrest totals were about 30 percent higher than white arrest totals. Within five years, they were more than 50 percent higher, and would persist at levels two to three times greater than white arrests until 1998, when the CPD effectively stopped arresting white people and drove black-to-white arrest disparities to rates of about 7:1.[41]

Those disparities were powerfully driven by the specific ways that police officers approached black people. A compendious study of police supervisory practices, conducted at the end of the 1960s by University of Illinois graduate student Larry Tifft, offers glimpses into these dynamics.[42] For his study, Tifft hired researchers who accompanied police officers out on their beats. Their nominal interest was to understand how supervisory systems influenced the dynamics of policing from beat to beat, but the data said just as much about officer interactions with community members. Young black men were officers' archetypical target. In the study's findings, officers were substantially more likely to search black suspects than white, and far more likely to do so with unsteady justification.[43] Officers working black neighborhoods were eight times more likely to approach suspects in "harassing" ways than were those working mixed, mostly white neighborhoods.[44] They were far less likely to try to establish a rapport with citizens they approached in black areas than in others.[45] And they routinely presumed black citizens' guilt when they stopped them, making them convince officers of their innocence.[46]

If and when people resisted these practices, they risked serious criminal charges. Prior to the *Terry* ruling, police hadn't shied away from using stop-and-frisk. After the ruling, though, they had even wider latitude to do so, and importantly, they were armed with the power to arrest people who protested such treatment. Indeed, lawyers in Chicago began increasingly to shorthand disorderly conduct, resisting arrest, and battery against a police officer as the "holy trinity" of charges officers would prefer against people protesting or resisting abusive and invasive treatment.[47]

Through mechanisms and practices like these, the CPD solidified its place as the piece of the state that black citizens came into contact with the most. By the early 1970s, as a report built on the back of community testimony put it: "Very few young Blacks and Browns have been spared the experience of having to swallow their pride and take a bullying insult from a police officer."[48] One young postal worker complained of having been stopped by police on twenty separate occasions in an eighteen-month span.[49] A paper written around the same time by black CPD officer Edward "Buzz" Palmer, cofounder of the Afro-American Patrolmen's League, lamented that "to grow up black and to be a man [means that it] is almost impossible not to have the ever present police record. Blacks standing on the corner in groups on hot, murky nights develop phobias in the minds of white policemen—blacks who later show up on police blotters as curfew violators."[50] One such young man might be the one identified in social work reports only as "James," who had by 1969 accumulated fourteen listed offenses with the CPD, the majority of them for curfew violations.[51] As a black man named Jackie Turner put it, after being manhandled by police while trying to do youth outreach and violence prevention in a South Side ghetto, "[If you're] a black man in his twenties living on the South Side . . . [and] you haven't met a cop by the time you're 18, you're a dude with a charmed life."[52]

"A Hard Line Police Approach": Chicago's War on Gangs

Part of the reason why so many young people by the late sixties and early seventies were invariably likely to "meet a cop" was because the department's surveillance apparatus was stretching aggressively outward toward the youth. This was true in its curfew enforcement, to be sure. But the most important piece of that matrix was the GIU.

The GIU had been formally constituted in March of 1967 by Orlando Wilson, who framed it as a means of confronting the gang violence that had escalated precipitously in the previous year.[53] Although Wilson officially organized the unit, he did so at such a late point in his career (with less than six months remaining, much of which would be spent transitioning operations to his successor) that ownership of the unit's actions and legacies lay more with Conlisk than with him.

From the outset, the GIU was deeply controversial. In the eyes of many members of the black community, it misdiagnosed the causes of gang violence and was extremely counterproductive in combating it. For instance, most activists and community members understood that better opportunities and a more supportive infrastructure for young people would be the best salve for violence. Indeed, during the summer of 1966, Martin Luther King, the SCLC, and the freedom movement more generally had tried to redirect the energies of black youth gangs to fight the city politically for better opportunities, rather than fighting each other. King's vision of the gangs working together toward achieving greater black freedom never came to fruition, but as we saw in the examples from the last chapter, gangs did labor to challenge structural inequalities, provide job training, and protest discrimination through the second half of the 1960s. Those efforts, if given time and followed to their logical conclusions of employment and educational opportunity, could have meant the elimination of gangs and cessation of gang violence. Instead, the GIU collaborated with the Daley machine to undercut those very same community betterment programs, because, according to many sympathetic observers of the gangs, any organizing successes that the gangs might have had "compromised [Daley's] power on the black South and West Sides."[54] As the historian Andrew Diamond notes, a survey of the GIU's records, which are housed together with those of the Red Squad, show plainly that the GIU infiltrated gangs involved in community betterment programs, "planted the seeds of destruction" within alliances that served such programs, and generally worked to sabotage those efforts.[55]

Meanwhile, the GIU also earned the scorn and resentment of many community members because of its reliance on brute force as a central operating principle. Initially slated as a ten-detective unit and headed by a black CPD lieutenant named Edward Buckney who would spend the next couple of years dramatically expanding it, the GIU was, in Buckney's words, reliant on "the hard-line police approach." It didn't matter if the gangs were a product of deprivation and desperation. As Buckney put it, "We're not concerned with sociological approaches."[56] The ensuing hard-line approach entailed many things. Some of them were constructive, including police-community meetings and weapons turn-ins. Most were far less so, including aggressive and sweeping arrest efforts, harassment, raids on gang strongholds and safe houses, and blunt physical force. The GIU also used coercion and subversion: infiltrating gangs, exacerbating intergang tensions, and in some cases working to cultivate a veritable war of extirpation. Gang members repeatedly reported being picked up by police officers who demanded information from them and, if they failed to give it, dropped them, vehicle-less, deep in a rival gang's turf.[57] Blackstone Ranger leader Jeff Fort's attorney, Marshall Patner, estimated in 1969 that Fort had been picked up by the GIU or other CPD officers more than 180 times, often with little apparent legal justification. Patner found such procedures to be so intrusive that he attempted to file a suit for injunctive relief in federal court.[58] Meanwhile, Charles Hurst, president of Malcolm X College, complained that GIU officers were harassing his students, disrupting their education and causing them to avoid the campus.[59]

Reports proliferated of gang unit officers profiling and rough-handling any young black men in the neighborhoods most closely under watch. In Englewood, officers were instructed to disperse any group of four or more teenagers, effectively crushing any chance of a normal social life that kids there might have had.[60] In the same neighborhood, an informant told a federal investigator trying to coordinate a gang weapons turn-in there that Englewood CPD officers had told the youths that they could just give the police officers the guns and they would in turn give them to the feds. But when the gang members kept their word and began bringing in their guns, the officers arrested them for possessing illegal weapons. According to the informant, the officers did so because they "needed the statistics."[61] A similar thing happened in Woodlawn. Local clergy and federal officials brokered a deal with gangs to turn in their weapons at First Presbyterian Church. When they did, police officers raided it, badly damaging bonds of trust that already hung by a thread, if there was indeed any connective tissue left there at all.[62]

The gangs' increasing body count could have been testimony to the negligible (at best) effect on gang violence that the GIU was offering. Nevertheless, the CPD continued to invest heavily in it. In 1968 alone, its projected strength increased from thirty-eight dedicated officers to two hundred.[63]

The next year, Daley and State's Attorney Ed Hanrahan collaboratively declared a "war on gangs" that would be mostly led by the gang unit.[64] In initiating that war, Daley and Hanrahan granted officers working in gang suppression an expansive set of powers. One of the unit's most careful contemporaneous observers, a black writer for the *Atlantic* named James Alan McPherson who spent six months researching the Blackstone Rangers and the GIU's relationship to it, labeled the GIU a "para-political force." "The relative ease with which its members operate within the police department," McPherson wrote, "and the cooperation they receive from the State's Attorney's Office and the Cook County jail, the influence they seem to have in the courts . . . all suggest that members of the Unit have more than ordinary police powers."[65]

Indeed, officials like Hanrahan and Conlisk conspired to give the GIU so much extraordinary power that the unit's function came to look more like the Red Squad than like a standard police unit. During CUCA's summer of action in 1969, CUCA representatives "charged police with the nighttime assault of gang members who participated in demonstrations," as well as with the unlawful arrests of numerous gang members, including Leonard Sengali— a key member of the Black P. Stone Nation and central cog in CUCA's organizing success.[66] Between the summer of 1969 and May of the following year, CUCA charged the police with murdering sixteen black youths, and gang members stood guard at the home of CUCA leader Reverend C. T. Vivian— a key figure in the civil rights movement both in Chicago and nationally— after receiving reports that the gang unit might come after him.[67] Such repression had the effect of undercutting CUCA's pursuit of jobs for young black men, gutting one of the most promising grassroots efforts to address the sort of inequality that produced gang violence in the first place.

The probability that the gang unit's war on CUCA was politically motivated was compounded by its attacks on black revolutionary movements more generally. Most prominent among these was the Black Panther Party, which, in addition to being targeted as a subversive group by the Red Squad and a general menace by the CPD broadly, was also targeted by the GIU. The gang unit's files are filled with panicked reports about the Panthers, largely culled from surveillance operations of and infiltrators inside the organization. Members of the GIU served among the FBI's approximately thirty informants funneling information to the bureau on the Chicago Panthers and the local party's leader, Fred Hampton.[68] They also almost assuredly contributed to the surveillance file that State's Attorney Edward Hanrahan assembled on the Panthers in the buildup to the police raid on Hampton's apartment in which CPD officers attached to Hanrahan's office assassinated Hampton and Mark Clark. Little wonder that in the wake of those assassinations, community outrage hammered the GIU, including fliers calling for Ed Buckney's "apprehension" for murder and conspiracy "in connection with the murder of Fred Hampton and the murder of other Black and Brown brothers in this here, Pig City."[69]

The point is not that gang violence wasn't a problem or that gangs were socially desirable. (They were not inherently *un*desirable, either, of course, as the example of CUCA demonstrates.) But the city opted to send in the police rather than deal seriously with the very real problems of socioeconomic inequality that conjured the gangs in the first place. The GIU became an instrument of almost unremitting repression that accomplished little of value for the community—and that, indeed, took a demonstrably adversarial stance to multiple groups working toward community betterment. And given the fact that gangs have repeatedly proved to be a wellspring of violence in black Chicago in the intervening years, the abject failure of Chicago to do anything constructive about gang violence in its infancy is a historical fact worthy of a reckoning.

A History of Violence: Officer-Involved Shootings in the Age of Black Power

Among the critiques people made of the GIU was that its officers were predisposed to violence, but this was actually true across the entire CPD. Contemporary observers argued, in fact, that violence was an expected outcome of aggressive preventive patrol—that the line between a nominally routine street interrogation and being subject to police violence in the process was perilously thin. As a 1972 report on police violence spearheaded by black Chicago congressman Ralph Metcalfe put it, "It is the basic law enforcement policy of the Police Department that aggressive police conduct toward citizens is desirable and legitimate. Abusive treatment of a citizen is viewed as merely over-zealous conduct within the scope of accepted police behavior."[70] Abuse, in other words, was a logical extension of police practices, not an aberration from them. And while violence had been central to the police department's operative DNA in black Chicago for years by that point, beyond the history and afterlives of past abuse, there was overwhelming evidence of its amplification in this moment. As early as 1967, studies showed that twice as many black Chicagoans as whites had seen the police use force or threats of force in handling civilians, and anecdotal evidence makes those figures seem very low.[71]

Perhaps worst and most notably, the volume of officer-involved killings went off the charts in the Conlisk years. Linda Anderson was nineteen when she died. Her husband, James, was in the army and stationed in Missouri, leaving Linda alone at their North Lawndale flat with their two infant children. In July of 1969, police responded to a potential assault against Linda taking place inside her apartment. Finding the thin plywood door locked when they arrived, one of the officers leveled a shotgun at the door and fired from less than four feet away. He failed to give verbal warning, missed the lock, and his buckshot hit Linda Anderson in the face. She died as her two kids watched. The CPD ruled the case an accident and suspended the officer for one day.[72]

Six weeks later, sixteen-year-old John Soto was shot in the back of the head by an officer on the Near West Side. Eyewitnesses insisted that Soto had been shot without provocation; police claimed he had been abusive toward the officer and that the gun had discharged in an ensuing scuffle.[73] Five days later, Soto's older brother Michael, a decorated army sergeant home on leave to attend John's funeral, was also shot dead by Chicago police. Department officers claimed the elder Soto had tried to rob a man, and confronted police with a gun when they tried to arrest him.[74] Both killings were ruled justifiable homicides by internal departmental review.

A month later, eighteen-year-old Steven Dixon died after an officer's bullet pulverized his chest as the officer worked to secure handcuffs on him. Witnesses said he lay wounded in the street for an hour before being taken to the hospital. He died on the way there. Justifiable homicide.[75]

Linda Anderson, Steven Dixon, the Soto brothers—these four lives were a small sample of a much larger pattern. All told, between 1969 and 1970 alone, the CPD killed at least fifty-six black men and three black women.[76] The rate at which black people died at the hands of the police was six times what it was for white Chicagoans, and was also the highest in the nation. Officers routinely claimed self-defense; in fifty-eight of the department's seventy-six total fatal-force cases over those two years, police alleged that the deceased had displayed a weapon. Yet in only six of the fifty-eight was fingerprint or ballistic evidence offered into evidence to substantiate the claims. Meanwhile, according to legal analyses conducted by the Northwestern University–housed Chicago Law Enforcement Study Group, in twenty-eight of the cases, there appeared to be "substantial evidence of police violation of administrative standards of conduct." In ten of those twenty-eight, evidence suggested "a substantial likelihood of criminal misconduct by the police officers during the fatal incident." Internal reviews exonerated the officers of wrongdoing in all but two of them.[77]

The scale of police violence in Chicago grew to such proportions that the FBI eventually began investigating whether or not CPD officers were actually *intentionally* killing black people. In May of 1972, bureau officials informed Conlisk that they were conducting a probe of five of his officers who together had allegedly murdered at least six black men between September of 1971 and February of 1972. Over the course of those six months, six bodies had turned up in the South Branch of the Chicago River—all of them shot in the back of the head execution-style, all of them black men. The FBI alleged that the murdered men had been drug dealers killed by police, who were operating as murderers for hire from rival drug dealers.[78]

All the officers in what the papers called this "hit squad" or "murder squad" were black. The limited benefits of black police had been evident to at least some degree since the days of Two-Gun Pete Washington, but this story reemphasized the fact. At the center of the FBI's investigation was Stanley Robinson, who had come up through the GIU. In June of 1972, Robinson's name leaked from the FBI investigation and landed in the *Tribune*'s reportage on the murder squad. A few days after, Robinson tried to fake his own kidnapping, calling in to the CPD and claiming to be an anonymous tipper who had seen him abducted on the West Side. In a bizarre collision of events, Robinson tried to frame three former Black Panthers for his kidnapping—all of whom happened to be informants working on the FBI's behalf.[79]

In February of 1973, a federal grand jury indicted Robinson, one other officer, and the man who'd allegedly hired them on ten counts, including conspiracy to commit murder and violating the civil rights of their victims.[80] In a public relations nightmare for Conlisk and the department, the trial played out day after day in the city newspapers. Some witnesses testified under oath that Robinson had kidnapped them and extorted money under threat of death.[81] William O'Neal, the infamous FBI informant who had helped facilitate the assassinations of Fred Hampton and Mark Clark in 1969, testified against Robinson alongside another Panther/FBI informant named Nathaniel Junior. Together, the two alleged that Robinson had confessed to having secured "murder contracts" where he would get cash for killing. (Robinson claimed to detest drug pushers, which was part of his rationale for deeming these things appropriate.[82]) O'Neal testified that he had actually been *with* Robinson the night that Robinson had killed twenty-two-year-old Jeff Beard. (Beard's family unsuccessfully sued O'Neal in the early 1980s, charging that as a federal informant, he had "a constitutional duty to prevent a killing that he knew was about to occur." A federal appeals court disagreed, although the incident likely furthered O'Neal's deep depression. He was entered into the federal Witness Protection Program in 1973, and lived secretively under the name William Hart from that point forward. He committed suicide in 1990.[83])

In October of 1973, a federal district court judge in Chicago sentenced Robinson to three life sentences, but the sentencing hardly closed the question of police violence.[84] That same year, the *Tribune* ran a series on police brutality, investigating hundreds of cases dating back to 1971. It eventually published detailed accounts of thirty-seven of them in an eight-part series in the newspaper, and bound the stories into a circulating pamphlet with an editorial introduction. The investigation's rationale was simple. As the introduction to the bound version put it, "The *Tribune* investigation was prompted by a glaring set of contradictions. In 1972 the Police Department's Internal Affairs Division, responsible for handling brutality complaints, received 827 such complaints but sustained only 29 cases against policemen. At the same time, this newspaper and scores of community organizations and civic leaders were receiving thousands of similar complaints that the department never seemed to act upon."

The *Tribune* intentionally downplayed the wages of race in the series, claiming that it "can happen to anyone" and trying to offer a diverse set of examples of brutality's victims. This wasn't true; there was no reasonable way to read the evidence and come away thinking that police brutality was a racially neutral social burden. But it made sense strategically, in trying to signal the severity of the problem to its majority-white readership. For its readers who perhaps didn't see themselves in Joshie Johnson, a black assembly line worker who received a fractured jaw and broken nose from an unprovoked attack by a CPD patrolman, the paper offered Irish immigrant, hospital janitor, and police beating victim Timothy Howard, or fourteen-year-old white teen Claude Bailey—a promising athlete who lost his left eye from a police beating in a case of mistaken identity.[85]

In both their particular details and broad findings, the investigations were scandalizing. As the *Tribune* summarized, "What emerged was a pattern of brutality by some policemen that could not be ignored." The investigation excoriated the department for "consistently ignor[ing] scathing criticism of half-hearted brutality investigations from such diverse groups as bar associations, federal study groups, and respected police organizations," as well as its discarding of the University of Chicago psychological screening system. It also highlighted the fact that "discipline against guilty policemen sometimes amounts to suspensions shorter than those levied against policemen who take an unauthorized lunch break."[86]

In the face of this years-long pattern of brutal and fatal force by the people under his command, Conlisk would simply remark that "brutality, like beauty, is in the eye of the beholder."[87]

"Occupational Paranoia": Police and Political Extremism

Conlisk's casual dismissal of the problem of brutality reflected police supporters' tendency to reject any and all criticisms as illegitimate by the late

1960s. The very fact that those criticisms existed at all made police resentful and angry, feeling alienated, persecuted, and harboring "an extreme sensitivity to criticism."[88] Majorities of the rank and file, in Chicago as elsewhere, felt disrespected and under siege. In Albert Reiss's study, 59 percent of the officers he interviewed said that they thought respect for the police was lower than twenty years previous; only 26 percent thought it was higher. That study was representative. Robert Fogelson termed this "the occupational paranoia of the big-city police," and as he summarized it, "In one interview after another the officers complained that . . . with few exceptions the citizens had little regard for the policemen's position and little sympathy for their problems."[89]

That persecution complex was heightened by the cascade of governmental reports in the mid- and late sixties that drew attention to the flawed and discriminatory nature of policing in black communities around the country. The most famous of these was the Kerner Commission report, which concluded that "white racism is essentially responsible for the explosive mixture which has been accumulating in our cities since the end of World War II." This included "pervasive discrimination and segregation," white flight, and ghettoization—with all the attending detriments and destructions.[90] But it also identified repressive policing as a primary culprit. "The police," the report's authors wrote, "are not merely a 'spark' factor. To some Negroes police have come to symbolize white power, white racism and white repression. And the fact is that many police do reflect and express these white attitudes. The atmosphere of hostility and cynicism is reinforced by a widespread belief among Negroes in the existence of police brutality and in a double standard of justice and protection—one for Negroes and one for whites." The assessment was accurate, even if it undersold just how historically embedded these problems had been. (Kenneth Clark testified to the committee that reading the postmortems of Chicago 1919, Harlem 1935, Harlem 1945, and Watts 1965 was "a kind of Alice in Wonderland—with the same moving picture reshown over and over again, the same analysis, the same recommendations, and the same inaction."[91])

Police bristled. Across the country, organizations like the International Conference of Police Associations, New York's Law Enforcement Group, and Los Angeles's Fire and Police Research Association lashed out at external critics of the police—whether they were groups they considered subversive like the ACLU or the CP, or formal governmental bodies like the Kerner or McCone Commissions.[92] They routinely based their cases on arguments that critics of the police were, essentially, hateful bigots who were just as bad as any other hateful bigot. The Chicago Confederation of Police's president complained that the police seemed to be the "only persons left in the entire country . . . being disciplined," and further framed the police as "a despised and hated minority" who were "S.O.B's and M.F's and whatever else an irate citizen chooses to call them."[93] A sympathetic police writer for the *Chicago Sun-Times* echoed the sentiment, arguing that "the only minority group that persons who consider themselves liberal would dare to stereotype" were police officers, and calling police critics "pigots."[94]

As leftist criticisms of police misconduct mounted, the police did two things. First, they targeted the Left for reprisals, and second, they themselves moved further to the right politically. It is, predictably, within the context of the Red Squad that these trends can be seen most clearly. The full content of the Red Squad's activities from this time will never be known. In 1973 an organization called the Alliance to End Repression sued the CPD (the proxy for the Red Squad in this case) and the FBI for infringing on the rights of its members and those of other organizations by conducting illegal surveillance on them in the name of national security. After years of litigation, the lawsuit ultimately bent the CPD toward a consent decree that, theoretically, sharply curtailed the Red Squad's activities. But in the process, fearing discovery of its activities, the CPD destroyed millions of pages of records about the Red Squad's actions—including files on at least 105,000 individuals and 1,300 organizations.[95] What was lost will never be fully recovered.

But we do know that the squad's surveillance and disruptive attention was trained squarely on Chicago's political Left, and routinely embraced its political Right.[96] An illustrative example is the squad's relationship to a Far Right organization called the Legion of Justice. The legion had its origins in opposing the CFM's 1966 open housing campaign, and gathered its organizational base from the failed 1968 Republican gubernatorial campaign of its founder, S. Thomas Sutton. By 1969 the legion claimed to have at least two hundred members in Chicago, and its primary occupation was to terrorize Chicago's Left into submission. It worked closely with the Red Squad in pursuing that goal. Legion activists burgled, bugged, harassed, and threatened leftists in the city, and turned over to the Red Squad a wide assortment of documents that they stole. In November of 1969, legion activists raided the offices of the Young Socialist Alliance, maced and clubbed YSA members, and stole money, books, and records from them. Police refused to arrest anyone from the legion. Routinely, legion members committed acts of violence against leftists, who found not only that the police were unwilling to punish legionnaires but also that they arrested their victims.[97]

That the legion was able to cultivate such a smoothly functioning relationship with the Red Squad is not surprising, but it is alarming. Much like their federal counterparts, undercover police officers made a habit of subverting the laws that they were charged with upholding in service of undermining the Left. One study on police subversion by leftist dissidents (which the Red Squad logged as "anti-police propaganda") reflected numerous accounts of agents provocateurs working inside antiwar organizations, trying to encourage leftists toward evermore extremist positions in order to damage their public image and stoke controversy. The same study collected testimony from peace groups whose offices had been burgled and raided and who suspected the Red Squad of being the perpetrators, echoing much of what is known about its affiliation with the Legion of Justice.[98]

Those flirtations and collaborations with right-wing extremists flared out into electoral politics, with many police officers embracing extremist politicians in exchange for support for law and order. Tellingly, by 1968, police were giving open support to the politician most synonymous with white supremacy in 1960s-era America, the archracist and segregationist Alabama-governor-turned-political-candidate George Wallace. Popular memory anoints Richard Nixon as the nation's law-and-order candidate in the 1968 election. Yet many of the actual agents *of* that law and order were drawn further to the extreme right, supporting Wallace instead. In the lead-up to that year's election, the national FOP invited Wallace to deliver the keynote speech at its national convention as part of his campaign circuit. In full-blown conspiracy theorist mode, Wallace hammered on the podium and railed against the breakdown of law and order and the riots of recent years, blaming them not on poverty and frustration with a broken social contract but on a secret "conference of world guerilla warfare chieftains [meeting] in Havana, Cuba" who were planning a Communist assault on the United States. He accused the Johnson administration of neglecting to do anything to "nip these plans in the bud," and demanded to know "Why weren't the revolutionaries arrested—prosecuted—and punished?" He accused the federal judiciary of gutting police officers' ability to contain crime, and declared that if "the police of this country could run it for about two years, then it would be safe to walk in the parks."[99] While Wallace ranted and raved and delivered bombastic mistruth after wild-eyed conspiracy, banners and buttons cheered his presidential run.[100] "Standing ovation followed standing ovation" as he spoke to the crowd of assembled police officers.[101] The FOP's president, John Harrington, personally endorsed Wallace for president, and confidently stated that he suspected most police officers would vote for him.[102]

Voting data doesn't exist that would tell us whether or not Harrington was right. But the embrace of Wallace, even if just in the moment of that room more so than in the voting booth, is an important marker of the FOP membership's political temperature. Whether they actively agreed with Wallace's racist and conspiracy-driven tirades, or were simply willing to look past them because Wallace promised them infinite resources and respect, police organizations like the FOP and the men and women they represented were very clearly and fully on board to dance with racist demagogues.

And none of this even yet touches the most extreme case of the CPD's ties to right-wing racist extremism. In the winter of 1967–68, an explosive story hit the newspapers showing that a Ku Klux Klan cell had been operating within the police department. The story's centerpiece was Donald Heath, a thirty-year-old white patrolman and six-year veteran of the force, who lived with his wife and children in the western section of Logan Square, and who was also the Illinois Klan's grand dragon.[103] Heath worked in the majority-black Fillmore District on Chicago's West Side. He despised black people and believed in segregation in all facets of life. Ever since the 1966 CFM had briefly threatened to destabilize Chicago's segregation and Orlando Wilson had tried to get CPD officers to protect movement activists, Heath had started courting other white officers to the Klan. Within a year, he'd successfully recruited at least five, including two others who worked the same district as he did.

It had been black CPD captain George T. Sims who first reported the Klan's operations to James Conlisk, after word leaked out within the ranks. (It is worth pointing out that Heath recruited among his white colleagues for over a year, with apparently none of them reporting him to their superiors.) Conlisk launched an investigation, and two days after Christmas, investigators were ready to move on their leads. They stormed through Heath's home and found an arsenal: an estimated 200,000 bullets and shells, many of them army-issue and designed to puncture through armor; seven hand grenades; a pump shotgun; a Winchester shotgun; an M-1 army rifle; a Ruger .22-caliber rifle; a .45-caliber automatic; two semiautomatic rifles; a zip gun; two smoke grenades; a gas mask; daggers, machetes, and swords; and two large crosses designed for burning.

Three of the six officers implicated in the ensuing investigation resigned almost immediately. Heath and two others—Ernest Semet and William Plogger—did not, and their refusal to resign posed problems for the city and the CPD. There was nothing technically illegal about Klan membership, nor was there anything in the police code of conduct that explicitly stated that such membership was a conduct or ethics violation. In order to bring the men forward for disciplinary hearings, then, the department was ultimately forced to rely on charges that Klan membership constituted a conflict of interest, and that because Heath and the others had refused to aid the investigation, they had breached departmental protocols.

As the winter dragged on, suspended from the force and with his hearing pending, Heath took to the local lecture circuit. In the month after his

'This way we get no police brutality complaints'

KU KLUX
KLAN KOPS

JENSEN

Political cartoonist
Cecil Jensen responds
to revelations of the
Ku Klux Klan operat-
ing within the CPD.
Clipping in American
Civil Liberties Union,
Illinois Division Rec-
ords, box 356, folder 1,
Special Collections
Research Center,
University of Chicago
Library.

suspension from the force, Heath claimed to have conducted more than twenty speaking engagements in Chicago and its suburbs. A *Chicago American* reporter, Frank Von Arx, followed Heath to one such event—a ninety-minute talk and Q&A with forty-five supporters in the Chicago suburb of Brookfield in late January of 1968. Ernest Semet and William Plogger, the two other suspended policemen/Klansmen, accompanied him. Heath told his audience that "it is no longer . . . a question of communism. It is now racism and whether the Black Power people will accomplish their plot to overrun the nation by 1972." Heath predicted riots in 1968, offering up "the brotherhood of klan membership, and the klan's network of neighborhood klaverns as the last reliable defense against Black Power."[104]

It was the end of February before Heath's hearing finally started. There, the extent of his hatred for black people, and his willingness to do anything in his power to undermine the black freedom movement, came fully out into the open. CPD officer James Tobin, who, at the encouragement of departmental investigators, had let Heath recruit him into the Klan, delivered the key testimony. According to Tobin, Heath had plans to muster "between 1,500 and 2,000 armed klansmen" if Martin Luther King tried to return to Chicagoland. He also detailed plans to dynamite the Chicago headquarters of the black nationalist Revolutionary Action Movement. And most shockingly, according to Tobin, Heath had concocted a plan to assassinate Mayor Daley and two top CPD officials, and to do it at a time of civil unrest so that it would be "blamed on the Negroes."[105] Heath called the charges lies, but in early April, he and his fellow Klansmen were fired from the police force. Heath subsequently moved to Milwaukee. Later that year he was investigated for conspiring to assassinate the entire United States Supreme Court.[106]

Chicago 1968: A Tale of Two Riots

Heath was right about one thing: 1968 would indeed be an explosive year in Chicago. But rather than the DNC riot, there was another event that year which was even more crucial for understanding the general tenor and content of policing. It erupted that April.

The evening TV newscasts beamed into Chicago's living rooms news that stunned the city. It was April 4, 1968. Five hundred miles to the southwest, in Memphis, Tennessee, Martin Luther King Jr. had been murdered.

King hadn't spent extended time in Chicago for a year and a half, yet the assassination hit the city hard. Many mourned as Walter Cronkite and other newsmen delivered the somber word of King's murder. In Chicago's black neighborhoods, people huddled around their TV sets—weeping, cursing, seething.[107]

When dawn broke on Chicago the following day, it was a gorgeous, picturesque Friday morning. Concerns had been raised about the possibility of protest actions and perhaps angry violence in response to King's murder, from black youth especially. Chicago Public Schools administrators made the choice to forge ahead with a school day.

Absenteeism was abnormally high that day, particularly in majority-black high schools on the West Side. Those students who showed up were furious—about King's assassination, and about their schools' decision to proceed as though everything was fine. Kids pulled fire alarms, which swelled and emptied school halls. Each time, fewer and fewer students came back. By midmorning, principals were calling in the police "for assistance in quelling vandalism and responding to some few actual and threatened physical assaults by black students on whites." By noon, most high schools on the West and South Sides had emptied out and closed for the weekend. Thousands of angry youth were sent out into the streets.

Those who didn't head home joined growing crowds outside. By the time the schools were closing, the many white storeowners who did business on the West Side had closed for the day. Targeting those white stores, which functioned as stand-ins for the larger economic extractions pummeling black neighborhoods, some black youth began busting out shop windows and damaging storefronts. Later that day, the looting of those same stores began, as did arson fires. Reports of sniper shots, directed at firefighters and police officers, were rarely confirmed but nevertheless potent. Daley requested the help of the National Guard. The next day he and Acting Governor Sam Shapiro asked the Johnson White House for federal troops to help contain and quell the uprising.

The uprising's first day was its most explosive, but throughout the weekend, Conlisk kept the CPD on high alert, and security in the streets was overwhelming. Conlisk extended police shifts from the standard eight hours to twelve hours on/twelve hours off, canceled officers' days off, and shifted nonuniformed officers over to uniformed duty.[108] More than three hundred task force officers flooded the West Side, and the department augmented their ranks with "incident control teams." Black CPD officer Renault Robinson recalled huge squads of officers, "maybe 50 of us at a time," would "just sweep down a block and grab everybody and fill up the police wagons. I mean everybody."[109] National Guard and federal army troops that numbered around eighteen thousand buttressed their ranks.

These security forces, and the CPD in particular, engaged the mostly young rioters seemingly in accordance with the dictates of war. In the far smaller conflagration on the West Side two years earlier, at least some citizens had fired on police in retaliation for officers' rough handling of black civilians. As a result, officers sent into the King riots were a potent mixture of angry, scared, and heavily armed. Many of them carried bayoneted guns. Jeeps crept through the West Side, machine guns attached and swiveling.[110] Numerous observers lamented the police use of guns in response to rioters that were seldom armed with serious weapons. At least one district commander facing a crowd of high school students fired his gun multiple times in the air to try to convince them to scatter.[111]

That sort of conduct took center stage as people tried to sort out what had happened in the uprising's aftermath. In total, eleven people died—all of them black, all of them men, all of them between sixteen and thirty-four years old.[112] Given the demographics of those participating, that isn't especially surprising. Nevertheless, a number of those deaths had happened at the hands of the police under suspicious circumstances, including four in a two-square-block radius within a few hours of one another. Concerning

CPD officer arrests a man during the 1968 West Side uprising. Chicago History Museum, ICHi-068945; Declan Haun, photographer.

those killings, the city committee that Daley convened to study the riot wrote that "allegedly two police cars containing two to four white police-men in each car who were armed with rifles were in the two block area at this time and were seen shooting on the level into stores" where two of the men died, and also shooting into the alley where the other two bodies were found.[113] In 2002 the journalist Christopher Chandler uncovered un-published newspaper investigations from the riot's aftermath that corrobo-rated the story. According to those investigations, one of the storeowners where the men were killed reported "hundreds of spent bullets on the floor of his shop the next morning." The investigator, Ben Heineman Jr., checked with the coroner, who told him that all four men had died "from shotguns whose shells had been packed with extra shot to be especially lethal." It ap-peared, as Chandler put it, that the four men had essentially been executed by a CPD "hit squad."[114]

Daley was unconcerned with reports of excessive force, however, and, in-stead, a week and a half later, he lashed out at his police department for being too *lenient* during the uprising. According to the mayor, earlier that day he had met with Conlisk, "and I gave him the following instructions, which I thought were instructions on the night of the fifth that were not car-ried out: I said to him very emphatically and very definitely that [he should issue an order] immediately and under his signature to shoot to kill any arsonist or anyone with a Molotov cocktail in his hand in Chicago because they're potential murderers, and to issue a police order to shoot to maim or cripple any arsonists and looters—arsonists to kill and looters to maim and detain."[115] Here was Daley—still one of the most powerful Democrats in America—offering one of the most extreme statements of law-and-order advocacy of the entire postwar era.

The order was a political lightning bolt. Virtually every major newspaper in America not only picked up the story but also took a stance on it within its editorial pages. Prominent political cartoonists Reginald Manning (of the *Arizona Republic*, syndicated by the prominent McNaught Syndicate) and Bill Mauldin (at that point, of the *Chicago Sun-Times*), with three Pulitzer Prizes between them, symbolized the split opinions well. To the conservative Man-ning, Daley's order functioned as a rational line in the sand. In a cartoon titled "Spare Some Sobs for Us," syndicated in dozens of papers across the United States, Manning characterized as "demagogues" those who would weep over Daley's order, while ghosts of "black and white victims of arson and mob murders" hung in the smoke above burned out buildings. To the civil libertarian Mauldin, meanwhile, the order was a slippery slope into the routinization of police violence. Casting Daley in a ten-gallon hat and Western sheriff-wear, giving him a revolver, and lending him the nickname

Political cartoonist Reginald Manning's cartoon takes opponents of Mayor Daley's "shoot-to-kill" order to task. Courtesy of Reg Manning Collection, Greater Arizona Collection, Arizona State University Library.

"Deadeye Dick," Mauldin depicted the mayor holding up a full-human-body "Chicago Police Target" that instructed officers to "kill arsonists" in the head and heart, "graze jostlers" in the elbow, "wing pickpockets" in the hands, and so on.

Citizens responded, too. Thousands of letters poured into Daley's office. *Time* magazine picked up the story about that correspondence, and Daley

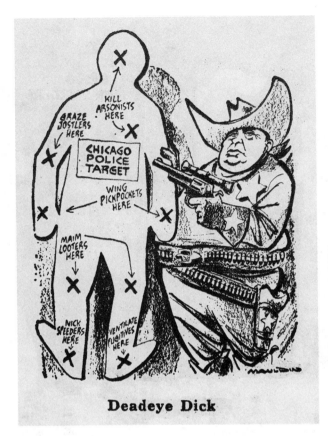

Political cartoonist Bill Mauldin's cartoon opposing Mayor Daley's "shoot-to-kill" order. Original source unknown; clipping found in American Civil Liberties Union, Illinois Division, Records, box 536, folder 1, Special Collections Research Center, University of Chicago Library.

told its reporters that the number of letters supporting him ran about fifteen to one against those opposing. (His personal papers, which contain numerous boxes stuffed full of letters to the mayor in the wake of the shoot-to-kill order, reflect a similar imbalance.) Those who offered dissent did so strongly. One letter writer asked Daley if the mayor "[planned] to issue his policemen hunting licenses for the summer season" and whether he planned to give patrol officers a raise since they were taking on new professional duties as "prosecuting attorney, chief witness, sole judge, and executioner."[116] Another writer, a Chicago woman, tellingly told Daley that he had "given some of the Police what they want" by insisting that they shoot to kill. "To give them this Judicial Power," she wrote, "is like putting the WHOLE COLORED RACE in front a firing squad."[117]

But such criticisms drowned in the flood of support. The order made Daley a star to the millions of whites across America (and the world) who saw the insurrection as symptomatic of black America's larger failings. Letters of praise flowed in from as far away as apartheid Southern Rhodesia, from which the white director of a safari company commended Daley for responding assertively to "the Hellish state of law and order."[118] Closer to home, a white Chicago woman praised Daley's order and excoriated Illinois Senator Charles Percy for opposing it, framing herself as one of many "white women who are prisoners in our own apartments," living in fear for their "safety and welfare."[119] A supportive Georgian similarly praised Daley's action, complaining that the only reason black people ever rioted was that "they wanted the Federal Government or Local Government to give them something."[120] A Pennsylvania man offered an unhinged letter of support in which he talked about the larger threats of "Negro COMMUNISM" and "CANNIBAL BLACK POWER NEGROS" who were seeking to "take over the United States, with their hidden guns."[121] A woman from the small town of Columbus, Wisconsin, applauded Daley as well, claiming that "'racism' for many negros is an excuse to loot and cause trouble."[122] Milwaukee resident Roy Hawkins, no doubt projecting his feelings about his own city's black freedom movement and its uprising of the year before, offered Daley only five sentences.[123] The last three of them were these: "It is about time somebody, somewhere starts talking the language that Niggers can understand— BULLETS. They don't seem to understand WORDS—so talk their language. I take a dim view of most, if not all Democrats, but I will back you 100% when it comes to a safe street to walk on."[124]

Responses to Daley's order in and around the CPD reflected a similar dynamic. Conlisk bent to Daley's pressure, issuing the requested shoot-to-kill/ shoot-to-maim order. In so doing, he also inadvertently showed who was in charge of police policy and explicitly established lethal violence as appropriate police procedure—even for property crimes.[125] Orlando Wilson had formalized a strict (and seemingly sensible) policy against firing into crowds, or firing warning shots if there was any risk of harming bystanders. That was now nullified, creating confusion and concern in the minds of some officers.[126] But most of those who were vocal on the matter supported the mayor. The clearest statement of such support came from local FOP president Joseph LeFevour, who telegrammed Daley: "I can assure you that you will have the fullest cooperation of the Chicago policemen in carrying out your orders. Also, you have our deepest respect and admiration for the unequivocal stand you have taken with respect to the anarchy that is threatening to destroy our society."[127]

For LeFevour and other officers, seeing Daley's violent directives as a noble line in the sand was not an abstraction. Rather, to them, what was happening in the country was professional and personal at once—not only

a culture run amok in lawlessness and immorality but one that actively rejected their personal legitimacy and authority as police officers. LeFevour's
vision of a properly functioning society may have been deeply narrow and
his politics provincial, but he was nevertheless channeling a common griev-
ance among many officers.

Such sentiments were amplified, not diminished, when the DNC riot exploded several months later. After the police riot in downtown Chicago,
officers routinely sounded both aggrieved and furious in describing their
nominal adversaries. One groused that "blacks used their plight to attack
the country and the war and we saw them the same as any of those longhairs
that were ruining the country."[128] Recalled another: "They were all against
our society; blacks and the antiwar crowd, they were all the same. . . . [They]
had declared war on us."[129] And another: "We were told not to take any prisoners, that we were in a war, and that the taxpayers were not going to pay us
to watch their city go down the shitter."[130]

Importantly, such police opinions held increasingly powerful sway in the
larger society. Like Daley's shoot-to-kill order, the DNC protests and police
riot simultaneously demonstrated America's heightening readiness for a
law-and-order agenda, placed Chicago at the middle of that emerging consensus, and amplified in people's minds the very state of lawlessness that
needed combating.[131] Conlisk critiqued the famous police-riot characterization of events at the DNC as out of touch: "To speak of a 'police riot' is to
distort the history of those August days. The world knows who the rioters
were."[132] America agreed. After the King riots, Daley had told *Time* that the
letters coming into his office offering comment were running fifteen-to-one
in favor of his shoot-to-kill order. Now, CBS similarly reported that the letters they were receiving editorializing on the CPD's DNC actions were running eleven-to-one in favor of the police.[133] A University of Michigan survey
found that 55 percent of respondents thought the police used "the right
amount" or "too little" force; only 19 percent said that they thought it had
been "too much."[134]

WHAT HAPPENED at the DNC riot was a critical moment in America's political history. But it was not a critical moment in the history of police and
state violence. To the degree that it matters to the story of policing, it is in
what it did to better pique the moral imagination of some white Americans
regarding the terrible realities of police violence.

But black people in Chicago already knew. Most of the protesters at the
DNC (most, though not all of them, white) eventually went home, and the
places they went home *to* were generally not communities both awash in

violence and stalked by police officers racking up arrests for minor offenses. And that is the crux of the matter: what was remarkable for the DNC demonstrators in Grant Park who have been lionized in the mythos of the sixties would have been painfully unremarkable if translated to the black West Side and parts of the South Side.

While the DNC protests dominate the public narrative about policing in late-sixties Chicago, the far more important story from that time was that the CPD's relationship to black Chicago dropped to its nadir. At a series of police-community meetings in 1972, Andrew Barrett, head of the Southside NAACP, called Jim Conlisk a "god damn liar," and no one spoke up on the superintendent's behalf; "in black neighborhoods," an advisor wrote to Daley after the meetings, "it has been hard to detect any local support" for the police.[135] The full and throttling power of the police force, constructed by Orlando Wilson, had now, with Wilson gone, been decoupled from any semblance of accountability and oversight. Over the course of the next decades, all of Chicago would deal with the consequences—whether directly (via abuse, harassment, torture, or incarceration) or indirectly (via taxpayer-funded cash settlements, to the tune of hundreds of millions of dollars, to the victims of police violence).

Beyond the King riots and on top of the constantly dysfunctional relationship it had with the community, arguably the deepest collective wound that the CPD opened for black Chicago was sliced in the winter of 1969, when police officers murdered two young men largely for the crime of trying to reimagine the social contract, and who in that reimagining assertively challenged the legitimacy of the city's police force to operate in accordance with its own status quo. That wound never healed. But it did help fuel the largest grassroots mobilizing for police reform and abolition that Chicago has ever seen—at least, perhaps, until the 2010s.

CHAPTER 7

Do You Consider Revolution to Be a Crime?

FIGHTING FOR POLICE REFORM

I t was freezing cold in the early morning hours of December 4, 1969. Chicago's sidewalks were laden with ice and salt, and outside Fred Hampton's apartment on Monroe Street, the snow was piled high above the curbs fronting the block's row houses. Inside, Hampton slept. Exhausted, he had fallen asleep while on the phone with his parents after midnight, leaving his eight-and-half-months-pregnant fiancée, Deborah Johnson, to wrap up the conversation.[1] Scattered throughout the rest of the apartment, seven other people slept, all of them members of the BPP, the Illinois chapter of which the twenty-one-year-old Hampton chaired.

Ever since rising to the Panther chairmanship the year before, Hampton had been direct and loud in his condemnations of the police. And those condemnations had only escalated in recent months as police violence and abuse had worsened, with Hampton excoriating the police killings of John and Michael Soto and others like them. This coincided with a deepening hostility between the Panthers and the CPD—one that included numerous attacks by the CPD on Panther offices, at least one unarmed Panther killed by the police, and a Panther affiliate killing two CPD officers in a deadly standoff in Washington Park that November.[2] The department had long considered Hampton, as the party's leader, to be one of its top public enemies, and had worked steadily to kill Hampton's growing influence. After the November deaths of the two officers in Washington Park, they decided to move.

At 4:30 on that cold December morning, the West Side blanketed in darkness, fourteen police officers assembled outside Hampton's apartment, nominally to serve a search warrant to look for illegal weapons. The officers were primarily from a special CPD detail attached to the office of Attorney General Edward Hanrahan, who would emerge as the face of the state's cover-up of what happened next.[3] The officers knew virtually every piece of information that there was to know about the apartment's layout, what weapons were inside, and who was there. They had obtained that information as part of a partnership between the CPD and the FBI, after FBI Special Agent Roy Mitchell, using pictures of the two officers killed in Washington Park, had convinced Chicago Panther Chief of Security and longtime bureau informant William O'Neal that it was time for the CPD to move on the Panthers. O'Neal drew detailed maps of Hampton's apartment for Mitchell, described the weapons kept there, and detailed the comings and goings of various people in and out of the place.[4]

At around 4:45, gunfire exploded the predawn darkness. For ten minutes, machine-gun, shotgun, and pistol fire punctured the quiet. Police fired more than one hundred shots into the apartment. The Panthers returned one solitary shot—one that, according to one survivor's testimony, was fired errantly by Mark Clark, a Peoria Panther leader visiting Chicago, when a police bullet hit him in the heart. At the end of the shooting, four Panthers— Verlina Brewer, Ronald Satchel, Blair Anderson, and Brenda Harris—had sustained multiple gunshot wounds but survived. Fred Hampton and Mark Clark both lay dead. Deborah Johnson testified that Hampton had survived the initial barrage of police gunfire but had then been executed by two shots to the back of the head when officers found him lying in bed, still breathing.[5] A haunting Associated Press photograph from after the raid shows city police officers smiling widely as they wheel Hampton's body away.

The city, CPD, and state's attorney's office all blamed the Panthers for what had happened. But the officers, at best, had been egregiously reckless with human life, and the evidence overwhelmingly suggests that they had effectively performed an execution. The city would later settle a multimillion-dollar civil suit with Hampton's family, and inquiries into the raid by outside parties laid out a fairly clear case that police and public officials had intentionally killed him. The consulting criminologist Herbert MacDonell, brought in to examine the scene as a ballistics expert, said without reservation that the police had clearly fired first and that the Panthers had only fired once.[6] David Spain, the director of pathology at the Brookdale Hospital Center in Brooklyn and a professor of clinical pathology at the New York University School of Medicine, performed one of the autopsies on Hampton's body, and concluded from the evidence at hand that "Fred Hampton was shot in full view of the killer while in a defenseless position, and not in a blind shoot-out."[7] The Commission of Inquiry into the Black Panthers and the Police—founded in the wake of Hampton and Clark's killings and made up of legal and intellectual luminaries like Marion Wright Edelman, Kenneth Clark, Roy Wilkins, and Ramsey Clark—concluded that police actions on that terrible December night "were more suited to a wartime military commando raid than the service of a search warrant."[8]

The very next day after Hampton and Clark's deaths, as black Chicago grieved, the CPD launched a second raid that looked eerily like what they had done at Hampton's apartment. This time their target was Bobby Rush, Hampton's second-in-command. (Rush is now a U.S. congressman representing Chicago.) The details were all the same: a predawn raid, a swarm of officers nominally there to serve a search warrant for illegal weapons, and forced entry on the premises.[9] The main difference was that no one was home at Rush's place. The day before, Louis Truelock, one of the Panthers who had survived the raid and been arrested by the CPD, reported to the Panthers' attorney Jeffrey Haas that he'd overheard one police officer tell another, "Rush is next."[10] Haas had relayed the information to Rush, who went into hiding with Jesse Jackson's Operation Breadbasket, and later remembered that "immediately after Fred was killed I was running for my life."[11] Running may indeed have saved his life.

The Chicago police went hunting Panthers at the end of the 1960s in part because they saw the party as a revolutionary organization. When James Conlisk was deposed by People's Law Office attorneys years later in lawsuits surrounding Hampton's death, he was asked, "Do you consider revolution to be a crime?" On the audiotapes, his discomfort is palpable. He finally answers with a long-winded version of "yes."[12]

But Conlisk and the men under his command also resented the fact that the Panthers represented the most assertive challenge to police power that Chicago had seen since at least the 1930s, and quite possibly ever. At both the local and national levels, critiquing the police was a staple of Panther rhetoric and a core tenet of their organizing strategy. This was in some ways what prompted J. Edgar Hoover to name the party as the most significant domestic security threat in the country, and what caused prominent police representatives like the FOP's Joseph LeFevour to decry them locally. As LeFevour said after Hampton's death, in a feverish chickens-come-home-to-roost justification, "The Black Panthers preach, every day, hate: Kill Whitey. Kill the police. Kill the pigs. Hate, hate, hate. That's all that you hear from 'em."[13]

There was no one in the organization who disproved LeFevour's lie better than Fred Hampton. To be sure, he was, first and foremost, concerned with black liberation and black freedom—a black revolutionary fiercely dedicated to his people. At the same time, he understood that oppression in America, despite the unique forms of savagery that it exacted upon the black poor and working poor, did not singularly confine itself to the black community. Eloquent, brilliant, and uncommonly effective at organizing people across racial lines, Hampton was the architect of Chicago's famed Rainbow Coalition, which united people from various marginalized and radical sections of Chicago around common grievances. In his hands, the traditional Panther axiom "Power to the People" became explicitly inclusive: "White Power to white people, Brown Power to brown people, Yellow Power to yellow people, Black Power to black people, X power to those we left out, and Panther Power to the Vanguard Party."[14]

But it is true that Hampton and those surrounding him were commonly aggrieved with and fundamentally opposed to police violence, harassment, and repression. Matching the rhetorical logics that pulsed through much of the larger Black Power moment, Hampton and others around him often spoke in twinned languages of community uplift and resistance to state and police power—of the police as an illegitimate occupying force, and of the need for community members to educate themselves on their rights and responsibilities to check the power of that force. These concerns were central, not peripheral. As Hampton explained the party's intellectual essence, the BPP was "dedicated to the overthrow of the brutal, racist American system. The only way to deal with the system is to deal with the enforcers of the system. The pigs are the enforcers. They come into the black community and brutalize and victimize black people. We intend to put a stop to that kind of violence."[15] He repeatedly denounced the CPD's "harassment of ghetto blacks," as the grand jury investigating his death reported, and promised self-defense of the community "if police brutality in the ghetto did not cease."[16]

Such talk alarmed police and city officials. As we have seen, even before the Illinois Panthers rose to prominence in the gloaming of 1968, the police were on edge—feeling under siege and alienated from the communities they were duty bound to at least nominally serve and protect. But the sense of alarm was heightened by the militant criticisms of the police that the Panthers leveled, and amplified still further by the fact that 1969 was a particularly dangerous year for police in Chicago, with seven officers killed in the line of duty, including the two killed on the South Side a few weeks before the CPD murdered Hampton and Clark.[17]

It is likely that officers and officials who celebrated Fred Hampton's death late in 1969 hoped that the revolutionary politics and square-jawed critiques of the police that he offered would die with him. His assassination did cripple the Panthers in many ways; according to Joshua Bloom and Waldo Martin, before his death, the Chicago branch's cross-racial "revolutionary coalition" that Hampton headed had been so promising that national party leaders had promoted it as a "national model."[18] His death was cataclysmal, then, for the Panthers as a whole, but especially for a local branch that was left without its symbol, mouthpiece, and best organizer. In many ways, the local Panthers were gutted by Hampton's assassination.

But before he died, Hampton and the Panthers were at the vanguard of a much larger swell of community activism, centered on bringing meaningful change to the CPD. And those efforts did not die with Hampton—indeed, his murder only intensified their mission. These efforts, unsurprisingly, co-incided with the steepening repression by the CPD in the late sixties and early seventies and the increasingly perilous nature of living in communities riddled with gun and gang violence. They comprised different priorities and took on different forms, involved different actors who deployed different tactics. The Panthers, gutted but not gone, played an important role. Black police did, too. So, too, did middle-class black individuals and organizations. The same with black politicians, who found their spines after years of quiescence to the Daley machine. And the same with thousands of other Chicagoans, black, Latinx, and white, operating under the aegis of dozens of varied organizations.

The sheer breadth of ways that citizens fought for a more responsive police system, more humane treatment, and a safer community is so expansive that it is impossible to capture all of it here. Some of it was intensely local, grassroots, and focused on the immediate improvement of material conditions in specific areas; some of it was broader in vision, more formalized, and seeking longer-term and more systematic changes. Some was animated almost singularly by concerns for public safety; some was governed by fears about police violence and anger about police harassment. But it must first and foremost be understood that all these disparate efforts had at their core a shared logic: the police were not serving the black community well. Activists may not have agreed about everything else, but that fact bound them together.

This chapter documents some of the disparate efforts by community members to challenge police authority, resist repression, and reconfigure the police system into something that would work better for all citizens. The sheer scope of actions on this front means that there are still other stories left to uncover beyond what I explore here. But even this slice of the larger whole is illustrative of some basic core truths, and these stories matter for many reasons.

For one, they challenge the standard narrative and chronology of the civil rights era in Chicago. The story we are often told of the black freedom struggle there is that the civil rights movement effectively died in 1966 after the Daley machine mostly defeated Martin Luther King.[19] But changing activism—in terms of strategy, scale, and focus—is not *no* activism. The broad set of police reform activism in the late sixties and early seventies requires reconsideration of the analysis that the civil rights movement died on the vine in the mid-sixties, and that what happened thereafter was not a new iteration and extension of that movement.

Relatedly, the dreams and activisms we see surrounding the police here challenge standard narratives that frame Black Power and civil rights as separate from and antagonist toward each other. To be sure, there were plenty of divergences between Black Power and civil rights, whether in Chicago or elsewhere, and acknowledging the distinctions between them is important. But what doesn't make sense is to ignore the ways that they also converged. Because the reality is that within the context of black Chicago's struggles concerning policing, Black Power activists worked fist-in-glove with activists aligned with more traditional civil rights frameworks. Churches, the heartbeat of the traditional movement, opened their doors to the Black Panthers, who held rallies supporting community control of the police and memorials to those dead and gone at the hands of the police. The CUL worked closely with militant black police officers who were explicit in their Black Power ethos, trying to collaboratively ameliorate the suffering of victims of crime and police violence. The NAACP spearheaded the most prominent investigation into the police killings of Black Panthers Fred Hampton and Mark Clark. And on and on. Black Power and civil rights were certainly different movements with different goals, but one of the most important political landscapes on which they found and forged common ground was in challenging and reimaging police power and what it would look like in black Chicago.

And finally, the stories told in this chapter matter for the present. Although the efforts of activists documented here almost uniformly failed to achieve their stated goals, that does not make their labors and dreams unimportant. If nothing else, in many ways, they are the ancestors of twenty-first-century movements for police reform, reparations, and abolition that have shaped the politics of the black community and its allies in Chicago and beyond. That, as much as anything, makes them a fitting place to close this book.

"Chairman Fred Lives": The Panthers and the Police

The killing of Fred Hampton and Mark Clark in December of 1969 came at the end of a tumultuous year. Hampton, Rush, and a few others chartered the Illinois Branch of the BPP late in 1968. From the beginning, Hampton was its heart and public face. A son of west suburban Maywood, Hampton had grown up with the black freedom struggle. When he was a small child, his mother, Iberia, had babysat a young Emmett Till, and Fred had been politically active from an early age. He had been a leader of the NAACP Youth Council in Maywood, and began accumulating an arrest record while in his teens for his participation in marches and demonstrations on behalf of racial equality and black liberation. Even in these early years, as the attorneys Flint Taylor and Dennis Cunningham wrote, "Fred displayed unique leadership qualities. Influenced by Malcolm X, the Student Nonviolent Coordinating Committee (SNCC), and the realities which he observed and experienced in the movement, Fred was radicalized and his politics became increasingly more militant."[20]

It was as a twenty-year-old leader of the Panthers, however, that Hampton emerged as a community standard-bearer for a new revolutionary politics, which included rejecting police authority in black Chicago. Building on the frameworks of the national Panthers' promises to police the police and to "[defend] our Black community from racist police oppression and brutality," Hampton was relentless in framing police power as a fundamentally illegitimate threat to Chicago's marginalized communities—especially (but not only) black and brown ones. To be sure, such criticisms of the police were not invented from whole cloth. We have seen throughout these pages the many ways that black activists, journalists, and community members had critiqued the CPD in many different ways for many years. Furthermore, activists in Jesse Jackson's Operation Breadbasket, the SCLC, and other organizations had continued to criticize the police throughout 1968, particularly after the uprising that April in the aftermath of the King assassination.[21] Indeed, while the FBI, CPD, and the press caricatured the Panthers as fomenting hatred against the police, they were as much *articulators* of community grievances as they were *shapers* of them. In characterizing the Panthers as inciting the community against city, state, nation, and law enforcement, what Joseph LeFevour, J. Edgar Hoover, and others were implicitly doing was disavowing the reality and history of the deep, historically informed, and organic community grievances that the BPP reflected and vocalized. Put differently, the Panthers didn't have to *tell* community members to dislike or distrust the police, as if those sorts of sentiments were foreign to the West or South Sides. Those sentiments were embedded in the experiences and ethos of wide swaths of those communities.

But what the Panthers *did* do was lift those grievances high into the public arena, infuse them with a more radical critique of capitalism and exploitation, and formulate specific strategies around them. Hampton and his colleagues (both women and men) undertook numerous efforts to curb law enforcement abuses and check criminal justice system authorities. Some-times these were in line with traditional modes of protest in Chicago. Dur-ing the infamous show trial of the "Chicago Eight," in which leftist leaders were charged with conspiracy for their supposed role in the chaos at the 1968 DNC, Judge Julius Hoffman ordered a defiant Bobby Seale, one of the key national leaders of the BPP, bound and gagged in the courtroom. After-ward, Hampton and the Panthers led demonstrations at the downtown Chi-cago federal building in protest of these actions. Hampton also attended public hearings on police brutality, such as one held by black legislators in late October 1969, and attended or sponsored other rallies that supported victims of police violence, like John and Michael Soto.[22]

Their efforts were pragmatic, too. The Chicago Panthers have never re-ceived the recognition that they deserve for trying to curb violence in the community, but they labored on this point incessantly, if in their own way. Because of their distrust in the police, the Panthers had no interest in trying to subvert the growing street gang violence propagated by the Rangers and rival groups by calling for more or nominally better policing. Rather, they sought to curb gang violence by "[negotiating] with Chicago street gangs, . . . attempting to convince them to give up their violent 'gangbanging,' and to focus on the true enemy—the government and the police."[23] Much like Mar-tin Luther King and the SCLC had done a couple of years prior, the Panthers sought to redirect the gangs' actions toward political, revolutionary ends. And, as they had when King had tried it, the police and federal officials panicked and tried to subvert such alliances. Federal agents sent Rangers leader Jeff Fort an anonymous letter from "A black brother you don't know," falsely warning him that the Panthers had put "a hit out for you," believing and hoping that Fort might order—as FBI documents put it—"retaliatory action against the Panthers."[24] The war against the Panthers didn't hap-pen, but the intention was clear. As black CPD officer and founding member of the Afro-American Patrolmen's League Howard Saffold remembered the CPD's panic, "The Panthers were pursuing an ideology that said 'We need to take these young minds, this young energy, and turn it into part of our movement in terms of black liberation and the rest of it.' And I saw a very purposeful, intentional effort on the part of the police department to keep that head from hooking up to that body. It was like, you know, 'Do not let this thing become part of what could ultimately be a political movement.' Because that's exactly what it was."[25]

While calling for the community to arm themselves in self-defense, the BPP also undertook grinding organizing work to democratize the police de-partment by way of gaining community control over it.[26] Under the logic of community control, the nature of policing—down to police policy, hiring, discipline, firing, and budgets—would be decentralized and overseen by civilian boards at the district level. Those living in Garfield Park, Englewood, or Woodlawn, in other words, would be granted the authority to determine what were appropriate strategies for the police to deploy within their community (and, as importantly, to determine that stop-and-frisk and similar strategies were *inappropriate*), to hire black residents of the district to police that district, and to fire officers who were found to be abusive or neglectful. And the call for community control was accompanied by calls to redirect budgetary investments away from policing and toward community uplift programs. While not technically a call for full police abolition, it was a radical reimagining of what the police presence in black communities could and should look like.

The campaign for community control never fully got off the ground during Hampton's lifetime, mostly because the Panthers spent the bulk of his brief leadership period fending off frontal assaults by the CPD. The FBI had begun actively monitoring the Panthers in 1968, and the CPD was not far behind.[27] While the bureau labored to surveil Hampton and disrupt his work, the CPD routinely harassed and arrested Panther members for everything from traffic violations to selling the party newspaper. Hampton himself was arrested by Maywood police for supposedly stealing ice cream from a vendor and distributing it to local children. State's Attorney Edward Hanrahan, using the power of his office and wielding heavy political pressure, successfully got Hampton sentenced to up to five years in prison.[28] He only spent a couple of months there before the state Supreme Court granted him an appeal bond, but it was nevertheless evidence of how far the state would go to undermine his power.

Indeed, while the constant harassment and raids that the police and FBI launched against the Panthers in the second half of 1969 reminded activists of the *need* for community control (David Hilliard, the national Panthers' chief of staff, argued for community control of the police precisely on the basis of the CPD's raids on the Panthers[29]), the relentless police assaults disrupted the party's everyday organizing. Nevertheless, the plan for community control itself lingered, and would be revived a few years later, with the anniversary of Hampton's assassination serving as a clarion call for that movement's launch in 1973. (More on that toward the end of this chapter.) The template for community control, in this way, became part of Chicago's radical zeitgeist.

Hampton's assassination also served as a mobilizing mechanism in the more immediate sense. In the days that followed, citizens held rallies and demonstrations in his memory, across Chicagoland from the North Shore suburbs to the Far South Side. Students at local schools walked out en masse and held memorials in his honor—including one that drew an estimated 1,200 students to a memorial at the Holy Angels Catholic Church in Kenwood-Oakland.[30] The Panthers themselves held a rally at the Church of the Epiphany on the Near West Side, for which they distributed pamphlets announcing that "Chairman Fred Lives" and calling for funds to help free the raid survivors who police had arrested.[31] The Organization for a Better Austin, a West Side consortium of block clubs and community groups, insisted that black Chicago had to stop tolerating "this kind of police oppression, brutality, harassment, and killing of black youths."[32] Meanwhile, as Hanrahan and other officials tried to construct an official narrative in which the Panthers were the primary aggressors, Bobby Rush and other Panthers led media and community members through the Monroe Street apartment, showing the evidence of the police assault and undermining the state's official story.[33] (They could do this because the authorities didn't seal the murder scene for weeks after Hampton was killed.) The lines of community members wishing to bear witness stretched so long that Mumia Abu-Jamal—a member of the Philadelphia Panthers who had flown in to Chicago after Hampton's killing, later to become one of postwar America's most famous political prisoners—remarked that it "made the apartment building resemble a movie theater."[34] And beyond trying to show the public what happened, almost immediately, local and national groups alike demanded inquiries and initiated legal action against the city.

None of this could resurrect Hampton, but it kept his assassination squarely in the public eye and consciousness for years. Lawsuits against the city in Hampton's death took the better part of a decade to settle, while the release of the grand jury report in 1970 and that of the Commission of Inquiry into the Black Panthers and the Police (tellingly titled *Search and Destroy*) in 1973 ensured that negative public assessments of the raid would stay in the news cycle. Successful public battles to rename the Maywood Pool, which Hampton had fought for back when he was in the NAACP Youth Council, in Hampton's honor showed the resonance of his memory.

So, too, did the unsuccessful 2006 campaign to have the block on which he was killed commemorated by an honorary street sign declaring it to be "Chairman Fred Hampton Way."[35] A two-story-high mural bearing Hampton's visage stands at Madison and California in East Garfield Park to this day, and is regularly visited by people who know where to seek it out. You can buy T-shirts online that read "The Chicago Police Department Killed Fred Hampton." In 2015, when activists won reparations from the city of Chicago for the victims of police torture in the 1970s, 1980s, and 1990s, Flint

Taylor—who had made his entry into fighting against police abuse in the aftermath of the Hampton and Clark assassinations—was one of the prominent faces of the legal team.

In this way, the fliers might have been right. Chairman Fred lives.

"Safe Streets": Fighting for Community Safety

Hampton and the Panthers' vision for a reimagined police system at that point in time was one piece of a patchwork quilt. Simultaneously with the Panthers' confrontations with the CPD, multiple other efforts emerged, high profile and not, that challenged the standard operating methods of the police department.

It is worth knowing that some of these were fundamentally opposed to the Panthers' model, working not to strip police power but to bring it further to bear in neglected areas of the black West and South Sides. By 1968 the federal government was making "safe streets" a central pillar of its vision for a better America, codifying the phrase into law in the Omnibus Crime Control and Safe Streets Act of that year and calling for a plan to make "law enforcement efforts . . . better coordinated, intensified, and . . . more effective at all levels of government."[36] For people on the ground, however, the campaign for safe streets was more urgent. In pockets of American cities, including Chicago, people were literally dying every day from gun violence. Therefore, many community members sought to make the CPD into something that would better serve their needs.

Scholars are only just beginning to fully come to grips with the seriousness and impact of black tough-on-crime politics in America, and must better reckon with the fact of community members' very real fears and frustrations about crime. This is true across much of the twentieth century and into the twenty-first, and is especially critical in making sense of a late-sixties and early-seventies moment in which homicide rates in urban America surged to all-time highs. The fact of the matter is that plenty of black citizens, contra the Panthers, wanted more, not less, police in their communities. For such advocates, it wasn't that they *only* wanted more police, of course; whereas national white attitudes on crime—expressed acutely in federal politics—were leaning away from social investment and toward social punishment, black community members offered a systematic analysis that correctly placed the blame for crime at the feet of cities' and the nation's political economies. Locally, they recognized that Chicago had failed hundreds of thousands of black and brown citizens, and that in doing so, had produced dangerous conditions for many black people, young people especially. But they also argued that police operations as currently constituted were not doing enough to keep people safe, and thus advocated for what James Forman calls an "all-of-the-above approach" to fighting crime, in which crime prevention meant interweaving tougher enforcement with compassionate and robust social investment.[37] As Ethel Payne, a black reporter and organizer of Chicago's Coalition of Concerned Women in the War on Crime (CCWWC), framed it, while crime was rooted in deep and durable racial inequalities, "on the other side, we have to deal with the immediate; that which threatens our public safety." She and others were determined "to make the police responsive to the people."[38]

Payne and the CCWWC, which emerged in the mid-1970s, were hardly pioneers on this issue. Anticrime politics had deep roots in black Chicago, and they blossomed dramatically at the close of the sixties as violent crime increased. Many of these efforts drew from the liberal traditions of Chicago's most prominent civil rights crusades, and emerged out of those crusades' networks. In the summer of 1970, for instance, the CUL convened meetings of black organizations in which they hoped to harness the grief and anger over Fred Hampton and Mark Clark's murders into some sort of constructive path forward for safer communities. Little consensus emerged on what needed to be done, although everyone agreed that gang violence was a clear and pressing problem.[39] The meetings produced a program and group known as Action for Survival, through which activists planned to lean on the CPD to reestablish foot patrols in black neighborhoods (believing auto patrols were less effective and undermined trust between residents and officers), hire more minorities on the police force, and build more bridges of communication with the black public to collaborate on crime control measures.[40] The group's founding programmatic statement "framed the question of crime broadly by highlighting various forms of violence and exploitation by white-dominated institutions—including the Police Department, the syndicate, slumlords, unfair merchants, the courts, white dealers in narcotics and illegal drugs—perpetuated *against* black Chicagoans." And it also, the historian Peter Pihos notes, "dealt head on with 'the most abhorrent and self-defeating' crime of 'Black people murdering Black people.'"[41]

That initial statement from Action for Survival highlights an important dynamic at work in virtually all these antiviolence campaigns. Beyond making structural assessments about the root causes of crime, they also refused to let the police off the hook for the repression and brutality that were wracking black communities. They ultimately had no choice, really, since one of the central obstacles to getting violent criminals off the streets was that so few community members trusted the police enough to approach them with information leading to someone else's arrest. As the *Defender* reporter Michael Culbert put it, "Many blacks are reluctant to report black criminals or wrongdoers to the 'proper authorities,'" and as former CUL executive Bill Berry argued, "Black people do want better police protection, but we want it fair and we want it equitable. We don't want black people beat to death for minor infractions of the law."[42]

The degree to which concerns about police repression were entangled in anticrime initiatives is perhaps best seen in a community phone service that was one of the centerpieces of Action for Survival's programming. Dubbed the Survival Line, it served the dual purpose of documenting both crime and failing police protection, and an as an outlet to report police abuse and harassment. Adopting the language of the Panthers, the founders envisioned the Survival Line as a means to "help the Black community to find ways to police the police so that they will be accountable to the community" and "to end crime in our streets."[43] They hoped that, "based on the calls, we could begin to see a pattern of the type of repressive acts taking place in our community. . . . We would have the facts to show exactly what is happening to us—the type of police service we are getting as well as the lack of service."[44] And sure enough, what they found was a deep mixture of flagging service and abusive treatment; in the first year alone, nearly one-third of the calls revolved around police abuse. Those who called in such reports were often referred to resources that might help them seek redress—including attorneys who volunteered their time to aid victims of crime and police abuse in getting the help they needed.[45]

Action for Survival workers also channeled Survival Line data toward another new organization called the Black Crime Commission (BCC).[46] Convened shortly after Action for Survival's founding by Laplois Shepard—Action for Survival's Agenda Committee chairman and the Chicago Urban League's director—the BCC was envisioned as a parallel institution to the Chicago Crime Commission. Recognizing the power and political influence that the CCC had harnessed over the past half century, the basic premise of the BCC was that the black community needed an advocacy group of its own to deal with the particular problems of crime and the failing city responses that it faced. Its founding documents posited that "the function of the Black Crime Commission will be to vigorously and unrelentingly stamp out crime in Black Chicago," and that it would "do this by investigating all allegations of crimes that are brought to its attention" and putting relevant information "in the hands of the proper authorities."[47] The commission would also work to expose public officials who deprived black people of their rights; guarantee that black people received fair and impartial trials; "develop the mechanics for creating accountability of law enforcement officials to the black community while ensuring that these officials truly serve and protect human rights, not property rights"; and hold public hearings about crime in the community.[48]

While the BCC hoped to successfully redirect public policy in ways that would make the streets safer, other citizens pursued similar goals at the neighborhood level. Groups like the Third Ward Committee on Crime Prevention focused on community uplift through combating criminal activity in the South Side Third Ward.[49] In Chatham, meanwhile, citizens led by black former CPD officer Lou Fitzgerald formed a citizen patrol group in which dozens of local residents agreed to use their own personal vehicles for patrolling neighborhood streets, augmenting the CPD's official presence there.[50] While that group dissolved, much to Fitzgerald's frustration, a few years later, in 1974, community leader Isaac Hawkins organized another citizens patrol that would do similar work, functioning essentially as a community watch program.[51]

When Hawkins organized the Chatham Community Patrol in 1974, it was one piece of a full-blown, loudly declared "War on Crime" that black Chicago's civil rights machinery was trying to execute. The lynchpin in those efforts was Ethel Payne and the CCWWC. In founding the CCWWC in February of 1974, Payne, Connie Seals, and other members laid out a draft of resolutions that included three preliminary goals: "1) While recognizing the existence of police brutality and corruption and the need for police reform, the basis of the struggle against crime must be made in police-citizen cooperation; 2) Citizens must be informed of their role in the fight against crime; and 3) a system, to be called 'Operation Dialog,' must be formed whereby these objectives can be implemented."[52] Less than a month after its founding, the CCWWC won a meeting with CPD Superintendent James Rochford (who replaced Conlisk), where they called for expanded human relations training for officers, faster response times to reported crimes, better witness protection, better psychological testing for officers, and the appointment of black policewomen who could help black rape victims.[53] They also held district-level community meetings between CPD officers and commanders and community members, at which community members recurrently complained that the police were too slow to respond to distress calls in their neighborhoods.[54]

Working in close partnership with the *Defender* (Payne was one of the paper's best and most popular journalists), the CCWWC mobilized black Chicago's liberal machinery with incredible success. The *Defender* ran story after story praising the organization's work and lauding the effects of its war on crime. The organization worked in close concert with churches, black politicians, the NAACP, the Illinois Commission on Human Relations, the

National Conference of Christians and Jews, and other groups that rallied behind their community-based crime war. The CCWWC held numerous mass meetings, including a major rally in June 1974 at the downtown civic center that drew city councilors, congressmen, and celebrities like Dick Gregory. That August, they accompanied Rochford on a walk through the West Side so that the superintendent could gain a better appreciation for conditions there. The following year, they worked with the CPD to try to get black citizens to engrave their belongings with their names and identifying information, believing that doing so would discourage theft and make stolen items easier to return.[55] All in all, the group considered itself to have "achieved a remarkable record of cooperation with the Chicago Police Department."[56] But proving the degree to which social problems couldn't be solved by policing alone, that record of cooperation didn't translate into any comparable impact on crime.

ORGANIZATIONS LIKE Action for Survival, the BCC, and the CCWWC achieved wide recognition in the black press and appreciation from the black community's most powerful sectors. This was partly because of the very nature of their labors, but it was also because they possessed the right sort of social resources. Middle-class, respectable, and steeped in the civil rights tradition, they fit a particular model of what civil rights activism in Chicago had traditionally looked like. But the fact is that these organizations were in some ways leading from behind, consciously or not, for they followed in the wake of grassroots anticrime initiatives waged by low-income families living in the city's housing projects, who operated largely outside the realm of formal politics and traditional civil rights organizing.

As part of the larger national postwar public housing boom, the Chicago Housing Authority had built a series of sprawling projects across Chicago. However, racially sculpted city policies and fears of political backlash over integration had meant that the CHA placed the projects largely in areas that were already mostly black and facing deep deprivation. Whereas their initial construction had been greeted with optimism, and while people moved in with high expectations, by the late sixties, many of the projects had become vertical manifestations of the city's broader landscapes of racial and socioeconomic inequality. As a result, poverty was concentrated into denser and denser areas that existed on a different tax and resource plane than much of the rest of the city.[57]

What resulted were real problems of public safety in some of the projects, especially as gangs that were producing much of Chicago's spiraling violence were starting to make inroads into them. This was particularly true at the famous Cabrini-Green Homes on the Near Northwest Side and the Robert Taylor Homes on the South, where residents increasingly identified safety as their primary concern in a long litany of grievances.[58] An August 1970 *Tribune* profile of one Cabrini-Green building described the project's descent from a "calm, friendly . . . place where a child could be raised" into "a Hydra's head of problems"—the worst of which was "gang terror."[59] This type of voyeuristic characterization ignored people's persistence and resilience and the vibrant social lives they cultivated, but it did capture the hazards.

When gangs first began operating inside the projects, they did so largely without any official city response. The CPD maintained no consistent presence in the projects at the time, despite the fact that its residents were taxpayers and that both Cabrini-Green and the Taylor Homes each had populations as big or bigger than numerous suburbs and medium-sized towns downstate. Instead, public safety was outsourced to private firms that were unequipped to handle the task, both in terms of their training and their enforcement powers.

Tenants thus mobilized to harness a better public safety system for themselves and their families. As they had throughout the long black freedom struggle, black women took the lead.[60] In the Taylor Homes, women organized themselves into informal groups they called "Mama's Mafias," banding together to thwart gang recruitment efforts.[61] Black women also largely made up and worked through elected tenant councils to lobby politicians and police officials for more and better protection. The success of their efforts was always uneven, and it was ultimately the murder of two police officers in Cabrini-Green that prompted the police to act as much as anything else.[62] Nevertheless, by 1971 the CPD had established "vertical patrol units" that ran around the clock at Cabrini-Green, with two-man patrols working the project's elevators, stairwells, halls, and grounds.[63] Those patrols were augmented by the installation of expensive security camera systems in common areas within the projects, resident action groups, and other smaller security measures.

This was a long stride toward hypersurveillance, and it still didn't help. Nor was it actually imported with any expediency into the Taylor Homes and other projects, where violence continued to escalate. By the spring of 1974, gang wars over narcotics traffic in the Taylor Homes were exploding constantly, and later that year, the alderman representing the district told police officials that "the vast majority of the project residents were begging for police protection because the high crime rate in the project is worsening and they live in constant fear and danger."[64] In response, Rochford pledged more manpower to patrol the area surrounding the Taylor Homes, while even at Cabrini-Green, where the CPD already maintained a sizable presence, things escalated. In July 1974, the *Defender* reported that the CPD, the Illinois Law Enforcement Commission, and the federal Department of Housing and Urban Development were collectively pledging $10 million to Cabrini-Green over the course of the following three years, earmarked expressly for safety. Those monies only further expanded the surveillance network: television cameras in the lobbies; guard stations; and redesigned and better-lit entryways.[65]

As this surveillance network failed, tenants continued to cast about for better options. Normal lobbying channels had proven to be largely fruitless, so they sought other avenues to secure their and their families' safety. Interviews with former tenants of the Taylor Homes showed that the most common and effective arrangement may have been for tenant councils and residents to broker cooperative arrangements not with the city or the CPD but with individual black police officers who would do their best to keep tenants within a particular project block safe. One-time Taylor Homes resident Tom Jenkins, for instance, became a CPD officer in the mid-1970s, and the connections he had there allowed tenants to call on him to ensure their safety. After he began coming around on a regular basis, gang recruitment reportedly declined, but this was only one part of one building of a sprawling project in a patchwork of community areas facing similar problems.[66] It was piecemeal and insufficient, and the projects remained perilously unsafe for too many of their residents.

The story of these activisms is deeply sad in many different ways. Grief and fear drove them—a consequence of the cascading violence, and the fear of it, that shaped so many black lives by this point in time. We should not lose sight of the fact that 1974, the same year that gang wars consumed the Taylor Homes, was the peak year for homicides in Chicago's history. Nearly one thousand people were murdered in the city in that year alone. When people fought for safer projects, streets, homes, and communities, they were not wrong in thinking of the fight as quite literally one of life and death. Although in hindsight their advocacy for a more expansive and aggressive police presence may strike some readers as misguided given the repressions described in this book, it bears remembering that they had few other options.

The fact that project tenant activism didn't yield safer projects does not, however, mean that the activism was of no consequence—especially over the long term. Activists' work in this vein reminds us of James Forman Jr.'s compelling argument that 1970s-era black activism for tougher anticrime measures inadvertently helped create the context for today's sprawling punitive state.[67] This was, of course, incremental, and there is no precise, direct line between this late-sixties and early-seventies project activism and what came later. But tenant activism on behalf of safer living spaces in the 1970s did preface if not produce an evermore invasive police presence in the projects. In subsequent years and decades, project residents essentially found their rights to privacy and the integrity of their homes abrogated by the CHA and the CPD. In 1988 and 1989 an ACLU lawsuit against the CHA program known as Operation Clean Sweep showed that the CHA's private security employees, in concert with the CPD, "have gone from residence to residence [in the projects], conducting unannounced, warrantless searches of tenants and their guests. These 'inspections,'" ACLU president Diane Geraghty wrote in a scathing editorial to the *Tribune*, "have included searches of the dresser drawers, bedding, and personal effects of tenants—unlikely places in which to find the squatters, gang members and drug dealers who are the alleged targets."[68] The housing authority also forbade residents from having guests after midnight, subjected them to stop-and-frisks, and claimed authority to request identification from anyone on the premises.[69] By 1990 the CHA had established its own police department, complete with substations in many of the projects.[70] Before they were finally torn down, the projects were thus by all appearances a form of police state, where residents literally lived on the same soil as the police department that surveilled their lives. And even that didn't work in ensuring residents' safety.

This was the double-bind in which activists found themselves. Despite citizens' dreams of safer homes, even police in the projects admitted that they couldn't fix the situation. As a black CPD commander named Charles Glass put it, "[Residents'] main complaint is a lack of simple police service . . . [but] the problems are more than just crime and violence. The problems are those of a poor community. There are not enough jobs. There is not enough recreation. There is not enough maintenance. There is not enough of anything."[71] The ethnographer Sudhir Venkatesh similarly summarized the "ubiquity of hardships" facing public housing tenants in his elegiac analysis of the Taylor Homes: a stagnant economy, falling employment rates due to mechanization and plant relocations and closings, poor job training, and few jobs that paid a living wage.[72]

Activists who pushed for safer communities, whether the low-income residents of the projects or middle-class members of the CCWWC, were engaged in a Sisyphean enterprise. What would solve the crises of public safety was not more and more aggressive police but, rather, meaningful social investment. Economic and opportunity inequality, racial antipathy, partisan politics, social isolation, and public policy had wrought the conditions that prevailed in the projects, and it was these that were to blame for those crises of crime. But the very nature of Chicago's political economy meant that there would be no forthcoming investments in actual measures to ameliorate the underlying conditions of poverty. Meaningfully confronting poverty and inequality was a nonstarter for the Daley machine. Much like how the federal government's funding of the War on Poverty evaporated over the second half of the 1960s and into the 1970s, first augmented and then replaced wholesale by funding for the War on Crime, the city threw increasing amounts of money at the police department while declining to invest in programs that would alleviate misery, reduce poverty, and enhance opportunity.[73] This brings to mind once again Bill Berry's furious 1966 argument before the Citizens' Committee to Study Police-Community Relations: in "a society without racial justice, the police bear the burden of policing an unjust order." For all intents and purposes, the city had abandoned its neglected and minority neighborhoods, and expected the police to play damage control.

"Black Power through Law": Black Police and the Afro-American Patrolmen's League

If the Panthers' rejection of police authority represented one thread of law-enforcement-focused community activism, and the labors for a more robust police presence in black communities represented another, the two were not always so separable. Indeed, what were ultimately the most influential and durable fights in the law enforcement arena held both in hand at the same time.

The earliest, longest-lasting, and best-remembered such campaign came out of the police department itself. On July 12, 1968, Renault Robinson, Edward "Buzz" Palmer, and Frank Lee—three young and black officers in the lower ranks of the CPD—held a press conference to announce the formation of a new organization called the Afro-American Patrolmen's League, which would work "to transform the role of the police in perpetuating racial domination in Chicago."[74]

The league's founding members had a special appreciation for how broken the police department was. Though they were, Pihos writes, "not activists who decided to become policemen, but policemen who became activists," their activism was contoured by the fierce urgency of the moment.[75] Starting in late 1967 or early 1968, they had begun meeting to discuss the double standards that the CPD applied to black officers, prompted especially by a case in which black officers were disciplined for allegedly meting out to a couple of white youths the sort of violence that white officers routinely used against black people without punishment.[76] Forged in the fires of the King riots, Daley's shoot-to-kill order, ubiquitous stop-and-frisk, police brutality, and worsening crime, the issues compelling AAPL members toward their activism were many, from the deep unsafety shaping the daily lives of black Chicagoans to the constant brutality those same communities were constantly subjected to.

More has been written about the AAPL than any other wing of black Chicago's police reform movement (other than the late-sixties Panthers, who were hardly reformist)—most notably by Pihos and other historians such as Beryl Satter, Tera Agyepong, and Megan Adams.[77] Those scholars have explored what the AAPL illuminates about the broader dynamics of Black Power, both in terms of social impact and cultural representation, what its labors can tell us about the rhythms and transformation of urban politics, how it fit within the larger context of Chicago's police organizations and unions, what was unique about the experiences of black officers, and, most basically, what it did in terms of fighting on the community's behalf. They have also documented the extreme repression and reprisals that members of the AAPL faced from the city and the CPD, including suspensions, docked pay, threats of termination, and the spreading of misinformation about the organization's goals and its leaders' intentions and reputations. This is all vital work that is of considerable value to scholars of policing and race, as well as to the struggles and experiences of black police officers generally. For our purposes here, however, I am mostly interested in sketching the programmatic philosophy and work of the AAPL, because it was instrumental in much of the activism surging through Chicago in the late sixties and early seventies that focused on reimagining and refashioning the CPD.

Arising from the same context and at essentially the same time as the local Black Panthers, the AAPL was deeply animated by many of the same Black Power ethics and ideas as the BPP. (Indeed, the group's logo was a clenched fist inside of a police star, its slogans variously "Black Power Policing" and "Black Power through Law.") From the beginning, members of the organization spoke in language reminiscent of Black Power's luminaries. They conjured up Malcolm X's ghost in pledging to stop the police from "daily . . . victimiz[ing] hundreds of Blacks and poor people of this city . . . by whatever means necessary."[78] In one of the earliest treatises affiliated with the AAPL, Buzz Palmer framed the police in the black community as serving no "service or protective function," but rather operating as "an elaborate control device to control black people" that constituted "an assault on our ideal of a democratic society."[79] Meanwhile, in another, the league's president, Renault Robinson, equated white policemen in black ghettos with slavery-era plantation overseers, and framed themselves as defenders of the community in opposition to those overseers. He described the CPD's relationship to the people as fundamentally "colonial" in nature, and part of a larger matrix shaped and dominated by white supremacy and exploitation.

"Police harassment, police brutality and the police acting as judge, jury and executioner is common practice in the black community," he wrote. "All of these abuses are not accidents or errors or simply acts of individual malice. They flow from the policemen's role as agents of an absentee white citizenry, which owns all the property in the black community and/or have a stake in the political and economic status quo and who are, therefore, continually demanding of the police that they prove their responsibility to and representation of the white power structure by the number of insults, assaults, arrests and kills, perpetrated against the black community." Mirroring the frequently masculinist rhetoric of the Panthers, he proposed that the league be an instrument "to stop white police from raping the black community in the name of 'law and order.'"[80]

Though by occupational definition agents of the state's power and machinery, AAPL members worked to radically subvert the very nature *of* that power and machinery, "embracing separatism without separation."[81] As Buzz Palmer put it at the announcement of the league's establishment, "We will no longer permit ourselves to be relegated to the role of brutal pawns in a chess game affecting the black community in which we serve."[82] Guided by the knowledge that the black community was both overpatrolled and underprotected, the league set out to address both problems head-on. They sought to ensure community safety by eliminating police violence and harassment toward black people on the one hand, and fighting crime and intracommunal violence through more effective policing on the other.

These fights were interconnected. It could hardly have been otherwise, since the communities they were fighting *for* were dealing with interconnected fears of abuse and struggles with neglect. The AAPL brought a broad-lens political analysis to their work, interpreting the entire enterprise of failing and abusive policing to be part of a larger macrostructure of white supremacy and exploitation. Cognizant of black Chicago's stunted political power in the machine city, league members advocated for the people to reject the political status quo and challenge its fundamental logics. As Robinson put it in one of his recurring early-seventies columns for the *Defender*, "The next time your precinct captain has the nerve to knock at your door and ask for your vote for King Daley remember what you are voting for: a police department that does nothing to stop serious crime in the black community—a police department that refuses to hire and promote black police officers—a police department that disrespects black people—a police department that kills black people—a police department that takes bribes which allow dope to be sold to black children—a police department that permits vicious gang activity."[83]

One of the pillars of the AAPL's labor lay in exposing, condemning, and gaining proper punishment for police brutality. Like all the league's work, these fights unfolded at multiple levels. On the one hand, they could be intensely microlocal, case-by-case affairs, as when league members would individually confront white colleagues and superiors in the moment when those colleagues were brutalizing black suspects.[84] They also used systematic approaches. They opened a referral and intake service for police brutality complaints so that they wouldn't get lodged in the abyss of Internal Affairs, and worked closely with Action for Survival on this project once the latter organization got its legs.[85] They lodged strident, public critiques of the CPD leadership and Daley, using the black press, and the *Defender* especially, as an ally in its struggle to expose and eliminate brutality. (Renault Robinson's recurring columns for the newspaper are the most obvious example.) Using these same forums, they worked to inform citizens of their rights vis-à-vis the police, so that people would be less likely to fall victim to overreaches of police power. They argued for police to stop carrying shotguns in their cars, especially after the CPD killed young Linda Anderson by shooting her in the face through her front door.[86] They also supported a civilian review panel that would hold both subpoena and investigatory powers in dealing with violent or corrupt officers, the results of which they could present directly to a special prosecutor.[87] George Clements, a black Catholic priest who had consulted the AAPL from the beginning, envisioned a time when CPD officers would no longer be armed.[88]

AAPL members viewed all of this as an extension of related abuses and harassments—from stop-and-frisk to unwarranted arrest to verbal disrespect. And it amounted to a police structure that was intensely and, importantly, *systematically* rotten and repressive. As Renault Robinson said in a letter to James Conlisk, the problems were not aberrational but embedded in the flawed structure and discretionary nature of the police system. "The problem that affects police relations with the black community is not caused by the individual policeman who acts improperly or misuses his authority," Robinson wrote to his boss in the summer of 1969. "Rather, it is the improperly constituted [police] structure that allows the individual policeman the relatively unrestricted personal discretion to act while under the color of [law] and, in many cases, within the legal limits of the law in a fashion that reflects prejudicial treatment."[89]

Moreover, while police violence and harassment were constant concerns for AAPL officers, so, too, was the intracommunal violence wreaking havoc across black Chicago. From the beginning, AAPL members believed that the problem of violence was partly bound up in a poor self-image and a lack of self-love inside the black community. Of police officers and larger sections of the community alike, Robinson wrote, "It will be necessary to convince them of the fact that black men, regardless of rank of office or station in life, can base a relationship on mutual respect and love." He also argued that because black police had "a unique knowledge of the problems of violence and self-hatred manifested in the conduct of black people toward each other," they were also uniquely positioned to help, partly by serving as positive role models for the rest of the community.[90]

But the problem of violence was also embedded in the fact that "the police are guilty of not giving black people full and complete police service," as Robinson contended. In an observation that is almost singular for the time in its historical insight, he wrote that "black people have never been given the service and protection white people receive."[91] Elsewhere, he commented that "the Black Community is hostile to the Chicago Police Department because we feel that we are victims of taxation without representation— we get neither the positions nor the protection White Communities receive in this City."[92]

It was in that light that the AAPL also embarked on an anticrime strategy to try to effect safer streets. Their efforts in this vein received less attention than their labors to challenge police authority. But the stakes were no less real. As homicide stats spiraled upward, Robinson and others inside the AAPL agonized over the "wanton taking of human lives," as well as the "liberal tolerance of criminal behavior" that "sentenced the peaceable hard-working blacks of the ghetto to a horrible . . . tyranny of hustlers, murders and extortionists in their midst."[93] And while they critiqued gang violence as a core menace to the community, they also understood its structural roots in Chicago's landscape of inequality. Moreover, they blamed the Daley machine for not doing more about the gangs, noting that despite their war of extirpation against the revolutionary Black Panthers, which posed frontal challenges to the political machine's legitimacy, "there is no concerted effort by Chicago police to end gang violence" because "the gangs pose no threat to Mayor Daley or white society in Chicago."[94]

Although the league won wide community support for its work on both the brutality and anticrime fronts, the CPD steadfastly refused its entreaties to reckon with itself. It levied massive reprisals against league members, Renault Robinson especially, and Conlisk refused to even meet with the AAPL to discuss their concerns and demands.

But that recalcitrance in some ways backfired when the AAPL stunned the city and police administration by taking its case to the federal government. The alliance between the government and the AAPL was an unlikely one. At a moment when law-and-order ideology was ascendant at the federal level, the league challenged the core logics of that ideology. If Richard Nixon's administration was intent on waging war on black "inner-city" communities, the AAPL was intent on keeping it from doing so. But the War on Crime made strange bedfellows, and in 1971 the AAPL landed on a means of harnessing federal power in order to bend the CPD to its demands. They would try to hit it where it hurt—its pocketbook.

The league had been engaged in legal battles with the CPD for roughly a year by that time, most prominently in *Robinson v. Conlisk*, in which Renault Robinson brought suit against the department for "unequal treatment, arbitrary suspension, other arbitrary discipline, and other forms of harassment."[95] But in 1971 the league escalated that legal assault, appealing directly to the LEAA to investigate the CPD. Their claim was not directly tethered to complaints about brutality or neglect. Rather, they argued that the department's hiring practices were discriminatory against black and Latino candidates for hiring and promotion, leaving them underrepresented at all levels of the force.[96]

The complaint's rationale was clear, especially within the larger context of the AAPL's philosophy. League members were too aware of the realities on the ground to think that all black police were good police, but they did fundamentally believe that one way to conjure a better and more just police system in Chicago was to stock black communities with black rather than white officers. As Robinson recalled, "We weren't gonna change these white guys. . . . We needed more black cops. Our belief was that more black cops would have empathy for their own community and would have more respect for black women and black kids and black people in general."[97]

The complaint's legal grounding was also clear. The basic premise was that the CPD's hiring and promotional policies violated Title VI of the 1964 Civil Rights Act, which prohibits programs receiving federal funds from discriminating on the basis of race. If the CPD was in violation of Title VI, it was ineligible to receive federal funds. The complaint touched off an investigation by the LEAA that while finding no evidence of "any intentional or planned program" to discriminate on the CPD's part, did find that "current personnel practices and procedures clearly have an adverse effect on minority group members, both as entry candidates and as members of the Department."[98] The CPD was found to be well short of minimal compliance with federal regulations, and investigators suggested that the department needed some sort of affirmative action program to rectify the situation.[99] The LEAA declined to cut off funds to the department, however, instead urging the CPD to come into voluntary compliance.[100]

Over time, the AAPL expanded its bid to hammer the city's pocketbook outward beyond the LEAA, filing a suit in Washington to get Chicago's eligibility for federal Revenue Sharing funds stripped away.[101] Revenue Sharing was a centerpiece of President Richard Nixon's approach to governing. It was effectively a block grant system, under which the federal government dispensed billions of dollars annually to states and local municipalities, who could do with it as they pleased, with little oversight.[102] By that point in time, the police department had overtaken such a massive amount of the city of Chicago's budget (fully one-quarter of it by the mid-seventies[103]) that the city devoted a large part of its revenue sharing dollars to the CPD.

In 1974 the AAPL filed a lawsuit which argued that racially discriminatory hiring and promotional practices within the CPD should make it ineligible to receive the funds. The federal Office of Revenue Sharing concurred, and sent a registered letter to Daley encouraging him to agree to a consent decree with the Department of Justice to resolve the matter.[104] Daley refused, and a week before Christmas, Federal Judge Prentice Marshall ordered the withholding of more than $76 million in federal funding to Chicago.[105] Still unswayed, Daley continued to fight for more than a year, rather than force a change to the department's discriminatory practices. He ended up having to borrow $55 million from local banks in order to offset the loss of funds, and explored raising real estate taxes, as well.[106] Not until March of 1977, after the city had had more than $114,000,000 withheld and after Daley died, did Marshall find the city's hiring practices suitable enough to restore funding.[107]

The league's labors did not, of course, end with that bid. But the work that it did in terms of confronting brutality and neglect, and forcing the CPD toward more equitable hiring policies (if not more humane policing practices) from the late 1960s to the mid-1970s yielded its ripest fruits. By working from the inside out to refashion the CPD, it rattled the department's cage and, through its appeals to the federal government, forced the department to account for itself before federal investigators.

This was important in endearing the AAPL to the community, too. At public hearings in the community just a year after the league's founding, people effusively praised its work while condemning the CPD.[108] Similarly, after its first year in existence, the Illinois ACLU presented the league with an award for "outstanding work in civil liberties."[109] Members of the Oakdale Civic Council and the neighborhood Parent Teachers Association wrote a letter affirming their support for the AAPL in "revolutionizing the most repressive institution in our decadent society."[110] And when the CPD levied heavy reprisals against league leaders, letters of support flooded into its offices from community members. Within black Chicago's social and political milieu, the AAPL's web of influence expanded widely and reached deeply, and created the space for important alliances to be forged.

The Machine and Its Discontents:
Police Reform and Black Elected Officials

Among the people with whom it curried favor, the AAPL won the respect and cooperation of key members of black Chicago's political leadership. The most well-known among these was Harold Washington, a state legislator who would later go on to become Chicago's first black mayor. With Washington in Springfield in the early 1970s, the league had a direct channel into the state's political machinery, with Washington routinely introducing to the Illinois House legislation meant to check police power. This included bills to overturn the state's stop-and-frisk statute, and another to create what was effectively a citizens' panel to investigate police misconduct.[111]

But while Washington's relationship with the AAPL was important and while his career arc has made him a (perhaps *the*) mainstay of black Chicago's political memory, on the matter of the early-seventies police reform movement, he is ultimately less important than his colleague, Ralph Metcalfe. Indeed, it was Metcalfe who initiated the process of shattering the Daley machine's hold on black Democratic politicians. And it was the issue of police violence that initiated the shattering.

This was far from preordained. A former Olympian and respectable member of the middle class, Metcalfe had ascended to an aldermanic position through the graces of the Democratic machine. He had ingratiated himself to Daley and the machine's other powerbrokers in order to obtain and keep his position. He had been one of the famous "Silent Six" black aldermen who were understood to be little more than a rubber stamp for Daley's projects and wishes.[112] In 1970 that loyalty had propelled him to the Democratic nomination for William Dawson's old seat representing the South Side in the U.S. House of Representatives. He remained active in local matters while in Washington, but almost never on issues that would make waves with the machine. While people close to him—most notably his son, Ralph Jr., whose politics were far more informed by Black Power than were his father's—urged him toward more responsive positions concerning community grievances around policing, in the 1960s he had chosen instead to align himself with the anticrime forces in the community. This was mostly a product of his real concerns with crime but, given his knowledge of Chicago's machine politics, was also surely a stance molded by his understanding of the political implications of attacking the CPD.

And then a friend of his, a prominent black dentist named Dr. Herbert Odom, was stopped one night in March 1972 by two CPD officers. The officers tried to frisk Odom on the street. When they started to do so, Odom requested that they go to a station instead to avoid embarrassment, at which point the officers handcuffed him, bent him over the hood of the car, and aggressively searched him. They then took him in and charged him with disorderly conduct, resisting arrest, battery, and driving without a rear license plate light.[113] While the treatment Odom received was relatively mundane compared to that meted out to other black Chicagoans by the police, the dentist's social position made his arrest and forceful handling a lightning rod for Metcalfe and other community leaders. And the outrage over his case would quickly be compounded by that of another friend of Metcalfe's, Dr. Daniel Claiborne (also a dentist), who just a month after Odom's arrest, died two weeks after suffering a stroke while driving, losing control of his car, and being arrested by CPD officers who assumed that he was drunk and placed him unconscious in a holding cell for six hours without any medical attention.[114]

Outraged by these incidents and responding to a groundswell from those around him, Metcalfe mobilized the powers of his office against Daley and the machine. He helped found a new organization called Concerned Citizens for Police Reform, which, among other things, excoriated the IAD for working more as an operation to protect officers than functioning as an actual tool of discovery, and demanded civilian oversight of the CPD and greater accountability to the community by the department. He also demanded meetings with police department officials and with city hall.[115]

When those requests proved fruitless, Metcalfe convened a Blue Ribbon panel into "the misuse of police authority" in Chicago, which included four public hearings in the summer of 1972. When Metcalfe called the hearings, the response was overwhelming. Community members, AAPL officials, medical professionals, and others showed up to testify against the police system and the treatment that it meted out. Black doctors, Latinx service workers, unemployed white laborers, career politicians—their stories haunted the proceedings: ghost stories of beloveds dead and gone, horror stories of torture and violence, indignant stories of harassment and abuse. They collectively and publicly agonized over a police system that was violent, unpredictable, and out of their control. Their complaints ran the gamut, from harassment to intimidation to violence to murder.[116] The refrain was familiar, pulsing with the same tenor of outrage as decades past. Richard Leftridge protested too loudly when a police officer hit a friend of his in the head with his blackjack, and reported being turned on by seven other officers who beat his head with such force that his left eye had to be removed three days later.[117] Widow Bennye Moon's son and daughter-in-law got into an argument one day that was loud enough for neighbors to call the police. The arriving officers became abusive toward her son, and when Ms. Moon protested, an officer pistol-whipped her and broke two ribs. Her pregnant seventeen-year-old daughter told the officer not to hit her mother; the officer turned around and slugged her in the stomach. The daughter's baby was then born prematurely—blind and with a perforated heart.[118] Such violence, according to testimony, was systematic: brutality as a part of the everyday, murder by police as commonplace.[119] Fear pervaded. As Lester Jackson, a contractor and community leader on the West Side, testified, "When I leave my home in the morning, I don't know if I'll ever see it again."[120] The hearings, in other words, laid bare many of the realities of what it was like to be policed in late-sixties and early-seventies Chicago.

They also demanded action. Even before the hearings, Metcalfe had begun to lean on the Daley administration to refashion the police department in a way that would make it more responsive and accountable. In a meeting with Conlisk several months before the hearings, Metcalfe had issued a series of demands to the superintendent that he thought would help stabilize the relationship between police and community. These included the termination of the task force, the establishment of district-level citizens' boards that would help set policy in those districts, the elevation of black people to positions of policy-making power, and the recruitment and hiring of more black people to the CPD.[121] The inauguration and aftermath of the hearings escalated those demands. Attorney Kermit Coleman and the ACLU produced an official report entitled "The Misuse of Police Authority in Chicago" that compiled all the hearings' testimony into one convenient, terrible, hundred-page bundle. It included an extensive list of nearly three dozen recommendations for reform, mostly focused on eliminating police harassment and brutality, implementing a civilian investigatory body into police abuse, and restructuring the disciplinary system.[122] The Urban League printed it for distribution, and the *Defender* serialized it, airing the department's dirty laundry in front of a wide public and bringing it under even more withering scrutiny.[123]

It is a testament to Daley and Conlisk's intransigence that they steadfastly refused to bend themselves to the mounting public pressure the hearings had produced. Law enforcement officials had been called to testify before the hearings, and had refused (although the Red Squad did send plainclothes officers in to covertly surveil the hearings).[124] When presented with the Metcalfe report's series of recommendations, they had largely declined to address them. For practical purposes, the cumulative impact of the Metcalfe wing of the police reform movement was pretty marginal.

Yet Metcalfe's public excoriation of the CPD and Daley over the issue of police brutality was a wedge that splintered Daley's hold on black elected officials in Chicago. Already in the summer of 1972, Keith Wilson, a judge and (unrelated) confidant of Orlando Wilson, wrote to the former superintendent that "Metcalfe is the spearhead of a 'police brutality' movement that has already passed the point of no return and will probably be the undoing of Mayor Daley's vaunted Democratic organization."[125] He wasn't far off, at least in terms of the 1970s-era black submachine. From that point forward until Daley's death in 1976, Metcalfe proved to be a consistent thorn in the mayor's side. In 1973 his Concerned Citizens for Police Reform joined with the AAPL, the Urban League, and seven individuals in a federal lawsuit against Conlisk and the CPD over ongoing problems of brutality, which almost certainly contributed to Conlisk's ultimate resignation later that year. He also opposed many of the mayor's political nominees from that point forward, most notably Cook County State's Attorney Edward Hanrahan, who Daley slated for reelection despite the community backlash for his role in helping orchestrate and cover up the killings of Fred Hampton and Mark Clark. When Hanrahan won the Democratic primary, Metcalfe went so far as to cross party lines to endorse his Republican opponent, Bernard Carey, who subsequently rode voting majorities in all but one of the black wards to a stunning upset victory over Hanrahan.[126] (From afar, the *New York Times* correctly reported that "crucial to Mr. Carey's victory was the first massive defection of the black voters who have long been the mainstay of Mr. Daley's organization."[127])

By 1975 Metcalfe himself was considering a run against Daley for mayor, and after ultimately deciding not to run, endorsed Daley's primary challenger. In response, Daley tried to undermine Metcalfe's congressional reelection campaign, sought to remove him as a Democratic Party committeeman, and stripped him of all his patronage benefits. Despite Daley throwing everything he had at Metcalfe, the congressman easily won reelection, and also managed to retain his committeeman post.[128] Emboldened either by Metcalfe or the general climate of political revolt he had helped foster, other black aldermen increasingly rebelled against the machine, injecting new life into black political power that would carry over past Daley and through to the election of Harold Washington as Chicago's mayor in 1983. Metcalfe had, the famous black *Tribune* columnist Vernon Jarrett crowed, helped launch a "plantation revolt"—one that would alter the character of black electoral politics in Chicago.[129]

The Police and the People: The Movement for Community Control

Above practically all these fights for police reform, the ghost of Fred Hampton hovered. Beloved as he'd been in black Chicago, his murder was a common reference point when people talked about police violence, and his dedication to the collective good of the people inspired countless activists in the struggle for a more equitable social arrangement, safer communities, and a police force that would actually be accountable to the people. In Hampton and Mark Clark's names, white liberals organized an Alliance to End Repression, which would eventually initiate the lawsuit against the CPD that would force the disbanding of the Red Squad. Researchers with the Northwestern University–based Law Enforcement Study Group began seriously investigating police violence in Chicago after Hampton and Clark's killings. (Theirs was the report that illuminated the sheer scale of fatal force at the close of the sixties, as documented in the previous chapter.) Action for Survival and its Survival Line similarly owe their origins to the killings of Hampton and Clark. By 1976 there were one hundred organizations in Chicago that were fighting for various forms of criminal justice reform.[130] Most of them had been born in the wake of Fred Hampton's murder.

But in closing this chapter, I want to return to one particular piece of the activist puzzle that stemmed from Hampton's murder—the fight for community control of the police that the Black Panthers waged in the years after his death, and in large part in his memory.

The idea of community control of the police, and control of other organizations, was a common ideological thread for a number of Black Power organizations. As Bobby Rush explained it, "The control of all institutions that directly affect the people's lives should be in the hands of those people. Justice comes through the attainment of power."[131] That the people should control the institutions that operated in their communities was essential to the task of subverting a white supremacist power structure that rigidly and abusively structured the lives and options of black people.[132] The national Black Panthers had tinkered with the idea of community control for years, and through the cross-organizational National Committee to Combat Fascism, put forward the first serious push for it in 1970, when they succeeded in getting the matter on the ballot in Berkeley, California.[133]

In Chicago, too, the idea of community control had emerged in fits and starts in the late sixties and early seventies. For instance, while it was never an explicit (or particularly coherent) piece of the AAPL's efforts, the animating logics behind it did influence the league. In 1969, after the editor of a local newspaper in Kenwood argued in favor of neighborhood-level police control, the league wrote to *Chicago Today* supporting his position.[134] Other documents from their files show the league discussing the merits of community control, as well. (Tellingly, in the sense that they knew the department would not go for the idea.[135])

But it was the Panthers who made it into something tangible and, for a time, seemingly within reach. The movement for community control in

Chicago began in August of 1972, when the Panthers convened a "Survival Conference" at George Clements's Holy Angels Church.[136] In keeping with the Panthers' ideological investment in community support, handbills distributed in advance of the one-day conference pledged that five thousand "free full bags of groceries (with a dozen large Grade A eggs in every bag)" would be given away, as would three thousand pairs of "brand new high quality children's back-to-school shoes." Free sickle-cell anemia tests would be administered, and attendees could expect to hear speeches from Bobby Rush, Renault Robinson, and Dick Gregory.[137] According to the conveners, more than five thousand people ended up participating, and a second, similar conference in Uptown in October drew another three thousand.[138] It was out of those two "survival conferences" that the Chicago Campaign for Community Control of Police (elsewhere called the Citywide Coalition for Community Control of Police—CCCCP, either way) was born, with a drafting committee developing a "basic ordinance that included some general principles for a more humane, effective community controlled police."[139] In keeping with the Panthers' larger turn from revolutionary to electoral politics across the country, CCCCP members hoped to bring that ordinance to the voters of Chicago.

On December 2, 1972, Bobby Rush held a press conference at the downtown Sherman House Hotel, where he announced that two days later, the campaign for community control would officially begin. The date was no coincidence. December 4 would mark the three-year anniversary of Fred Hampton's murder, and the CCCCP would hold a memorial rally in his honor that would serve as the campaign's formal launch. At the press conference, Rush mapped out the campaign's core logic: "Community control of police is necessary because the police department has developed into a segment of government that has isolated itself from the community. It has shown callousness toward solving some of the real problems of the community and has become a major threat to the very existence of people in the community." Echoing the long-standing language of occupation, he explained that "the police occupy our communities like foreign troops occupy territory."[140]

As the movement got underway, these precise comments would be printed as the opening salvo on pamphlets distributed in the community, explaining the rationale of the community control movement as well as its basic mechanics.[141] The campaign called for the creation of twenty-one local police districts, each governed by a district board that would comprise nine citizens, elected in "non-partisan, low-budget elections," that "should reflect the composition of the community." Stripping policy-making power from a centralized superintendent's office, each district board would have its own power to set policy guidelines for police operations in that district.

The boards would also hold public hearings on citizen grievances against the police; would select a district commander to oversee the police in that district; and would have oversight over personnel matters, including hiring and firing privileges. The president of each district board would serve on a citywide police commission, which would oversee matters not confined to the district level (traffic, police training, and so on).[142] Through these initiatives, "the tyranny of a police apparatus neither responsive nor responsible to the people in the community will not continue in Chicago."[143]

Moreover, the campaign envisioned a dramatic reduction and redistribution of the city's police budget. The hundreds of millions of dollars that the city spent on the CPD, Rush wrote, "is too much money for the inadequate services we receive."[144] Choosing social investment over social punishment, the CCCCP would reduce the CPD's budget, and "free some of our tax money to come back to our communities to provide jobs which will establish an economic base for our community existence."[145] Establishing community control of the police, in other words, was the first piece of a set of freedom dreams that included economic and political independence.

And these were freedom dreams that, at least in the beginning, appeared to capture the imagination of wide swaths of Chicago's activist community. The CCCCP's coalition kept expanding, weaving together groups with diffuse ideologies and diverse backgrounds who found common cause in bending the police department to the will of the people. Joining the Panthers in the movement were organizations like the NAACP, Operation PUSH (People United to Serve Humanity), the American Indian Movement, and the Midwest Latino Conference, as well as numerous organizations that were dominated by white progressives and radicals. Barbershops, record stores, cleaning companies, doctors, and individuals alike also signed on to the movement as financial patrons in the push for control.[146]

The centerpiece of the CCCCP's mobilizing strategy was a conference in June of 1973 at the University of Illinois at Chicago campus, which activists hoped would translate into greater community interest and involvement. With sessions spread out across a Friday afternoon and evening and all day Saturday, the conference featured numerous workshops on various aspects of community control, voter registration, and grassroots organizing, as well as meals and entertainment. But the main draw was probably the speakers' roster, which was a veritable who's who of the 1960s-era black freedom struggle. In addition to local leaders like Bobby Rush, activists from across the country, including Julian Bond, Fannie Lou Hamer, Ralph Abernathy, Dick Gregory, Richard Hatcher, Benjamin Spock, and Bobby Seale (replacing Huey Newton, who was initially slated to come), descended on Chicago for the event.[147] The attendees sang variations on freedom songs ("This little vote of mine, I'm gonna let it shine"), pledged themselves to do the work necessary for community control, and, on Saturday evening, were dispatched by Bobby Rush with a pledge to build "the baddest people's political machine in the history of the U.S."[148] Infiltrators from the Red Squad looked on from the crowd.[149]

But that was as far as it got. Rush and the CCCCP had envisioned the 1973 conference as the movement's opening salvo. It ended up instead being its high-water mark. Efforts for community control, in Chicago as elsewhere, were fiercely resisted not just by the political establishment but also by "businessmen, lawyers, academics, public officials, police chiefs, and other upper-middle and upper-class Americans."[150] Although plenty of black, brown, and poor citizens knew the police department to be an organization that did not work for them, those with greater social and political capital had increasingly come to see the police department as an ally and social asset. Moreover, and logistically speaking, the bar for getting the community control ordinance on the ballot was always going to be high. The CCCCP would have had to get some hundred thousand voters to sign a petition before it could go to the citywide vote, which was a massive grassroots undertaking.[151] Activists never successfully put in place an organizing infrastructure for mobilizing that sort of campaign, which meant that it withered on the vine in the months that followed the conference. Those who had hoped that it would end up on the ballot in 1975 hoped in vein. Despite its promise, the campaign died.

THE FACT THAT movements for community control of the police failed in the early 1970s should not blind us to their vision. Critics of the movement elsewhere in the United States argued that it was tantamount to abolition, but that is not quite right. In the movement's Berkeley iteration, activists *had* called for the abolition of the Berkeley Police Department, although they wished to see it subsequently replaced with smaller, separate police forces.[152] So, too, in Chicago, where activists envisioned a new arrangement in which police power would be dramatically reduced, decentralized, and redistributed but did not seek the elimination of the police altogether.

But even if community control of the police did not mean full abolition, it was nevertheless a radical reimagining of the possible. In the mind's eye of community control activists, after years of abuse, harassment, and neglect, the police force would at best finally be for black and brown and poor people the social good that others took for granted. At worst, it would at least be an instrument of lesser repression. Activists' labors on this front were an effort to refashion the police—the face of local state power—from something that was repressive and destructive into something that was responsive and supportive.

In this, their efforts were very much aligned with the broader currents of social activism surrounding the police in the late sixties and early seventies— whether those currents emanated from the city's housing projects or the offices of a congressman. Across differences of vision, critique, and approach, thousands upon thousands of Chicagoans in that extended moment labored toward something better. *Better* could mean a police force that helped keep them safer. *Better* could mean a police force that stopped harassing them and abusing them. *Better* could (and usually did) mean some combination of the two.

What these various organizations and individuals shared, then, was not a consensus on how to forge ahead. What they shared, lodged inside their work for something better, was an acknowledgment, tacit or explicit, that Chicago's police department simply did not work for them. That, as much as anything, is testament to the durability and intractability of these ruptures between police and community over the generations, from then to now.

Epilogue

Black Chicago's relationship to the department that polices it sunk to its nadir by the late 1960s. Despite the efforts of thousands of citizen-activists in the city, it has not climbed out of it since.

Police practices that accumulated during the early and middle parts of the twentieth century became further entrenched in the century's closing decades, as the United States and Chicago both invested themselves more and more in a bipartisan tough-on-crime race to the bottom. This was most apparent in the escalation of the War on Drugs and antigang initiatives that brought spiking arrest rates in the city—which, notably, happened in the most pronounced fashion during the administration of Chicago's first black and most progressive mayor, Harold Washington, in the early 1980s.[1] Since that time, the number of arrests has fallen, but the racial disjunctures that were established during the postwar era have not. Black arrest totals eclipsed white ones early in the 1960s, and the two diverged later in the decade. They have never come close to one another since then. In 2010 (the last year of publicly available records), the CPD logged more than 160,000 arrests, of which African Americans constituted nearly 72 percent. Black arrest rates were high for serious crimes such as homicide and other public-safety offenses, but they were also high for narcotics violations (black people were 78 percent of those arrested), gambling charges (99 percent), "other municipal code violations" (90 percent), and other minor, quality-of-life crimes.[2] The CPD also effectively stopped arresting white people at all—the practice of racialized policing having reached its logical conclusion, the police force having become singularly invested in policing black and brown people.

And that's just a small piece of the story. Over one four-month span in the middle of 2014, the CPD logged more than 250,000 stop-and-frisk encounters in which no arrest was made—police encounters with men and women who, Langston Hughes might have said, the law simply "had a bad opinion of." Spread out over a full year, this places no-arrest stop-and-frisk's frequency somewhere around three-quarters of a million people. Unsurprisingly, according to the Illinois ACLU, black people, still roughly a third of the city population, accounted for about three-quarters of those stopped and frisked. At that time, Chicago's per-capita rate of stop-and-frisks was more than four times greater than that of the New York Police Department—the department that often serves as the gold standard in such repression.[3] And while the overall numbers of stop-and-frisks have declined since then because of legal action by the ACLU, the likelihood that the person stopped would be black still sits at over 70 percent.[4]

Through these mechanisms, cities like Chicago have become the prime culprits in exacting mass incarceration's racial toll. When paired with stricter and longer sentencing policies that were brought into being during the 1970s and beyond, the fundamentally racist contours of urban policing that were already in place at that point have meant that astounding numbers of black women and men have spent astounding amounts of their lives in jail or prison. The federal crime and drug wars *did* incentivize the expansion and honing of police practices that targeted marginalized communities for the sake of generating arrest numbers, but it was more tweak than revolution. Modern practices of stop-and-frisk, profiling, neighborhood sweeps and saturation, the logics of "broken windows" policing and COMPSTAT crime assessment—all borrow from ideas and practices established long before their current practitioners were even part of the police force (or even, in many cases, born). And it is those practices that govern and guide who gets initiated into the carceral trap in the first place. This is history at work in the present: if we look at history's long arc, it is depressingly unsurprising that mass incarceration is so deeply racialized. It relies on the police system to provide the grist for its mill. And the police system has been targeting black people for punishment in extreme disproportion for generations.

Meanwhile, officer-involved violence remains embedded inside police culture, too. Bettie Jones, Rekia Boyd, Laquan McDonald, and dozens of others have lost their lives to reckless and excessive police force in the past few years alone. This, too, is history in the present. These patterns have held for generations, with black Chicagoans being forced to bear violence's keenest agonies. Beyond what is documented in these pages, the history of such violence stretches from the 1970s into our own time. To the historian, the records of organizations fighting police violence and repression during the 1970s and after, Citizens Alert's records foremost among them, read like an archive of devastation and death: arrested teenagers killed in the Cook County Jail, people killed in CPD squad cars or in the city's housing projects, a fourteen-year-old accidentally shot in the back of the head by an officer conducting a routine stop-and-frisk.[5] The most infamous were the crimes of Jon Burge and the men under his command. A young Vietnam veteran from the Marionette Manor neighborhood, Burge was promoted to detective in 1972 and placed in charge of a group of men working on the South Side. His team began torturing black South Siders roughly around that time, using electrical shocks to genitals and other body parts, beatings, suffocation, and other abuses to torture confessions out of at least 118 people. The city is still paying settlement claims for these torture victims. It was also still paying a nearly $50,000-per-year pension to Burge until he died in 2018.[6]

In more recent years, evidence has also come to light of the CPD continuing its long history of hiding away detainees, out of contact and out of normal due process procedures, at its infamous Homan Square "Black Site."[7] Meanwhile, the FOP fights to have officers' disciplinary records destroyed, continuing long-standing police practices of obfuscation, nondisclosure, and unaccountability.[8] And at the same time, Chicago's political and police machinery have continuously dodged and dismissed efforts to meaningfully reform the department.[9] The police department remains governed by a system that holds officers stunningly unaccountable for their actions, dismisses the legitimacy of citizens' grievances, and seems perfectly comfortable with its terrible reputation for violence and corruption.

None of this is surprising. These are the predictable results of a racialized, repressive, and violent police system a century in the making. As should be clear by now, that system is not a new invention. Its lineage is clear. It has changed some under the influence of the Wars on Crime and Drugs, but only incrementally, not foundationally. We as a society are kidding ourselves if we think that we can look to a pre–crime war model for how policing and criminal justice ought to look. It isn't working well for black people now, but it also hasn't worked well for black people in any of our lifetimes.

OTHER VOICES HAVE more significantly shaped my thinking on this history, but Bill Berry's has lingered in my mind constantly as I have written this book. Berry was not, by any stretch of the imagination, a radical. But in 1966, he acknowledged that the police had not performed their function well or equitably in black communities. They had been brutal, negligent, harassing, and abusive. And at the same time, he argued that this was as much a social problem as a police one, noting that "in a society without racial justice, *the police must bear the burden of policing an unjust order*."[10]

American cities must transform their police forces, or else they must reckon with social movement voices that call for total abolition *of* those forces. But when thinking about Bill Berry's formulation, it doesn't make sense to talk *only* about transforming the police. For the police are symptomatic; they reflect and protect the larger economic, political, and social arrangements that this country has decided it wants (or, at least, can live with). Over the span of decades, Chicago's police, political powerbrokers, and social and business elites have made choices that organized patterns of deprivation and crime in ways that lodged them disproportionately in black districts. To say this is not conspiracy theory. It is to cite evidence. The clearest choice was budgetary: decisions to dump billions of dollars into a system of punishment that would surveil, harass, and arrest people, instead of conjuring a plan of social investment that would ameliorate problems of poverty and crime in the first place. Consider, too, the placement of the Levee, the willingness to let bootleggers operate on the South Side, politicians' complicity in forced segregation and their unwillingness to address the public health crisis of the postwar heroin epidemic and instead treat it as a punishable crisis of public disorder, the entire apparatus's willingness to execute people like Fred Hampton when they challenged its precepts, and any number of other examples from these pages of the ways in which Chicago's political system wielded its police force to do its dirty work. The political system generally and the Democratic Party especially have failed black citizens—relentlessly, mercilessly. (Modern Republicans, it is worth stating, offer even worse solutions than modern Democrats do.)

This was neither inevitable nor organic. It was a function of political choice, political economy, and public policy. And it is also the past in the present, not mere artifact. Policymakers continue to abandon their responsibilities to the disadvantaged, whether those responsibilities entail properly funding schools, controlling guns, or building the economic infrastructure of marginalized neighborhoods. Instead, they choose to give police the unenviable and essentially impossible task of being an unjust society's arbiters and executioners. Indeed, advocates of community-controlled policing in the 1970s who said that the police budget should be reduced and redistributed would surely be dismayed today to have seen it grow to $1.5 billion annually (that number is worth dwelling on), while it eviscerates other public services. A cash-starved Chicago Public Schools system is asked to close fifty schools while also paying $25 million *per year* to the cash-rich CPD in order to station police officers in city high schools.[11] The city closes half of its mental health clinics in the name of saving $3 million—a savings of less than 0.02 percent of the CPD's annual budget.[12] The evidence of the city's failure is overwhelming, the logical conclusions about what and who it cares about condemnatory. Indeed, whoever has a functioning right to the city, it is surely not the racially and economically marginalized.

At the same time, the other half of Bill Berry's point is true, too. The police have done a bad job with the responsibilities conferred on them. The problems are both systematic and individualized. Police policy in the city's low-income black and brown neighborhoods traverses a web of hypersurveillance, containment, and neglect today that is strikingly familiar in its fundamental premises to what we see mapped in the pages of this book. Data collected from recent CPD personnel files shows hundreds of cases of explicitly racist verbal assaults by officers against citizens, some of which also descended into physical assault.[13] The numbers of fatal officer-involved shootings today rivals what it was in the 1960s, and the situations under which those shootings occur remain shrouded in suspicion. Meanwhile, to walk the streets of the South and West Sides is to feel constantly under watch, whether from the police presence there or the nearly one thousand video cameras installed throughout the neighborhoods to record what people there are doing. You will see police squad cars flitting about the city's poor black and brown neighborhoods, particularly on the peripheries where they jut up against areas of commerce, white residence, and greater affluence: surrounding the University of Chicago, near U.S. Cellular Field where the White Sox play, around the United Center on event nights. Their function here is clear: they are there to contain.

And all that disciplining, all that punishing—none of it has made Chicago a safer place to live for black and brown poor people. Arguments to the contrary do not compute. Too many people have died (and die) too many violent deaths, both at the hands of the police or other community members, to say that the police mission in black Chicago can be considered anything remotely like a success.

Acknowledging that fact means we must reach for something more. What is required in the more ideological sense is what Martin Luther King called a "radical revolution of values"—reorienting ourselves "from a thing-oriented society to a person-oriented society." It is only that sort of revolution that can subvert the fundamentally unjust society that conjures so much misery in the first place. It is that sort of revolution—a hard look in our collective mirror—that might convince us, once and for all, that it is an unforgivable absurdity for a city like Chicago, which reflects the larger society, to complain that it can't afford to provide basic human necessities for its citizens while at the same time spending $1.5 billion every year to surveil and police those same citizens. More people must reflect more deeply and more honestly about the circumstances society has cultivated for millions of their countrypeople. They must be honest with themselves that it is an almost uniquely ugly picture.

More immediately and pragmatically, we must also reimagine what police departments can be or should look like. Numerous organizations and individuals in Chicago are doing this hard work already, and have been for a long time. Mariame Kaba has been researching the prison industrial complex and organizing to dismantle it for years.[14] She and others helped form the intergenerational organizing group We Charge Genocide, which takes its name and much of its mission exposing and opposing police violence from the Civil Rights Congress's petition to the United Nations more than half a century ago. Meanwhile, activists organizing under a banner call of "Reparations Now!" won a stunning victory in 2015 that forced the city of Chicago not only to pay reparations to victims of police torture but also to add the history of Jon Burge's torture regime to the curriculum of Chicago Public Schools. And members of Black Lives Matter Chicago, the Black Youth Project, Assata's Daughters, and the For the People Artists Collective continue to do the work of figuring out ways to dismantle the repressive burden that the CPD (and the larger political system) hoists on black and brown communities in Chicago.

A number of these activists would argue that police departments like the CPD shouldn't exist at all, so great has the human misery been that they have wrought. One can disagree with these arguments, but their sincerity and urgency requires a reckoning. Short of abolition, it is worth taking seriously the political project of dramatically scaling back the size of police departments like the CPD and turning more authority over them to the people themselves. Community control activists in the 1970s did not get what they sought, and they faced avalanching and disingenuous criticisms that civilians could not be trusted to effectively oversee police operations. But that sort of argument presupposes that police departments have done a good job of overseeing themselves, when almost precisely the opposite is true. The only time that Chicago has come close to having a functioning accountability system was for a brief six-year window in the 1960s, and that one was fought tooth and nail from within the department and was accompanied by some of the worst unleashing of police power in the city's history. It's worth asking, then, what precisely there is to be lost by actually democratizing the police and giving individual communities a voice in what the mechanics and foundations of policing look like within their neighborhoods.

Regardless, we must be very clear on one thing: the issues we confront today have germinated for a very long time. They are not going to magically revert back to some better and more equitable state, because they did not originate in a better or more equitable state. We must face that first, before anything else.

"HISTORY," Saidiya Hartman has written, "is how the secular world attends to the dead."[15] But history can also be a vehicle for attending to the living.

The history written in these pages must force us not only to look backward but to look forward as well. It must force us to reckon not only with the history of the policing arrangement in this country but also with the reality of the one that we live with today. Maybe by reckoning we can begin reimagining, and perhaps by reimagining, we can make the reality of the past and present not be the reality of the future. Both past and present are ugly. Perhaps the future can be less so. With this book, I hope to have made some contribution to the reckoning, to aid the reimagining.

ACKNOWLEDGMENTS

Many academics share their lives with partners who are in the same field, and acknowledgments sections often seem to become forums to thank their partners for reading drafts, talking through ideas, and generally improving the quality of the book. That type of relationship seems lovely. At the same time, I feel just as fortunate to share my life with a partner who is outside the academy and with whom I rarely talk about the mechanics of my work. Leah—thank you for helping me pull myself away from the labor when I'm in too deep, for listening when I *do* need to talk about my work and the ideas behind it, and for tolerating the late nights and long weekends that I have spent writing this book. More generally, thank you for your tireless support of everything that I dream and do, and for building a life with me that is far more than I ever expected I would have.

My mom and dad also deserve pride of place in this long line of thank-yous. I'm a child of the adoption process, and it was by some massive stroke of good fortune that I was plucked from the service by Barbara and Irving Balto. When I reflect on the long arc of my life, I appreciate more fully just how much they shaped who I am and what I do—from the hours spent on the couch reading with my mom to those spent at protests demanding a better world. For my eighteenth birthday my mom and dad gave me a copy of James Baldwin's *The Fire Next Time*. The inside cover of that book bears an inscription from my mom. In part: "James Baldwin stands for what is the finest in writing and in humanity. Let his life and his work be an inspiration to you." Ma passed away three months later and never got to see my evolution into a scholar of the freedom struggle. But I think that this book and its titular borrowing from Baldwin prove her prescience. I hope she'd be proud.

Thanks here, also, to the many other people in my life outside of academia that helped shape who I am and the life that I have. A full list would be a book unto itself, so I beg forgiveness from those not explicitly included here. But special shout-outs to my brother Sam and his lovely family, my own extended family on both sides, my dad's long-time partner Karen Sherman, Lori and Doug Schubert, Nell and Randy Hull, Karen and Simcha Prombaum, and the entire Starkey crew—Rick, Janie, Joel, Travis, and Dana—who for the better part of two decades have been, functionally, my second family. All of you have been instrumental in shaping me in some way or another. The same is true of my wider network of friends who keep me grounded and laughing. I'm blessed to have you all.

I've also been fortunate to have people in my working life who have lent me more of their friendship, insight, and support over the past decade than I probably deserve. For starters, none of this would have happened were it not for Erik Gellman. (Thanks or curses, Erik, depending on the day that you ask me.) Erik was the first mentor I had in this line of work, when he was my instructor for a couple of graduate courses I took at Roosevelt University while working days as a cook at a Chicagoland restaurant. He saw something in me that I did not at all see in myself, encouraged me to pursue a PhD, and assured me that I had the intellectual tools to do so. More than a decade later, I'm fortunate to call him not only a teacher and mentor but also a collaborator and friend. He also read an early version of this manuscript in full and pushed me to flesh out a number of incomplete thoughts and challenged me on a few half-baked ideas and arguments. He is as good a mentor as anyone could ever hope to have.

In 2008 I left Chicago and enrolled in a joint master's (African American studies) and PhD (history) program at my undergraduate alma mater, the University of Wisconsin–Madison. (Go Badgers.) The list of people who shaped me as a scholar, teacher, and person there seems endless. Christina Greene and Brenda Gayle Plummer served, respectively, as my MA and PhD advisers. Both were tremendous shepherds of my ideas and important supporters of my work and goals. It is not at all an overstatement to say that I wouldn't be where I am without their presence in my life. The same is true of a number of people who didn't function in any formal advisory role but who pushed me and taught me and encouraged me. Jim Sweet stands tall as one of the best mentors and strongest cheerleaders that a young scholar could ever hope to have. His influence on me in some ways mirrors Erik's, in that Jim saw things in me that I did not see in myself and worked to help cultivate them. He was instrumental in my development as a scholar, and I am grateful to count him among my friends. So, too, with Will Jones and Steve Kantrowitz, both of whom deeply shaped my ideas, my teaching, and my life with their mentorship and friendship. Christy Clark-Pujara, Nan Enstad, John Hall, Neil Kodesh, Al McCoy, Franco Scarano, and Alexander Shashko all teach or taught at the University of Wisconsin, and in various ways have helped hone my thinking and expand my understanding of both history and the present world. Meanwhile, Leslie Abadie is the glue that holds Wisconsin's Department of History together. She has counseled, advised, prodded, and helped countless numbers of graduate students, myself included, during her time in Madison. There aren't enough superlatives to describe how good she is at what she does and how much she meant to my career development.

All told, between my undergraduate and graduate degrees, I spent more than ten years in school at Madison. Throughout that time, I never took a single class from Karl Shoemaker or David McDonald—probably to their benefit. Nevertheless, I cherish their friendship. Everyone's lives would be enriched by time spent listening to David tell stories about Russian history, pop culture, or whatever topic emerges as his muse in that moment. Karl is similarly as funny as he is brilliant. I've benefited greatly from his friendship, and also from the many conversations that we've had over beers about my work, his work, sports, music, and all manner of things. The community of scholar-mentors at Wisconsin is, truly, next level.

A final note on that community: I am at a loss when I try to say how much I miss the late Camille Guérin-Gonzales. She was an incredible teacher, a brilliant scholar, and a fierce believer in the young scholars who worked with her. I will always be thankful that she was a part of my life, and mourn how briefly she was.

Among the many blessings that graduate school bestowed on me, none was more important than introducing me to some of the best and most brilliant people who inhabit my life. Faron Levesque is my spirit animal and a supremely kindred soul. I love her and all the joyful times and stimulating and deep conversations that having her in my life has yielded. Charles Hughes has counseled me throughout my career and taught or modeled for me about 90 percent of what I know about teaching and about being a gracious and giving academic. More importantly, he has been an invaluable friend and has tipped me to some of my favorite singers and bands. Naomi Williams has taught me a great deal about history, politics, and whiskey. Her tenacious defense of breakfast food is insane, but she is brilliant. Brian Hamilton, Jesse Gant, and I entered graduate school as part of the same cohort and have grown and thought together ever since. The three of us were in a writing group back in 2014 and 2015, so they've read a lot of what became this book and greatly improved the quality of it. Brian, Jesse, and Faron were also part of an earlier writing group that I was in, which we dubbed the Weary Writing Collective after the bar we traditionally met in. (Shout-out to the Weary Traveler in Madison.) Leah Webb-Halpern and Jackie Cooney-Birch were part of the group, too. I learned as much from these women and men as I have from any formal teacher that I ever had, and had many, many laughs along the way. Finally, the late Doria Johnson was a constant resource and an unwavering friend throughout and after my graduate school years. I miss her and promise to keep telling truths about the history of racism, racial exploitation, and freedom struggles in Chicago in her honor. Doria—Chairman Fred lived in you.

Beyond Wisconsin, the list of academics who have influenced me for the better is vast. I want to be Heather Ann Thompson when I grow up. Until that happens, I'll satisfy myself with calling her a friend and learning constantly from the model she offers as a scholar-activist. Charles McKinney is fiercely devoted to building a more just world, but I also appreciate him for his hilarious sense of humor, his unwavering mentorship, and his willingness to go eat fried catfish with me every time I'm in Memphis. Max Felker-Kantor and I lived a mile apart in Indianapolis for three years and convened frequently for conversations about both work and life. I'm grateful that he's in my life and our conversations made this a better book. (We probably also owe thanks to Twenty Tap for providing our convening space.) Lionel Kimble and Sam Mitrani commented on a draft of this book's first chapter for a seminar at the Newberry Library, and improved it as a consequence. The Newberry also introduced me to stellar scholar-activists Liesl Orenic, Leon Fink, and Peter Cole, and I've benefited from my conversations with them all. Martha Biondi, Danielle McGuire, and Tim Tyson have also made important contributions to my intellectual development, and I am privileged to consider them friends.

I feel fortunate to be researching the history of the carceral state at a time when so many other scholars are doing similar labors. I'm fortunate to have had the opportunity to think about my work alongside an entire cohort of brilliant thinkers who are also down in the trenches doing the work. Among the most significant for me: Chris Agee, Tera Agyepong, Andy Baer, Dan Berger, Anne Gray Fischer, Elizabeth Hinton, Julilly Kohler-Hausman, Nora Krinitsky, Toussaint Losier, Melanie Newport, Peter Pihos, Carl Suddler, and Keeanga-Yamahtta Taylor. Max and Heather—you, too.

Much of this book was written while I worked at Ball State University, with the latter parts of the work done as I transitioned to the University of Iowa. In both places, I have been fortunate to work with some truly incredible colleagues who provided invaluable friendship as well as crucial questions and advice. A full list would stretch this book's page count to untenable lengths, but I want to offer special recognition to Jim Connolly, who offered important comments on huge portions of this manuscript and counseled me through a variety of life and career decisions, as well as to Abel Alves, Yaron Ayalon, Sarah Drake Brown, Colin Gordon, Lisa Heineman, Lena Hill, Michael Hill, Emily Johnson, Liza Lawrence, Kristen McCauliff, Jessica Reuther, Emily Rutter, Doug Seefeldt, Kevin Smith, Scott Stephan, Landon Storrs, Chris Thompson, and Kiesha Warren-Gordon.

A number of people in Chicago were also instrumental to the development of this book. In particular, I need to thank Amanda, Susan, and Mike Klonsky for opening up their home and offering me access to their own ideas and those of many other brilliant and radical thinkers from across the city. Timuel Black is a true inspiration and a fount of wisdom. Ralph Metcalfe Jr. offered many off-the-record insights into the life of his father, as well as his own thoughts on Chicago's past and present. Jeff Coleman taught me a lot about the legal community in Chicago and its past. Monica Trinidad and Page May asked me to join them on their podcast to talk about Chicago's activism, and it challenged me to think more deeply about some of the issues I explore here. This only scratches the surface, but I am grateful for these Chicagoans, all of whom are extraordinary ambassadors for the city and its radical traditions.

Outside of my home office, this book was mostly written in libraries, coffee shops, and bars in Chicago, Indianapolis, Madison, Iowa City, and Muncie. Thank you to everyone affiliated with these places and the work that you do to ensure the vibrancy of public spaces.

Similarly, thanks to a number of editors who have offered me space to flesh out my ideas in their pages and on their websites. This includes the editorial staffs at *TIME*, the *Washington Post*, the *Progressive*, the *Washington Spectator*, the *Journal of African American History*, *Labor*, and History News Network. In 2017 I started writing for the Lawyers, Guns, and Money blog and have been pushed in useful directions by my blogmates and the commentariat there. Thinking through ideas on the page and having a large community of smart people offering comment on them is a scary experience. It is also a joy.

Thanks to all the archivists who have dedicated their lives to preserving the past and have helped me research this book. This includes the archivists with whom I worked very extensively at the Chicago History Museum, the University of Chicago, the University of Illinois at Chicago, the Newberry Library, and the numerous branches of the Chicago Public Library. It also includes those at the Schomburg Center in Harlem, the Library of Congress in Washington, and the Bancroft Library in Berkeley. You all are unsung heroes, and we need to sing about you more.

The research and writing of this book was funded by grants and fellowships from the National Endowment for the Humanities; the Andrew Mellon Foundation; the Black Metropolis Research Consortium; the Doris Quinn Foundation; the Benjamin V. Cohen Memorial Endowment Fund; the University of Wisconsin's African American Studies Department, History Department, and Graduate School; the Sponsored Projects Administration at

Ball State University; and the University of Iowa's College of Liberal Arts and Sciences. We are fortunate to have generous funders of scholarly research that expands our understanding of the world. Please fight to ensure that they continue.

Thanks also to everyone at the University of North Carolina Press for supporting this project. When I first started conjuring the idea that became this book, I dreamed that it would end up with UNC Press and what was, then, a very young but robust Justice, Power, and Politics series. And now here we are. Thank you to Mary Caviness, Dylan White, Dino Battista, and everyone else on the editorial, production, and marketing teams at UNC Press, as well as to Karen Carroll, who served as an attentive and thorough copyeditor. Special thanks are owed to my editor, Brandon Proia, whom I first met years ago, when this book was still in the most germinal of stages. He believed in it from the beginning, and over the years has shepherded and edited it with keen insight and boundless grace. I'm grateful for his friendship and the working relationship we have. Among the many smart choices that he made in improving the book was recruiting readers who would be able to identify and comment on the manuscript's strengths and, more important, weaknesses. This book is much, much stronger for the insights of Beryl Satter and Jordan Camp. I am humbled that they were willing to offer such careful reads of the book.

Finally, I want to thank everyone, in Chicago and elsewhere, who is fighting for us all. In Chicago this means thanking activists with Black Lives Matter, We Charge Genocide, Assata's Daughters, the Black Youth Project, Reparations Now, the For the People Artists Collective, and so many others. I started this book before most of these organizations existed, but I am inspired and fortified by their labors. I hope that you find this history useful.

And to you, reader—thank you. I see you. I appreciate you.

NOTES

Abbreviations Used in the Notes

AAPLR   Afro-American Patrolmen's League Records, Chicago History Museum, Chicago, IL

ACLUR   American Civil Liberties Union, Illinois Division Records, Special Collections Research Center, University of Chicago

CHM   Chicago History Museum, Chicago, IL

CULR   Chicago Urban League Records, Special Collections and University Archives, Richard J. Daley Library, University of Illinois at Chicago

MRC   Municipal Reference Collection, Chicago Public Library, Harold Washington Branch, Chicago, IL

NAACPR   Records of the National Association for the Advancement of Colored People, Library of Congress, Manuscript Division, Washington, DC

WSSC   Woodlawn Social Services Center Records, Special Collections Research Center, University of Chicago

Introduction

1. Blue Ribbon Panel, *Metcalfe Report*, 20.

2. Ibid., 2–18.

3. Renault Robinson, "Black Police: A Positive Means of Social Change," n.d., ca. early 1970s, series 4, box 115, folder 1305, CULR.

4. Chicago Police Department, *Annual Reports*: 1970–1979, MRC.

5. *Chicago Daily Defender*, July 18, 1972.

6. Ralph Knoohuizen, Richard P. Fahey, and Deborah J. Palmer, "The Police and Their Use of Fatal Force in Chicago: A Report of the Chicago Law Enforcement Study Group," 1972, single file, CHM.

7. Chicago Police Department, List of Charges against Donald Heath, January 23, 1968, box 536, folder 1, ACLUR; *Chicago Defender*, December 29, 1967; *Chicago American*, December 30, 1967; *Chicago Daily News*, December 30, 1967; *Chicago Sun-Times*, December 30, 1967.

8. United States Department of Justice: Bureau of Justice Statistics, "Correctional Populations in the United States, 2014," http://www.bjs.gov/content/pub/pdf/cpus14.pdf.

9. Thompson, "How Prisons Change the Balance of Power in America."

10. The Sentencing Project, "Racial Disparity: Corrections Population Statistics," http://www.sentencingproject.org/map/map.cfm#map (accessed March 30, 2018).

11. Alexander, *New Jim Crow*. James Forman Jr. makes a number of points about

why Michelle Alexander's book tells us less than a full story about today's carceral project. Perhaps the largest intellectual ones are that Alexander does little to resolve the matter of the extraordinary numbers of Latinx, Indigenous, and poor white people caught up in the system of mass incarceration, and does nothing to deal with the problem of violent offenders who fall outside the range of her War on Drugs–centric focus. Forman, "Racial Critiques of Mass Incarceration."

12. The body of scholarship on mass incarceration and the carceral state by policy analysts, legal scholars, and social scientists is immense. Foundational studies exploring mass incarceration's origins and the political, economic, and social impulses that drove it include R. Kennedy, *Race, Crime and the Law*; Parenti, *Lockdown America*; Mauer, *Race to Incarcerate*; Garland, *Culture of Control*; Gottschalk, *Prison and the Gallows*; McLennan, *Crisis of Imprisonment*; Simon, *Governing through Crime*; and Tonry, *Malign Neglect*.

Whereas much of the received common sense surrounding mass incarceration has assumed it to be a product of conservative politics generally and the War on Drugs in particular, an important branch of the carceral state scholarship has challenged that thesis. Heather Ann Thompson's important *Journal of American History* article links the carceral state's rise to the larger urban crisis reshaping postwar America. See Thompson, "Why Mass Incarceration Matters." Ruth Wilson Gilmore examines mass incarceration as a response to capitalism's creation of "surplus" populations that need to be contained and controlled. See R. Gilmore, *Golden Gulag*. Naomi Murakawa, Elizabeth Hinton, Jordan T. Camp, and Loïc Wacquant each make compelling but markedly different arguments for the ways that liberal and/or neoliberal politics have driven the development of mass incarceration. See Murakawa, *First Civil Right*; Hinton, *From the War on Poverty to the War on Crime*; Camp, *Incarcerating the Crisis*; Wacquant, *Punishing the Poor*; Wacquant, *Prisons of Poverty*; and Wacquant, "Class, Race and Hyperincarceration." Meanwhile, James Forman Jr. and Michael Javen Fortner examine how black fears about crime led black political leaders and some community members to support tough-on-crime politics in and after the 1970s. See Forman, *Locking Up Our Own*; and Fortner, *Black Silent Majority*. Julilly Kohler-Hausmann explores how the demonization and criminalization of welfare recipients in the 1970s prompted the prison boom. See Kohler-Hausmann, *Getting Tough*. Kelly Lytle Hernández uses a settler colonialist lens to explore the rise of "human caging" in Los Angeles over the course of several centuries. See Hernández, *City of Inmates*.

Other scholars examine the consequences of mass incarceration on contemporary communities and politics. Among others, see Western, *Punishment and Inequality*; Pager, *Marked*; Frampton, López, and Simon, *After the War on Crime*; Clear, *Imprisoning Communities*; Rios, "Hyper-Criminalization of Black and Latino Male Youth"; Rios, *Punished*; Goffman, *On the Run*; and Gottschalk, *Caught*. Nell Bernstein has done important work in this area that specifically examines the treatment of children's relationships (direct and indirect) to incarceration. See N. Bernstein, *All Alone in the World* and *Burning Down the House*.

13. On racial condemnation, see Muhammad, *Condemnation of Blackness*. For books on older historical regimes that prefigured the current one, see LeFlouria,

Chained in Silence; Haley, *No Mercy Here*; Malka, *The Men of Mobtown*; Agyepong, *The Criminalization of Black Children*; Oshinsky, *"Worse Than Slavery"*; Lichtenstein, *Twice the Work of Free Labor*; Curtin, *Black Prisoners and Their World*; Shapiro, *New South Rebellion*; Blackmon, *Slavery by Another Name*; Gross, *Colored Amazons*; Hicks, *Talk with You Like a Woman*; and Perkinson, *Texas Tough*. Other historians have also studied the ways that prisoners have responded to and resisted their confinement and degradation. See esp. Chase, "Civil Rights on the Cell Block," and Berger, *Captive Nation*.

14. R. Gilmore, *Golden Gulag*; Hernández, *City of Inmates*; and Felker-Kantor, *Policing Los Angeles*.

15. Overwhelmingly, studies of mass incarceration begin in or after the 1960s and the era of the wars on crime and drugs. Those that reach back further often lose historical nuance, falling into a teleological trap that treats racialized mass incarceration as an outgrowth or new manifestation of old modes of racial repression. The work of Michelle Alexander, Loïc Wacquant, and Randall Kennedy are all representative of how that trap works. Notable exceptions to this general trend include Hernández's *City of Inmates* and Murakawa's *First Civil Right*.

16. Scott Lassar, "The Administration of Law Enforcement Assistance Administration Grants in Illinois, 1969–1971: A Report of the Chicago Law Enforcement Study Group," ca. 1972, single file, MRC; Illinois Law Enforcement Commission, Annual Report: 1970, MRC.

17. CPD, *Annual Reports*: 1920, 1970, MRC; CPD, *Annual Report*: 2010, https://portal .chicagopolice.org/portal/page/portal/ClearPath/News/Statistical%20Reports/Annual %20Reports/10AR.pdf (accessed March 30, 2018).

18. Militarization is a popular term for the implementation of SWAT teams and the outfitting of police forces with military-grade equipment—or even equipment furnished directly from the military. It also references the troubling way of talking about cities as if they're war zones. Scholars write of "warrior cops" and "cities under siege," and aren't talking about far-flung authoritarian regimes. Drawing from the work of Tim Blackmore, Stephen Graham notes that in today's world and in the mind's eye of the American military and political elite, everything is "battlespace"—perpetual, constant, endless danger and war. "Nothing," he writes, "lies outside battlespace, temporally or geographically. Battlespace has no front and no back, no start nor end. It is 'deep, high, wide, and simultaneous.'" Nowhere does this sense of danger and justified war exist in greater measure than in the cities. Thus, in an urbanized, battlespaced world in which everything looks like a nail, the state swings its hammer hard and often. And the most vital hammer on the domestic front is the police. See Graham, *Cities under Siege*, 31. See also Balko, *Rise of the Warrior Cop*. It's worth acknowledging that the term "militarization" is not uncontroversial. See, for example, judicial scholar and navy veteran Gilbert Rivera's article in the *Berkeley Journal of Criminal Law* arguing, essentially, that saying that American police are militarized is an insult to the military. Rivera, "Armed Not Militarized."

19. Daniel D. Howard Associates, "A Study Defining the Selection Problem of the Task Force," February 1969, single file, CHM.

20. J. Baldwin, "Report from Occupied Territory."

21. Ibid.

22. A. Davis, "Political Prisoners, Prisons, and Black Liberation."

23. Seale, *Seize the Time*, 96.

24. Haas, *Assassination of Fred Hampton*, 65.

25. Levy, *Great Uprising*.

26. National Advisory Commission on Civil Disorders, *Kerner Report*, 11.

27. Other important studies of policing, and police relationships to urban governance and politics, include Fogelson, *Big-City Police*; Mitrani, *Rise of the Chicago Police Department*; Malka, *The Men of Mobtown*; Agee, *Streets of San Francisco*; Monkkonen, *Police in Urban America*; Donner, *Protectors of Privilege*; Moore, *Black Rage in New Orleans*; M. Johnson, *Street Justice*; and K. Johnson, "Police-Black Community Relations in Postwar Philadelphia."

28. Lefebvre's vision of the conflict over the right to the city is complex and multi-faceted. Complicating factors more is the fact that it's been expanded on and bent in innumerable directions by other urban theorists, social theorists, sociologists, and geographers. The context of capitalism, neoliberalization, and the commodification of the commons is usually central to their definitions—wherein the struggle to gain a right to the city is a collective endeavor against broader socio-political-economic forces, rather than one between differing groups of working-class citizens. But given the differentials in social power between, say, black migrants on the one hand, and on the other, white youth gangs in the 1920s who were enmeshed in the local political machine and protected by the police, the idea is intellectually useful here. Among the most influential articulations of the right to the city are Lefebvre, *Writings on Cities*; Harvey, "Right to the City"; Harvey, *Rebel Cities*; and Boggs and Boggs, "City Is the Black Man's Land."

29. Harvey, "Right to the City," 23.

30. LeRoy Martin, interview by Timuel Black, in Black, *Bridges of Memory*, 459.

31. Nguyen, *Nothing Ever Dies*, 8.

32. Scholarship on the carceral state that more fully utilizes gender analysis includes Ritchie, *Invisible No More*; Hicks, *Talk with You Like a Woman*; Gross, *Colored Amazons*; Gross, *Hannah Mary Tabbs*; Haley, *No Mercy Here*; LeFlouria, *Chained in Silence*; Fischer, "Arrestable Behavior"; Woolner, "Woman Slain in Queer Love Brawl"; Greene, "She Ain't No Rosa Parks"; and Mustakeem, "Armed with a Knife in Her Bosom."

33. Lilia Fernández offers some very useful insights into Puerto Rican and Mexican experiences with the CPD within her larger history of brown life in postwar Chicago. Fernández, *Brown in the Windy City*, esp. 159–72.

34. Van Cleve, *Crook County*, 11. John Pfaff's recent book on prosecutorial behavior, *Locked In*, is a new and important addition to the aforementioned studies on the causes and consequences of mass incarceration.

35. Vitale, *End of Policing*. It should be obvious that I quibble with Vitale's assessment that the major problems with American policing have grown in the past forty years, but his book is nevertheless an excellent primer on the problems of American policing.

36. Taylor, *From #BlackLivesMatter to Black Liberation*, 181.

Prologue

1. Brooks, "Kitchenette Building." The title of this chapter, "Devil's Sanctum," is a play on L. O. Curren's *Chicago, Satan's Sanctum*, in which he wrote, "I believe that Chicago is the devil's headquarters." Quoted in Adler, *First in Violence, Deepest in Dirt*, 8.

2. Algren, *Chicago: City on the Make*, 72–73.

3. Terkel, *Studs Terkel's Chicago*, 10.

4. Bellow, "Civilized Barbarian Reader"; Wright, *Black Boy*, 307.

5. Sandburg, "Chicago."

6. Cisneros, *House of My Own*. Cisneros talks about her Chicago experiences elsewhere, as well, notably in the introduction to the twenty-fifth anniversary edition of her classic *House on Mango Street*.

7. On Burnham's plan for Chicago, see C. Smith, *Plan of Chicago*. On the ways that black Chicagoans utilized the city's natural spaces, see McCammack, *Landscapes of Hope* and, to a lesser extent, Fisher, *Urban Green*.

8. Cronon, *Nature's Metropolis*, 23–35. On the Battle of Fort Dearborn's significance to Chicago's rise, see Keating, *Rising Up from Indian Country*.

9. On the early planning for the reversal of the Chicago River, see Pacyga, *Chicago*, 45–46.

10. Ibid., 39–40.

11. See Lewis, *Chicago Made*. On the history of the Union Stock Yard in particular and its significance in the story of industrial America, see Pacyga, *Slaughterhouse*.

12. Garb, *Freedom's Ballot*, 21.

13. On the patterns of ethnic group organization, see Cohen, *Making a New Deal*, esp. chap. 2.

14. On the supposed problems of social order during this period, see Mitrani, *Rise of the Chicago Police Department*; Avrich, *Haymarket Tragedy*; and J. Green, *Death in the Haymarket*.

15. Mitrani, *Rise of the Chicago Police Department*, 2. See also Monkkonen, *Police in Urban America*.

16. Mitrani, *Rise of the Chicago Police Department*, 3.

17. Ibid., 27.

18. Ibid., 32.

19. On this consensus, see Mitrani, *Rise of the Chicago Police Department*, chap. 5. On the Great Railroad Strike more broadly, see Stowell, *Streets, Railroads, and the Great Strike of 1877*.

20. Mitrani, *Rise of the Chicago Police Department*, 133.

21. J. Green, *Death in the Haymarket*, 5; Mitrani, *Rise of the Chicago Police Department*, 188.

22. J. Green, *Death in the Haymarket*, 5–8.

23. On the effects of Haymarket on the CPD, see Mitrani, *Rise of the Chicago Police Department*, 194–207; quote on 200.

24. On whiteness and the process of "becoming white," see Ignatiev, *How the Irish Became White*; Jacobson, *Whiteness of a Different Color*; Roediger, *Wages of Whiteness*;

and Roediger, *Working toward Whiteness*. On the particular dynamics of whiteness and its boundaries in Chicago, see Guglielmo, *White on Arrival*.

25. Mitrani, *Rise of the Chicago Police Department*, 168.

26. Christopher Robert Reed has written numerous books on the early history of black Chicago that cover the years preceding this study. See Reed, *Black Chicago's First Century, All the World Is Here!*, and *Knock at the Door of Opportunity*.

27. Garb, *Freedom's Ballot*, 22–23.

28. Ibid., 33.

29. Ibid., 69.

30. Ibid.

31. The phrase "freedom dreams" is taken from Kelley, *Freedom Dreams*.

32. Grossman, *Land of Hope*, 4.

33. The literature on Jim Crow terror is immense. For a small sampling, see Woodward, *Strange Career of Jim Crow*; Litwack, *Been in the Storm So Long*; Wood, *Lynching and Spectacle*; Feimster, *Southern Horrors*; Parsons, *Ku-Klux*; Ward, *Hanging Bridge*; and Allen, *Without Sanctuary*.

34. Grossman, *Land of Hope*, 96; Bougere, "Exodus Train."

35. Drake and Cayton, *Black Metropolis*, 31.

36. Ibid., 60.

37. Michaeli, *Defender*, 76.

38. Citizens' Police Committee, *Chicago Police Problems*, 150.

39. For a sustained, if notably antiquated, contemporaneous account of Chicago's meatpacking industry in the early twentieth century and African Americans' roles and experiences within it, see Herbst, *Negro in the Slaughtering and Meat-Packing Industry in Chicago*.

40. Quoted in Pacyga, *Slaughterhouse*, 22.

41. For an excellent overview of the working, home, and associational lives of members of many of these immigrant blocs in the first decades of the twentieth century, see Cohen, *Making a New Deal*.

42. Wilkerson, *Warmth of Other Suns*, 225.

43. Hughes, *Not without Laughter*, 278.

44. Wright, *Black Boy*, 307.

45. W. E. B. Du Bois, "Hopkinsville, Chicago, and Idlewild," *Crisis*, August 1921, 158.

46. Bachin, *Building the South Side*, 247. For an especially rich accounting of "the Stroll" and early-century black cultural life in Chicago more generally, see D. Baldwin, *Chicago's New Negroes*.

47. On the Great Migration in a broader view, see Wilkerson, *Warmth of Other Suns*; Gregory, *Southern Diaspora*; Lemann, *Promised Land*; and Berlin, *Making of African America*, chap. 4.

48. On the influence of black Chicago on the cultural life of the city (and nation), see Hine and McCluskey, *Black Chicago Renaissance*; Bone and Courage, *Muse in Bronzeville*; and Mullen, *Popular Fronts*.

49. On Sellin's theory and its relationship to race-making and the condemnation of blackness, see Muhammad, *Condemnation of Blackness*, 2–3.

50. McWhirter, *Red Summer*, 118.

51. "Outline of Interview with Juvenile Officer. Station 2A," ca. 1927, box 274, folder 4, Ernest Burgess Addenda; F. R. Jenkins, "Cases of Negro Families," summer 1926, box 257, folder 26, Burgess Addenda; both in Special Collections Resource Center, University of Chicago.

52. Andrew A. Bruce, draft of an "Introduction to Survey on Organized Crime," January 1929, box 9, folder 4, Ernest Burgess Papers, Special Collections Resource Center, University of Chicago. Bruce was also part of the 1929–1930 survey of the CPD entitled *Chicago Police Problems*. J. B. Crossley to Julius Rosenwald, March 12, 1929, box 39, folder 4, Julius Rosenwald Papers, Special Collections Resource Center, University of Chicago.

53. Historians still disagree somewhat on the degrees to which agency and constraint respectively shaped the process and outcome of this ghettoization. Exclusion and proscription weighed heavy on the housing question, as migrants found themselves hemmed in by the machinations of white supremacist housing policies, threats, and economic deprivation. Writing in 1967, the historian Allan Spear hedged no bets on the matter—especially on antiblack racism's role in the ghetto's creation story: "The development of the physical ghetto in Chicago, then, was not the result chiefly of poverty; nor did Negroes cluster out of choice. The ghetto was primarily the product of white hostility." Spear, *Black Chicago*, 26. Two decades later, the historian James Grossman, while allowing significant social power to the effects of racism, also argued for some degree of choice at work in black people's residential choices: "Exclusion aside, many migrants sought their first homes in areas populated by other blacks, where they could be more comfortable and find familiar institutions." Grossman, *Land of Hope*, 127.

The Chicago historian Christopher Reed is the most authoritative voice of which I know who suggests that Black Chicago ca. the 1920s did not, in fact, constitute a ghetto. He cites the extraordinary diversity of class and sensibility that characterized black neighborhoods, the fact that some very wealthy African Americans *did* move out of that area, as well as the fact that a sizable number of white people still lived intermingled with the black population. This is all true, as Reed's scholarship here and elsewhere has made clear. It might be countered, however, that the majority of black people lacked the ability to move out of this section of the city, whether as a consequence of racial terrorism, the threats of same, or economic deprivation, the roots of which were also bound up with the history of racism both locally and nationally. In turn, the neighborhoods in which they lived were deprived in terms of resources, opportunities, and material relative to others in the city. And it seems to me that this arrangement—proscribed mobility, combining with and exacerbating inequality—is, in many ways, a ghetto in an almost classically defined sense. See Reed, *Rise of Chicago's Black Metropolis*.

Finally, it is worth pointing out that the very meaning and application of the term "ghetto" is and has long been contested. For a historical contextualization of the term, see Duneier, *Ghetto*.

54. Frazier, *Negro Family in Chicago*, 205–6.

55. Grossman, *Land of Hope*, 181–207; Drake and Cayton, *Black Metropolis*, 219–21.

56. Chatelain, *South Side Girls*, chap. 1.

57. Chicago Commission on Race Relations, *Negro in Chicago*, 153.

58. Ibid., 152.

59. Ibid., 185.

60. Grossman, *Land of Hope*, esp. 123–60; quote on 152.

61. Drake and Cayton, *Black Metropolis*, 56; Bachin, *Building the South Side*, 258; and Blair, *I've Got to Make My Livin'*, chap. 4.

62. Bachin, *Building the South Side*, 259.

63. Drake and Cayton, *Black Metropolis*, 178.

64. Ibid.

65. Krist, *City of Scoundrels*, 103.

66. CCRR, *Negro in Chicago*, 34.

67. Morris Lewis to Walter White, January 21, 1922, Records of the National Association for the Advancement of Colored People, Library of Congress, Washington, DC, microfilm reproduction, series 12, reel 1.

Chapter 1

1. Chicago Commission on Race Relations, *Negro in Chicago*, 38–39. Detailed narratives of the riot, complete with varying degrees of analyses, include the CCRR report; Sandburg, *Chicago Race Riots*; and Tuttle, *Race Riot*.

2. Transit disruptions caused by the riot were compounded and eventually completed by striking transit workers. Krist, *City of Scoundrels*, esp. 205–6.

3. CCRR, *Negro in Chicago*, 35.

4. Krugler, *1919*, 122.

5. The stories of Wellington Dunmore, John Slovall, and William Thornton are from CCRR, *Negro in Chicago*, 34–35. That of Joseph Scott is from Tuttle, *Race Riot*, 43.

6. Descriptions of and information about these police lockups are taken from a 1947 investigation of such facilities, conducted by the John Howard Association (JHA), a Chicago-based prisoner rights organization. That report, in turn, makes detailed reference to a similar study conducted in 1912 by a special City Council Committee on Schools, Fire, Police, and Civil Service, the complete report of which has proven impossible to locate. I arrived at the above portrait of the lockups at the time of the 1919 riot by cross-referencing the JHA's detailed observations in 1947 with its summation of those of the City Council in 1912. Eugene S. Zemens, "Held without Bail: Physical Aspects of the Police Lockups of the City of Chicago, 1947–48," single file, CHM. See also Beeley, *Bail System in Chicago*, 32.

7. Travis, *Autobiography of Black Chicago*, 26.

8. Tuttle, *Race Riot*, 243.

9. *Chicago Defender*, March 20, 1920.

10. Timuel D. Black, interview by author, Chicago, August 21, 2013.

11. See Tuttle, *Race Riot*; Krist, *City of Scoundrels*, 169–71.

12. Consider, for instance, that black officers were forced into segregated sleeping quarters by department superiors. The riot's outbreak roughly coincided with the trial of three black CPD officers before the department's Merit Committee, on charges that they refused to use the Jim Crow sleeping quarters. CCRR, *Negro in Chicago*, 34.

13. Ibid., 4.

14. *Broad Ax*, August 2, 1919.

15. CCRR, *Negro in Chicago*, 5.

16. *Chicago Tribune*, July 30, 1919.

17. CCRR, *Negro in Chicago*, 451.

18. Ibid., 5.

19. Ibid., 572; Tuttle, *Race Riot*, 49.

20. Chicago Commission on Race Relations, "Public Opinion and the Negro," box 114, folder 746, Victor Lawson Papers, Newberry Library, Chicago.

21. Bukowski, *Big Bill Thompson*, 104.

22. *New York Times*, July 31, 1919.

23. Abu-Lughod, *Race, Space, and Riots*, 61.

24. CCRR, *Negro in Chicago*, 37–38.

25. *Chicago Defender*, March 20, 1920.

26. Biles, *Richard J. Daley*, 22.

27. On the decentralization of big city police departments more generally during this period, see Fogelson, *Big-City Police*, esp. 97–98.

28. Former CPD officer Joseph Sevick details the ways his brother John was able to manipulate political connections in order to join the department, despite technically being ineligible because he fell short of the height requirements. John was also given an answer sheet for the department's mental exam, which helped him earn a spot in the department. Joseph Sevick, untitled document, Joseph Sevick Papers, CHM.

29. For an example of this in action, see Lindberg, *To Serve and Collect*, 128. As Robert Fogelson puts it, most officers "could . . . ignore [central] headquarters with virtual impunity, provided that they kept on good terms with the superior officers and ward bosses." Fogelson, *Big-City Police*, 99.

30. Comments of Commissioner William Russell at a Meeting of the Citizens' Police Committee, May 13, 1919, box 1 folder 1, Chicago Citizens' Police Committee Records, Special Collections Research Center, University of Chicago.

31. Cohen and Taylor, *American Pharaoh*, 28.

32. *Chicago Tribune*, July 31, 1919.

33. Krugler, *1919*, 111.

34. *Chicago Tribune*, July 31, 1919.

35. Krugler, *1919*, 104.

36. CCRR, *Negro in Chicago*, 39.

37. Ibid., 35.

38. Ibid., 35. The grand jury's statement is meaningful, though it did not stay out of session long. Its members resumed hearing cases the following day, when they voted in favor of indictments against twenty-three African Americans. *Chicago Tribune*, August 8, 1919.

39. CCRR, *Negro in Chicago*, 34. Hoyne was a political aspirant who despised Mayor Bill Thompson, and thus had great cause to try to undermine the legitimacy of Thompson's police force. He also possessed exceedingly low opinions of African Americans, made oddly manifest in wild conspiracy theories that black people had consorted to incite the riot, and his prosecutorial efforts held evidence of racial bias at almost every turn. Nevertheless, the extent to which his opinions were corroborated makes them worthy of attention.

40. Ibid., 36.

41. *Chicago Tribune*, August 15, 1919.

42. For example, the black-owned *Broad Ax* published a laudatory eulogy the week after the riot for black CPD Officer John Simpson, who lost his life during the riot, "protecting life and property irrespective of color," and Simpson was not alone in performing his sworn duty well. *Broad Ax*, August 9, 1919.

43. On the rise, crest, and fall of homicide rates, see Adler, "Less Crime, More Punishment." In the wake of the infamous St. Valentine's Day Massacre in 1929—in which members of Al Capone's South Side gang donned CPD uniforms and ambushed members of a North Side Irish gang, murdering seven of them execution-style in a Lincoln Park garage—University of Chicago sociologist Ernest Burgess estimated that in the four years previous, 215 gangsters had been killed. Ernest Burgess, "Crime and Law Enforcement," n.d., ca. mid-1929, box 28, folder 11, Ernest Burgess Papers, Special Collections Research Center, University of Chicago.

44. The number of home stills was so huge in the case of Chicago's Little Italy that the neighborhood reputedly reeked of alcohol fumes. Okrent, *Last Call*, 128.

45. McGirr, *War on Alcohol*.

46. Ibid., 55-56.

47. The sociologist Robert Lombardo has made a case for the existence of a "black mafia" in Chicago at this point in time. But even he acknowledges that black underworld powerbrokers—no matter their strengths—weren't able to touch the lucrative bootlegging industry. The major mob bosses were too powerful, too ruthless, and too well connected. The great majority of black Chicagoans themselves were totally uninvolved in bootlegging in any capacity. Those who were involved were largely only peripherally so, at the same levels as poor white ethnics: small-scale distillers, low-level numbers runners, saloonkeepers, and, most of all, consumers. Lombardo, "Black Mafia."

48. Reckless, *Vice in Chicago*, 90.

49. Ibid., 71.

50. Ibid., 92.

51. Blair, *I've Got to Make My Livin'*, 232-33.

52. CCRR, *Negro in Chicago*, 202.

53. Muhammad, *Condemnation of Blackness*, 226.

54. For a sketch of this history over a longer term, see Spillane, "Making of an Underground Market."

55. Reckless, *Vice in Chicago*, 97.

56. D. Baldwin, *Chicago's New Negroes*, 106.

57. Illinois Association for Criminal Justice, *Illinois Crime Survey*, 615-19.

58. *Chicago Defender*, July 17, 1920.

59. Mumford, *Interzones*, 33.

60. Bougere, "Exodus Train," 259.

61. *Chicago Defender*, September 11, 1920.

62. CCRR, "Public Opinion and the Negro"; emphasis added.

63. See Muhammad, *Condemnation of Blackness*.

64. Adler, "Less Crime, More Punishment," 40. The effects of this nationally mani-

fested in a barrage of punitive forms: in the expansion of both federal and state prison systems; the passage of laws like New York's Baumes laws, which mandated minimum sentences and other "get tough" policies; the establishment of the chain gang system in the South; and the expanding police budgets of many American cities. See also Gottschalk, *Prison and the Gallows*; and McLennan, *Crisis of Imprisonment*, esp. chap. 10.

65. For a particularly astute exploration of this uneven enforcement in a national context and through the lens of Prohibition, see McGirr, *War on Alcohol*. As both McGirr and Linda Gordon note, rabid anti-Catholicism undergirded Prohibition enforcement, and Prohibition enforcement coincided with the resurgence of the Ku Klux Klan. See Gordon, *Second Coming of the KKK*.

66. Ibid.

67. CPD, *Annual Report*: 1920, MRC.

68. Frazier, *Negro Family in Chicago*, 210.

69. *Chicago Defender*, April 11, 1925.

70. CPD, *Annual Report*: 1930, MRC.

71. Moses, "Community Factors in Negro Delinquency," 224.

72. CPD, *Annual Reports*, 1920–1929, MRC. The annual reports are the proper source for sifting this information, but Dianne Pinderhughes's *Race and Ethnicity in Chicago Politics* offers a fairly stunning graphic display of these patterns. See Pinderhughes, *Race and Ethnicity in Chicago Politics*, 151.

73. Moses, "Community Factors in Negro Delinquency," 227.

74. As Mitchell Duneier writes, the Chicago School to which Burgess was central still, at this point in time, "had no meaningful conception of racism." He was thus constantly looking for other explanations for seemingly unique challenges faced by black people. Eduardo Bonilla-Silva notes that this was characteristic of white sociologists of the time, and long after. Duneier, *Ghetto*, 47; Bonilla-Silva, "What We Were."

75. Ernest Burgess, "Questions of Master's Thesis—Earl R. Moses," n.d., box 134, folder 5, Ernest Burgess Papers, Special Collections Research Center, University of Chicago.

76. *Chicago Defender*, September 3, 1921; CCRR, "Negro and Crime," 126, box 114, folder 738, Victor Lawson Papers, Newberry Library.

77. CCRR, "Negro and Crime," 127.

78. Ibid., 115.

79. Ibid., 116.

80. On the congestion of the criminal courts and the consequences, see Chicago Crime Commission, Fourth Annual Report of the Chicago Crime Commission: 1922, Chicago Crime Commission Collection, CHM.

81. On the stiffening of sentencing policies, see Adler, "Less Crime, More Punishment."

82. National Commission on Law Observance and Enforcement, *Lawlessness in Law Enforcement*; Hopkins, *Our Lawless Police*, 218–19; and Chafee, Pollak, and Stern, *Third Degree*, 128n84.

83. Lavine, *Third Degree*, 82–83.

84. Ibid., 62–64.

85. National Commission on Law Observance and Enforcement, *Lawlessness in Law Enforcement*, 188.

86. Ibid., 131–32.

87. Ibid., 136.

88. Ibid., 158. The report does not specify which cities.

89. Elizabeth Dale offers a few glimpses of these earlier forms of police torture in Chicago, although her book on the case of Robert Nixon very much hinges around that one 1938 case. See Dale, *Robert Nixon*.

90. *Chicago Defender*, March 29, 1924.

91. *Chicago Defender*, July 23, 1927.

92. *Chicago Defender*, February 2, 1929.

93. For these four years for which these numbers are available, the total number of justifiable/excusable killings ran to 147, sixty of whom were black. See CPD, *Annual Reports* for 1923, 1926, 1928, and 1929, MRC.

94. *Chicago Defender*, October 26, 1929.

95. Muhammad, *Condemnation of Blackness*, 249.

96. Reed, *Rise of Chicago's Black Metropolis*.

97. St. Clair Drake, "Black Communities in Urban Areas of the United States: Some Observations on Uniformities and Diversities," March 1969, b 22, folder 21, p. 31, St. Clair Drake Papers, Schomburg Center for Research in Black Culture, New York Public Library.

98. Gosnell, *Negro Politicians*, 250.

99. Comparison to total force strength is done by using the CPD, *Annual Report*: 1930, MRC.

100. Gosnell, *Negro Politicians*, 246.

101. Ibid., 246–47.

102. Ibid., 255–56.

103. Ibid., 256–57.

104. J. Connolly, *An Elusive Unity*, 222.

105. Pinderhughes, *Race and Ethnicity in Chicago Politics*.

106. *Chicago Defender*, February 21, 1920.

107. Branham, "Transformation of Black Political Leadership," 330–32.

108. Reed, *Rise of Chicago's Black Metropolis*, 154.

109. In the buildup to the 1919 riot, for instance, Wells had implored the city to do something to punish white terrorists targeting black homes for bombing. As we have seen, they did nothing. Tuttle, *Race Riot*, 240.

110. *Chicago Defender*, November 28, 1925.

111. See Fogelson, *Big-City Police*, 67–92.

112. On the proliferation of crime commissions, see Fogelson, *Big City Police*, 43, 67–92.

113. Included in the CCC's original self-vision was that it would be "engaged in the work of gathering data to make clear the reason for the prevalence of crime in Chicago"; "obtain legislation sufficient to enable the various duly authorized departments and branches of the government to properly function"; and ensure that all agencies related to the administration of law "are acting in good faith and are free

from the demoralizing effects of politics." This would be the narrowest vision that the CCC would ever hold for itself. See Chicago Crime Commission, *Bulletin of the Chicago Crime Commission*, no. 4 (June 1919), Chicago Crime Commission Collection, CHM.

114. Willrich, *City of Courts*, 294.

115. The Crime Commission's bulletins, available at the Chicago History Museum, are a trove of information on the organization's activities during and after this period.

116. *Chicago Defender*, November 20, 1920; Citizens' Police Committee, *Chicago Police Problems*, 1.

117. Citizens' Police Committee, *Chicago Police Problems*, 1.

118. Ibid., vii–viii.

119. Citizens' Police Committee, Meeting of the Operating Committee May 9, 1929, box 1, folder 1, Chicago Citizens Police Committee Records, Special Collections Research Center, University of Chicago.

120. Andrew A. Bruce, draft of an "Introduction to Survey on Organized Crime," January 1929, box 9, folder 4, Ernest Burgess Papers, Special Collections Resource Center, University of Chicago. Bruce also was also part of the study that culminated in *Chicago Police Problems*. J. B. Crossley to Julius Rosenwald, March 12, 1929, box 39, folder 4, Julius Rosenwald Papers, Special Collections Resource Center, University of Chicago.

Chapter 2

1. J. Adams, *Epic of America*, xx.

2. Cohen, *Making a New Deal*, 217.

3. Schlesinger, *Age of Roosevelt*, 168.

4. I. Bernstein, *Turbulent Years*, 14.

5. Ethan Blue's study of Depression-era prisons and prisoners' lives is a notable exception. Blue, *Doing Time in the Depression*.

6. Johnson, Kantor, and Fishback, "Striking at the Roots of Crime."

7. Naomi Murakawa and Dan Berger both make this case strongly. See Murakawa, *First Civil Right*, and Berger, *Captive Nation*, esp. chap. 1.

8. Biles, *Big City Boss*, 61.

9. Quoted in Drake and Cayton, *Black Metropolis*, 83.

10. In his 1981 book *Black Marxism*, Cedric Robinson mapped out a theory of racial capitalism in which he illuminated the ways that "racialism . . . permeate[d] the social structures emergent from capitalism." The two systems were, Robinson argued, inextricable from the beginning and continued to systematically inform one another. Robinson, *Black Marxism*, 2.

11. On "slave labor camps," see Baptist, *Half Has Never Been Told*. On race and capitalism in real estate, see N. D. B. Connolly, *World More Concrete*. On sharecropping and racial division (and efforts to overcome it), see Kelley, *Hammer and Hoe*. On Wall Street's colonization of the Caribbean, see Hudson, *Bankers and Empire*. The 2017 *Boston Review* forum on "Race, Capitalism, and Justice" is an essential resource for thinking about racial capitalism, with Walter Johnson's lead essay and

Peter James Hudson's tracing of the longer intellectual history of the racial capitalism being especially important to my own thinking. W. Johnson, "To Remake the World"; Hudson, "Racial Capitalism and the Dark Proletariat." See also R. Gilmore, *Golden Gulag*; W. Johnson, *River of Dark Dreams*; and Camp, *Incarcerating the Crisis*.

12. Reed, *Chicago's Black Metropolis*.

13. Rick Halpern documents those Depression-era solidarities in Chicago's packinghouses—and the fragmentation that preceded them—in *Down on the Killing Floor*.

14. See Cohen, *Making a New Deal*.

15. Drake and Cayton, *Black Metropolis*, 83.

16. I. Bernstein, *Lean Years*, 298; D. Kennedy, *Freedom from Fear*, 87.

17. Drake and Cayton, *Black Metropolis*, 84.

18. Ibid., 88.

19. Earl B. Dickerson, interview by Studs Terkel, in Terkel, *Hard Times*, 393.

20. Cayton, *Long Old Road*, 179.

21. Ibid.

22. Thomas Ellis, interview by Timuel D. Black, in Black, *Bridges of Memory*, 27.

23. Gottfried, *Boss Cermak of Chicago*, 219.

24. Ibid.

25. Ibid., 235.

26. Grimshaw, *Bitter Fruit*; Rakove, *Don't Make No Waves*; and Royko, *Boss*.

27. Gellman, "'Carthage Must Be Destroyed,'" 88.

28. Branham, "Transformation of Black Political Leadership," 331.

29. Reed, *Chicago NAACP*, 85.

30. *Chicago Tribune*, October 21, 1950.

31. Biles, *Big City Boss*, 92, 126–27; Cohen and Taylor, *American Pharaoh*, 55–56.

32. The reasons black voters gravitated toward the Democratic Party during the 1930s and after included the party's control of patronage opportunities, the appeal of New Deal programs, and the recognition that as it lost power, the Republican Party in Chicago could offer little to help them. Grimshaw, *Bitter Fruit*; Haller, "Policy Gambling," 729.

33. This is one of the central theses of Grimshaw's *Bitter Fruit*.

34. Gottfried, *Boss Cermak of Chicago*, 238–87.

35. Biles, *Big City Boss*, 23.

36. D. Kennedy, *Freedom from Fear*, 163.

37. Joseph Sevick, untitled document, Joseph Sevick Papers, CHM.

38. Biles, *Big City Boss*, 88–89.

39. Gottfried, *Boss Cermak of Chicago*, 259.

40. Ibid., 279.

41. *Chicago Tribune*, August 16, 1931; Gottfried, *Boss Cermak of Chicago*, 280.

42. CPD, *Annual Report*: 1932, MRC.

43. Gottfried, *Boss Cermak of Chicago*, 282.

44. Virgil Peterson, "Re: Chicago Police Department," January 28, 1947, box 57, folder 11, Virgil Peterson Papers, CHM.

45. Grimshaw, *Bitter Fruit*, 84.

46. Simpson et al., "Chicago: Still the Capital of Corruption."

47. Fogelson, *Big-City Police*, 168.

48. Deutsch, "The Plight of the Honest Cop."

49. The series ran from at least mid-May to mid-June of 1946. See clippings in box 57, folder 1, Virgil Peterson Papers, CHM.

50. Virgil Peterson to Guy Reed, September 17, 1945, box 57, folder 11, Virgil Peterson Papers, CHM.

51. Scholars in a number of contexts have shown how problematic crime statistics can be. This is a central piece of Muhammad's *Condemnation of Blackness*, but see also Maltz, "Bridging Gaps in Police Crime Data," and Pepper and Petrie, *Measurement Problems*.

52. CPD, *Annual Report*: 1931, MRC.

53. While Allman reported to Cermak that his new system of measurement made it so that "for the first time in the history of the Chicago Police Department, an accurate picture of criminal offenses committed over the entire city is available," there was no adjusting for the fact that a large number of crimes—then as now—were never reported in the first place. CPD, *Annual Report*: 1931, MRC.

54. CPD, *Annual Reports*: 1929, 1930, 1931, MRC.

55. Andrew Bruce to L. B. White, December 5, 1930, box 1, folder 2, Chicago Citizens' Police Committee Records, Special Collections Research Center, University of Chicago.

56. CPD, *Annual Report*: 1931, MRC.

57. *Chicago Defender*, December 5, 1931.

58. *Chicago Tribune*, December 8, 1931.

59. The game had been around on the South Side since as early as the 1890s, when John "Mushmouth" Johnson had brought it in, but had grown markedly during the late 1920s.

60. Biles, *Big City Boss*, 90.

61. Drake and Cayton, *Black Metropolis*, 486.

62. Duneier, *Ghetto*, 52.

63. Gottfried, *Boss Cermak of Chicago*, 281.

64. Biles, *Big City Boss*, 89.

65. Ibid., 89–90.

66. Cohen and Taylor, *American Pharaoh*, 52. See also Biles, *Big City Boss*, 89–90.

67. Biles, *Big City Boss*, 89–90.

68. CPD, *Annual Report*: 1931, MRC.

69. Haller, "Organized Crime in Urban Society, 219. Beyond that fact, other forms of gambling, ones that were just as destructive (or harmless, depending on the vantage) as policy, were either ignored altogether by police and policymakers, or were given explicit legal sanction. In the case of the latter, for instance, in 1927 the state of Illinois legalized racetrack betting, a sport popular with the white sporting set. Moreover, according to the historian John C. Burnham, games like craps and other dice games had exploded in popularity during and after World War I, when servicemen brought them back from the barracks. But those dice games, at least when played within white homes, were never a preoccupation of politicians or policymakers. Instead, the CPD bloated the gambling columns of its arrest rolls with black policy players, while nonblack players of other games partook freely. Burnham, *Bad Habits*, 154.

70. Biles, *Big City Boss*, 90.

71. CPD, *Annual Reports*: 1933-1945, MRC.

72. Storch, *Red Chicago*, 18-30.

73. Ibid., 36, 219.

74. Ibid., 36.

75. G. Gilmore, *Defying Dixie*, 42.

76. Storch, *Red Chicago*, 27.

77. Reed, *Depression Comes to the South Side*, 80; Gellman, "'Carthage Must Be Destroyed,'" 88; and Storch, *Red Chicago*, 113.

78. Drake and Cayton, *Black Metropolis*, 86.

79. As Michael Dennis correctly writes of the CPD's antilabor drives later in the 1930s, "Strikebreaking and antilabor activity reflected the assumption that the resort to police violence was necessary to maintain order." Dennis, *Memorial Day Massacre*, 77.

80. Cayton, *Long Old Road*, 178-81.

81. I borrow the language of "plunder" from Ta-Nehisi Coates. See Coates, *Between the World and Me* and "Case for Reparations."

82. See N. D. B. Connolly, *World More Concrete*.

83. Storch, *Red Chicago*, 99.

84. On the conflict over Diane Gross's eviction, see *Chicago Defender*, August 8, 1931; *Chicago Tribune*, August 4, 1931; Haywood, *Black Communist*, 212-13; Cayton, *Long Old Road*, 178-82; and Reed, *Depression Comes to the South Side*, 86.

85. *Chicago Defender*, August 8, 1931.

86. *Chicago Tribune*, August 4, 1931; *Chicago Tribune*, August 5, 1931.

87. Haywood, *Black Communist*, 212.

88. Storch, *Red Chicago*, 100.

89. Ibid.

90. Ibid.

91. Cayton, *Long Old Road*, 182.

92. Storch, *Red Chicago*, 100-101.

93. Reed, *Depression Comes to the South Side*, 112.

94. *Chicago Tribune*, August 7, 1931.

95. Ibid.

96. Donner, *Protectors of Privilege*, 32.

97. Ibid., 49-50.

98. The historian Randi Storch provides a thorough accounting of what such antiradical police violence (often spearheaded by the Red Squad) looked like in early-1930s Chicago. Storch does not really get Make Mills's character correct, however, casting him as a far more reasonable person and administrator than he in fact was. Storch, *Red Chicago*, 115-20.

99. Dennis, *Memorial Day Massacre*, 77-79.

100. *Chicago Defender*, May 26, 1934.

101. Ibid.

102. *Chicago Defender*, December 31, 1932.

103. *Chicago Defender*, November 2, 1935.

104. Gellman, *Death Blow to Jim Crow*, 27–28.

105. *Chicago Tribune*, August 21, 1932; *Chicago Tribune*, March 22, 1934; and *Chicago Tribune*, August 23, 1935.

106. See Dennis, *Memorial Day Massacre*.

107. *Chicago Tribune*, December 30, 1935.

108. *Chicago Tribune*, February 13, 1937.

109. In the early 1970s, the CPD purged huge portions of the Red Squad files. For a partial list of what was destroyed, see folder 91, folder labeled "Purge Records," CPD Red Squad Files, CHM.

110. Storch, *Red Chicago*, 53.

111. Ibid., 54.

112. *Chicago Defender*, July 1, 1933; *Chicago Defender*, July 15, 1933; Storch, *Red Chicago*, 167–68; and Bates, *Pullman Porters*, 120–21.

113. Kimble, *New Deal for Bronzeville*, 37.

114. H. A. Turner to Walter White, Western Union telegram, August 4, 1931, part 1: G50, folder 6, NAACPR.

115. Reed, *Chicago NAACP*, 84.

116. *Chicago American*, August 5, 1931; *Chicago Daily News*, August 5, 1931.

117. The problems of the NAACP during this period are well documented. See, for example, Halpern, *Down on the Killing Floor*, 106–7.

118. Theophilus Mann to NAACP Press Service, December 30, 1931, part 1: G50, folder 1; NAACP Press Release, July 8, 1933, part 1: G51, folder 10; both in NAACPR.

119. Among others, see Plummer, *Rising Wind*; Dudziak, *Cold War Civil Rights*; and Horne, *Black and Red*.

120. Gellman, *Death Blow to Jim Crow*, 2.

121. Bates, *Pullman Porters*, 124.

122. Halpern, *Down on the Killing Floor*, 126–29.

123. Gellman, *Death Blow to Jim Crow*, 25.

124. For the long PWOC struggle in the packinghouses, see Halpern, *Down on the Killing Floor*, 96–166.

125. Halpern, *Down on the Killing Floor*, 215.

126. Gellman, *Death Blow to Jim Crow*, 31; Gellman, "'Carthage Must Be Destroyed,'" 111.

127. Gellman, *Death Blow to Jim Crow*, 44.

128. Ibid.

129. Zeiger, *CIO, 1935–1955*, 62–63.

130. Carol Quirke offers an insightful deep dive into the video footage of the massacre. See Quirke, "Reframing Chicago's Memorial Day Massacre."

131. Halpern, *Down on the Killing Floor*, 154.

132. Ibid.

133. *Chicago Tribune*, March 22, 1941; *Chicago Tribune*, October 23, 1941.

134. *Chicago Tribune*, December 28, 1945.

135. Halpern, *Down on the Killing Floor*, 229–30.

136. Helgeson, *Crucibles of Black Empowerment*, 56.

137. Ibid., 56–59.

138. Ibid., 59, 61.

139. Cahill, *Revised Statutes*, 1470. See also Brundage, "Illinois Attorney General's Report for the Biennium 1919–1920."

140. *Chicago Tribune*, March 18, 1930. Their primary targets appear to have been suspected mob gunmen (one of the highest profile arrests under the statute's auspices was of Frank Maritote, a gunman in the Capone syndicate), but this constituted an important turn in application. Many judges declared that such measures violated the Constitution, but the sentiment was far from unanimous. Unsurprisingly, police officials took such judicial uncertainties as carte blanche to forge ahead with the practice.

141. *Chicago Tribune*, March 18, 1930.

142. Theophilus Mann to NAACP Press Service, December 30, 1931, box 1: G50, folder 1, NAACPR.

143. Associated Negro Press, Press Release, December 2, 1931, box 8, folder 1, Claude Barnett Papers, CHM.

144. *Chicago Tribune*, November 25, 1932; *Chicago Tribune*, January 2, 1933.

145. Moses L. Walker to Walter White, Western Union telegram, March 2, 1930; Walter White to Herbert Turner, Postal telegraph, March 3, 1930; both in box 1: G50, folder 6, NAACPR.

146. Theophilus Mann to NAACP Press Service, December 30, 1931, box 1: G50, folder 1, NAACPR.

147. *Chicago Defender*, December 5, 1931.

148. Ibid.

149. Ibid.

150. *Chicago Defender*, October 31, 1931.

151. *Chicago Defender*, December 27, 1930.

152. *Chicago Defender*, January 16, 1932.

153. *Chicago Defender*, March 26, 1932.

154. *Chicago Defender*, April 30, 1932.

155. *Chicago Defender*, September 23, 1939.

156. Stewart-Winter, *Queer Clout*, 74–81.

157. Mantler, *Power to the Poor*, 235.

Chapter 3

1. Joseph Beauharnais to Martin Kennelly, August 14, 1953, box 21, folder 12, Robert Merriam Papers, Special Collections Research Center, University of Chicago.

2. Chicago Commission on Human Relations, "Documentary Report of the Anti-Racial Demonstrations and Violence against the Home and Persons of Mr. and Mrs. Roscoe Johnson, 7153 St. Lawrence Ave., July 25, 1949," single file, CHM. See also Chicago Commission on Human Relations, "A Preliminary Report on Racial Disturbances in Chicago for the Period July 21 to August 4, 1957," single file, CHM.

3. On the relationship between privilege and the police in earlier eras, see, among others, Mitrani, *Rise of the Chicago Police Department*; Monkkonen, *Police in Urban America*; and Donner, *Protectors of Privilege*.

4. Fogelson, *Big-City Police*, 12. Emphasis added.

5. Gallup Poll, "Confidence in Institutions," June 2016, http://www.gallup.com/poll /1597/confidence-institutions.aspx.

6. Fogelson, *Big-City Police*, 147.

7. Hahn and Jeffries, *Urban America and Its Police*, 98.

8. Ibid.; Hindelang, "Public Opinion Regarding Crime."

9. On the public relations campaigns of police organizations in the sixties, see M. Adams, "Patrolmen's Revolt."

10. Buntin, *L. A. Noir*, 190–91.

11. Felker-Kantor, "Liberal Law-and-Order"; Fogelson, *Big-City Police*, 140.

12. Sugrue, *Origins of the Urban Crisis* and *Sweet Land of Liberty*; Thompson, *Whose Detroit*, "Urban Uprisings: Riots or Rebellions?," and "Understanding Rioting."

13. Muhammad, *Condemnation of Blackness*.

14. *Crusader*, March 22, 1958.

15. Hirsch, *Making the Second Ghetto*, 17.

16. Jackson, "Race, Ethnicity, and Real Estate Appraisal," 431.

17. Jackson, "Race, Ethnicity, and Real Estate Appraisal."

18. Ibid., 436.

19. *Oakland-Kenwood Outlook*, May 20, 1943.

20. *Oakland-Kenwood Outlook*, June 17, 1943.

21. Mayor's Commission on Human Relations, "Human Relations in Chicago: Inventory in Human Relations, 1945–1948: Recommendations for the Future," January 13, 1949, single file, CHM.

22. On the larger history of struggle over restrictive covenants, see Gonda, *Unjust Deeds*.

23. Patillo, *Black on the Block*, 49.

24. *Chicago Defender*, October 21, 1944.

25. *Chicago Defender*, May 19, 1945.

26. *Chicago Defender*, November 10, 1945.

27. *Chicago Defender*, July 6, 1946; Henry McGee to Madison Jones, August 12, 1946, pt. 2: C45, folder 1, NAACPR.

28. Mayor's Commission on Human Relations, "Human Relations in Chicago: Inventory in Human Relations, 1945–1948: Recommendations for the Future," single file, CHM.

29. Flier issued by Community Book Store, "Stop Hoodlumism in Hyde Park NOW!," n.d., ca. 1955, box 56, folder 1, St. Clair Drake Papers, Schomburg Center for Research in Black Culture, New York Public Library.

30. Hirsch, *Making the Second Ghetto*, esp. 40–99.

31. Halpern, *Down on the Killing Floor*, 215.

32. Biles, *Big City Boss*, 126–27; Cohen and Taylor, *American Pharoah*, 55–56; and Gellman, "'Armed Arbiters," 13–14.

33. Mayor's Commission on Human Relations, "Human Relations in Chicago: Inventory in Human Relations, 1945–1948: Recommendations for the Future," single file, CHM.

34. Ibid.

35. Hirsch, *Making the Second Ghetto*, 96.

36. Ibid., 97.

37. *Chicago Sun-Times*, November 16, 1949.

38. Letter to the Editor, November 16, 1949, box 7, folder 56, St. Clair Drake Papers, Schomburg Center for Research in Black Culture, New York Public Library.

39. Commission on Human Relations, "Monthly Report of the Executive Director," May 1950, box 58, folder 1, St. Clair Drake Papers, Schomburg Center for Research in Black Culture, New York Public Library.

40. *Chicago Tribune*, July 2, 1976.

41. Waitstill H. Sharp to Edgar Bernhard and Edward Meyerding, July 26, 1951, box 499, folder 2, ACLUR.

42. *Chicago Sun-Times*, November 16, 1949.

43. Hirsch, *Making the Second Ghetto*, 97.

44. *Chicago Sun-Times*, July 31, 1957.

45. Research Department to Executive Director, "Report on Trial of Some Individuals Arrested in Connection with the Race Riot of July 28, 1957—Calumet Park, Chicago," September 13, 1957, series 3, box 170, folder 1846, CULR.

46. Biles, *Big City Boss*, 147–48.

47. Chandler Owen, "A Program for Solution of the Trumbull Housing Conflict," 1954, box 21, folder 9, Robert Merriam Papers, Special Collections Research Center, University of Chicago.

48. Kennelly, for instance, tried to declare in 1949 that "there is no such thing as a white neighborhood in Chicago." Jack, "Chicago's Violent Armistice"; *Chicago Defender*, September 2, 1950.

49. Biles, *Richard J. Daley*, 65.

50. Notes from the meeting of the Committee on Racial Tensions in Housing Projects, November 3, 1953, box 21, folder 9, Robert Merriam Papers, Special Collections Research Center, University of Chicago.

51. "Statement to the People by Mayor Richard J. Daley," August 19, 1966, box 85, folder 4, Richard J. Daley Papers, Special Collections and University Archives, Richard J. Daley Library, University of Illinois at Chicago.

52. Hirsch's *Making the Second Ghetto* is a classic in showing how urban renewal and housing policies made the "second ghetto," the walls of which were even stronger than the original.

53. Patterson, *We Charge Genocide*, 8–9. See also Plummer, *Rising Wind*; Dudziak, *Cold War Civil Rights*; and Anderson, *Eyes Off the Prize*.

54. Patterson, *We Charge Genocide*.

55. Copies of all handbills, creators unattributed, are found in box 565, folder 4, ACLUR.

56. *Chicago Defender*, February 16, 1946.

57. *Chicago Defender*, July 19, 1947.

58. *Chicago Defender*, July 2, 1949; *Chicago Defender*, August 6, 1949; and Civil Rights Congress, "Fact Sheet: Hitlerite Mob Violence at 56th and Peoria St.," box 56, folder 9, St. Clair Drake Papers, Schomburg Center for Research in Black Culture, New York Public Library.

59. *Chicago Defender*, July 2, 1949.

60. [Commission on Human Relations] to Edgar Bernhard, November 19, 1949, box 551, folder 3, ACLUR.

61. Edgar Bernhard to Martin Kennelly, November 21, 1949, box 551, folder 3, ACLUR.

62. *Sun-Times*, December 1, 1949; *Sun-Times*, December 18, 1949.

63. Jack, "Chicago's Violent Armistice."

64. Prendergast's plan for improving mob control may be found in the *Chicago Daily News*, December 1, 1949.

65. Hirsch, "Massive Resistance, 522.

66. Ibid.

67. *Freedom's Call*, May 1954, pt. 2: C46, folder 7, NAACPR.

68. Ibid.

69. Ibid.; News Release, "An Ultimatum Will Be Presented to Mayor Kennelly," May 11, 1954, pt. 2: C46, folder 7, NAACPR.

70. News Release, "NAACP Delegation Meets with Police Commissioner," May 19, 1954, pt. 2: C46, folder 7, NAACPR.

71. News Release, "NAACP to Observe Negro Newspaper Week at March Meet," March 23, 1954, pt. 2: C46, folder 7, NAACPR.

72. Scholars of the southern black freedom struggle like Akinyele Omowale Umoja, Charles Cobb, and Nicholas Johnson have, in recent years, offered compelling evidence showing the importance of armed resistance in helping propel and support black freedom dreams. Umoja, *We Will Shoot Back*; Cobb, *This Nonviolent Stuff'll Get You Killed*; and N. Johnson, *Negroes and the Gun*.

73. Hirsch, "Massive Resistance," 533.

74. *Chicago Tribune*, April 11, 1954.

75. Hirsch, "Massive Resistance," 533; *Chicago Tribune*, May 24, 1954.

76. News Release, "NAACP Files Suits for Civil Damages against Trumbull Rioters," August 2, 1954, pt. 2: C47, folder 2, NAACPR.

77. Ibid.

78. *Chicago Defender*, August 14, 1954.

79. Christopher Reed calls this period "the apex of militant activism" for the local NAACP. See Reed, *Chicago NAACP*, 161–94.

80. See Tyson, *Blood of Emmett Till*.

81. A. Green, *Selling the Race*, 179–212.

82. Tyson, *Blood of Emmett Till*, 198.

83. News Release, "Chicago NAACP Calls for Federal Troops to Occupy Mississippi," October 10, 1955, pt. 2: C47, folder 3, NAACPR.

84. Ibid.

85. "Recommendations of the Chicago Branch of the NAACP, Offered to Honorable Richard J. Daley, Mayor of the City of Chicago and to the Commission on Community Welfare as a Solution to the Trumbull Park Situation," n.d., pt. 2: C47, folder 3, NAACPR.

86. Robert L. Birchman, "News from Chicago Branch of the National Association for the Advancement of Colored People: NAACP to Stage Mass Protest Meeting on Till Lynching," September 20, 1955, pt. 2: C47, folder 3, NAACPR.

87. Ibid.

88. Ibid.

89. "Resolution Presented and Adopted at NAACP Mass Meeting," Sunday, September 25, 1955; Resolution on Trumbull Park and Racial Tensions in Chicago," Sunday, September 25, 1955; both in pt. 2: C47, folder 3, NAACPR.

90. Flier for Washington Park Rally, September 1, 1957, pt. 2: C47, folder 3, NAACPR.

91. News from Chicago Branch NAACP, "Statement of Willoughby Abner, President Chicago Branch NAACP Setting Forth NAACP Action, Program and Policy in Re: Calumet Park Disturbances and Other Racial Disorders in Chicago," September 1, 1957, pt. 2: C47, folder 3, NAACPR.

92. Ibid.

93. Edwin Berry to Richard J. Daley, July 30, 1957, box 499, folder 1, ACLUR.

94. Chicago Urban League, "A Working Paper on Reported Incidents of Racial Violence in Chicago: 1956 and 1957," November 1958, series 3, box 170, folder 1848, CULR.

95. Chicago Conference on Civic Unity, "Human Relations in Chicago 1949: Inventory in Human Relations, 1945–1948, Recommendations for the Future," single file, CHM.

96. *Freedom's Call*, October 1956, pt. 3: C29, folder 6, NAACPR; News Release, "Appeal to Appellate Court Filed in Case of Six Fined for Disorderly Conduct in Café Fracas Over Denial of Service," ca. September/October, 1956, pt. 3: C29, folder 6, NAACPR.

97. Gerald Bullock, "An Eyewitness Account of the Trianon Incident," March 29, 1950, box 499, folder 3, ACLUR. See also Edgard Bernhard to John Prendergast, May 23, 1950, box 499, folder 3, ACLUR.

98. Gerald Bullock, "The enclosed being true one is impelled to ask a few pertinent 'Whys?,'" ca. March 1950, box 499, folder 3, ACLUR.

99. Ibid.

100. In this, they were hardly unique. As Marvin Dulaney wrote in his study of *Black Police in America*, "as early as the 1860s, African Americans believed that police officers of their own race would enforce the law impartially and even at times protect them from the racially biased system under which they lived in American society." Dulaney, *Black Police in America*, xv.

101. There were 222 black police officers in 1945, constituting about 3 percent of the force. In 1949 there were 185, less than 2.4 percent of it.

102. *Chicago Defender*, August 30, 1952.

103. *Chicago Tribune*, July 21, 2013.

104. Ibid.

105. *Chicago Tribune*, July 21, 2013.

106. Dulaney, *Black Police in America*, 106.

107. "Why I Killed 11 Men," *Ebony*, January 1950.

108. *Chicago Tribune*, July 21, 2013.

109. Timuel D. Black, interview by author, Chicago, August 21, 2013.

110. "Diary—2nd District," February 1953, box 58, folder 3, Virgil Peterson Papers, CHM.

111. Timuel D. Black, interview by author.

Chapter 4

1. Langston Hughes, "Simple and the Law," *Chicago Defender*, January 13, 1945.

2. Timuel D. Black, interview by author, Chicago, August 21, 2013.

3. Prominent examples include Simon, *Governing through Crime*; Hinton, *From the War on Poverty to the War on Crime*; and Flamm, *Law and Order*.

4. Drake and Cayton, *Black Metropolis*, 799.

5. In 1947 alone, more than four times as many housing units were constructed in Chicago's suburbs as in the city itself. Bowly, *Poorhouse*, 49. The black population in Chicago's suburbs grew by 53,000 between 1940 and 1960—a not-insignificant number, but one that pales in comparison to the more than 500,000-person growth to the city proper. Wiese, *Places of Their Own*, 118. On the larger history of suburbanization in America, see Jackson, *Crabgrass Frontier*.

6. Diamond's *Chicago on the Make* paints this story with special vividness.

7. The historian Thomas Sugrue first popularized the theory of the urban crisis in his classic study of post–World War II Detroit, *Origins of the Urban Crisis*. Sugrue flipped popular assumptions about what had caused the supposed post–civil rights "crisis" in American cities. He rejected the thesis that black anger and sixties-era urban uprisings had provoked capital abandonment of the city and white flight to the suburbs, which had in turn provoked the city's economic decline and the evisceration of black neighborhood infrastructure. Instead, the opposite was true. Sugrue, *Origins of the Urban Crisis*.

8. Drake and Cayton, *Black Metropolis*, 807.

9. W. Wilson, *When Work Disappears*, esp. 18–20.

10. On the growth of school inequality in Chicago, see Neckerman, *Schools Betrayed*.

11. Drake and Cayton, *Black Metropolis*, 812.

12. Ibid., 828.

13. Sugrue, *Origins of the Urban Crisis*, 4.

14. Sampson, *Great American City*; Sampson and Lauritsen, "Racial and Ethnic Disparities."

15. For this picture of major crimes across the city, I use statistics found in the CPD's Annual Reports, as well as those that the CPD submitted to the FBI for its Uniform Crime Reports. See CPD, *Annual Reports*: 1945–1958 (1959 unavailable), MRC; Uniform Crime Reports, 1945–1959; and Peterson, "Crime Conditions in the Fifth Police District."

16. One can look at CPD Annual Reports from any given year and see this dynamic at work.

17. Peterson, "Crime Conditions in the Fifth Police District."

18. Ibid.

19. Ibid.

20. Ibid.

21. The series began on May 28, 1946, and ran through June 9.

22. *Chicago Tribune*, June 23, 1946; *Chicago Tribune*, June 25, 1946.

23. *Chicago Defender*, July 6, 1946; A. W. Wright, "Memorandum for the Operating Director Re: 5th Police District," September 30, 1946, box 58, folder 4, Virgil Peterson Papers, CHM.

24. Ibid.

25. See the report of a CCC informant inside the CPD from 1946. Virgil Peterson, "Memoranda for the Files Re: Fifth Police District," October 2, 1946, box 58, folder 4, Virgil Peterson Papers, CHM.

26. Memorandum "Re: the $5,000,000 increase in the appropriation for the Police

Department from 1945 to 1946"; List of personnel and patrolmen annually: 1946–1953, as of December 1, 1953; both in box 48, folder 802, Martin H. Kennelly Papers, Special Collections and University Archives, Richard J. Daley Library, University of Illinois at Chicago.

27. "Motor Equipment," ca. 1953, box 48, folder 802, Martin H. Kennelly Papers, Special Collections and University Archives, Richard J. Daley Library, University of Illinois at Chicago.

28. Information on Robert Merriam's early career and campaign against Daley is taken from Cohen and Taylor, *American Pharaoh*, as well as from his obituary in the *Tribune* after his death. See Cohen and Taylor, *American Pharaoh*, 130–32; *Chicago Tribune*, August 26, 1988.

29. Cohen and Taylor, *American Pharaoh*, 130.

30. Virgil Peterson, "Memorandum Re: 5th Police District," October 12, 1946, box 58, folder 4, Virgil Peterson Papers, CHM.

31. Robert Merriam to Dwight S. Strong, December 3, 1954, box 28, folder 4, Robert Merriam Papers, Special Collections Research Center, University of Chicago. On the details of Gross's murder, see *Chicago Tribune*, February 8, 1952; and *Chicago Tribune*, February 22, 1952.

32. Robert Merriam to John Yowell, May 25, 1954, box 28, folder 1, Robert Merriam Papers, Special Collections Research Center, University of Chicago; *Chicago Tribune*, February 7, 1954.

33. Robert Merriam to Henri Wolbrette, July 19, 1954, box 28, folder 2, Robert Merriam Papers, Special Collections Research Center, University of Chicago.

34. John Gutknecht to Martin Kennelly, March 19, 1955, box 18, folder 19, Robert Merriam Papers, Special Collections Research Center, University of Chicago.

35. Special Committee, *Kefauver Committee Report*, 31.

36. Deutsch, "The Plight of the Honest Cop."

37. Ibid.

38. Merriam letter re: better police protection, n.d., box 28, folder 7, Robert Merriam Papers, Special Collections Research Center, University of Chicago.

39. Cohen and Taylor, *American Pharaoh*, 131.

40. Ibid., 113–30. On the Dawson submachine, see Manning, *William L. Dawson*.

41. Cohen and Taylor, *American Pharaoh*, 136; *Chicago Tribune*, March 19, 1955.

42. "Memo—Police Advisory Board," n.d., ca. 1954/5; "Memo—Police," n.d., ca. 1954/5. For campaign speeches by Daley that emphasize the point, see, among others, Richard J. Daley address at the City Club, February 14, 1955; and Richard J. Daley Address to the Independent Voters of Illinois, n.d., ca. 1955. All in box 29, folder 3, Richard J. Daley Papers, Special Collections and University Archives, Richard J. Daley Library, University of Illinois at Chicago.

43. Cohen and Taylor, *American Pharaoh*, 130.

44. Ibid., 134.

45. CPD, *Annual Reports*: 1945, 1965, MRC.

46. Citizens Alert, "Annual Report Card on James M. Rochford, Police Superintendent, Chicago, Illinois, 1975," box 32, folder 545, Citizens Alert Records, Special Collections and University Archives, Richard J. Daley Library, University of Illinois at Chicago.

47. Seligman, *Chicago's Block Clubs*, 195.

48. Seligman, *Block by Block*, 34.

49. "Fact Sheet: Greater Lawndale Conservation Commission," n.d., ca. 1955, box 2, folder 3, GLCC Records, CHM.

50. On these conflicts, see Seligman, *Chicago's Block Clubs*, 170-72.

51. Jerome Braverman to the *Chicago Sun-Times*, December 11, 1956, box 3, folder 4, GLCC Records, CHM.

52. Allen Williams to A. R. Cox, August 3, 1955, box 2 folder 1, GLCC Records, CHM.

53. *Chicago Tribune*, November 11, 1954.

54. *Chicago Tribune*, December 2, 1954.

55. Sidney D. Deutsch, Address to the meeting of the Greater Lawndale Conservation Commission, April 19, 1955, box 1, folder 6, GLCC Records, CHM; Allan C. Williams to A. R. Cox, August 3, 1955, box 2, folder 1, GLCC Records, CHM; *Lawndale Times* (Chicago), December 15, 1955; *Chicago Tribune*, April 28, 1955; and *Chicago Tribune*, May 7, 1955.

56. Progressive Block Club to Police Commissioner O'Connor, October 29, 1958, box 7, folder 7; Resident Petition to Richard J. Daley, Mayor, March 15, 1959, box 9, folder 5; both in GLCC Records, CHM.

57. Jerome Braverman to Joseph Lohman, November 23, 1956, box 3, folder 4, GLCC Records, CHM.

58. "Confidential Report—Civil Rights Department: Case no. 58-70," June 20, 1958, box 7, folder 2; C. J. Peck to Timothy O'Connor, August 13, 1958, box 7, folder 3; both in GLCC Records, CHM.

59. Captain Joseph [Illegible] to Commissioner Timothy O'Connor, File No. 21074," August 19, 1958, box 7, folder 3, GLCC Records, CHM.

60. "Case 58-70," box 10, folder 4, GLCC Records, CHM.

61. Civil Rights Services Department to Frederick D. Pollard, May 26, 1959, box 10, folder 4, GLCC Records, CHM.

62. "Meeting with white residents of south side of street on 4100 block," July 13, 1960, box 14, folder 2, GLCC Records, CHM.

63. A. W. Wright, "Memorandum for the Operating Director Re: 5th Police District," September 30, 1946, box 58, folder 4, Virgil Peterson Papers, CHM.

64. *Chicago Tribune*, June 24, 1946.

65. Forman, *Locking Up Our Own*, 12.

66. Christopher Wimbish, *"Crime Prevention—The Solution—A New Approach*, Broadcast by State Senator Christopher C. Wimbish, Third District, Illinois, Monday, November 13, 1945, Station W.H.F.C., at the Request of the Illinois State Division of Crime Prevention, Lawrence Morrell Gross, Superintendent," box 1, folder 6, Christopher Wimbish Papers, CHM. Emphases are in original.

67. Drake and Cayton, *Black Metropolis*, 799.

68. *Chicago Defender*, July 27, 1946.

69. *Chicago Tribune*, June 24, 1946.

70. A. W. Wright, "Memorandum for the Operating Director Re: 5th Police District," September 30, 1946, box 58, folder 4, Virgil Peterson Papers, CHM.

71. See Courtwright, *Dark Paradise*, chap. 6.

72. Ibid., 150.

73. Illinois Institute for Juvenile Justice and the Chicago Area Project, "Drug Addiction among Young Persons in Chicago," October 1953, box 247, folder 3, Ernest Burgess Papers, Addenda, Special Collections Research Center, University of Chicago.

74. Ibid.; Schneider, *Smack*, 37–40.

75. Schneider, *Smack*, 37.

76. Ibid., 38.

77. See various documents authored by the "Dope Must Go" Committee in box 32, folder 14, Robert Merriam Papers, Special Collections Research Center, University of Chicago.

78. *Chicago Defender*, July 7, 1951.

79. Report of Investigator #1, May 12, 1952, box 18, folder 13, Robert Merriam Papers, Special Collections Research Center, University of Chicago; *Chicago Defender*, July 7, 1951.

80. *Chicago Tribune*, September 30, 1949.

81. Schneider, *Smack*, 42.

82. *Chicago Tribune*, October 3, 1949.

83. *Chicago Tribune*, September 30, 1949.

84. *Chicago Tribune*, December 3, 1950.

85. Special Committee, "Kefauver Committee Final Report."

86. *Chicago Tribune*, November 10, 1950.

87. *Chicago Tribune*, November 18, 1950.

88. *Chicago Defender*, July 7, 1951.

89. Milton Deas Jr., interview by Timuel Black, in Black, *Bridges of Memory*, 419.

90. Lois Higgins, "Make Drug Addiction a Crime." (Elsewhere, Higgins suggested that the rising tide of narcotics in America was part of a Communist plot.) Higgins, "Status of Narcotic Addiction in the United States."

91. Illinois Institute for Juvenile Justice and the Chicago Area Project, "Drug Addiction among Young Persons in Chicago."

92. Illinois Institute for Juvenile Justice and the Chicago Area Project, "Drug Addiction among Young Persons in Chicago," 25–26.

93. Ibid., 28.

94. CPD, *Annual Report*: 1955, MRC.

95. Ibid.

96. Muhammad, "Where Did All the White Criminals Go?"

97. All these statistics are taken directly from CPD Annual Reports.

98. Cohen and Taylor, *American Pharaoh*, 253.

99. *Chicago Tribune*, June 25, 1955.

100. "Housing Problems (Interviews with Family of Mrs. R)," ca. 1969/1970, box 7, folder 4, WSSC.

101. Agee, *Streets of San Francisco*.

102. Kenneth Culp Davis was the most prominent voice here. See K. Davis, *Discretionary Justice*.

103. *Chicago Tribune*, March 23, 1956; *Chicago Tribune*, March 24, 1956; and *Los Angeles Times*, July 2, 1956.

104. *Chicago Defender*, April 26, 1958.

105. *Crusader*, May 12, 1956.

106. *Chicago Defender*, April 26, 1958.

107. *Chicago Defender*, May 20, 1958.

108. As reported in a pamphlet by the national ACLU circa the late 1960s. See American Civil Liberties Union, *Police Power and Citizens' Rights*, ca. 1967, box 571, folder 4, ACLUR.

109. People deep in the Chicago legal system at the time remember this well. In the context of a recently prosecuted case concerning police torture in 1952, retired attorney, Circuit Court Judge, and First District Appellate Court Judge R. Eugene Pincham was asked by People's Law Office attorney John Stainthorp to assess the frequency of both torture and such illegal detention during the early 1950s, when he was working at an attorney's office before opening his own private practice in 1955. Of illegal detention, he wrote, "The Chicago Police Department practice of secreting arrestees from their family, friends, and attorneys, and keeping these arrestees incommunicado, was well established in 1952. . . . The law [calling for quick access to a judge] was consistently ignored by the Chicago Police Department, since it allowed them time to interrogate the prisoner." R. Eugene Pincham to John L. Stainthorp, August 6, 2007. Letter is in author's possession, provided by Flint Taylor of the People's Law Office, Chicago, IL.

110. Mariame Kaba, foreword to Ritchie, *Invisible No More*, xii.

111. Rob Warden, "Oscar Walden, Jr.," Bluhm Legal Clinic Center on Wrongful Convictions, Northwestern University, http://www.law.northwestern.edu/legalclinic/wrongfulconvictions/exonerations/il/oscar-walden-jr.html (accessed March 30, 2018).

112. Flint Taylor, "80-Year-Old Chicago Police Torture Victim About to Obtain His Final Vindication," *Huffington Post*, November 11, 2012, http://www.huffingtonpost.com/g-flint-taylor/oscar-walden-settlement_b_1872852.html.

113. *Chicago Tribune*, August 28, 1960.

114. *Chicago Tribune*, March 29, 1960.

115. Ibid.

116. Martin, "Rights of the Accused."

117. Ibid.

118. Bernard Weisberg to *Chicago Daily News* Editor, March 4, 1959, box 591, folder 12, ACLUR.

119. Lindberg, *To Serve and Collect*, 295–317.

120. *Chicago Defender*, January 17, 1959.

121. Ibid.

Chapter 5

1. Bopp, *O. W.*; Statement from the Office of the Mayor, Richard J. Daley, March 2, 1960, box 37, folder 13, Richard J. Daley Papers, Special Collections and University Archives, Richard J. Daley Library, University of Illinois at Chicago.

2. Bopp, *O. W.*, 149n34.

3. Richard Daley to Orlando Wilson, Western Union telegram, January 23, 1960, box 1 [no folder], Orlando Winfield Wilson Papers, Bancroft Library, University of California.

4. See Richard J. Daley to Orlando W. Wilson, March 2, 1960. While this was the

official appointment, the decision was reached the previous week. See, among others, Dolores L. Sheehan to Orlando Wilson, February 25, 1960; and John Melaniphy to Orlando Wilson, February 26, 1960. All in box 1 [no folder], Orlando Winfield Wilson Papers, Bancroft Library, University of California.

5. *Chicago Defender*, August 6, 1960.

6. *Chicago Defender*, February 29, 1960

7. Pihos, "Policing, Race, and Politics in Chicago," 47.

8. Lindberg, *To Serve and Collect*, 312.

9. CPD, *Annual Report*: 1968, MRC.

10. CPD, *Annual Report*: 1965, MRC.

11. Chicago Commission on Human Relations, "Human Relations News of Chicago," March 1961, box 58, folder 3, St. Clair Drake Papers, Schomburg Center for Research in Black Culture, New York Public Library.

12. *Chicago Tribune*, February 23, 1960; Bopp, *O. W.*

13. O. W. Wilson, Address to the Annual Meeting of the American Society of Criminology, December 29, 1961, carton 1, Orlando Winfield Wilson Papers, Bancroft Library, University of California.

14. O. Wilson, "Police Arrest Privileges," 399.

15. O. Wilson, "Police Authority in a Free Society."

16. Kamisar, "On the Tactics of Police-Prosecution Oriented Critics," 436.

17. CPD Staff Meeting minutes, May 3, 1963, CPD Collection, CHM.

18. CPD, *Annual Report*: 1964, MRC.

19. CPD, "A Review of Foot Patrol Utilization and Distribution in the Chicago Police Department," May 10, 1961, MRC; CPD Staff Meeting minutes, February 21, 1964, CPD Collection, CHM.

20. CPD Staff Meeting minutes, February 21, 1964, CPD Collection, CHM.

21. CPD Staff Meeting minutes, March 5, 1964, CPD Collection, CHM.

22. CPD, "A Review of Foot Patrol Utilization and Distribution in the Chicago Police Department," May 10, 1961, MRC.

23. *Chicago Tribune*, March 21, 1961; *Southeast Economist*, May 18, 1961.

24. CPD Staff Meeting minutes, March 15, 1963, April 19, 1963, CPD Collection, CHM.

25. *Southeast Economist*, May 18, 1961.

26. *Chicago Tribune*, January 13, 1963; *Chicago Tribune*, April 26, 1965; *Chicago Tribune*, June 4, 1965; and *Chicago Tribune*, June 9, 1965.

27. Milton Davis to John McKnight, April 4, 1962, box 565, folder 5, ACLUR.

28. Report of M. Zimbalist Hayes III, February 12, 1966, box 571, folder 6, ACLUR.

29. Uptown Goodfellows, "Fact Sheet on Policeman Sam Joseph, Badge Number 11383," August 11, 1966, box 566, folder 2, ACLUR.

30. Statement of Montgomery H. Williams, ca. March 1962, box 566, folder 13, ACLUR.

31. *Chicago Defender*, December 7, 1967.

32. *Chicago Defender*, May 20, 1967.

33. *Chicago Defender*, August 24, 1968.

34. "The Police, Riots, and the Committee System," box 571, folder 2, ACLUR.

35. *Chicago Sun-Times*, May 17, 1966. This move on Wilson's part was perhaps

the most literal incarnation of legal scholar Kenneth Davis's depiction of police-as-policymakers, and of police exercising "an unlawful assumption of power." See K. Davis, *Discretionary Justice*, 87. CPD Commander Edward Egan is quoted in Ward Wallingford to Jay Miller, January 11, 1967, box 566, folder 2, ACLUR. On stop-and-frisk signed into law, see *Chicago Tribune*, August 22, 1968.

36. Mill, *On Liberty*, 6. Bernard Harcourt offers an important rendering of how the harm principle has been not so much resurrected as completely redefined in the modern age. See Harcourt, "Collapse of the Harm Principle."

37. Christopher Agee provides one classic example of harm principle policing in action in his analysis of sixties-era San Francisco, when liberal citizens and politicians began to see value in getting police officers to beg off arresting people for "untraditional cultural, sexual, and racial perspectives" because doing so was seen as a threat against the city's vibrancy. Moreover, it constituted a misplacing of priorities to police cultural and sexual mores rather than address "the citizenry's common interest in reducing violence." Agee, *Streets of San Francisco*, 14.

38. Minutes of the Chicago Police Department Staff Meeting, November 19, 1964, CPD Collection, CHM.

39. Kelling and Wilson, "Broken Windows."

40. *Chicago Tribune*, January 21, 1961.

41. Orlando Wilson, Address to the Annual Meeting of the American Society of Criminology, December 29, 1961.

42. *Chicago Tribune*, October 21, 1961; *Chicago Tribune*, November 11, 1961.

43. Chicago Police Department, "Report on Chicago Population Trends and Their Effect on Criminal Activity," n.d., ca. 1964, carton 2, Orlando Winfield Wilson Papers, Bancroft Library, University of California.

44. Ibid.

45. CPD, *Annual Reports*: 1965–70, https://home.chicagopolice.org/inside-the-cpd /statistical-reports/annual-reports/.

46. Ibid.

47. Marable, *How Capitalism Underdeveloped Black America*, 124.

48. Hinton, *From the War on Poverty to the War on Crime*, 94.

49. Scott Lassar, "The Administration of Law Enforcement Assistance Administration Grants in Illinois, 1969–1971: A Report of the Chicago Law Enforcement Study Group," ca. 1972, single file, MRC.

50. CPD, *Annual Reports*: 1957, 1967, MRC.

51. CPD, *Annual Report*: 1965, MRC.

52. Ibid.

53. The possibility that aggressive preventive patrol had neutral or even negative impacts on crime rates was a constant point of debate in the 1960s. See Hahn and Jeffries, *Urban America and Its Police*, 20.

54. *Chicago Tribune*, February 23, 1960; Orlando Wilson, Statement to the Illinois State Legislature, ca. May 1960, carton 1, Orlando Winfield Wilson Papers, Bancroft Library, University of California.

55. "Proceedings of the *Chicago American*: Press Conference with Superintendent Wilson," July 19, 1960, carton 2, Orlando Winfield Wilson Papers, Bancroft Library, University of California.

56. Biles, *Richard J. Daley*, 68.

57. *Chicago Tribune*, June 18, 1967.

58. "Address by Orlando W. Wilson, Superintendent of Police of the Chicago Police Department, to a mass meeting of police officers, March 12th, 1960 at the amphitheater—morning session," carton 1, Orlando Winfield Wilson Papers, Bancroft Library, University of California.

59. "Prospectus for the Chicago Metropolitan Area Citizen's Alert," ca. 1966, box 571, folder 3, ACLUR.

60. Virgil Peterson to Lloyd Wendt, August 17, 1961, box 60, folder 2, Virgil Peterson Papers, CHM.

61. Address by Col. Minor K. Wilson at the 11th Annual Conference of Citizens Crime Commissions, November 14, 1961, box 60, folder 6, Virgil Peterson Papers, CHM.

62. *Chicago Sun-Times*, March 17, 1961; *Chicago Tribune*, April 8, 1961.

63. *Chicago Tribune*, April 5, 1961.

64. *Chicago Sun-Times*, March 17, 1961; *Chicago Tribune*, April 8, 1961.

65. *Chicago Tribune*, April 29, 1962.

66. Samuel Walker noted nearly ten years ago that the literature on police unions is startlingly limited, and that hasn't changed much. S. Walker, "Neglect of Police Unions." Megan Adams's dissertation is one useful corrective to this trend.

67. See, for example, Simon Balto, "Why Police Cheered Trump's Dark Speech," *Washington Post*, July 31, 2017; Friedersdorf, "How Police Unions and Arbitrators Keep Abusive Cops on the Street"; Editorial Board, "When Police Unions Impede Justice," *New York Times*, September 3, 2016.

68. James Surowiecki, "Why Are Police Unions Blocking Reform?," *New Yorker*, September 19, 2016.

69. M. Adams, "Patrolmen's Revolt."

70. *Chicago Tribune*, September 13, 1970.

71. M. Adams, "Patrolman's Revolt," 56, 58, 32.

72. *Chicago Tribune*, August 5, 1960.

73. Inserra, *C-1 and the Chicago Mob*, 82.

74. S. Smith, "You Can't Expect Police on the Take to Take Orders."

75. Ibid.

76. Bernard Weisberg to Orlando Wilson, March 8, 1965, box 539, folder 11, ACLUR.

77. Richard A. Crane and Gregory J. Schlesinger, "Citizen Complaints of Police Misconduct and the Internal Affairs Division of the Chicago Police Department: Analysis and Evaluation of the System," May 15, 1971, box 533, folder 8, ACLU Records.

78. Alexander Polikoff to Members of the ACLU Police Brutality Subcommittee, March 17, 1965, box 565, folder 4, ACLUR.

79. Charles Andrew Pfeiffer, "The Police and the Woodlawn Community," box 10, folder 23, WSSC.

80. Chicago Commission on Human Relations, Minutes of Research Advisory Committee meeting, March 29, 1961, box 59, folder 3, St. Clair Drake Papers, Schomburg Center for Research in Black Culture, New York Public Library.

81. Reiss, *Patterns of Behavior in Police and Citizen Transactions*, 136.

82. For example, see *Chicago Defender*, November 5, 1960.

83. John Stuckey, interview by Rafike (formerly Ron Woodard), October 12, 1988, box 2, A/V file 001, CORE Records; *Chicago Defender*, August 13, 1963.

84. Chicago Police Department Press Release, August 14, 1963, box 499, folder 5, ACLUR.

85. M. Adams, "Patrolman's Revolt," 20–21.

86. *Chicago Defender*, November 25, 1961.

87. Lorraine Greenhouse, Recorders Reports: Police and Criminal Law Workshop, ACLU Annual Meeting, May 13, 1961, box 47, folder 3, ACLUR.

88. George Leighton to Alexander Polikoff, November 30, 1963, box 565, folder 4, ACLUR; *Woodlawn Booster*, January 29, 1964.

89. The "red record" referenced here is Ida B. Wells's famous documenting of the realities of lynching in the Jim Crow South. See Wells, *The Red Record*.

90. Howard N. Gilbert to CPD Internal Investigation Division, May 8, 1964, box 567, folder 6, ACLUR.

91. *Chicago Defender*, October 14, 1961.

92. *Chicago Defender*, February 20, 1964.

93. *Chicago Defender*, October 3, 1966.

94. "List of Police Brutality Complaints Made to the Chicago Branch, NAACP During Twelve Month Period Beginning December 1, 1962 and Ending December 1, 1963," box 565, folder 3, ACLUR.

95. *Chicago Daily Defender*, March 25, 1964.

96. Minutes of the Chicago Police Department Staff Meeting, December 10, 1963, CPD Collection, CHM.

97. Orlando Wilson, "pax 501," June 1, 1964, box 565, folder 4, ACLUR.

98. On the Burge cases, see Baer, "Men Who Lived Underground."

99. Minutes of the Chicago Police Department Staff Meeting, December 10, 1963, CPD Collection, CHM.

100. Anonymous to Orlando Wilson, January 14, 1963, box 565, folder 4, ACLUR.

101. *Chicago Daily Defender*, March 24, 1964.

102. W. Wilson, *When Work Disappears*, 29–30.

103. See esp. Satter, *Family Properties*.

104. Blau and Blau, "Cost of Inequality," 126. The Blaus relied on data from 1970.

105. National Advisory Commission on Civil Disorders, *Kerner Report*, 267.

106. CPD, *Annual Reports*: 1966–1970, MRC.

107. *Chicago Defender*, June 13, 1966.

108. *Presbyterian Life*, February 15, 1968.

109. Cooley, "'Stones Run It,'" 912.

110. Diamond, *Mean Streets*, 272.

111. Ibid., 274.

112. Ibid., 275.

113. Ibid., 265.

114. On the history of CUCA's activism and the gangs' place within it, see Gellman, "'Stone Wall Behind.'"

115. Ibid., 114.

116. Ibid., 126.

117. Ibid., 127.

118. *Chicago Tribune*, May 14, 1968; *Chicago Sun-Times*, April 26, 1968.

119. CPD, *Annual Reports*: 1965, 1970, 1974, MRC.

120. *Presbyterian Life*, February 15, 1968.

121. Daniel D. Howard Associates, "A Study Defining the Selection Problem of the Task Force," February 1969, CHM.

122. Satter, "Cops, Gangs, and Revolutionaries," 1119.

123. Ralph, *Northern Protest*, 34.

124. CORE, Minutes of the Executive Committee, March 18, 1964, box 1, folder 5, CORE Records.

125. SNCC Flier, box 135, file 939-A, CPD Red Squad Files, CHM.

126. *Chicago Defender*, April 24, 1965.

127. SNCC Flier, box 137, file 940, CPD, Red Squad Files, CHM.

128. Statement of Claude Lightfoot and James West, July 1, 1965, box 2, folder 9, Richard J. Daley Papers, Special Collections and University Archives, Richard J. Daley Library, University of Illinois at Chicago. The entire folder here is instructive for understanding the diverse reactions to the local movement. The folder contains fan and hate mail directed to Daley, variously accusing him of trying to discredit the movement and of doing right to stand up to it.

129. On the leaking of dossiers to the press, see Donner, *Protectors of Privilege*, 139.

130. Ralph, *Northern Protest*, 88.

131. *Chicago Sun-Times*, January 28, 1966.

132. Ralph, *Northern Protest*, 105–7.

133. Ibid., 108.

134. Ibid., 108–9.

135. Ibid., 109–11.

136. Anderson and Pickering, *Confronting the Color Line*, 219.

137. Ralph, *Northern Protest*, 120–21.

138. Ibid., 124.

139. Ibid., 123.

140. Anderson and Pickering, *Confronting the Color Line*, 270.

141. Chicago Police Department, "Equal Rights for All Citizens," n.d., ca. 1960s, box 59, folder 3, St. Clair Drake Papers, Schomburg Center for Research in Black Culture, New York Public Library.

142. Ralph, *Northern Protest*, 164–65.

143. Statement to the People by Mayor Richard J. Daley, August 19, 1966, box 85, folder 4, Richard J. Daley Papers, Special Collections and University Archives, Richard J. Daley Library, University of Illinois at Chicago.

144. Ralph, *Northern Protest*, 160.

145. Royko, *Boss*, 164.

146. Testimony of Edwin C. Berry before the Citizens' Committee to Study Police-Community Relations, November 23, 1966, single folder, CHM.

147. Ibid.

Chapter 6

1. Farber, *Chicago '68*, 16.

2. Gitlin, *Sixties*, 324.

3. My narrative of the DNC conflicts is drawn from the famous "Walker Report." See D. Walker, *Rights in Conflict*.

4. H. Johnson, "1968 Democratic Convention."

5. Quoted in Pihos, "Policing, Race, and Politics in Chicago," 92.

6. Schultz, *No One Was Killed*, 89.

7. Ransby, *Ella Baker*, 335.

8. McPherson, "Chicago's Blackstone Rangers, Part II."

9. Charles Andrew Pfeiffer, "The Police and the Woodlawn Community," December 1, 1968, box 10, folder 23, WSSC.

10. Quoted in Barbara A. Caulfield, "The Chicago Police Department: Access to Information, Personnel Practices and Internal Control—A Review of Major Reports: A Report of the Chicago Law Enforcement Study Group," 1973, single file, CHM.

11. National Advisory Commission on Civil Disorders, *Kerner Report*, 1.

12. "A Faithful Servant" to Richard Daley, June 21, 1969, series 1, box 84, folder 5, Richard J. Daley Papers, Special Collections and University Archives, Richard J. Daley Library, University of Illinois at Chicago.

13. John C. Bucher to O. W. Wilson, June 30 1972, box 3 [no folder], Orlando Winfield Wilson Papers, Bancroft Library, University of California.

14. Minor Keith Wilson to O. W. Wilson, June 29, 1972, box 3 [no folder], Orlando Winfield Wilson Papers, Bancroft Library, University of California.

15. *Chicago Sun-Times*, May 16, 1967.

16. Ibid.

17. Royko, *Boss*, 164.

18. Minor Keith Wilson to O. W. Wilson, June 29, 1972.

19. Deposition of James Conlisk in *Hampton v. Chicago*.

20. Royko, *Boss*, 6.

21. Perlstein, *Nixonland*, xi.

22. For some overview and analysis of these urban rebellions/riots and their impact on localities and the nation, see, among others, Levy, *Great Uprising*; Mumford, "Harvesting the Crisis"; Mumford, *Newark*; Thompson, "Understanding Rioting"; Elfenbein et al., *Baltimore '68*; Gilje, *Rioting in America*; and Horne, *Fire This Time*.

23. Perlstein, *Nixonland*, 105.

24. Flamm, *Law and Order*, 36.

25. Ibid., 165.

26. Ibid., 167.

27. Ibid., 170.

28. Mantler, *Power to the Poor*, 50–52.

29. Thompson, *Blood in the Water*, 563–65.

30. Kohler-Haumann, *Getting Tough*, chap. 4.

31. Citizens Alert, "The Case for a Comprehensive Psychological Screening Program in the Chicago Police Department," August 2, 1973, box 31, folder 524, Citizens Alert Records, Special Collections and University Archives, Richard J. Daley Library, University of Illinois at Chicago; *Chicago Tribune*, January 8, 1974.

32. *Chicago Tribune*, January 8, 1974.

33. The array of tests given during officers' probationary period is found in Daniel D. Howard Associates, "A Study Defining the Selection Problem of the Task Force for Police Department, City of Chicago," February 1969, single file, CHM.

34. *Chicago Tribune Magazine*, January 7, 1979.

35. Blue Ribbon Panel, *Metcalfe Report*, 20.

36. Ibid., 34.

37. Royko quoted in Kusch, *Battleground Chicago*, 9.

38. Total arrest figures are taken from the CPD's *Annual Reports*.

39. CPD, *Annual Reports*: 1968 and 1975, MRC.

40. On the likelihood of finding arrest-worthy evidence, see Tifft, "Comparative Police Supervision Systems," 353.

41. All arrest data here is pulled from CPD Annual Reports from 1953 (the first year that racial data on arrests themselves became available) through 2010.

42. Tifft, "Comparative Police Supervision Systems."

43. Ibid., 342.

44. Ibid., 316–17.

45. Ibid., 332–33.

46. Ibid., 262–64.

47. Blue Ribbon Panel, *Metcalfe Report*, 31.

48. Ibid.

49. "The Police, Riots, and the Committee System," box 571, folder 2, ACLUR.

50. Edward "Buzz" Palmer, "What Can We Do?," series 4, box 115, folder 1304, CULR.

51. "Housing Problems (Interviews with Family of Mrs. R)," ca. 1969/1970, box 7, folder 4, WSSC.

52. *Chicago Tribune*, April 16, 1972.

53. On the founding of the GIU, see *Chicago Tribune*, March 22, 1967.

54. Diamond, *Mean Streets*, 276.

55. Ibid., 277.

56. McPherson, "Chicago's Blackstone Rangers, Part I."

57. Balto, "MLK's Forgotten Plan."

58. McPherson, "Chicago's Blackstone Rangers, Part II."

59. *Chicago Defender*, October 9, 1971.

60. U.S. Government Special Investigator to Supervisor, August 4, 1966, box 423, folder 2, CPD, Red Squad Files, CHM.

61. Ibid.

62. Moore and Williams, *Almighty Black P Stone Nation*, 63.

63. McPherson, "Chicago's Blackstone Rangers, Part I."

64. A partial copy of this report is available on the scholar John Hagedorn's "Gang Research" webpage. See www.gangresearch.net/ChicagoGangs/blackstonerangers /Daley.html.

65. McPherson, "Chicago's Blackstone Rangers, Part II."

66. Gellman, "Stone Wall Behind," 127.

67. Ibid., 128.

68. Cohen and Gottlieb, "Was Fred Hampton Executed?"

69. Information Report, [Redacted], December 10, 1969, box 408, folder 2, CPD, Red Squad Files, CHM.

70. Blue Ribbon Panel, *Metcalfe Report*, 34.

71. Excerpt from Albert J. Reiss Jr., "Public Perceptions and Recollections about Crime, Law Enforcement, and Criminal Justice," box 570, folder 7, ACLUR.

72. Ralph Knoohuizen, Richard P. Fahey, and Deborah J. Palmer, "The Police and

Their Use of Fatal Force in Chicago: A Report of the Chicago Law Enforcement Study Group," 1972, single file, CHM.

73. *Chicago Defender*, October 7, 1969.

74. *Chicago Sun-Times*, January 7, 1970.

75. *Chicago Defender*, November 10, 1969; *Chicago Defender*, November 11, 1969; *Chicago Sun-Times*, January 11, 1970.

76. Ralph Knoohuizen, Richard P. Fahey, and Deborah J. Palmer, Police and Their Use of Fatal Force in Chicago: A Report of the Chicago Law Enforcement Study Group," 1972, 55–56, single file, CHM.

77. Ibid.

78. *Chicago Tribune*, June 24, 1972; *Chicago Tribune*, July 28, 1973; *Chicago Tribune*, February 2, 1973; and *Chicago Tribune*, February 4, 1973.

79. *Chicago Tribune*, July 10, 1973.

80. *Chicago Tribune*, February 24, 1973.

81. *Chicago Tribune*, June 26, 1973.

82. *Chicago Tribune*, June 19, 1973.

83. O'Neal's uncle was with him the night he committed suicide. He provided an account of what happened, and O'Neal's larger mental health crisis, to the *Chicago Reader*. See Michael Ervin, "The Last Hours of William O'Neal," *Chicago Reader*, January 25, 1990. See also the *Chicago Tribune*'s article on O'Neal's death, from January 18, 1990.

84. *Chicago Tribune*, October 3, 1973.

85. *Chicago Tribune, Police Brutality*, bound pamphlet, ca. November 1973, box 20, folder 337, Citizens Alert Records, Special Collections and University Archives, Richard J. Daley Library, University of Illinois at Chicago.

86. Ibid.

87. *Chicago Tribune Magazine*, January 7, 1979.

88. Fogelson, *Big-City Police*, 238–39.

89. Ibid.

90. National Advisory Commission on Civil Disorders, *Kerner Report*, 91.

91. Ibid., 13.

92. Fogelson, *Big City Police*, 239–40.

93. M. Adams, "Patrolmen's Revolt," 52.

94. Ibid.

95. *Chicago Tribune*, October 27, 1976.

96. Donner, *Protectors of Privilege*, 145.

97. Ibid., 145–50.

98. Scott Allswang and Michael F. Youdovin, "The Law and Police Infiltration and Surveillance of Dissident Groups," October 28, 1968, box 159, file 989, CPD, Red Squad Files, CHM.

99. Carter, *Politics of Rage*, 305.

100. Lesher, *George Wallace*, 405.

101. Flamm, *Law and Order*, 164.

102. M. Adams, "Patrolman's Revolt," 20; *Chicago Tribune*, October 29, 1968.

103. The story of the Klan's operation within the CPD is pieced together from the following: Chicago Police Department, List of Charges against Donald Heath,

January 23, 1968, box 536, folder 1, ACLUR; *Chicago Daily News*, December 29, 1967; *Chicago Defender*, December 29, 1967; *Chicago Sun-Times*, December 29, 1967; *Chicago American*, December 30, 1967; *Chicago Daily News*, December 30, 1967; *Chicago Sun-Times*, December 30, 1967; *Chicago American*, December 31, 1967; and *Chicago Sun-Times*, January 3, 1968.

104. *Chicago American*, January 24, 1968.

105. *Chicago Defender*, March 1, 1968; *Chicago Tribune*, March 1, 1968; and *Chicago Tribune*, March 2, 1968.

106. *Daily Banner* (Greencastle, IN), December 28, 1968. Heath's conspiracies to initiate a race war and to wage violent assaults on state institutions predate by a few years the larger white power movement's efforts to do the same, as outlined by the historian Kathleen Belew in her stunning book *Bring the War Home*. Nevertheless, this is a striking antecedent to those efforts.

107. Unless otherwise noted, descriptions of Chicago in the throes of the King riots are captured from the report of the Chicago Riot Study Committee, convened by Daley later that summer to study what had transpired. As with all committee reports such as this, its conclusions and analysis should be approached with some degree of caution. Nevertheless, its multiracial character and serious commitment to both condemning violent responses and insisting that Chicago needed to understand the wells from which those responses came make it probably the most useful primary source available on these particular events. See "Report of the Chicago Riot Study Committee to the Hon. Richard J. Daley," August 1, 1968, box 116, folder 1314, CULR.

108. "Report of the Chicago Riot Study Committee."

109. Quoted in Pihos, "Policing, Race, and Politics in Chicago," 9.

110. Gary Rivlin, "The Night Chicago Burned," *Chicago Reader*, August 25, 1988.

111. "Report of the Chicago Riot Study Committee," 47.

112. Christopher Chandler, "Shoot to Kill . . . Shoot to Maim, *Chicago Reader*, April 4, 2002; Cohen and Taylor, *American Pharaoh*, 454.

113. "Report of the Chicago Riot Study Committee," 50.

114. Chandler, "Shoot to Kill."

115. Cohen and Taylor, *American Pharaoh*, 455.

116. Peter A. Facione to Richard Daley, April 25, 1968, box 60, folder 8, Richard J. Daley Papers, Special Collections and University Archives, Richard J. Daley Library, University of Illinois at Chicago.

117. Miss Remell Lee to Richard Daley, box 60, folder 8, Richard J. Daley Papers, Special Collections and University Archives, Richard J. Daley Library, University of Illinois at Chicago.

118. Jacques P. Lott to Richard Daley, April 26, 1968, box 60, folder 9, Richard J. Daley Papers, Special Collections and University Archives, Richard J. Daley Library, University of Illinois at Chicago.

119. Mrs. William B. Austin to Richard Daley, April 25, 1968; Mrs. William B. Austin to Charles Percy, n.d., likely April 25, 1968; both in box 61, folder 2, Richard J. Daley Papers, Special Collections and University Archives, Richard J. Daley Library, University of Illinois at Chicago.

120. Steve Gibson to Richard Daley, April 24, 1968, box 60, folder 9, Richard J. Daley

Papers, Special Collections and University Archives, Richard J. Daley Library, University of Illinois at Chicago.

121. Byron C. Brown Sr. to Richard Daley, April 26, 1968, box 60, folder 9, Richard J. Daley Papers, Special Collections and University Archives, Richard J. Daley Library, University of Illinois at Chicago. Brown's emphasis.

122. Mrs. Charles E. King to Richard Daley, April 25, 1968, box 60, folder 9, Richard J. Daley Papers, Special Collections and University Archives, Richard J. Daley Library, University of Illinois at Chicago.

123. On the Milwaukee movement, see Jones, *Selma of the North*.

124. Roy Hawkins to Richard Daley, n.d. ca. April 1968, box 60, folder 9, Richard J. Daley Papers, Special Collections and University Archives, Richard J. Daley Library, University of Illinois at Chicago. Hawkins's emphasis.

125. *Chicago Tribune*, April 16, 1968.

126. Ibid.

127. Ibid.

128. Kusch, *Battleground Chicago*, 28.

129. Ibid., 27–28.

130. Ibid., 25–26.

131. As the editor Lewis Gillenson put it in the version of the Walker Report that was bound and printed for public distribution, the violence in Chicago "doubtlessly made melodramatic and obligatory upon the three candidates to heighten the campaign issue of 'law and order.'" Lewis W. Gillenson, Editorial Comment, preface to D. Walker, *Rights in Conflict*.

132. Quoted in Kusch, *Battleground Chicago*, 155.

133. Ibid.

134. Ibid.

135. Frank Sullivan to Richard Daley, "Report on First Five Police-Community Meetings," May 19, 1972, series 1, box 113, folder 110, Richard J. Daley Papers, Special Collections and University Archives, Richard J. Daley Library, University of Illinois at Chicago.

Chapter 7

1. Commission of Inquiry into the Black Panthers and the Police, *Search and Destroy*, 67; Testimony of Deborah Johnson in draft of Commission of Inquiry Report, ca. 1970, 52, box 3, folder 3, Kenneth Clark Papers, Schomburg Center for Research in Black Culture, New York Public Library.

2. Special Committee of Black Congressman, "Exhibit No. 1: Arrests and Harassments," December 20, 1969, box 26, folder 6, Richard Newhouse Papers, CHM; Bloom and Martin, *Black against Empire*, 236–37.

3. On the relationship between the state's attorney's office and the CPD, see United States District Court, Northern District of Illinois, Eastern Division, *Report of the January 1970 Grand Jury*, 27–28.

4. Pollard et al., PBS Home Video, *Eyes on the Prize*, 1992, "A Nation of Laws?"

5. Details of the raid can be found in Commission of Inquiry into the Black Panthers and the Police, *Search and Destroy*, 4–14.

6. Herbert Leon MacDonell, "Report on the Investigation of the Premises at 2337 West Monroe Street, Chicago, Illinois, and the Examination of Evidence Removed Therefrom," box 3, folder 1, Kenneth Clark Papers, Schomburg Center for Research in Black Culture, New York Public Library.

7. David M. Spain to The Commission of Inquiry, December 29, 1970, box 3 folder 1, Kenneth Clark Papers, Schomburg Center for Research in Black Culture, New York Public Library.

8. Commission of Inquiry into the Black Panthers and the Police, *Search and Destroy*, vii.

9. *Chicago Tribune*, December 6, 1969.

10. Haas, *Assassination of Fred Hampton*, 82.

11. The December 4th Committee, "Fred Hampton: 20th Commemoration" booklet, available online at the People's Law Office website, http://peopleslawoffice.com/wp-content/uploads/2012/02/Hampton.-20th-Anniversary-Booklet-1989.pdf.

12. Deposition of James Conlisk in *Hampton v. Chicago*.

13. Pollard et al., PBS Home Video, *Eyes on the Prize*, 1992, "A Nation of Laws?"

14. Haas, *Assassination of Fred Hampton*, 4.

15. Williams, *From the Bullet to the Ballot*, 92–93.

16. United States District Court, Northern District of Illinois, Eastern Division, *Report of the January 1970 Grand Jury*, 6.

17. Ibid., 12.

18. Bloom and Martin, *Black against Empire*, 292.

19. Anderson and Pickering's analysis of the 1966 movement in Chicago, *Confronting the Color Line*, is the clearest example.

20. The December 4th Committee, "Fred Hampton: 20th Commemoration."

21. On some of these protests, see Williams, *From the Bullet to the Ballot*, 82–85.

22. Intelligence Division Interview Report: Police Brutality Hearing, 28 October 1969; Intelligence Division Interview Report, RE: Memorial Services for the Soto Brothers, November 17, 1969; both in box 159, file 989-B, CPD, Red Squad Files, CHM.

23. The December 4th Committee, "Fred Hampton: 20th Commemoration."

24. Pollard et al., PBS Home Video, *Eyes on the Prize*, 1992, "A Nation of Laws?"

25. Ibid.

26. Haas, *Assassination of Fred Hampton*, 39; The December 4th Committee, "Fred Hampton: 20th Commemoration."

27. The December 4th Committee, "Fred Hampton: 20th Commemoration."

28. Haas, *Assassination of Fred Hampton*, 47–51.

29. Bloom and Martin, *Black against Empire*, 235.

30. *Chicago Tribune*, December 6, 1969.

31. Submitted into evidence with Information Report, [Redacted], December 5, 1969, box 408, folder 2, CPD, Red Squad Files, CHM.

32. *Chicago Tribune*, December 6, 1969.

33. Haas, *Assassination of Fred Hampton*, 90–91.

34. Ibid., 91.

35. *New York Times*, March 5, 2006.

36. Omnibus Crime Control and Safe Streets Act, Public Law 90–351.

37. Forman, *Locking Up Our Own*, 12.

38. Quoted in Pihos, "Policing, Race, and Politics in Chicago," 319.

39. Pihos, "Policing, Race, and Politics in Chicago," 183.

40. Laplois Ashford to James Conlisk, October 1, 1970, series 2, box 218, folder 2157, CULR.

41. Pihos, "Policing, Race, and Politics in Chicago," 183.

42. *Chicago Defender*, March 17, 1973.

43. Action for Survival Meeting Minutes, June 26, 1970, series 2, box 242, folder 2392, CULR.

44. Quoted in Pihos, "Policing, Race, and Politics in Chicago," 131.

45. *Chicago Defender*, November 18, 1970.

46. Ibid.

47. "Recommendations for the Black Crime Commission," ca. June 1970, series 4, box 115, folder 1307, CULR.

48. Ibid.

49. Third Ward Committee on Crime Prevention, "Program for Action," October 1971, series 2, box 218, folder 2155, CULR.

50. *Chicago Defender*, July 10, 1971; *Chicago Defender*, September 11, 1971.

51. *Chicago Defender*, September 4, 1974.

52. *Chicago Defender*, September 7, 1974.

53. Ibid.

54. *Chicago Defender*, April 20, 1974.

55. *Chicago Defender*, June 4, 1975.

56. *Chicago Defender*, November 9, 1974.

57. For the consequences of public housing's vision in Chicago, see, among others, Bowly, *Poorhouse*; Polikoff, *Waiting for Gautreaux*; Whitaker, *Cabrini-Green*; and Petty, *High Rise Stories*.

58. In a two-year-long study of CHA housing, conducted by the Welfare Council of Metropolitan Chicago and released in the summer of 1970, residents repeatedly cited fears for the physical safety of themselves and their families as of utmost concern. *Chicago Tribune*, July 26, 1970.

59. *Chicago Tribune*, August 2, 1970.

60. On women's leadership in the long black freedom struggle, see, among others, R. Williams, *The Politics of Public Housing*; Greene, *Our Separate Ways*; McGuire, *At the Dark End of the Street*; Blain, *Set the World on Fire*; Farmer, *Remaking Black Power*; Cooper, *Beyond Respectability*; Lindsey, *Colored No More*; Gore et al., *Want to Start a Revolution?*; Collier-Thomas and Franklin, *Sisters in the Struggle*; and Taylor, *How We Get Free*.

61. Venkatesh, *American Project*, 30.

62. *Chicago Defender*, July 3, 1974.

63. *Chicago Tribune*, January 16, 1971.

64. *Chicago Defender*, May 4, 1974; *Chicago Defender*, October 10, 1974.

65. *Chicago Defender*, July 3, 1974.

66. Venkatesh, *American Project*, 73.

67. Forman, *Locking Up Our Own*.

68. *Chicago Tribune*, January 4, 1989.

69. Ibid.

70. Popkin et al., *Hidden War*, 34.

71. *Chicago Tribune*, August 16, 1970.

72. Venkatesh, *American Project*, 45.

73. The replacement of War on Poverty funding with War on Crime funding is a key insight of Hinton's *From the War on Poverty to the War on Crime*.

74. Pihos, "Policing, Race, and Politics in Chicago," 8.

75. Ibid.

76. Ibid., 69.

77. Pihos, "Policing, Race, and Politics in Chicago"; Satter, "Cops, Gangs, and Revolutionaries"; Agyepong, "In the Belly of the Beast"; M. Adams, "Patrolmen's Revolt."

78. Renault Robinson to Jay Miller, June 19, 1969, box 3, folder 8, AAPLR.

79. Edward (Buzz) Palmer, "What Can We Do?," ca. 1968, series 4, box 115, folder 1304, CULR.

80. Renault Robinson, "Black Police: A Positive Means of Social Change," ca. 1968, series 4, box 115, folder 1305, CULR.

81. Satter, "Cops, Gangs, and Revolutionaries," 1111.

82. *Chicago Tribune*, July 13, 1968; see also Robinson, "Black Police."

83. Renault Robinson quoted in Pihos, "Policing, Race, and Politics in Chicago," 23.

84. For an example, see Pihos, "Policing, Race, and Politics in Chicago," 7–8.

85. Pihos, "Policing, Race, and Politics in Chicago," 130–31.

86. *Chicago Sun-Times*, June 25, 1969; *Chicago Tribune*, June 25, 1969; Samuel Nolan to Sherri Goodman, box 1, folder 3, AAPLR.

87. Pihos, "Policing, Race, and Politics in Chicago," 306.

88. *Chicago American*, n.d., clipping in series 4, box 115, folder 1306, CULR.

89. Renault Robinson to James Conlisk, July 15, 1969, box 1, folder 3, AAPLR.

90. Robinson, "Black Police."

91. Ibid.

92. Renault Robinson, "Press Release," May 4, 1971, series 1, box 100, folder 11, Richard J. Daley Papers, Special Collections and University Archives, Richard J. Daley Library, University of Illinois at Chicago.

93. Satter, "Cops, Gangs, and Revolutionaries," 1118.

94. Ibid.

95. Quoted in Pihos, "Policing, Race, and Politics in Chicago," 211.

96. Renault Robinson to Jerris Leonard, June 2, 1971, box 3, folder 11, AAPLR.

97. Agyepong, "In the Belly of the Beast," 271.

98. Paul M. Whisenand, Robert E. Hoffman, and Lloyd Sealy, "The Chicago Police Department: An Evaluation of Personnel Practices, Prepared for the Law Enforcement Assistance Administration, United States Department of Justice," box 31, folder 521, Citizens Alert Records, Special Collections and University Archives, Richard J. Daley Library, University of Illinois at Chicago.

99. Pihos, "Policing, Race, and Politics in Chicago," 248–49.

100. Afro-American Patrolmen's League, "Narrative Statement Concerning LEAA's Findings of Racial Discrimination in the Chicago Police Department and the Unsuccessful Attempt to Secure Voluntary Compliance," ca. 1973, box 8, folder 2, AAPLR.

101. *Chicago Sun-Times*, April 22, 1974.

102. Pihos, "Policing, Race, and Politics in Chicago," 224–25.

103. Citizens Alert, "Annual Report Card on James M. Rochford, Police Superintendent, Chicago, Illinois, 1975," box 32, folder 545, Citizens Alert Records, Special Collections and University Archives, Richard J. Daley Library, University of Illinois at Chicago.

104. *Chicago Sun-Times*, April 22, 1974

105. *Chicago Tribune*, December 21, 1974.

106. *Chicago Tribune*, January 4, 1975; *Chicago Tribune*, December 20, 1975.

107. *Chicago Tribune*, March 22, 1977.

108. Satter, "Cops, Gangs, and Revolutionaries," 1111.

109. Jay Miller to Renault Robinson, May 27, 1969, box 3, folder 8, AAPLR.

110. Percy Fleming et al. to Renault Robinson, May 20, 1970, box 3, folder 9, AAPLR.

111. Pihos, "Policing, Race, and Politics in Chicago," 306.

112. Grimshaw, *Bitter Fruit*, 95.

113. Blue Ribbon Panel, *Metcalfe Report*, 82; *Chicago Defender*, March 15, 1972.

114. Blue Ribbon Panel, *Metcalfe Report*, 83–84.

115. Blue Ribbon Panel, *Metcalfe Report*.

116. *Chicago Defender*, July 3, 1972.

117. Blue Ribbon Panel, *Metcalfe Report*, 6.

118. Ibid., 7.

119. *Chicago Tribune*, July 18, 1972; *Chicago Defender*, July 18, 1972.

120. *Chicago Defender*, July 18, 1972.

121. *Chicago Defender*, April 25, 1972.

122. Blue Ribbon Panel, *Metcalfe Report*, 60–77.

123. Pihos, "Policing, Race, and Politics in Chicago," 131; *Chicago Defender*, July 7. 1973.

124. Intelligence Division Interview Report, July 5, 1972, box 159, file 989-B, CPD, Red Squad Files, CHM.

125. Minor Keith Wilson to O. W. Wilson, June 29, 1972, box 3 [no folder], Orlando Winfield Wilson Papers, Bancroft Library, University of California.

126. Chicagoan and longtime progressive operative Don Rose offers a great account of the buildup to this upset in Finley et al., *Chicago Freedom Movement*, 263–73.

127. *New York Times*, November 9, 1972.

128. Grimshaw, *Bitter Fruit*, 137–38.

129. *Chicago Tribune*, January 8, 1975.

130. Pihos, "Policing, Race, and Politics in Chicago," 113.

131. *Chicago Defender*, December 2, 1972.

132. As David Goldberg and Trevor Griffey write, "Seizing control of the political, economic, and social institutions whose everyday operation allowed white people to exercise control over black urban communities, activists believed, would harness the rise in black militancy that followed the outbreak of the urban rebellion in a common struggle to end 'internal colonization' and establish black self-determination and 'community control.'" Goldberg and Griffey, *Black Power at Work*, 9.

133. Fogelson, *Big-City Police*, 296.

134. Renault Robinson to Luke Carroll, July 14, 1969, box 3, folder 8, AAPLR.

135. Afro-American Patrolmen's League of Chicago, "Police Public Relations Programs (a concerted effort), n.d., box 3, folder 8, AAPLR.

136. CCCCP, Conference Program and Conference Schedule, June 1 and 2, 1973, box 89, folder 18, Timuel D. Black Papers, Vivian Harsh Collection, Chicago Public Library, Carter G. Woodson Branch.

137. A photocopy of the handbill appears on typed letter from Mel Lawrence to Orlando Wilson, August 8, 1972, box 3 [no folder], Orlando Winfield Wilson Papers, Bancroft Library, University of California.

138. CCCCP, Conference Program and Schedule.

139. Ibid.

140. *Chicago Defender*, December 2, 1972.

141. CCCCP, pamphlet, *Community Control of Police*, series 4, box 115, folder 1308, CULR.

142. CCCCP, Draft of "An Ordinance to Establish Community Control of Police," box 115, folder 1308, CULR.

143. Ibid.; CCCCP, "Community Control: What It Means," box 89, folder 18, Timuel D. Black Papers, Vivian Harsh Collection, Chicago Public Library, Carter G. Woodson Branch.

144. CCCCP, Conference Program and Schedule.

145. Ibid.

146. CCCCP, Conference Program and Schedule.

147. Ibid.

148. *Chicago Defender*, June 5, 1973.

149. *Chicago Defender*, March 26, 1975.

150. Fogelson, *Big-City Police*, 299.

151. CCCCP, pamphlet, *Community Control of Police*, series 4, box 115, folder 1308, CULR.

152. Fogelson, *Big-City Police*, 296.

Epilogue

1. On policing during the Washington years, see Pihos, "Policing, Race, and Politics in Chicago"; and Losier, "Public Does Not Believe the Police Can Police Themselves."

2. CPD, *Annual Report*: 2010, MRC.

3. Don Babwin, "ACLU: Chicago Police Had Higher Stop-and-Frisk Rate than NYC," March 23, 2015, https://apnews.com/714e4a12d04e49d3b19bac97b804cfba/aclu-chicago-police-had-higher-stop-and-frisk-rate-nyc.

4. *Chicago Tribune*, March 24, 2017.

5. Press Release re: "The Lucas Case" and "The Watts Case," n.d., box 74, folder 1279, Citizens Alert Records, Special Collections and University Archives, Richard J. Daley Library, University of Illinois at Chicago; *Chicago Daily News*, October 28, 1975; *Chicago Defender*, July 13, 1976; *Chicago Daily News*, October 21, 1977.

6. The descriptions of Burge and the tortures by his men are taken from John Conroy, "Tools of Torture," *Chicago Reader*, February 3, 2005. Also see Baer, "Men Who Lived Underground."

7. Spencer Ackerman, "The Disappeared: Chicago Police Detain Americans at Abuse-Laden 'Black Site,'" *Guardian*, February 24, 2015, https://www.theguardian.com/us-news/2015/feb/24/chicago-police-detain-americans-black-site.

8. Austin Berg, "Chicago Police Unions Are Fighting to Destroy Decades of Complaint Records," *Illinois Policy*, December 14, 2015, https://www.illinoispolicy.org/chicago-police-unions-are-fighting-to-destroy-decades-of-complaint-records/.

9. *Chicago Tribune*, June 2, 2017, http://www.chicagotribune.com/news/local/breaking/ct-chicago-police-independent-monitor-met-20170602-story.html.

10. Testimony of Edwin C. Berry before the Citizens' Committee to Study Police-Community Relations, November 23, 1966, single folder, CHM. Emphasis mine.

11. Kaba and Edwards, "Policing Chicago Public Schools," 3.

12. *Chicago Sun-Times*, December 28, 2011; City of Chicago, *2018 Budget Overview*, 108, https://www.cityofchicago.org/content/dam/city/depts/obm/supp_info/2018Budget/2018_Budget_Overview.pdf.

13. Citizens Police Data Project, https://cpdb.co/data/D3JoG1/citizens-police-data-project (accessed March 30, 2018).

14. Kaba blogs at http://www.usprisonculture.com/blog/. Her work there is an essential resource for readers interested in reconsidering and/or abolishing the criminal justice system as it currently functions.

15. Hartman, *Lose Your Mother*, 18.

BIBLIOGRAPHY

Manuscript Collections

Berkeley, California
    Bancroft Library, University of California
        Orlando Winfield Wilson Papers
Chicago, Illinois
    Chicago History Museum
        Afro-American Patrolmen's League Records
        Alliance to End Repression Records
        Claude Barnett Papers
        Joseph Bibb Papers
        Chicago Commission on Human Relations Files
        Chicago Committee to Defend the Bill of Rights Records
        Chicago Crime Commission Collection
        Chicago Law Enforcement Study Group Records
        Chicago Police Department Collection
        Chicago Police Department Red Squad Files
        Harold Gosnell Papers
        Greater Lawndale Conservation Commission Records
        Richard Newhouse Papers
        Virgil Peterson Papers
        Joseph Sevick Papers
        Christopher Wimbish Papers
        The Woodlawn Organization Records
    Chicago Public Library, Harold Washington Branch
        Municipal Reference Collection
            Chicago Law Enforcement Study Group Reports
            Chicago Police Department Collection
            Illinois Law Enforcement Commission Records
    Chicago Public Library, Carter G. Woodson Branch
        Vivian Harsh Collection
            Timuel D. Black Papers
            Horace R. Cayton Papers
            Chicago SNCC History Project Records
            Congress on Racial Equality Records (Chicago Branch)
            Illinois Writers Project Records
            Ishmael Flory Papers
            Alice and Edward Palmer Papers

        Howard Saffold Papers
        Reverend Al Sampson Papers
        Reverend Addie and Claude Wyatt Papers
     National Archives at Chicago
        Case files for *Iberia Hampton, et al. v. City of Chicago, et al.*
     Newberry Library
        Victor Lawson Papers
     People's Law Office (provided to author by Attorney Flint Taylor)
        Court Transcripts and Legal Briefs Surrounding the Case of Oscar Walden
     University of Chicago
        Special Collections Research Center
           American Civil Liberties Union, Illinois Division Records
           Chicago Citizens' Police Committee Records
           Ernest Burgess Papers (and Addenda)
           Robert Merriam Papers
           Julius Rosenwald Papers
           Woodlawn Social Services Center Records
     University of Illinois at Chicago
        Special Collections and University Archives, Richard J. Daley Library
           Chicago Urban League Records
           Citizens Alert Records
           Martin H. Kennelly Papers
           Richard J. Daley Papers
New York, New York
  New York Public Library
     Schomburg Center for Research in Black Culture
        Kenneth Clark Papers
        St. Clair Drake Papers
Washington, DC
  Library of Congress, Manuscript Division
     Records of the National Association for the Advancement of Colored People

Periodicals

Atlantic
Broad Ax
Chicago American
Chicago Daily News
Chicago Defender
Chicago Reader
Chicago Sun-Times
Chicago Tribune
Chicago Tribune Magazine
Crisis
Crusader
Daily Banner (Greencastle, IN)

Ebony
Freedom's Call
Lawndale Times
Life
Los Angeles Times
Nation
New York Times
New Yorker
Oakland-Kenwood Outlook
Presbyterian Life
Saturday Evening Post
Smithsonian
Southeast Economist
Washington Post
Woodlawn Booster

Interview

Timuel D. Black. Interview by the author, Chicago, IL, August 21, 2013.

Video Recording

Samuel D. Pollard, Sheila Curren Bernard, James A. DeVinney, and Madison Davis Lacey, *Eyes on the Prize*, PBS Home Video, 1987–1990.

Selected Books, Articles, Dissertations, and Reports

Abu-Lughod, Janet L. *Race, Space, and Riots in Chicago, New York, and Los Angeles.* Oxford: Oxford University Press, 2007.

Adams, James Truslow. *The Epic of America.* 1931. Reprint, New Brunswick, NJ: Transaction, 2012.

Adams, Megan Marie. "The Patrolmen's Revolt: Chicago Police and the Labor and Urban Crises of the Late Twentieth Century." PhD diss., University of California, Berkeley, 2012.

Adler, Jeffrey S. *First in Violence, Deepest in Dirt: Homicide in Chicago, 1875–1920.* Cambridge, MA: Harvard University Press, 2006.

———. "Less Crime, More Punishment: Violence, Race, and Criminal Justice in Early Twentieth-Century America." *Journal of American History* 102, no. 3 (December 2015): 34–46.

Agee, Christopher Lowen. "Crisis and Redemption: The History of American Police Reform since World War II." *Journal of Urban History.* Online First, 2017.

———. *The Streets of San Francisco: Policing and the Creation of a Cosmopolitan Liberal Politics, 1950–1972.* Chicago: University of Chicago Press, 2014.

Agyepong, Tera. *The Criminalization of Black Children: Race, Gender, and Delinquency in Chicago's Juvenile Justice System, 1899–1945.* Chapel Hill: University of North Carolina Press, 2018.

———. "In the Belly of the Beast: Black Policemen Combat Police Brutality in Chicago, 1968–1983." *Journal of African American History* 98, no. 2 (Spring 2013): 253–76.

Alexander, Michelle. *The New Jim Crow: Mass Incarceration in an Age of Colorblindness.* New York: New Press, 2010.

Algren, Nelson. *Chicago: City on the Make.* 1951. 60th Anniversary ed. Chicago: University of Chicago Press, 2011.

Allen, James, ed. *Without Sanctuary: Lynching Photography in America.* Santa Fe, NM: Twin Palms, 2000.

Anderson, Alan, and George W. Pickering. *Confronting the Color Line: The Broken Promise of the Civil Rights Movement in Chicago.* Athens: University of Georgia Press, 1986.

Anderson, Carol. *Eyes Off the Prize: The United Nations and the African American Struggle for Human Rights, 1944–1955.* Cambridge: Cambridge University Press, 2003.

Avrich, Paul. *The Haymarket Tragedy.* Princeton, NJ: Princeton University Press, 1986.

Bachin, Robin F. *Building the South Side: Urban Space and Civil Culture in Chicago, 1890–1919.* Chicago: University of Chicago Press, 2004.

Baer, Andrew S. "The Men Who Lived Underground: The Chicago Police Torture Cases and the Problem of Quantifying Victims of Police Violence, 1970–2016." *Journal of Urban History* 44, no. 2 (March 2018): 262–77.

Baldwin, Davarian. *Chicago's New Negroes: Modernity, the Great Migration, and Black Urban Life.* Chapel Hill: University of North Carolina Press, 2007.

Baldwin, James. "A Report from Occupied Territory." *Nation,* July 11, 1966.

Balko, Radley. *Rise of the Warrior Cop: The Militarization of America's Police Forces.* New York: Public Affairs, 2013.

Balto, Simon. "MLK's Forgotten Plan to End Gun Violence." *History News Network,* July 8, 2013. https://historynewsnetwork.org/article/152489.

———. "'Occupied Territory': Police Repression and Black Resistance in Postwar Milwaukee." *Journal of African American History* 98, no. 2 (Spring 2013): 229–52.

Baptist, Edward E. *The Half Has Never Been Told: Slavery and the Making of American Capitalism.* New York: Basic Books, 2014.

Bates, Beth Tompkins. *Pullman Porters and the Rise of Protest Politics in Black America, 1925–1945.* Chapel Hill: University of North Carolina Press, 2001.

Beeley, A. L. *The Bail System in Chicago.* Chicago: University of Chicago Press, 1927.

Belew, Kathleen. *Bring the War Home: The White Power Movement and Paramilitary America.* Cambridge, MA: Harvard University Press, 2018.

Berger, Dan. *Captive Nation: Black Prison Organizing in the Civil Rights Era.* Chapel Hill: University of North Carolina Press, 2014.

Berlin, Ira. *The Making of African America: The Four Great Migrations.* New York: Penguin, 2010.

Bernstein, Irving. *The Lean Years: A History of the American Worker, 1920–1933.* 1969. Reprint, Chicago: Haymarket Books, 2010.

———. *The Turbulent Years: A History of the American Worker, 1933–1940.* 1969. Reprint, Chicago: Haymarket Books, 2010.

Bernstein, Nell. *All Alone in the World: Children of the Incarcerated.* New York: New Press, 2005.

⸺. *Burning Down the House: The End of Juvenile Prison.* New York: Perseus, 2014.

Biles, Roger. *Big City Boss in Depression and War: Mayor Edward J. Kelly in Chicago.* DeKalb: Northern Illinois University Press, 1984.

⸺. *Richard J. Daley: Politics, Race, and the Governing of Chicago.* DeKalb: Northern Illinois University Press, 1995.

Black, Timuel D. *Bridges of Memory: Chicago's First Wave of Black Migration.* Evanston, IL: Northwestern University Press, 2005.

Blackmon, Douglas. *Slavery by Another Name: The Re-Enslavement of Black People in America, from the Civil War to World War II.* New York: Doubleday, 2008.

Blair, Cynthia M. *I've Got to Make My Livin': Black Women's Sex Work in Turn-of-the-Century Chicago.* Chicago: University of Chicago Press, 2010.

Blain, Keisha N. *Set the World on Fire: Black Nationalist Women and the Global Struggle for Freedom.* Philadelphia: University of Pennsylvania Press, 2018.

Blau, Judith R., and Peter M. Blau. "The Cost of Inequality: Metropolitan Structure and Violent Crime." *American Sociological Review* 47, no. 1 (February 1982): 114–29.

Bloom, Joshua, and Waldo E. Martin Jr. *Black against Empire: The History and Politics of the Black Panther Party.* Berkeley: University of California Press, 2013.

Blue, Ethan. *Doing Time in the Depression: Everyday Life in Texas and California Prisons.* New York: New York University Press, 2012.

Blue Ribbon Panel convened by the Honorable Ralph H. Metcalfe. *The Metcalfe Report on the Misuse of Police Authority in Chicago.* Chicago, 1972.

Boggs, James, and Grace Lee Boggs. "The City Is the Black Man's Land." *Monthly Review* 17, no. 11 (April 1966).

Bone, Robert, and Richard A. Courage. *The Muse in Bronzeville: African American Creative Expression in Chicago, 1932–1950.* New Brunswick, NJ: Rutgers University Press, 2011.

Bonilla-Silva, Eduardo. "What We Were, What We Are, and What We Should Be: The Racial Problem of American Sociology." *Social Problems* 64, no. 2 (May 2017): 179–87.

Bopp, William J. *O. W.: O. W. Wilson and the Search for a Police Profession.* Port Washington, NY: Kennikat Press, 1977.

Bougere, Joseph. "The Exodus Train" (1942). In *The Negro in Illinois: The WPA Papers*, edited by Brian Doliner, 248–49. Urbana: University of Illinois Press, 2013.

Bowly, Devereux. *The Poorhouse: Subsidized Housing in Chicago.* 1978. 2nd ed. Carbondale: Southern Illinois University Press, 2012.

Branham, Charles Russel. "The Transformation of Black Political Leadership in Chicago, 1864–1942." PhD diss., University of Chicago, 1981.

Brundage, Edward J. *Illinois Attorney General's Report for the Biennium 1919–1920.* Springfield: Illinois State Journal, 1921.

Bukowski, Douglas. *Big Bill Thompson, Chicago, and the Politics of Image.* Urbana: University of Illinois Press, 1997.

Buntin, John. *L. A. Noir: The Struggle for the Soul of America's Most Seductive City.* New York: Broadway Books, 2010.

Burnham, John C. *Bad Habits: Drinking, Smoking, Taking Drugs, Gambling, Sexual Misbehavior, and Swearing in American History.* New York: New York University Press, 1994.

Cahill, James C., ed. *Revised Statutes of the State of Illinois: Embracing All General Laws of the State of Illinois in Force January 1, 1922.* Chicago: Callaghan, 1922.

Camp, Jordan T. *Incarcerating the Crisis: Freedom Struggles and the Rise of the Neoliberal State.* Berkeley: University of California Press, 2016.

Camp, Jordan T., and Christina Heatherton. *Policing the Planet: Why the Policing Crisis Led to Black Lives Matter.* New York: Verso, 2016.

Carter, Dan T. *The Politics of Rage: George Wallace, the Origins of the New Conservatism, and the Transformation of American Politics.* New York: Simon & Schuster, 1995.

Cayton, Horace R. *Long Old Road: Back to Black Metropolis.* 1963. Reprint, Piscataway, NJ: Transaction, 2010.

Chafee, Zechariah, Jr., Walter H. Pollak, and Carl S. Stern. *The Third Degree: Report to the National Commission on Law Observance and Enforcement.* 1931. Reprint, New York: Arno Press, 1969.

Chase, Robert T. "Civil Rights on the Cell Block: Race, Reform, and Violence in Texas Prisons and the Nation, 1945–1990." PhD diss., University of Maryland, 2009.

Chatelain, Marcia. *South Side Girls: Growing Up in the Great Migration.* Durham, NC: Duke University Press, 2015.

Chicago Commission on Race Relations. *The Negro in Chicago: A Study of Race Relations and a Race Riot.* Chicago: University of Chicago Press, 1922.

Chronopoulos, Themis. "Police Misconduct, Community Opposition, and Urban Governance in New York City, 1945–1965." *Journal of Urban History.* Online First, 2015.

Cisneros, Sandra. *A House of My Own: Stories from My Life.* New York: Knopf, 2015.
———. *The House on Mango Street.* 1984. Reprint, New York: Vintage, 2009.

Citizens' Police Committee. *Chicago Police Problems.* Chicago: University of Chicago Press, 1931.

Clear, Todd. *Imprisoning Communities: How Mass Incarceration Makes Disadvantaged Neighborhoods Worse.* Oxford: Oxford University Press, 2009.

Coates, Ta-Nehisi. *Between the World and Me.* New York: Spiegel & Grau, 2015.
———. "The Case for Reparations." *Atlantic*, June 2014.

Cobb, Charles. *This Nonviolent Stuff'll Get You Killed: How Guns Made the Civil Rights Movement Possible.* New York: Basic Books, 2014.

Cohen, Adam, and Elizabeth Taylor. *American Pharaoh: Mayor Richard J. Daley; His Battle for Chicago and the Nation.* Boston, MA: Little, Brown, 2000.

Cohen, Jeff, and Jeff Gottlieb. "Was Fred Hampton Executed?" *Nation*, December 25, 1976.

Cohen, Lizabeth. *Making a New Deal: Industrial Workers in Chicago, 1919–1939.* 1990. Reprint, Cambridge: Cambridge University Press, 2008.

Collier-Thomas, Bettye, and V. P. Franklin, eds., *Sisters in the Struggle: African-*

American Women in the Civil Rights–Black Power Movement. New York: New York University Press, 2001.

Commission of Inquiry into the Black Panthers and the Police. *Search and Destroy: A Report by the Commission of Inquiry into the Black Panthers and the Police*. New York: Metropolitan Applied Research Center, 1973.

Connolly, James J. *An Elusive Unity: Urban Democracy and Machine Politics in Industrializing America*. Ithaca, NY: Cornell University Press, 2010.

Connolly, N. D. B. *A World More Concrete: Real Estate and the Remaking of Jim Crow South Florida*. Chicago: University of Chicago Press, 2014.

Cooley, Will. "'Stones Run It': Taking Back Control of Organized Crime in Chicago, 1940–1975." *Journal of Urban History* 37, no. 6 (2011): 911–32.

Cooper, Brittney C. *Beyond Respectability: The Intellectual Thought of Race Women*. Urbana: University of Illinois Press, 2017.

Courtwright, David T. *Dark Paradise: A History of Opiate Addiction in America*. 1982. 2nd ed. Cambridge, MA: Harvard University Press, 2001.

Cronon, William. *Nature's Metropolis: Chicago and the Great West*. New York: W. W. Norton, 1992.

Curtin, Mary Ellen. *Black Prisoners and Their World: Alabama, 1865–1900*. Charlottesville: University of Virginia Press, 2000.

Dale, Elizabeth. *Robert Nixon and Police Torture in Chicago, 1871–1971*. DeKalb: Northern Illinois University Press, 2016.

Davis Angela. "Political Prisoners, Prisons, and Black Liberation." In *If They Come in the Morning: Voices of Resistance*, ed. Angela Davis, 19–38. New York: Third Press, 1971.

Davis, Kenneth Culp. *Discretionary Justice: A Preliminary Inquiry*. Baton Rouge: Louisiana State University Press, 1969.

Deutsch, Albert. "The Plight of the Honest Cop." *Collier's*, September 18, 1953.

Dennis, Michael. *The Memorial Day Massacre and the Movement for Industrial Democracy*. New York: Palgrave Macmillan, 2010.

Diamond, Andrew. *Chicago on the Make: Power and Inequality in a Modern City*. Berkeley: University of California Press, 2017.

———. *Mean Streets: Chicago Youths and the Everyday Struggle for Empowerment in the Multiracial City, 1908–1969*. Berkeley: University of California Press, 2009.

Donner, Frank. *Protectors of Privilege: Red Squads and Police Repression in Urban America*. Berkeley: University of California Press, 1990.

Drake, St. Clair, and Horace R. Cayton. *Black Metropolis: A Study of Negro Life in a Northern City*. 1945. Reprint, Chicago: University of Chicago Press, 1993.

Du Bois, W. E. B. "Hopkinsville, Chicago, and Idlewild." *Crisis*, August 1921, 158–60.

Dudziak, Mary L. *Cold War Civil Rights: Race and the Image of American Democracy*. Princeton, NJ: Princeton University Press, 2000.

Dulaney, W. Marvin. *Black Police in America*. Bloomington: Indiana University Press, 1996.

Duneier, Mitchell. *Ghetto: The Invention of a Place, the History of an Idea*. New York: Farrar, Straus and Giroux, 2016.

Elfenbein, Jessica, Elizabeth Nix, and Thomas Hollowak, eds. *Baltimore '68: Riots and Rebirth in an American City*. Philadelphia: Temple University Press, 2011.

Farmer, Ashley D. *Remaking Black Power: How Black Women Transformed an Era.* Chapel Hill: University of North Carolina Press, 2018.

Farber, David. *Chicago '68.* Chicago: University of Chicago Press, 1988.

Feimster, Crystal N. *Southern Horrors: Women and the Politics of Rape and Lynching.* Cambridge, MA: Harvard University Press, 2011.

Felker-Kantor, Max. "Liberal Law and Order: The Politics of Police Reform in Los Angeles. *Journal of Urban History.* April 28, 2017. http://journals.sagepub.com /eprint/9SwXk4TBxKVYCbR3hUkA/full.

———. *Policing Los Angeles: Race, Resistance, and the Rise of the LAPD.* Chapel Hill: University of North Carolina Press, 2018.

Fernández, Lilia. *Brown in the Windy City: Mexicans and Puerto Ricans in Postwar Chicago.* Chicago: University of Chicago Press, 2012.

Finley, Mary Lou, Bernard Lafayette Jr., James R. Ralph Jr., and Pam Smith, eds. *The Chicago Freedom Movement: Martin Luther King Jr. and Civil Rights Activism in the North.* Lexington: University of Kentucky Press, 2016.

Fischer, Anne Gray. "Arrestable Behavior: Women, Police Power, and the Making of Law-and-Order America, 1930s–1980s." PhD diss., Brown University, 2018.

Fisher, Colin. *Urban Green: Nature, Recreation, and the Working Class in Industrial Chicago.* Chapel Hill: University of North Carolina Press, 2015.

Flamm, Michael W. *Law and Order: Street Crime, Civil Unrest, and the Crisis of Liberalism in the 1960s.* New York: Columbia University Press, 2007.

Fogelson, Robert. *Big-City Police.* Cambridge, MA: Harvard University Press, 1977.

Forman, James, Jr., *Locking Up Our Own: Crime and Punishment in Black America.* New York: Farrar, Straus and Giroux, 2017.

———. "Racial Critiques of Mass Incarceration: Beyond the New Jim Crow." *New York University Law Review* 87 (April 2012): 101–46.

Fortner, Michael Javen. *Black Silent Majority: The Rockefeller Drug Laws and the Politics of Punishment.* Cambridge, MA: Harvard University Press, 2015.

Foucault, Michel. *Discipline and Punish: The Birth of the Prison.* Translated by Alan Sheridan. New York: Vintage, 1995.

Frampton, Mary Louise, Ian Haney López, and Jonathan Simon, eds. *After the War on Crime: Race, Democracy, and a New Reconstruction.* New York: New York University Press, 2008.

Frazier, E. Franklin. *The Negro Family in Chicago.* Chicago: University of Chicago Press, 1932.

Friedersdorf, Conor. "How Police Unions and Arbitrators Keep Abusive Cops on the Street." *Atlantic,* December 2, 2014.

Garb, Margaret. *Freedom's Ballot: African American Political Struggles in Chicago from Abolition to the Great Migration.* Chicago: University of Chicago Press, 2014.

Garland, David. *The Culture of Control: Crime and Social Order in Contemporary Society.* Chicago: University of Chicago Press, 2002.

Gellman, Erik S. "'Armed Arbiters and Scrupulous Pioneers': The Chicago NAACP's Quest for Status, Welfare, and Dignity, 1933–1957." Paper presented at the NAACP: A Centenary Appraisal Conference, University of Sussex, UK, September 24–25, 2009.

———. "'Carthage Must Be Destroyed': Race, City Politics, and the Campaign to Integrate Chicago Transportation Work, 1929–1943." *Labor: Studies in Working-Class History of the Americas* 2, no. 2 (2005): 81–114.

———. *Death Blow to Jim Crow: The National Negro Congress and the Rise of Militant Civil Rights*. Chapel Hill: University of North Carolina Press, 2012.

———. "'The Stone Wall Behind.'" In Goldberg and Griffey, *Black Power at Work*, 112–33.

Gilje, Paul A. *Rioting in America*. Bloomington: Indiana University Press, 1996.

Gillenson, Lewis W. Editorial Comment, preface to Daniel Walker, *Rights in Conflict*.

Gilmore, Glenda Elizabeth. *Defying Dixie: The Radical Roots of Civil Rights, 1919–1950*. New York: W. W. Norton, 2008.

Gilmore, Ruth Wilson. *Golden Gulag: Prisons, Surplus, Crisis, and Opposition in Globalizing California*. Berkeley: University of California Press, 2007.

Gitlin, Todd. *The Sixties: Years of Hope, Days of Rage*. New York: Bantam Books, 1993.

Goffman, Alice. *On the Run: Fugitive Life in an American City*. Chicago: University of Chicago Press, 2014.

Goldberg, David A., and Trevor Griffey, eds. *Black Power at Work: Community Control, Affirmative Action, and the Construction Industry*. Ithaca, NY: Cornell University Press, 2010.

Gonda, Jeffrey. *Unjust Deeds: The Restrictive Covenant Cases and the Making of the Civil Rights Movement*. Chapel Hill: University of North Carolina Press, 2015.

Gordon, Linda. *The Second Coming of the KKK: The Ku Klux Klan of the 1920s and the American Political Tradition*. New York: Liveright, 2017.

Gore, David F., Jeanne Theoharis, and Komozi Woodard, eds., *Want to Start a Revolution? Radical Women in the Black Freedom Struggle*. New York: New York University Press, 2009.

Gosnell, Harold F. *Negro Politicians: The Rise of Negro Politics in Chicago*. Chicago: University of Chicago Press, 1935.

Gottfried, Alex. *Boss Cermak of Chicago: A Study of Political Leadership*. Seattle: University of Washington Press, 1962.

Gottschalk, Marie. *Caught: The Prison State and the Lockdown of American Politics*. Princeton, NJ: Princeton University Press, 2015.

———. *The Prison and the Gallows*. Cambridge: Cambridge University Press, 2006.

Graham, Stephen. *Cities under Siege: The New Military Urbanism*. New York: Verso, 2010.

Green, Adam. *Selling the Race: Culture, Community, and Black Chicago, 1940–1955*. Chicago: University of Chicago Press, 2009.

Green, James. *Death in the Haymarket: A Story of Chicago, the First Labor Movement, and the Bombing That Divided Gilded Age America*. New York: Anchor Books, 2006.

Greene, Christina. *Our Separate Ways: Women and the Black Freedom Movement in Durham, North Carolina*. Chapel Hill: University of North Carolina Press, 2005.

———. "'She Ain't No Rosa Parks': The Joan Little Rape-Murder Case and Jim Crow Justice in the Post–Civil Rights South." *Journal of African American History* 100, no. 3 (Summer 2015): 428–47.

Gregory, James N. *The Southern Diaspora: How the Great Migrations of Black and White Southerners Transformed America*. Chapel Hill: University of North Carolina Press, 2005.

Grimshaw, William. *Bitter Fruit: Black Politics and the Chicago Machine*. Chicago: University of Chicago Press, 1992.

Gross, Kali Nicole. "African American Women, Mass Incarceration, and the Politics of Protection." *Journal of American History* 102, no. 1 (June 2015): 25–33.

———. *Colored Amazons: Crime, Violence, and Black Women in the City of Brotherly Love, 1880–1910*. Durham, NC: Duke University Press, 2006.

———. *Hannah Mary Tabbs and the Disembodied Torso: A Tale of Race, Sex, and Violence in America*. Oxford: Oxford University Press, 2016.

Grossman, James R. *Land of Hope: Chicago, Black Southerners, and the Great Migration*. Chicago: University of Chicago Press, 1989.

Guglielmo, Thomas A. *White on Arrival: Italians, Race, Color, and Power in Chicago, 1890–1945*. Oxford: Oxford University Press, 2004.

Haas, Jeffrey. *The Assassination of Fred Hampton: How the FBI and the Chicago Police Murdered a Black Panther*. Chicago: Lawrence Hill Books, 2010.

Hahn, Harlan, and Judson L. Jeffries. *Urban American and Its Police: From the Postcolonial Era through the Turbulent 1960s*. Boulder: University Press of Colorado, 2003.

Haley, Sarah. *No Mercy Here: Gender, Punishment, and the Making of Jim Crow Modernity*. Chapel Hill: University of North Carolina Press, 2016.

Haller, Mark H. "Organized Crime in Urban Society: Chicago in the Twentieth Century." *Journal of Social History* 5, no. 2 (Winter 1971–72): 210–34.

———. "Policy Gambling, Entertainment, and the Emergence of Black Politics: Chicago from 1900 to 1940." *Journal of Social History* 24, no. 3 (Summer 1991): 719–39.

Halpern, Rick. *Down on the Killing Floor: Black and White Workers in Chicago's Packinghouses, 1904–1954*. Urbana: University of Illinois Press, 1997.

Harcourt, Bernard E. "The Collapse of the Harm Principle." *Journal of Criminal Law and Criminology* 90, no. 1 (Fall 1999): 109–94.

Hartman, Saidiya. *Lose Your Mother: A Journey along the Atlantic Slave Route*. New York: Farrar, Straus and Giroux, 2007.

Harvey, David. *Rebel Cities: From the Right to the City to the Urban Revolution*. New York: Verso, 2013.

———. "The Right to the City." *New Left Review* 53 (September–October 2008): 23–40.

Haywood, Harry. *A Black Communist in the Freedom Struggle*. 1978. Reprint, Minneapolis: University of Minnesota Press, 2012.

Helgeson, Jeffrey. *Crucibles of Black Empowerment: Chicago's Neighborhood Politics from the New Deal to Harold Washington*. Chicago: University of Chicago Press, 2014.

Herbst, Alma. *The Negro in the Slaughtering and Meat-Packing Industry in Chicago*. Boston, MA: Houghton Mifflin, 1932.

Hernández, Kelly Lytle. *City of Inmates: Conquest, Rebellion, and the Rise of Human Caging in Los Angeles, 1771–1965*. Chapel Hill: University of North Carolina Press, 2017.

Hicks, Cheryl. *Talk with You Like a Woman: African American Women, Justice, and Reform in New York, 1890–1935.* Chapel Hill: University of North Carolina Press, 2010.

Higgins, Lois. "Make Drug Addiction a Crime." *Dopeology: A Publication of the Crime Prevention Bureau* (1953): 100–104.

———. "Status of Narcotic Addiction in the United States." *American Biology Teacher* 16, no. 4 (April 1954): 94–98.

Hindelang, Michael J. "Public Opinion Regarding Crime, Criminal Justice, and Related Topics." *Journal of Research in Crime and Delinquency* 11, no. 2 (1974): 101–16.

Hine, Darlene Clark, and John McCluskey Jr., eds. *The Black Chicago Renaissance.* Urbana: University of Illinois Press, 2012.

Hinton, Elizabeth. "Creating Crime: The Rise and Impact of National Juvenile Delinquency Programs in Black Urban Neighborhoods." *Journal of Urban History* 41, no. 5 (September 2015): 808–24.

———. *From the War on Poverty to the War on Crime: The Making of Mass Incarceration in America.* Cambridge, MA: Harvard University Press, 2016.

———. "'A War within Our Own Boundaries': Lyndon Johnson's Great Society and the Rise of the Carceral State." *Journal of American History* 102, no. 1 (June 2015): 100–112.

Hirsch, Arnold R. *Making the Second Ghetto: Race and Housing in Chicago, 1940–1960.* 1983. Reprint, Chicago: University of Chicago Press, 1998.

———. "Massive Resistance in the Urban North: Trumbull Park, Chicago, 1953–1966." *Journal of American History* 82, no. 2 (September 1995): 522–50.

Hopkins, Ernest Jerome. *Our Lawless Police: A Study of the Unlawful Enforcement of the Law.* New York: Viking Press, 1931.

Horne, Gerald. *Black and Red: W.E.B. Du Bois and the Afro-American Response to the Cold War, 1944–1963.* Albany: SUNY Press, 1985.

———. *Fire This Time: The Watts Uprising and the 1960s.* New York: Da Capo Press, 1997.

Hudson, Peter James. *Bankers and Empire: How Wall Street Colonized the Caribbean.* Chicago: University of Chicago Press, 2017.

———. "Racial Capitalism and the Dark Proletariat." *Boston Review,* Forum 1 (2017): 59–65.

Hughes, Langston. *Not without Laughter.* 1930. Reprint, New York: Scribner Paperback Fiction, 1995.

Ignatiev, Noel. *How the Irish Became White.* New York: Routledge, 1995.

Illinois Association for Criminal Justice. *Illinois Crime Survey.* Chicago: Blakely Printing, 1929.

Inserra, Vincent L. *C-1 and the Chicago Mob.* Bloomington, IN: XLIBRIS, 2014.

Jack, Homer. "Chicago's Violent Armistice." *Nation,* December 10, 1949.

Jackson, Kenneth T. *Crabgrass Frontier: The Suburbanization of the United States.* Oxford: Oxford University Press, 1987.

———. "Race, Ethnicity, and Real Estate Appraisal: The Home Owners Loan Corporation and the Federal Housing Administration." *Journal of Urban History* 6, no. 4 (August 1980): 419–52.

Jacobson, Matthew Frye. *Whiteness of a Different Color: European Immigrants and the Alchemy of Race*. Cambridge, MA: Harvard University Press, 1999.

Johnson, Haynes. "1968 Democratic Convention: The Bosses Strike Back." *Smithsonian Magazine*, August 2008.

Johnson, Karl E. "Police-Black Community Relations in Postwar Philadelphia: Race and Criminalization in Urban Social Spaces, 1945–1960." *Journal of African American History* 89, no. 2 (Spring 2004): 118–34.

Johnson, Marilynn S. *Street Justice: A History of Police Violence in New York City*. Boston, MA: Beacon Press, 2004.

Johnson, Nicholas. *Negroes and the Gun: The Black Tradition of Arms*. Amherst, NY: Prometheus Books, 2014.

Johnson, Ryan S., Shawn Kantor, and Price V. Fishback. "Striking at the Roots of Crime: The Impact of Social Welfare Spending on Crime during the Great Depression." National Bureau of Economic Research Working Paper #12825, 2007. http://www.nber.org/papers/w12825.pdf.

Johnson, Walter. *River of Dark Dreams: Slavery and Empire in the Cotton Kingdom*. Cambridge, MA: Belknap Press, 2013.

———. "To Remake the World: Slavery, Racial Capitalism, and Justice." *Boston Review*, Forum 1 (2017): 11–31.

Jones, Patrick D. *The Selma of the North: Civil Rights Insurgency in Milwaukee*. Cambridge, MA: Harvard University Press, 2010.

Kaba, Mariame, and Frank Edwards, "Policing Chicago Public Schools: A Gateway to the School-to-Prison Pipeline." January 2012. https://policeinschools.files .wordpress.com/2011/12/policing-chicago-public-schools-final2.pdf.

Kamisar, Yale. "On the Tactics of Police-Prosecution Oriented Critics of the Courts." *Cornell Law Review* 49, no. 3 (Spring 1964): 436–77.

Keating, Ann Durkin. *Rising Up from Indian Country: The Battle of Fort Dearborn and the Birth of Chicago*. Chicago: University of Chicago Press, 2012.

Kelley, Robin D. G. *Freedom Dreams: The Black Radical Imagination*. Boston, MA: Beacon Press, 2002.

———. *Hammer and Hoe: Alabama Communists during the Great Depression*. Chapel Hill: University of North Carolina Press, 1990.

Kelling, George L., and James Q. Wilson. "Broken Windows: The Police and Neighborhood Safety." *Atlantic*, March 1982.

Kennedy, David M. *Freedom from Fear: The American People in Depression and War, 1929–1945*. Oxford: Oxford University Press, 1999.

Kennedy, Randall. *Race, Crime and the Law*. New York: Pantheon, 1997.

Kimble, Lionel. *A New Deal for Bronzeville: Housing, Employment and Civil Rights in Black Chicago, 1935–1955*. Carbondale: Southern Illinois University Press, 2015.

Kohler-Haumann, Julilly. *Getting Tough: Welfare and Imprisonment in 1970s America*. Princeton, NJ: Princeton University Press, 2017.

Krist, Gary. *City of Scoundrels*. New York: Broadway Books, 2012.

Krugler, David. F. *1919, the Year of Racial Violence: How African Americans Fought Back*. Cambridge: Cambridge University Press, 2015.

Kusch, Frank. *Battleground Chicago: The Police and the 1968 Democratic National Convention*. Westport, CT: Praeger, 2004.

Lassiter, Matthew D. "Pushers, Victims, and the Lost Innocence of White Suburbia." *Journal of Urban History* 41, no. 5 (September 2015): 787–807.

Lavine, Emanuel H. *The Third Degree: A Detailed Account of Police Brutality*. New York: Vanguard Press, 1930.

Lefebvre, Henri. *Writings on Cities*. Translated by Elenore Kofman and Elizabeth Lebas. New York: Wiley-Blackwell, 1996.

LeFlouria, Talitha L. *Chained in Silence: Black Women and Convict Labor in the New South*. Chapel Hill: University of North Carolina Press, 2016.

Lemann, Nicholas. *The Promised Land: The Great Black Migration and How It Changed America*. New York: Vintage, 1992.

Lesher, Stephan. *George Wallace: American Populist*. Cambridge: Perseus, 1994.

Levy, Peter. *The Great Uprising: Race Riots in Urban America during the 1960s*. Cambridge: Cambridge University Press, 2018.

Lewis, Robert. *Chicago Made: Factory Networks in the Industrial Metropolis*. Chicago: University of Chicago Press, 2008.

Lichtenstein, Alex. *Twice the Work of Free Labor: The Political Economy of Convict Labor in the New South*. New York: Verso, 1996.

Lindberg, Richard C. *To Serve and Collect: Chicago Politics and Police Corruption from the Lager Beer Riot to the Summerdale Scandal*. Carbondale: Southern Illinois University Press, 1998.

Lindsey, Treva B. *Colored No More: Reinventing Black Womanhood in Washington, D.C.* Urbana: University of Illinois Press, 2017.

Litwack, Leon. *Been in the Storm So Long: Black Southerners in the Age of Jim Crow*. New York: Vintage, 1999.

Lombardo, Robert M. "The Black Mafia: African-American Organized Crime in Chicago, 1890–1960." *Crime, Law, and Social Change* 38, no. 1 (2002): 33–65.

Losier, Toussaint. "'The Public Does Not Believe the Police Can Police Themselves': The Mayoral Administration of Harold Washington and the Problem of Police Impunity." *Journal of Urban History*. Online First, 2017.

Malka, Adam. *The Men of Mobtown: Policing Baltimore in the Age of Slavery and Emancipation*. Chapel Hill: University of North Carolina Press, 2018.

Maltz, Michael D. "Bridging Gaps in Police Crime Data: A Discussion Paper from the BJS Fellows Program." Bureau of Justice Statistics, September 1999, NCJ 176365. https://www.bjs.gov/content/pub/pdf/bgpcd.pdf.

Manning, Christopher. *William L. Dawson and the Limits of Black Electoral Leadership*. DeKalb: Northern Illinois University Press, 2009.

Mantler, Gordon K. *Power to the Poor: Black-Brown Coalition and the Fight for Economic Justice, 1960–1974*. Chapel Hill: University of North Carolina Press, 2013.

Marable, Manning. *How Capitalism Underdeveloped Black America: Problems in Race, Political Economy, and Society*. 1983. Reprint, London: Pluto Press, 2000.

Martin, John Bartlow. "The Rights of the Accused." *Saturday Evening Post*, August 20, 1960.

Mauer, Marc. *Race to Incarcerate*. 1999. Reprint, New York: New Press, 2006.

McCammack, Brian. *Landscapes of Hope: Nature and the Great Migration in Chicago*. Cambridge, MA: Harvard University Press, 2017.

McGirr, Lisa. *The War on Alcohol: Prohibition and the Rise of the American State*. New York: W. W. Norton, 2015.

McGuire, Danielle L. *At the Dark End of the Street: Black Women, Rape and Resistance—A New History of the Civil Rights Movement from Rosa Parks to Black Power*. New York: Knopf, 2010.

McLennan, Rebecca. *The Crisis of Imprisonment: Protest, Politics, and the Making of the American Penal State, 1776–1941*. Cambridge: Cambridge University Press, 2008.

McPherson, James Alan. "Chicago's Blackstone Rangers, Part I." *Atlantic*, May 1969.

———. "Chicago's Blackstone Rangers, Part II." *Atlantic*, June 1969.

McWhirter, Cameron. *Red Summer: The Summer of 1919 and the Awakening of Black America*. New York: St. Martin's Griffin, 2012.

Michaeli, Ethan. *The Defender: How the Legendary Black Newspaper Changed America*. Boston, MA: Houghton Mifflin Harcourt, 2016.

Mill, John Stuart. *On Liberty*. London: Longmans, Green, 1867.

Mitrani, Sam. *The Rise of the Chicago Police Department: Class and Conflict, 1850–1894*. Urbana: University of Illinois Press, 2013.

Monkkonen, Erik. *Police in Urban America, 1860–1920*. Cambridge: Cambridge University Press, 1980.

Moore, Leonard. *Black Rage in New Orleans: Police Brutality and African American Activism from World War II to Hurricane Katrina*. Baton Rouge: Louisiana State University Press, 2010.

Moore, Natalie Y., and Lance Williams. *The Almighty Black P Stone Nation: The Rise, Fall, and Resurgence of an American Gang*. Chicago: Chicago Review Press, 2012.

Moses, Earl R. "Community Factors in Negro Delinquency." *Journal of Negro Education* 5, no. 2 (April 1936): 220–27.

Muhammad, Khalil Gibran. *The Condemnation of Blackness: Race, Crime, and the Making of Modern Urban America*. Cambridge, MA: Harvard University Press, 2010.

———. "Where Did All the White Criminals Go?: Reconfiguring Race and Crime on the Road to Mass Incarceration." *Souls: A Critical Journal of Black Politics, Culture, and Society* 13, no. 1 (2011): 72–90.

Mullen, Bill. *Popular Fronts: Chicago and African-American Cultural Politics, 1935–1946*. Urbana: University of Illinois Press, 1999.

Mumford, Kevin. "Harvesting the Crisis: The Newark Uprising, the Kerner Commission, and Writing on Riots." In *African American Urban History since World War II*, edited by Kenneth L. Kusmer and Joe W. Trotter, 203–18. Chicago: University of Chicago Press, 2009.

———. *Interzones: Black/White Sex Districts in Chicago and New York in the Early Twentieth Century*. New York: Columbia University Press, 1997.

———. *Newark: A History of Race, Rights, and Riots in America*. New York: New York University Press, 2007.

Murakawa, Naomi. *The First Civil Right: How Liberals Built Prison America*. Oxford: Oxford University Press, 2014.

Murch, Donna. "Crack in Los Angeles: Crisis, Militarization, and Black Response to the Late Twentieth-Century War on Drugs." *Journal of American History* 102, no. 1 (June 2015): 162–73.

———. *Living for the City: Migration, Education, and the Rise of the Black Panther Party in Oakland*. Chapel Hill: University of North Carolina Press, 2010.

Mustakeem, Sowande' M. "'Armed with a Knife in Her Bosom': Gender, Violence, and the Carceral Consequences of Rage in the Late 19th Century." *Journal of African American History* 100, no. 3 (Summer 2015): 385–405.

National Advisory Commission on Civil Disorders. *The Kerner Report*. 1968. Reprint, Princeton, NJ: Princeton University Press, 2016.

National Commission on Law Observance and Enforcement. *Lawlessness in Law Enforcement*. Vol. 11 of *Report of the National Commission on Law Observance and Enforcement*. Washington, DC: Government Printing Office, 1931.

Neckerman, Kathryn M. *Schools Betrayed: Roots of Failure in Inner-City Education*. Chicago: University of Chicago Press, 2010.

Nguyen, Viet Thanh. *Nothing Ever Dies: Vietnam and the Memory of War*. Cambridge, MA: Harvard University Press, 2016.

Okrent, Daniel. *Last Call: The Rise and Fall of Prohibition*. New York: Scribner, 2010.

Oshinsky, David. *"Worse Than Slavery": Parchman Farm and the Ordeal of Jim Crow Justice*. New York: Free Press, 1996.

Pacyga, Dominic A. *Chicago: A Biography*. Chicago: University of Chicago Press, 2009.

———. *Slaughterhouse: Chicago's Union Stock Yard and the World It Made*. Chicago: University of Chicago Press, 2015.

Pager, Devah. *Marked: Race, Crime, and Finding Work in an Age of Mass Incarceration*. Chicago: University of Chicago Press, 2008.

Parenti, Christian. *Lockdown America: Police and Prisons in the Age of Crisis*. New York: Verso, 1999.

Parsons, Elaine Frantz. *Ku-Klux: The Birth of the Klan during Reconstruction*. Chapel Hill: University of North Carolina Press, 2016.

Patillo, Mary. *Black on the Block: The Politics of Race and Class in the City*. Chicago: University of Chicago Press, 2007.

Patterson, William, ed. *We Charge Genocide: The Historic Petition to the United Nations for Relief from a Crime of the United States Government against the Negro People*. 1951. Reprint, New York: International Publishers, 1970.

Pepper, John V., and Carol V. Petrie, eds. *Measurement Problems in Criminal Justice Research: Workshop Summary*. Washington, DC: National Academies Press, 2003.

Perkinson, Robert. *Texas Tough: The Rise of America's Prison Empire*. New York: Picador, 2010.

Perlstein, Rick. *Nixonland: The Rise of a President and the Fracturing of America*. New York: Scribner, 2008.

Peterson, Virgil W. "Crime Conditions in the Fifth Police District: Survey Made in 1945 to Determine Reasons for High Crime Rate." *Criminal Justice: Journal of the Chicago Crime Commission* (May 1946).

Petty, Audrey, ed. *High Rise Stories: Voices from Chicago Public Housing*. San Francisco, CA: McSweeney's, 2013.

Pfaff, John F. *Locked In: The True Causes of Mass Incarceration and How to Achieve Real Reform*. New York: Basic Books, 2017.

Pihos, Peter Constantine. "Policing, Race, and Politics in Chicago." PhD diss., University of Pennsylvania, 2015.

Pinderhughes, Dianne M. *Race and Ethnicity in Chicago Politics*. Urbana: University of Illinois Press, 1987.

Plummer, Brenda Gayle. *Rising Wind: Black Americans and U.S. Foreign Affairs, 1935–1960*. Chapel Hill: University of North Carolina Press, 1996.

Polikoff, Alexander. *Waiting for Gautreaux: A Story of Segregation, Housing, and the Black Ghetto*. Evanston, IL: Northwestern University Press, 2005.

Popkin, Susan J., Victoria E. Gwiasda, Lynn M. Olson, Dennis P. Rosenbaum, and Larry Buron. *The Hidden War: Crime and the Tragedy of Public Housing in Chicago*. New Brunswick, NJ: Rutgers University Press, 2000.

Quirke, Carol. "Reframing Chicago's Memorial Day Massacre, May 30, 1937." *American Quarterly* 60, no. 1 (March 2008): 129–57.

Rakove, Milton L. *Don't Make No Waves . . . Don't Back No Losers: An Insider's Analysis of the Daley Machine*. Bloomington: Indiana University Press, 1975.

Ralph, James R. *Northern Protest: Martin Luther King, Jr., Chicago, and the Civil Rights Movement*. Cambridge, MA: Harvard University Press, 1993.

Ransby, Barbara. *Ella Baker and the Black Freedom Movement: A Radical Democratic Vision*. Chapel Hill: University of North Carolina Press, 2003.

Reckless, Walter C. *Vice in Chicago*. Chicago: University of Chicago Press, 1933.

Reed, Christopher Robert. *All the World Is Here!: The Black Presence at White City*. Bloomington: Indiana University Press, 2000.

———. *Black Chicago's First Century*. Vol. 1, *1833–1900*. Columbia, MO: University of Missouri Press, 2005.

———. *The Chicago NAACP and the Rise of Black Professional Leadership, 1910–1966*. Bloomington: Indiana University Press, 1997.

———. *The Depression Comes to the South Side: Protest and Politics in the Black Metropolis, 1930–1933*. Bloomington: Indiana University Press, 2011.

———. *Knock at the Door of Opportunity: Black Migration to Chicago, 1900–1919*. Carbondale: Southern Illinois University Press, 2014.

———. *The Rise of Chicago's Black Metropolis, 1920–1929*. Urbana: University of Illinois Press, 2011.

Reiss, Albert, Jr. *Patterns of Behavior in Police and Citizen Transactions*. Washington, DC: Government Printing Office, 1967.

Rios, Victor M. "The Hyper-Criminalization of Black and Latino Male Youth in the Era of Mass Incarceration." *Souls* 8, no. 2 (September 2006): 40–54.

———. *Punished: Policing the Lives of Black and Latino Boys*. New York: New York University Press, 2011.

Ritchie, Andrea J. *Invisible No More: Police Violence Against Black Women and Women of Color*. Boston, MA: Beacon Press, 2017.

Rivera, Gilbert. "Armed Not Militarized: Achieving Real Police Militarization." *Berkeley Journal of Criminal Law* 20, no. 2 (Fall 2015): 1–33.

Robinson, Cedric. *Black Marxism: The Making of the Black Radical Tradition*. 1983. Reprint, Chapel Hill: University of North Carolina Press, 2000.

Roediger, David R. *The Wages of Whiteness: Race and the Making of the American Working Class.* New York: Verso, 1991.

———. *Working toward Whiteness: How America's Immigrants Became White; The Journey from Ellis Island to the Suburbs.* New York: Basic Books, 2006.

Royko, Mike. *Boss: Richard J. Daley of Chicago.* New York: Plume, 1976.

Sampson, Robert J. *Great American City: Chicago and the Enduring Neighborhood Effect.* Chicago: University of Chicago Press, 2013.

Sampson, Robert J., and Janet L. Lauritsen. "Racial and Ethnic Disparities in Crime and Criminal Justice in the United States." *Crime and Justice* 21 (1997): 311–74.

Sandburg, Carl. "Chicago." *Poetry* 3, no. 6 (March 1914).

———. *The Chicago Race Riots: July 1919.* 1919. Reprint, New York: Harcourt, Brace, & World, 1969.

Satter, Beryl. "Cops, Gangs, and Revolutionaries in 1960s Chicago: What Black Police Can Tell Us about Power." *Journal of Urban History* 42, no. 6 (2016): 1110–34.

———. *Family Properties: Race, Real Estate, and the Exploitation of Black Urban America.* New York: Metropolitan Books, 2009.

Schlesinger, Arthur M., Jr. *The Age of Roosevelt: The Crisis of the Older Order, 1919–1933.* Boston, MA: Houghton Mifflin, 1957.

Schneider, Eric C. *Smack: Heroin and the American City.* Philadelphia: University of Pennsylvania Press, 2011.

Schneider, Eric C., Christopher Agee, and Themis Chronopoulos. "Dirty Work: Police and Community Relations and the Limits of Liberalism in Postwar Philadelphia." *Journal of Urban History.* Online First, 2017.

Schultz, John. *No One Was Killed: The Democratic National Convention, August 1968.* 1969. Reprint, Chicago: University of Chicago Press, 2009.

Seale, Bobby. *Seize the Time: The Story of the Black Panther Party and Huey P. Newton.* 1970. Reprint, Baltimore: Black Classic Press, 1991.

Seligman, Amanda I. *Block by Block: Neighborhoods and Public Policy on Chicago's West Side.* Chicago: University of Chicago Press, 2005.

———. *Chicago's Block Clubs: How Neighbors Shape the City.* Chicago: University of Chicago Press, 2016.

Shabazz, Rashad. *Spatializing Blackness: Architectures of Confinement and Black Masculinity in Chicago.* Urbana: University of Illinois Press, 2015.

Shapiro, Karen. *A New South Rebellion: The Battle against Convict Labor in the Tennessee Coalfields, 1871–1896.* Chapel Hill: University of North Carolina Press, 1998.

Simon, Jonathan. *Governing through Crime: How the War on Crime Transformed American Democracy and Created a Culture of Fear.* Oxford: Oxford University Press, 2009.

Simpson, Dick, Thomas J. Gradel, Melissa Mouritsen, and John Johnson. "Chicago: Still the Capital of Corruption; Anti-Corruption Report Number 8." May 28, 2015. https://pols.uic.edu/docs/default-source/chicago_politics/anti-corruption_reports /corruption-rpt-8_final-052715.pdf?sfvrsn=0.

Smith, Carl. *The Plan of Chicago: Daniel Burnham and the Remaking of the American City.* Chicago: University of Chicago Press, 2007.

Smith, Sandy. "You Can't Expect Police on the Take to Take Orders." *Life*, December 6, 1968.

Soss, Joe, and Vesla Weaver. "Police Are Our Government: Politics, Political Science, and the Policing of Race-Class Subjugated Communities." *Annual Review of Political Science* 20 (2017): 565–91.

Spear, Allan H. *Black Chicago: The Making of a Negro Ghetto, 1890–1920*. Chicago: University of Chicago Press, 1967.

Special Committee to Investigate Organized Crime in Interstate Commerce. "Kefauver Committee Final Report, August 1931, 1951." Washington, DC: Government Printing Office, 1951.

———. *The Kefauver Committee Report: Organized Crime*. New York: Didier, 1951.

Spillane, Joseph. "The Making of an Underground Market: Drug Selling in Chicago." *Journal of Social History* 32, no. 1 (Autumn 1998): 27–47.

Stewart-Winter, Timothy. *Queer Clout: Chicago and the Rise of Gay Politics*. Philadelphia: University of Pennsylvania Press, 2016.

Storch, Randi. *Red Chicago: American Communism at Its Grassroots, 1928–1935*. Urbana: University of Illinois Press, 2007.

Stowell, David O. *Streets, Railroads, and the Great Strike of 1877*. Chicago: University of Chicago Press, 1999.

Sugrue, Thomas J. *The Origins of the Urban Crisis: Race and Inequality in Postwar Detroit*. Princeton, NJ: Princeton University Press, 2014.

———. *Sweet Land of Liberty: The Forgotten Struggle for Civil Rights in the Urban North*. New York: Random House, 2008.

Taylor, Keeanga-Yamahtta. *From #BlackLivesMatter to Black Liberation*. Chicago: Haymarket Books, 2016.

———, ed. *How We Get Free: Black Feminism and the Combahee River Collective*. Chicago: Haymarket Books, 2017.

Terkel, Studs. *Hard Times: An Oral History of the Great Depression*. 1970. Reprint, New York: New Press, 2005.

———. *Studs Terkel's Chicago*. 1985. Reprint, New York: New Press, 2012.

Thompson, Heather Ann. *Blood in the Water: The Attica Prison Uprising of 1971 and Its Legacy*. New York: Pantheon: 2016.

———. "How Prisons Change the Balance of Power in America." *Atlantic*, October 7, 2013.

———. "Understanding Rioting in Postwar Urban America." *Journal of Urban History* 26, no. 3 (March 2000): 391–402.

———. "Urban Uprisings: Riots or Rebellions?" In *The Columbia Guide to America in the 1960s*, edited by David Farber and Beth Bailey, 109–17. New York: Columbia University Press, 2001.

———. *Whose Detroit?: Politics, Labor, and Race in a Modern American City*. Ithaca, NY: Cornell University Press, 2001.

———. "Why Mass Incarceration Matters: Rethinking Crisis, Decline, and Transformation in Postwar American History." *Journal of American History* 97, no. 3 (December 2010): 703–34.

Tifft, Larry Lowell. "Comparative Police Supervision Systems: An Organizational Analysis." PhD diss., University of Illinois, 1970.

Tonry, Michael. *Malign Neglect: Race, Crime, and Punishment in America*. Oxford: Oxford University Press, 1995.

Travis, Dempsey. *An Autobiography of Black Chicago*. Rev. ed. Evanston, IL: Agate Bolden, 2014.

Tuttle, William M., Jr. *Race Riot: Chicago in the Red Summer of 1919*. New York: Atheneum, 1970.

Tyson, Timothy B. *The Blood of Emmett Till*. New York: Simon & Schuster, 2017.

Umoja, Akinyele Omowale. *We Will Shoot Back: Armed Resistance in the Mississippi Freedom Movement*. New York: New York University Press, 2014.

United States District Court, Northern District of Illinois, Eastern Division. *Report of the January 1970 Grand Jury*. Washington, DC: Government Printing Office, 1970.

Van Cleve, Nicole Gonzalez. *Crook County: Racism and Injustice in America's Largest Criminal Court*. Stanford, CA: Stanford University Press, 2016.

Venkatesh, Sudhir Alladi. *American Project: The Rise and Fall of a Modern Ghetto*. Cambridge, MA: Harvard University Press, 2000.

Vitale, Alex S. *The End of Policing*. New York: Verso, 2017.

Wacquant, Loïc. "Class, Race and Hyperincarceration in Revanchist America." *Daedalus* 139, no. 3 (Summer 2010): 74–90.

———. *Prisons of Poverty*. Minneapolis: University of Minnesota Press, 2009.

———. *Punishing the Poor: The Neoliberal Government of Social Insecurity*. Durham, NC: Duke University Press, 2009. Original French edition, 2004.

Walker, Daniel. *Rights in Conflict: Chicago's 7 Brutal Days*. New York: Grosset & Dunlap, 1968.

Walker, Samuel. "The Neglect of Police Unions: Exploring One of the Most Important Areas of American Policing." *Police Practice and Research* 9, no. 2 (May 2008): 95–112.

Ward, Jason Morgan. *Hanging Bridge: Racial Violence and America's Civil Rights Century*. Oxford: Oxford University Press, 2016.

Washington, Sylvester. "Why I Killed 11 Men." *Ebony*, January 1950.

Wells, Ida B. *The Red Record: Tabulated Statistics and Alleged Causes of Lynching in the United States*. Chicago: Donohue and Hansberry, 1895.

Western, Bruce. *Punishment and Inequality in America*. New York: Russell Sage Foundation, 2007.

Whitaker, David T. *Cabrini-Green in Words and Pictures*. Chicago: W3 Chicago, 2000.

Wiese, Andrew. *Places of Their Own: African American Suburbanization in the Twentieth Century*. Chicago: University of Chicago Press, 2004.

Williams, Jakobi. *From the Bullet to the Ballot: The Illinois Chapter of the Black Panther Party and Racial Coalition Politics in Chicago*. Chapel Hill: University of North Carolina Press, 2013.

Williams, Rhonda Y. *The Politics of Public Housing: Black Women's Struggles against Urban Inequality*. Oxford: Oxford University Press, 2005.

Willrich, Michael. *City of Courts: Socializing Justice in Progressive Era Chicago*. Cambridge: Cambridge University Press, 2003.

Wilkerson, Isabel. *The Warmth of Other Suns: The Epic Story of America's Great Migration*. New York: Random House, 2010.

Wilson, Orlando Winfield. "Police Arrest Privileges in a Free Society: A Plea for Modernization." *Journal of Criminal Law and Criminology* 51, no. 4 (Winter 1960): 395–401.

———. "Police Authority in a Free Society." *Journal of Criminal Law and Criminology* 54, no. 2 (Summer 1963): 175–77.

Wilson, William Julius. *When Work Disappears: The World of the New Urban Poor.* New York: Vintage, 1996.

Wood, Amy Louise. *Lynching and Spectacle: Witnessing Racial Violence in America, 1890–1940.* Chapel Hill: University of North Carolina Press, 2011.

Woodward, C. Van. *The Strange Career of Jim Crow.* Oxford: Oxford University Press, 1955.

Woolner, Cookie. "'Woman Slain in Queer Love Brawl': African American Women, Same-Sex Desire, and Violence in the Urban North, 1920–1929." *Journal of African American History* 100, no. 3 (Summer 2015): 406–27.

Wright, Richard. *Black Boy.* 1944. Reprint, New York: Harper Perennial, 1993.

Zeiger, Robert H. *CIO, 1935–1955.* Chapel Hill: University of North Carolina Press, 1995.

INDEX

Page numbers in italics refer to illustrations.

Dixon, Steven, 205
Donner, Frank, 9
Draine, Ernest, 87
Drake, St. Clair, 20, 49, 61, 69, 100, 115, 125–26, 138
drug trade, 40, 124–25, 137–49, 206, 233, 237, 239
Du Bois, W. E. B., 21
Duke, Charles, 25
Dulaney, Marvin, 119
Duneier, Mitchell, 69
Dunmore, Wellington, 27
du Sable, Jean Baptiste Point, 14, 18

Ebony magazine, 119
Edelman, Marion Wright, 224
Edwards, Staddie, 111
Ellis, Thomas, 62
Escobedo v. Illinois, 158
Everett Dirksen Federal Building (Chicago), 1–2
evictions. *See* housing evictions

Farmer, James, 117
fascism, 82, 91
Federal Bureau of Investigation (FBI), 154, 170–71, 203, 205–6, 209, 223, 228, 230
Federal Bureau of Narcotics (FBN), 140, 144. *See also* drug trade
Federal Housing Administration (FHA), 96–98
federal policy, 4–6, 57, 114, 125, 132, 141, 165, 173, 177, 197, 232, 240, 245–46. *See also* New Deal
Felker-Kantor, Max, 4
Fifteenth Amendment (1870), 19
Fitzgerald, Lou, 235
Fitzmorris, Charles, 46
Fogelson, Robert, 93, 101, 208
Forman, James, Jr., 138, 233, 238, 269–70n11
Fort, Jeff, 177, 202, 229
Fort Dearborn, 14
For the People Artists Collective, 261
Foster, A. L., 99

Fraternal Order of Police (FOP), 160–61, 170, 210–11, 219, 224, 258
Frazier, E. Franklin, 43

Gaines, Irene McCoy, 138
Garfield Park (Chicago, IL), 182, *183*, 230–31
Garner, Richard, 180
Garrity, John, 25, 32–33
Gebert, Bill, 75
Geeter, Joseph, 129
Gellman, Erik, 82
gender, 4, 10, 60
Geraghty, Diane, 239
Gilmore, Glenda, 72
Gilmore, Ruth Wilson, 4
Gitlin, Todd, 190
Gladney, Ida Mae Brandon, 21
Glass, Charles, 239
Glen, Ivan, 47–48, 54
Goldwater, Barry, 196–97
Gonzalez Van Cleve, Nicole, 11
Gorney, Jay, 56
Gosnell, Harold, 49
Goss, Bernard, 22
Grant Park (Chicago, IL), 191, 221
Great Depression, 55–90, 94, 180
Great Migration: First, 8, 11, 19–24, 50, 54; Second, 8, 19, 90–91, 95–97, 125–27, 138
Great Railroad Strike (1877), 17
Greater Lawndale Conservation Commission (GLCC), 135–37, 139, 146
Green, Adam, 113
Green, Walter, 106–8
Gregory, Dick, 236, 252–53
Grey, Abe, 75, 87
Gross, Charles, 131
Gross, Dianna, 75, 80
Guthrie, Woody, 56

Haas, Jeffrey, 224
Hamer, Fannie Lou, 253
Hampton, Fred, 192, 203–4, 206, 222–40, 250–52, 259
Hampton, Iberia, 228